MIND DESIGN

Philosophy, Psychology, Artificial Intelligence

MIND
DESIGN

Philosophy
Psychology
Artificial Intelligence

edited by

JOHN HAUGELAND

A Bradford Book

The MIT Press
Cambridge, Massachusetts
London, England

First MIT Press edition, 1981

Library of Congress Catalog Card Number 81-83996
Printed in the United States of America

ISBN   0-262-08110-5 (hard)
           0-262-58052-7 (paper)

for Barbara and John III

Acknowledgments

This book is conceived as a sequel to Alan Ross Anderson's *Minds and Machines* (1964), augmenting it and bringing it up to date. All of the essays included here were written after that work appeared, and I daresay most of them were directly or indirectly influenced by it. There is, of course, no duplication of contents, and there could be no replacing the classic articles in that little volume; I can only hope to have chosen as well from the burgeoning subsequent literature.

For assistance and/or moral support while designing the book and writing the introduction, I am indebted to Paul Benacerraf, Daniel Dennett, Hubert Dreyfus, Jay Garfield, Barbara Haugeland, Pat Hayes, John McCarthy, Robert Moore, Zenon Pylyshyn, and William Rohwer. For financial support, I am indebted to the Center for Advanced Study in the Behavioral Sciences, the National Endowment for the Humanities, the Alfred P. Sloan Foundation, and the National Science Foundation (BNS 78–24671). Finally, I am indebted to the Stanford Artificial Intelligence Laboratory for the use of its wonderful editing tools and toys.

Each of the articles that follow has been published previously (though, sometimes in a slightly different version), and each is reprinted here with the kind permission of the author(s).

1. "Computer Science as Empirical Inquiry: Symbols and Search," by Allen Newell and Herbert A. Simon, was the tenth Turing Award Lecture, delivered to the annual conference of the Association for Computing Machinery in

1975, and published in *Communications of the Association for Computing Machinery,* 19 (March 1976) 113–126. It is reprinted by permission of the ACM.

2. "Complexity and the Study of Artificial and Human Intelligence," by Zenon W. Pylyshyn, was presented (in an earlier version) at a conference on Objectives and Methodologies for Artificial Intelligence, in Canberra, Australia (May 1974), and first published in *Philosophical Perspectives in Artificial Intelligence,* edited by Martin Ringle (Atlantic Highlands, N.J.: Humanities Press, 1979). It is reprinted here (with modest revisions) by permission of Humanities Press.

3. "A Framework for Representing Knowledge," by Marvin Minsky, was originally published as Memo 306 of the Artificial Intelligence Laboratory at MIT. Excerpts were reprinted in *The Psychology of Computer Vision,* edited by Patrick H. Winston (New York: McGraw Hill, 1975); and other excerpts were reprinted in the Proceedings of the 1975 TINLAP Conference, in Cambridge, Massachusetts. Still other excerpts are reprinted here by permission of Professor Minsky.

4. "Artificial Intelligence—A Personal View," by David Marr, was first published in *Artificial Intelligence,* 9 (1977) 37–48. It is reprinted here by permission of North-Holland Publishing Company.

5. "Artificial Intelligence Meets Natural Stupidity," by Drew McDermott, was first published in the *SIGART Newsletter* (of the Special Interest Group on Artificial Intelligence, of the Association for Computing Machinery), No. 57 (April 1976). It is reprinted here by permission of Professor McDermott.

6. "From Micro-Worlds to Knowledge Representation: AI at an Impasse," by Hubert L. Dreyfus, is excerpted (with minor revisions) from the Introduction to the second edition of his *What Computers Can't Do* (New York: Harper and Row, 1979). It is reprinted here by permission of Harper and Row.

7. "Reductionism and the Nature of Psychology," by Hilary Putnam, was first published in *Cognition,* 2 (1973) 131–146. It is reprinted here (somewhat abridged) by courtesy of Elsevier Sequoia, Lausanne.

8. "Intentional Systems," by Daniel C. Dennett, was first published in *The Journal of Philosophy,* 68 (1971) 87–106; it has been reprinted in Professor Dennett's *Brainstorms* (Montgomery, Vermont: Bradford Books, 1978). It is reprinted here by permission of *The Journal of Philosophy.*

9. "The Nature and Plausibility of Cognitivism," by John Haugeland, was first published in *The Behavioral and Brain Sciences,* 1 (1978) 215–226. Copyright © 1978 Cambridge University Press. Reprinted (with minor revisions) by permission of the publisher.

10. "Minds, Brains, and Programs," by John R. Searle, was first published in *The Behavioral and Brain Sciences,* 3 (1980), 417–424. Copyright © 1980 Cambridge University Press. Reprinted by permission of the publisher.

11. "Methodological Solipsism Considered as a Research Strategy in Cognitive Psychology," by Jerry A. Fodor, was first published in *The Behavioral and Brain Sciences,* 3 (1980), 63–73. Copyright © 1980 Cambridge University Press. Reprinted by permission of the publisher.

12. "The Material Mind," by Donald Davidson, was first published in *Logic, Methodology and Philosophy of Science IV,* edited by Pat Suppes, et al. (Amsterdam: North-Holland, 1973). It is reprinted by permission of North-Holland Publishing Company.

Contents

(continued)

MIND DESIGN

Semantic Engines:

An Introduction to Mind Design

JOHN HAUGELAND

I. Cognitive Science

"Reasoning is but reckoning," said Hobbes (1651, ch. V), in the earliest expression of the computational view of thought. Three centuries later, with the development of electronic "computers," his idea finally began to catch on; and now, in three decades, it has become the single most important theoretical hypothesis in psychology (and several allied disciplines), and also the basis of an exciting new research field, called "artificial intelligence." Recently, the expression *cognitive science* has been introduced to cover all these varied enterprises, in recognition of their common conceptual foundation. This term, therefore, does not apply to every scientific theory of cognition, but only to those sharing a certain broad outlook—which is sometimes called the "information processing" or "symbol manipulation" approach. Perhaps, at last, Hobbes's philosophical insight has found its home in a proper scientific paradigm (Kuhn, 1970).

Collected here are a dozen major papers in the *philosophy of cognitive science*—efforts by philosophers and scientists alike to understand the basic structure, assumptions, and prospects of this vigorous young field. Mostly, these essays are nontechnical, and intended for a wide audience of nonspecialists. Sometimes, however, they do presuppose familiarity with a few elementary ideas and distinctions from cognitive science itself; consequently, I shall introduce the volume with a brief survey of the relevant background.

Often (here and elsewhere) the discussion focuses on *artificial intelligence*—"AI," among friends—because it amounts to a kind of distilled essence of cognitive science. But again, it is important to realize that "AI" (like "cognitive science") is more specific in its meaning than the words themselves might suggest. Crudely, we can put the point in terms of different technologies: a project at IBM to wire and program an intelligent robot would probably be AI, whereas a project at DuPont to brew and mold a synthetic-organic android probably would not. But this can be misleading; the crucial issue is not protoplasm versus semiconductor ("wet-ware" versus "hardware"), but rather whether the product is designed and specified in terms of a computational structure. If it is, then a working model could probably be manufactured much more easily by means of electronics and programming; and that's the *only* relevance of the technology. Indeed, the guiding inspiration of cognitive science is that, at a suitable level of abstraction, a theory of "natural" intelligence should have the same basic form as the theories that explain sophisticated computer systems. It is this idea which makes *artificial* intelligence seem not only possible, but also a central and pure form of *psychological* research.

A better perspective on all the excitement can be gained by asking why it took three hundred years for Hobbes's original proposal to be appreciated. Mainly, three famous philosophical dilemmas stood in the way: (i) the metaphysical problem of mind interacting with matter; (ii) the theoretical problem of explaining the relevance of meanings, without appealing to a question-begging homunculus; and (iii) the methodological issue over the empirical testability (and, hence, respectability) of "mentalistic" explanations. The computational idea can be seen as slicing through all three dilemmas at a stroke; and this is what gives it, I think, the bulk of its tremendous gut-level appeal.

Descartes, a contemporary of Hobbes, gave the mind/matter problem its modern form in his doctrine of metaphysical *dualism*. Mind and body, he said, are two entirely different *kinds* of substance: the one can have (as distinguishing characteristics) various thoughts and feelings, whereas the other can have shapes, motions, and the causal interactions described by physical laws (and not vice versa). Intuitively, this is much more appealing than *materialism* (the main alternative to dualism), according to which everything, including minds, is really just matter, in one form or another. Not only are we reluctant to ascribe thought and feeling to "mere" matter, but we also find it very hard to ascribe shape and location to minds or ideas. There is, however, one basic problem, which no dualist has ever really solved: how can mind and body *interact?* On the one hand, they certainly *seem* to interact, as when a mental decision leads to a physical action, or when a physical stimulus leads to a mental perception; indeed, it's not clear how perception and action could be possible at all without mind/body interaction. On the other hand, however, physical laws are supposed to describe all motions of all bodies *completely* in terms of their interactions with one another.[1] In other words, physics leaves no room for causal intervention by the mental; hence the price of mind/body interaction is violation of the laws of physics—a price that few philosophers (or scientists) are willing to pay.

Thought itself (quite apart from matter) is not static and not random: it progresses and develops in ways that obey (at least much of the time) various rules of inference and reason. Superficially, this suggests an analogy with material particles obeying the laws of physics. But the analogy breaks down at a crucial point: particles have neither choice nor difficulty in "obeying" physics—it happens infallibly and automatically. People, on the other hand, often have to work to be reasonable; following the rules of reason is hardly infallible and can be very difficult. But this means there cannot be an explanatory dynamics of thought, which is at all comparable to physical dynamic theories; the respective roles of rules and laws in the two cases are deeply different. In particular, since correct application of the rules of reason to particular thoughts depends on what those thoughts *mean*, it seems that there must be some active rule-applier, which (or: who) *understands* the thoughts (and the rules), and which

---

1. There remain, of course, quantum indeterminacies, even in physics; but these are no consolation to interactionism. It is generally best, in fact, to forget about quantum mechanics in any discussion of mind/body metaphysics.

applies the rules to the thoughts as well as it can. If the activity of this rule-applier, following the rules of reason, is to explain the rationality of our thought processes, then it must be regarded as a complete little person—or *homunculus* (in Latin)—inside the head, directing the thoughts like a traffic cop. The trouble is: a theory that invokes an homunculus to *explain* thinking, has begged its own question, because the homunculus itself has to think, and *that* thinking has *not* been explained.

Finally, there is the question of how the psychology of thought could ever be properly scientific. Thoughts, it seems, cannot be observed; and the diffculty is not that, like electrons or distant galaxies, they are too small or too far away. Rather, they are somehow essentially subjective—we don't even know what it would be like to observe (or measure) them objectively. So all that science has to go on, even in principle, is objective *behavior* (which might include internal "physiological behavior"); hence, thoughts can enter the picture only as inferred or hypothesized intermediates. Unfortunately, in any given case, invoking beliefs and desires to explain an action is just too easy. Whatever an organism does, one can always trump up a million different ideas and motives that would explain it. If there can be, in principle, no independent, empirical check on which of these hypotheses is the right one, it seems scientifically disreputable to accept any of them, even tentatively. This, roughly, is the stance taken by *behaviorism.* The other half of the story, however, is that explaining behavior *without* invoking intervening mental processes is just too hard. In general, the subtle regularities, connections, and nonrandom variations in real-life behavior cannot so much as be *described* in nonmentalist (pure behaviorist) terms, let alone *explained*—hence, the overwhelming mechanicalness and stupidity of all the phenomena that the behaviorists were ever really able to account for.[2] The upshot is another philosophical standoff, with mentalists and behaviorists gleefully accusing one another of scientific bankruptcy.

Cognitive scientists can be materialists (nondualists) and mentalists (nonbehaviorists) at the same time; and they can offer

2. Which is not to say, by any means, that those accounts themselves were stupid, or scientifically worthless.

explanations in terms of meaning and rule-following, without presupposing any unexplained homunculus. It all depends on a marvellously rich analogy with computers—the outlines of which we can see with a quick look at everybody's favorite example: a chess-playing machine. It would be very awkward and peculiar to start assigning geometrical shapes and locations to the internal program routines and operations (decision processes and data structures, say) of such a system; yet we are quite confident it has no immaterial soul. These same decisions clearly cause physical behavior (e.g., in teletypewriters or TV screens), yet no one is worried that the laws of physics are being violated. When the machine plays, it follows rules in at least two senses: it always abides by the rules of the game, and it employs various reasonable rules of thumb to select plausible moves. Though these rules are in no way laws of nature, the machine's behavior is explained (in part) by citing them—and yet, no unexplained "compunculus" is presupposed. Finally, this explanation will necessarily invoke the system's internal reasoning processes; yet it is far from easy to figure out (or design) processes that will consistently lead to the observed (or desired) behavioral responses. Moreover, for any given machine, on any given occasion, there seems to be a determinate right answer about which reasonings it in fact went through.

That may have been a bit swift, but still, *what an inspiration!* If there are no philosophical dilemmas about chess-playing computers, then why should there be any about chess-playing people— or, indeed, about human intelligence in any other form? To put it coldly: why not suppose that people *just are* computers (and send philosophy packing)? Well . . . nothing very interesting is ever that simple. Various questions come up, among the first of which is: What exactly is being proposed, anyway?

II. Formal Systems

To start at the beginning, we must first say a little bit more carefully what a computer is. It is an automatic formal system. To see what this means, we first consider what a formal system is, and then what it is to automate one.

A *formal system* is like a game in which tokens are manipulated according to rules, in order to see what configurations can be obtained. Basically, to define such a game, three things have to be specified:

(1) what the tokens are;
(2) what the starting position is; and
(3) what moves are allowed in any given position.

Implicit in (2) and (3) is a specification of what positions are possible (for instance, what the board is, if it's a board game). Also, there is sometimes a specified *goal* position, which the player (or each player) is trying to achieve—such as a "winning position."

For example, there is a familiar solitaire game in which the tokens are pegs, arranged as follows in the starting position:

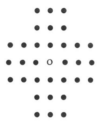

The solid dots are the tokens (pegs), and the circle in the middle is an empty space, into which a token could fit. The only move allowed by the rules is jumping one token over an adjacent one into an empty space, and then removing the token jumped over. This game has a goal: to perform such jumps until only one token remains, and it is in the center space.

Three points should be noticed about this (simple-minded) formal system. First, it is entirely *self-contained*. Only its own tokens, positions, and moves make any difference to it, and these only insofar as they matter to the application of the rules. In other words, the "outside world" (the weather, the state of the economy, whether the building is on fire, and so on) makes no difference whatsoever in the game. And, further, any aspects of the tokens and positions themselves which are irrelevant to determining which moves are legal—e.g., (in this game) color, size, weight, market value—are equally outside the game. Politics and courtship, by contrast, are not at all self-contained (even though they are sometimes called games) because just about anything could be relevant in some situation or other. Second, every relevant feature of the game is *perfectly definite;* that is, barring outright mistakes or breakdowns, there are no ambiguities, approximations, or "judgment calls" in determining what the position is, or whether a certain move is legal. For each peg and slot, that peg is either definitely (obviously and 100 percent) in that slot, or definitely (obviously and 100 percent) not in that slot—there are no in-between or borderline cases. Third, the moves are *finitely checkable,* in the sense that for each position and each candidate move, only a finite number of things has to be checked to see whether that move would be legal in that position. This is pretty trivial for our example, but it's nontrivial and very important for more complicated formal systems. Obviously, being self-contained, perfectly definite, and finitely checkable go nicely hand-in-hand; we will say that a game or system that has all three properties is *digital.* All formal systems are digital in this sense.

The digitalness of formal systems has the following important consequence: two systems that seem to be quite different may nevertheless be essentially the same. Clearly, the peg-jumping game would be essentially unchanged if the pegs were replaced by marbles, or even by helicopters (given a big enough board)—so long as the same rules were followed. But the differences can be more dramatic. Imagine a game played with two baskets and thirty-three dominoes, each with one letter and one numeral written on it. At the beginning, all the dominoes are in the start basket, except the one marked D4, which is in the finish basket; and the object of the game is to reverse that situation, by a process of "switching triads." A *triad* is three dominoes which have the same letter and sequential numerals, or the same numeral and sequential letters—so B4, C4, and D4 form a triad, because they have the same numeral and sequential letters. *Switching* a triad is just moving each of its members to the opposite basket; and this is legal whenever the middle member and one other are in the start basket and the third is in the finish basket. Though one would hardly suspect it at first, it turns out that this game (played with a certain domino set) is essentially the same as the peg-jumping game. It is easy to see why as soon as the members of that domino set are listed in the following revealing order:

A3, A4, A5,
B3, B4, B5,
C1, C2, C3, C4, C5, C6, C7,
D1, D2, D3,   D5, D6, D7,   D4,
E1, E2, E3, E4, E5, E6, E7,
F3, F4, F5,
G3, G4, G5.

Thus switching the D2-D3-D4 triad in the starting position would be equivalent to jumping the peg in slot D2 over the peg in slot D3, thereby emptying both of those slots and filling slot D4.

This kind of essential sameness among formal systems is called *formal equivalence*. Two formal systems are formally equivalent if they can be translated back and forth in roughly the following sense:

(1) for each position in one system, there is a unique corresponding position in the other system;

(2) the two starting positions correspond; and

(3) whenever you can get from one position to another in one system, you can get from the corresponding position to the corresponding position in the other system.

Actually, this definition is a little more stringent than necessary; but it gives the right idea. In particular, it leaves room for equivalent systems to be *very* different on the surface, so long as appropriate correspondences can be found.

There are, of course, an unlimited number of formal systems; and most of the interesting ones are significantly more complicated than our peg-jumping example (or its domino-switching equivalent). Two forms of complication are especially widespread and important; we introduce them by considering chess and algebra. The first is that there can be different *types* of tokens, such that what the rules permit depends on the type(s) of token(s) involved. Thus, in chess, each side begins with sixteen tokens of six different types; and whether it would be legal to move a certain token to a certain square always depends (among other things) on what type it is—what would be legal for a rook would not be legal for a bishop, and so on. In fact, whether two tokens are treated equally by the rules (in the same circumstances) is what determines whether they are tokens of the same type. For example, in some fancy chess sets, the pawns are little figurines, each one different from the next; but they are all the same type (namely, pawns), *because* the rules specify the same moves (namely, pawn moves) for all of them. To put it another way, tokens of the same type are formally interchangeable. Note, by the way, that the type of each token has to be perfectly definite (and also finitely checkable, and independent of the outside world) if the overall system is to remain digital.[3]

The second complication is that the *positions* of one formal system can function as the *tokens* in another ("higher level") system. We can see both how this works and why it is important, by considering high-school algebra as a formal system. Though one would not usually call algebra a game, the rules have actually been formalized to the point where it can be played like one. In the algebra game the tokens are equations or formulae, and the rules specify various transformations that can be made in these formulae—or (what comes to the same thing) various new formulae that can be written down, given some that are already written down. The starting position consists of a collection of formulae that are "given" (including, of course all the *axioms*); and making a "move" is adding a formula (*theorem*) to this list, by following the rules—that is, giving a formal *deduction* or *proof* (or, at least, a step in one). Now, the difficulty is that each different algebraic formula is a different type of token in this system, and there are indefinitely many of them—so how can the moves be finitely checkable? And the answer, of course, is that all these different tokens are built up in a systematic way out of a comparatively small collection of letters and standard symbols.

More specifically, each algebra-game token is a legal position in another game, which we might call the "well-formed-formula game." The tokens of the latter (i.e., the letters and symbols) are usually called "simple" or "atomic" tokens, to distinguish them

3. The number of different types of tokens is not a "deep" property of a formal system, as can be seen from the fact that the peg-jumping game has only one type, whereas the domino-switching game has 33 types—yet, in a deep sense, they are the same game. In effect, the domino version trades more sophisticated token discriminations for less sophisticated position discriminations.

from the tokens of the algebra game (i.e., the well-formed equations), which are "compound" or "molecular" tokens. The point is that the rules of the algebra game can apply to the various (molecular) tokens in terms of their structure; thus for *any* equation that has the same addend on both sides, you can "cancel" that addend. So, the same rule can apply in a parallel fashion to tokens of indefinitely many different types, so long as they have the specified structural features; hence, finitely many rules can suffice for the algebra game, even though there are indefinitely many types of well-formed algebraic formulae. This general strategy of using the positions of one formal system as the tokens of another makes large complicated systems much easier to deal with, and it is found throughout mathematics, formal logic, and virtually everywhere else that formal methods are used.

It might seem odd to include mathematics and logic here in the same category with chess and the peg-jumping game—because, roughly, their tokens *mean* something (and thus might be true or false, say). But their inclusion is perfectly serious and very important. Most mathematical and logical systems are *formal* in *exactly the same sense* that chess, checkers, and the like are formal: they have starting positions, and rules for making moves in any given position, and they are digital, in the sense explained above. From this point of view, any meanings that their tokens might have are utterly irrelevant; meaning has to do with the outside world, and is in no way part of any self-contained formal system, as such. There are, of course, other points of view, in which meaning is very important (we will discuss some of these when we come to interpretation and semantics). But, considered only *as formal systems*, games, logic, and mathematics are all equally meaningless, and entirely on a par.

III. Automatic Formal Systems (Turing Machines and Computers)

An *automatic* formal system is a physical device (such as a machine) which automatically manipulates the tokens of some formal system according to the rules of that system. It is like a chess set that sits there and plays chess *by itself*, without any intervention from the players, or an axiomatic system that writes out its own proofs and theorems, without any help from the mathematician. The exciting and astonishing fact is that such systems can be built. Looked at in the right way, this is exactly what computers are. There are two fundamental problems in building an automatic formal system. The first is getting the device to obey the rules (in principle, this problem has already been solved, as will be explained in the remainder of this section). The second is the "control" problem—how the device selects which move to make when there are several legal options. We will consider this briefly in the next section.

The theoretical ancestor of all automatic formal systems is a class of devices invented (in the abstract) by the mathematician Alan Turing and now called *Turing machines.* A Turing machine has:

(1) an unlimited number of *storage bins;*

(2) a finite number of *execution units;* and

(3) one *indicator unit.*

The indicator unit always indicates one execution unit (the "active" unit), and two storage bins (the "in" and "out" bins, respectively). Each storage bin can contain one formal token (any token, but only one at a time). Each execution unit has its own particular rule, which it obeys whenever it is the active unit. What that rule specifies will depend on what token is in the current in-bin; and in each case it will specify two things: first, what token to put in the current out-bin (discarding the previous contents, if any), and second, what the indicator unit should indicate next. The machine proceeds by steps: the active execution unit checks the in-bin, and then, according to what it finds there and what its rule is, it refills the out-bin and resets the indicator unit; then the next step begins. Usually there is one execution unit which does nothing; so if it ever gets activated, the machine stops.[4]

---

4. This is a slight generalization of Turing's original definition (Turing, 1937). In his version, the storage bins are all connected in a row, called a "tape"; each bin can hold only a *simple* token; the in-bin and the out-bin are always the same bin; and this in/out-bin is always either the same as or right next to the in/out-bin for the previous step. So Turing's machine chugs back and forth along the tape, one bin at a time, dealing with one simple token at a time. The surprising and important point, as we shall see shortly, is that (apart from convenience and efficiency) these differences don't make any difference.

Clearly, any Turing machine is an automated version of some formal system or other. The starting position is the initial contents of the storage bins, the moves are the machine steps, and the rules are those which the execution units obey (the control problem is handled in the rules for resetting the indicator unit). Not so obvious, but almost certainly true, is the converse: any automatic formal system can be formally imitated by some Turing machine.[5] "Formal imitation" is like formal equivalence, except for two things. First, since we are talking about *automatic* systems—that is, systems that actually "choose" which move to make—an imitating system has not merely to offer corresponding legal options in each corresponding position, but also to make the corresponding choice in each case. Let's call systems which are formally equivalent, and which make equivalent choices in each position *dynamically* equivalent. Second, the imitating system is often divided into two parts: the part which directly corresponds to the system being imitated, and another part which works behind the scenes, making everything come out right. The first part is called the *virtual machine*, and the second part the *program*.

For example, suppose some automatic formal system, *A*, is being formally imitated by some Turing machine, *T*. Then there is some virtual machine, *V*, which is both a part of *T*, and dynamically equivalent to *A*. So some portion (say half) of *T*'s storage bins will be allocated to *V*, as *V*'s storage bins; the tokens that appear in these bins will constitute *V*'s positions (which, in turn, correspond to *A*'s positions). The rest of *T*'s storage bins contain the *program* (and perhaps some "scratchpad" workspace). The reason a program is necessary is that in general *V*'s rules will be different from *T*'s rules. The program is a (finite) set of tokens so contrived that when *T* obeys its own rules with respect to *all* of its storage bins, it will, in effect, obey *V*'s rules with respect to the tokens in those bins that have been allocated to *V*. Intuitively, we can think of the program as "translating" *V*'s rules into *T*'s

5. This is a way of expressing *Church's thesis* (named after the logician, Alonzo Church); it has been proven true for all known, well-defined kinds of automatic formal system; but it cannot be proven in general, in part because the general idea of "automatic formal system" is itself somewhat intuitive, and not precisely definable.

rules, or even as "telling" *T* what *V's* rules are, so that *T* can follow them in moving the tokens in *V's* bins. In fact, it's not quite that straightforward, and *T's* rules have to have a certain versatility in the first place, in order to make such an imitation possible. But the point is: for any formal system, there is a Turing machine that can be programmed to imitate it.

But the fundamental importance of Turing machines rests on yet another truly amazing fact—a theorem first proved by Turing—which has, perhaps more than any other single result, shaped modern computer science. It is that there are special Turing machines, called *universal Turing machines*, which can be programmed to imitate any other Turing machine. In particular, one could imitate a Turing machine that was itself imitating some other automatic formal system—which means that, indirectly, the universal machine is also imitating that other automatic formal system. So, combining Church's thesis and Turing's theorem, a universal Turing machine can (suitably programmed) imitate any automatic formal system whatsoever! To put it another way: if you have just one universal Turing machine, and you are prepared to do some programming, you can have (a formal imitation of) any automatic formal system you care to specify.

It was soon discovered that there are a number of different kinds of universal machine, which are not (in the strict sense) Turing machines. But since they are universal, they can formally imitate any Turing machine; and, of course, any universal Turing machine can formally imitate any of them. In principle, therefore, it doesn't matter which one you have—*any* universal machine will do as well as any other (except for differences in efficiency, elegance, and the like). The reason this is important is that, with one qualification, universal machines can be built; that is what digital computers are. The one qualification is that a true universal machine must have unlimited storage, whereas any actual machine will have only a certain fixed amount (though it can be very large). So, aside from limitations of memory size, any standard digital computer can, with appropriate programming, formally imitate any automatic formal system yet discovered; that, basically, is why computers are so powerful.

Interestingly, computer programmers almost never program any of the machines that are actually constructed out of transistors, wires, and so on; rather, most programs are written for *virtual* machines, which are themselves merely being *imitated* by the hardware machine. The reason is that some universal machines are cheaper to build, while others are more convenient to use. The sensible course for a manufacturer, therefore, is to build the cheaper one, hire a few experts to write complicated programs (called "interpreters" or "compilers") which will make it imitate the more convenient ones, and then sell the package. The computer "languages" that you hear about—BASIC, FORTRAN, PASCAL, LISP, and so on—are really just some of these more convenient universal machines, which are widely imitated by various hardware machines. In fact, there are often more layers than that: thus the hardware directly imitates some intermediate virtual machine, which, in turn, is programmed to imitate the higher level machines, like those mentioned above. And, of course, when a programmer programs the latter, he or she is really designing yet another (virtual) machine, which the FORTRAN or LISP machine, or whatever, will formally imitate. This last machine, incidentally, will typically be designed for some special purpose, and so probably will not be a universal machine (though it could be).

A fundamental point should now be obvious: a particular physical object can be, at one and the same time, any number of *different machines.* There is no single correct answer to the question: which machine is that (really)? Of course, at the hardware level it is some particular model from some manufacturer; but at the same time it *is* (just as "really") all the other machines that are being imitated at various other levels. So a particular object is a particular machine (or automatic formal system) only at a particular level of description—at other levels of description it is other machines. Once we see this point, we see how foolish it is to say that computers are nothing but great big number crunchers, or that all they do is shuffle millions of "ones" and "zeros." Some machines are basically numerical calculators or "bit" manipulaters, but most of the interesting ones are nothing like that. And the fact that most actual commercial equipment can be described as such machines (e.g., most can be described as bit manipulators, on some level) is of no theoretical consequence. The machine one cares about—perhaps several levels of imitation up from the hardware—may have nothing at all to do with bits or numbers; and that is the only level that matters. For instance, an automatic system that played the peg-jumping game would probably not refer to numbers. Part of the reason for using the expression "automatic formal system" in place of "computer" is that the latter suggests a device which only "computes," and that is just wrong.

IV. The Control Problem

In the last section we considered systems in which each move is completely determined by the rules and the current position. This is essential in the design of an *automatic* system, because each step has to be made "automatically"—that is, it must be completely fixed by the state of the machine at the time.[6] But in most positions in most formal systems, any one of various moves would be legal; usually, that is what makes them interesting, as games or whatever. Does it follow that such interesting formal systems cannot be automated? No; it only follows that some device for deciding among the several legal options at any point must be automated as well.

The easiest way to think about it is to consider the machine as divided into two parts or "sub-machines": one to generate a number of legal options, and another to choose from among them. This, of course, is just an extension of the basic point that a given device can be various machines, depending on how you look at it; only now we are looking at it as *two* separate (virtual) machines, interacting with each other on the same level. The advantage is that we can see how the above dilemma is resolved: the move-generating submachine automates an "interesting" system, in which a variety of moves might be legal at any point; but the combined machine, with both parts together, satisfies the requirement that some *particular* next move be determined by the overall state of the device at each step. Designing the second submachine—the one that makes the choices, given the options—is the *control problem*. In most cases, control design turns out to be the hardest part of automating an interesting formal system.

In an average chess position, for example, a player will have 30

6. We ignore the possibility of "randomizers"—they don't affect the point.

or 35 legal possibilities to choose from. A beginning chess player could discover and list all of them without too much trouble; and designing a machine to do the same would not be terribly difficult either. The hard part—the entire difference between amateurs and world champions—is deciding *which* move to make, given these few possibilities; and that is the hard part to program as well. At first it might seem that big modern computers, with their tremendous speed and memory, could just look ahead to every possible outcome and see which moves lead to ultimate victory. In principle, this would be possible, since chess is technically finite; and such a machine would be literally invincible. In practical terms, however, such a computation is nowhere near possible. Assuming an average of 31.6 options per play gives a thousand (31.6×31.6) possible combinations per full move (each side having a turn). Thus looking ahead five moves would involve a quadrillion (10^{15}) possibilities; forty moves (a typical game) would involve 10^{120} possibilities. (For comparison, there have been fewer than 10^{18} seconds since the beginning of the universe.) These numbers are just preposterously large for any physically conceivable computer. They get that big because the number of choices at each additional step *multiplies* the total humber of possible combinations so far. For understandable reasons, this is called the *combinatorial explosion;* it plagues control design for all but the most straightforward problems.

Obviously, human chess-players don't make that many calculations either; in fact, the available evidence indicates that they make rather few. The trick is to consider only the *relevant* possibilities and ignore the rest. Thus most of those 30 or 35 options in a typical chess position would be totally pointless or manifestly stupid; hence, it would be a waste of time to consider all the possible developments that could follow after them. If the number of relevant alternatives could be reduced, say, to three at each stage, then looking ahead five complete moves would involve only 59,049 possible combinations—still too many for a person to consider (consciously, anyway), but well within reach of computers. So, the approach to the control problem in this case will almost certainly concentrate on determining which possible moves are the relevant ones, deserving further consideration.

Unfortunately, there is no fail-safe way to tell what is and isn't relevant. Everybody knows how a seemingly pointless or terrible move can turn out to be a brilliant stroke (once the opponent takes the bait). Any method that systematically bypasses certain moves as not worth pursuing will inevitably overlook some of these brilliancies. What we want is a method that is efficient at by-passing moves that *really are* worthless, but not easily fooled into ignoring moves that only *seem* worthless. Such methods in general are called "heuristics" (from the Greek word for "discover"), in contrast to "algorithms" (from the Latin word for the Arabic system of numerals, named after an Arabic mathematician). In current usage, the essential difference is this: an *algorithm* is a rule or procedure that is guaranteed to give a result meeting certain conditions (you just turn the crank and out it pops); a *heuristic,* on the other hand, is a rule or procedure that is more or less reliable, but not infallible—just a rule of thumb. We have algorithms for multiplying integers, arranging words in alphabetical order, and finding a checkmate in certain chess end-games (king and rook against king, for example). But there are no feasible algorithms for finding the best move in most other chess positions, or arranging words into poetry, or discovering proofs of arbitrary theorems in number theory. In these cases people proceed by intuition, inspiration, and a few explicit heuristic rules of thumb. (Intuition and inspiration might just be unconscious heuristics, of course—that's a disputed point among psychologists.)

Automatic systems, in any case, *must* proceed according to explicit rules (explicit, at least, in the program of the virtual machine). And in one sense these rules have to be algorithms—they have to determine the next move of the machine definitively, at each step. But often, whether a given rule is an algorithm or a heuristic depends on how the desired result is specified. Thus a reasonable rule of thumb for winning chess games is: never trade your queen for a pawn. Occasionally, of course, a queen sacrifice is a brilliant play; so this rule is only a heuristic when the result is specified as "Find the best move." But if the specified result is "Avoid swapping a queen for a pawn," then this rule is (trivially) infallible. The point is that the rules followed by the machine only *have to* be algorithms in this trivial sense. That is, it can perfectly well follow a bunch of inconclusive rules of thumb, relative to the interesting result specification (winning, say), so long as there are algorithms defining the heuristics themselves. The machine can infallibly follow quite fallible rules.

This shows, by the way, what's wrong with the idea that a (properly functioning) computer never makes a mistake. It just depends on what counts as a mistake—i.e., relative to which result specification. A chess-playing computer can function perfectly, never making a single mistake in following its internal heuristics but making lots of mistakes *in the game*, because its heuristics are rather clumsy. It is only at special tasks (like arithmetic and sorting), where there are algorithms for the interesting results, that a (perfect) computer can be infallible.

If we construe "heuristics" broadly to include any methods that improve a system's chances of making "correct" decisions while leaving some possibility of "mistakes," then any techniques for providing default assignments (standard assumptions), jumping to conclusions, or reading between the lines will be heuristic procedures. In this broad sense, a major part of the effort in artificial intelligence research goes toward finding better heuristics—ones that are more efficient and harder to fool—and better ways of implementing them on the machines (i.e., better algorithms for defining the heuristics). Indeed, in certain specialized areas, like game playing, theorem proving, and most tasks in "micro-worlds," work on heuristics is most of the problem. These areas are distinguished by the fact that the desired result is already known, and easy to specify in formal terms; for instance, in chess the goal is winning, and winning positions (checkmates) can be defined precisely. Many other forms of intelligent behavior, however, like writing good poetry (to take an extreme case) or carrying on a normal conversation (to take a case that does not *seem* so extreme) are not well defined in this way. In these areas, a major effort is required even to characterize the results toward which the heuristics are supposed to guide the system—and this involves the semantic and pragmatic issues to which we will turn shortly.

V. Digital and Analog

Automatic formal systems are, by definition, *digital* computers. There is another kind of device, sometimes called an *analog* computer, which is really quite different. Digital systems, remember, are self-contained, perfectly definite, and finitely checkable—all with regard to which moves are legal in which positions, according to the rules. An analog device, on the other hand, doesn't even have clearly defined moves, rules, and positions—though it may have states (which may change), and there is usually some way that it is supposed to work. The crucial difference is that in analog systems the relevant factors have not been defined and segregated to the point where it is always *perfectly definite* what the current state is, and whether it is doing what it is supposed to do. That is, there will often be slight inaccuracies, and marginal judgment calls, even when the device is working normally. To take the very simplest example, it is like the difference between a multiposition selector switch and a continuous tuning dial on a stereo. A switch has a number of click-stops, and it is always set definitely at one or another of them—you cannot set it between AM and FM. Of course, when you rotate it, it passes through intermediate angles; but these are irrelevant to its function, and (if it is a good switch) can be ignored. A tuning dial, on the other hand, moves smoothly without click-stops, and each angle tunes a different frequency. It is perfectly possible to set the dial between two stations, and, in fact, getting it "right on" a station can require a sensitive judgment call.

For some purposes, analog devices are very convenient. Scale models are a case in point. Suppose an architect wants to find out how the light and shadows will fall on a complicated structure at different times of day. A good analog approach is to build a model, illuminate it with a spotlight from various directions, and then *look* at it from various directions. A trickier but similar case is the use of laboratory animals in medical research. To estimate the physiological effects of weird drug combinations, experimenters can give corresponding (or exaggerated) doses to rats and then just wait to see what happens. Other common examples of analog devices are slide rules, electronic harmonic systems (modeling mechanical harmonic systems), and string-net pathfinders for railroad or highway networks. Though "analog" is itself a rather ill-defined notion, it clearly encompasses quite valuable tools.

Digital systems, however, have several inherent advantages. First, of course, universal machines are, by their very nature, extremely versatile; and that makes them more economical for each application. Second, analog systems can themselves often be *digitally simulated*—which makes the digital system even more versatile. For example, the architect's model could be simulated by writing equations for all the opaque surfaces in the building, and then calculating the paths of individual light rays at, say, one-inch intervals (for various positions of the sun). The whole thing might then drive a TV display, set for various viewing angles; and if all the intervals are small enough, the result can be pretty good. The amount of calculation involved can be prodigious, and the general technique has all the theoretical elegance of sandblasting; but computers are cheap, fast, and tireless, so it often works nicely.

It is sometimes said (with a grand air) that *any* analog device can be digitally simulated to *any* desired precision; but this is grossly misleading. Digital simulation is possible only when all the operative relationships in the analog system can be described in a relatively compact and precise way—e.g., not too many equations with not too many variables. The architectural simulation, for example, depends on assuming that all the light comes from the same direction and travels in a straight line until it's blocked by one of the few specified opaque surfaces. Without this simple structure to work from, the simulation could not get off the ground. Thus there is no comparable general description of the physiology of laboratory rats pumped full of odd chemicals— there are billions of potentially relevant subtle interactions and responses in a complex organic system, and the scope for combinatorial explosion is essentially indescribable. Hence, digital simulation is out of the question, except in very special cases where it is known in advance that only a certain few variables and relationships are relevant. It might seem that, in principle, simulation must be possible anyway, because rats are made of atoms, and each atom obeys known equations. But such a principle is utterly out to lunch. A single large molecule may have so many interdependent degrees of freedom, that no computer yet built could simulate it reliably in reasonable time; and one rat contains more molecules than there would be minicomputers if the entire volume of the earth were packed solid with them.

The real theoretical advantage of digital systems lies in quite another direction, and depends specifically on their digital nature. Consider two conventions for keeping track of money in a poker game. Each uses different colors for different denominations:

blue, red, and white for a hundred, ten, and one, respectively. But in one system, the unit of each denomination is a colored plastic disk (i.e., a poker chip), whereas in the other system it is a table-spoon of colored sand. The latter arrangement does have some merits—particularly the fact that *fractional* bets are possible—using less than a full tablespoon of white sand. But the chip system has one overwhelming advantage: all the bets are *exact.* By contrast, in measuring volumes of sand, there is always some small error, no matter how careful you are. Using the chips, and a very modest degree of care, it is possible to wager *exactly* 13 units (plus or minus zero); but with the sand this is impossible, even given the finest instruments in the world. The difference is that the chip system is digital; each token is perfectly definite, and there is no need for judgment calls.

The more complex and interdependent a system becomes, the more vulnerable it is to errors that propagate and get out of control. A small error in one component, affecting a more sensitive component, can result in a larger error going to the next component, and so on. We can see a rudimentary form of this, even in the poker example. Suppose the measurement error on sand volumes is ±2 percent; then it would be perverse to try to bet, say, 613 units, because the measurement error on the six blue tablespoons is worth four times as much (on the average) as all three white tablespoons—the latter simply drop out as irrelevant. There are ways to control such errors, of course, but only to a certain extent, and they tend to get expensive. The perfect defi-niteness of digital tokens, though confining in some cases, pays off in the elimination of this sort of error; thus, though you can-not bet a fraction of a unit with poker chips, there is no problem in betting 613 units—since six blue chips can be counted exactly, the white chips remain perfectly significant. This advantage is progressively more important for larger and more complicated systems—hence the contemporary predominance of digital methods.

VI. Semantics

Formal systems (and computers) can be more than mere games, because their tokens can have interpretations that relate them to the outside world. This is the domain of semantics and pragmatics.

Sometimes we say that the tokens in a certain formal system

mean something—that is, they are "signs," or "symbols," or "expressions" which "stand for," or "represent," or "say" something. Such relations connect the tokens to the outside world (what they are "about"), making it possible to use them for purposes like record-keeping, communication, calculation, and so on. A regular, systematic specification of what all the tokens of a system mean is called an *interpretation;* and the general theory of interpretations and meanings is called *semantics.* Accordingly, what any token means or says, and hence also whether it is true or false, and so on, are all *semantic properties* of that token.

Semantic properties are not formal properties. A formal system as such is completely self-contained and, viewed in that way, is just a meaningless game. In strictly formal terms, interpretation and meaning are entirely beside the point—they are extraneous "add ons" that are formally irrelevant. (When discussing a system that is to be interpreted, we call its purely formal characteristics and structure its *syntax;* "syntactical" is just another word for "formal," but it is generally used only when a contrast to "semantic" is relevant.)

So, formal tokens can lead two lives: *syntactical* (formal) *lives,* in which they are meaningless markers, moved according to the rules of some self-contained game; and (if the system is interpreted) *semantic lives,* in which they have meanings and significant relations to the outside world. The story of how these two lives get together is the foundation of modern mathematics and logic; and it is also the philosophical inspiration of cognitive science. We review the mathematical/logical case first, however, because it is better understood and there are fewer complications.

Consider a formal system (like the algebra game, discussed above in section 2) in which the positions are just sets of tokens, and the legal moves are just to add more tokens to the current position (depending, of course, on what is already in it). And suppose this system is interpreted in such a way that each of its (well-formed, complete) tokens "asserts" something—that is, each token (according to the meaning assigned to it by the interpretation) expresses some claim about the world. Then, depending on what the claim is and what the world is like, each of these tokens will be either true or false (relative to that interpretation).

Now, the *rules* of such a system will have the semantic property of being *truth-preserving* if and only if they meet the following condition: for any position which already contains *only* true tokens, any other token which can be added to that position (according to the rules) will also be true. In other words, if you start with tokens which are all true (under the interpretation), and if you obey the (purely formal) rules, then you can be sure there are no false tokens in any position you ever reach.

The rules of standard logical and mathematical systems, relative to their standard interpretations, are all truth-preserving; and, of course, the tokens in their starting positions (i.e., their axioms) are all true. Therefore, any token in any legal position of one of these systems is guaranteed also to be true! That is why we know in advance that their *theorems* (which are defined in purely syntactical/formal terms) are all *true* (which is a semantic property). Or, what comes to the same thing, in order to establish the semantic truth of a token in such a system, it suffices merely to prove it formally (play the game). This is how the "two lives" of the tokens get together; and it is the basic idea behind the formalization of modern logic and mathematics. In effect, given an interpreted formal system with true axioms and truth-preserving rules, if you take care of the syntax, *the semantics will take care of itself.*[7]

Most mathematical and logical systems are only partially interpreted, in the sense that some of their atomic tokens are left as variables, whose exact interpretation is to be specified by the user (in certain allowable ways). For example, in ordinary algebra, you can specify what the letters (variables) stand for in any way you want—so long as they stand for numbers. The important thing

---

7. Unfortunately, even in mathematics, formalization is not all that one might have hoped. Ideally, one would like a system such that not only were all its theorems true, but also all its true tokens were theorems (i.e., *only* theorems were true); such a system is *semantically complete*. But it has been shown (originally by Kurt Gödel, in 1931) that no consistent formalization of arithmetic can be complete; and the same applies to many other important axiomatic systems. Most people are agreed, however, that this result doesn't make any difference to cognitive science. (For a possibly dissenting view, see Lucas, 1961).

is that the rules are still truth-preserving, no matter what specific interpretation is given to the variables. For example, if a user knows, relative to some specific interpretation of the variables (as values in a physics problem, say) that the token

$$\frac{a - b}{c} + c = \frac{d - b}{c} + \frac{e(1 + e) - e}{c}$$

is true, then he or she can apply the purely *formal* rules for multiplying through, deleting parentheses, collecting terms, etc., and be assured that the token

$$a + c^2 = d + e^2$$

is also *true* (relative to the same interpretation). This is a vivid example of how useful it can be to have the semantics "take care of itself," if only one plays the syntactical game correctly.

An even more vivid example is computers, because precisely what an automatic formal system can do is "take care of the syntax"—i.e., play by the rules. The machine does not have to pay any attention to the interpretation or meaning of any of its tokens. It just chugs along purely formally; and if the starting position, rules, and interpretation happen to be of the sort we have been discussing, then it will automatically produce only truths. Given an appropriate formal system and interpretation, the semantics takes care of itself. This, fundamentally, is why computers can be so useful for calculations and the like—why they can be *computers* and not just electronic toys.

An automatic formal system with an interpretation such that the semantics will take care of itself is what Daniel Dennett (1981) calls a *semantic engine.* The discovery that semantic engines are possible—that with the right kind of formal system and interpretation, a machine can handle meanings—is the basic inspiration of cognitive science and artificial intelligence. Needless to say, however, mathematics and logic constitute a very narrow and specialized sample of general intelligence. People are both less and much more than automatic truth-preservers. Consequently, our discussion of interpretation needs to be expanded and generalized considerably; unfortunately, the issues will get messier and murkier as we go.

VII. Interpretation and Truth

Interpretation is especially straightforward in the special case of logic and mathematics because, in the final analysis, the only semantic property that matters is truth. Hence, it suffices if the theorems are guaranteed true, given the truth of the axioms (and special assumptions, if any)—that is, it suffices if the rules are truth-preserving. We shall see in the next section that there are many other cases where truth is far from all that matters in judging interpretations. But it is worth staying with the special case a little longer, to ask *why* truth has the importance it does; then it will be clearer why other considerations are important in other cases.

Imagine finding an automatic formal system that uses ordinary numerical tokens, and generates "theorems" (i.e., outputs) like the following:

$$= 5 = 1 \div \qquad = \div\, 3 - 1 - 8 \qquad + 1 - 5940$$
$$71 \div 92 \times \qquad = 61 = 040 \qquad 84 - 1 \times 5 =$$

Formally, of course, there is nothing wrong with these tokens; we can imagine any number of (strange and boring) games in which they would be perfectly legal moves. *Semantically,* on the other hand, they look like nonsensical, random gibberish—"arithmetic salad." That is, it seems impossible to construe them as expressing claims about the relationships among numbers (e.g., equations). But hold on: this reaction depends on a tacit adoption of the familiar Arabic interpretation of what the numerals and signs mean (the digit '1' stands for the number one, the '+' sign stands for addition, and so on). Formally, however, these numerals and signs are just neutral marks (tokens), and many other (unfamiliar) interpretations are possible (as if the outputs were in a code). Suppose, for instance, we construed the atomic tokens according to the following noncustomary scheme (using '⇒' to abbreviate "stands for"):

'1' ⇒ equals	'6' ⇒ zero	'+' ⇒ five
'2' ⇒ plus	'7' ⇒ one	'−' ⇒ six
'3' ⇒ minus	'8' ⇒ two	'X' ⇒ seven
'4' ⇒ times	'9' ⇒ three	'÷' ⇒ eight
'5' ⇒ div. by	'0' ⇒ four	'=' ⇒ nine

Then, with this table, we could translate the system's outputs back into the familiar notation as

$9 \div 9 = 8$	$98 - 6 = 62$	$5 = 6 \div 3 \times 4$
$1 = 83 + 7$	$90 = 94 \times 40$	$2 \times 6 = 7 \div 9$

Superficially, these look more like equations, and hence not nearly as random or crazy as the raw (untranslated) outputs. Unfortunately, they're all false—*wildly* false. In fact, on closer inspection, the digits look just as random as before; we still have arithmetic salad, only disguised in regular equation format.

But there are over a trillion possible ways to interpret these fifteen atomic tokens (even sticking to permutations of the ordinary one). Here is just one more possibility, together with the translations it would yield for the original outputs

'1' ⇒ equals	'6' ⇒ zero	'+' ⇒ five
'2' ⇒ div. by	'7' ⇒ nine	'−' ⇒ four
'3' ⇒ times	'8' ⇒ eight	'X' ⇒ three
'4' ⇒ minus	'9' ⇒ seven	'÷' ⇒ two
'5' ⇒ plus	'0' ⇒ six	'=' ⇒ one

$1 + 1 = 2$	$12 \times 4 = 48$	$5 = 4 + 7 - 6$
$9 = 27 \div 3$	$10 = 16 - 6$	$8 - 4 = 3 + 1$

What a difference! These not only look like equations, they *are* equations—they are *true*. And, intuitively, that strongly inclines us to prefer this interpretation—to think it "better" or "righter" than the ones which yield random nonsense as readings. This intuition has several theoretical considerations behind it.

In the first place, formal tokens in themselves never intrinsically favor one interpretation scheme over any other—from their point of view, all interpretations are equally extraneous and arbitrary. So if some particular interpretation is to be adopted, over all the other possibilities, there must be something distinctive about it, which makes it stand out in the crowd. But, as our example suggests, an interpretation that renders a system's theorems as truths is a rare and special discovery (the alternatives yield mostly gibberish). Hence, such an interpretation is distinctive.

Second, if we regard an interpretation as *relating* or *connecting* a formal system to the outside world (i.e., to whatever its tokens are "about"), then the distinctiveness of the preferred interpretation should lie in that relation. But if a system's theorems are all true under an interpretation, then there is, in fact, a relation strong enough to support inferences about the world from the theorems, and about the theorems from (knowledge of) the world. Thus we can discover new facts about numbers, using an interpreted formalization of arithmetic; likewise, the above-noted (practical) utility of the semantics "taking care of itself" depends on the *truth*-preservingness of the rules. In the other direction, we (sometimes) can predict theorems, given what we know about numbers. For instance, if our example system produced the theorem fragment '7401 . . .', we would be hard pressed to guess its completion, from its form alone. The first interpretation scheme (which gives '1 X 4 = . . .') is no help either, because its "translations" come out randomly false. But knowing that the second scheme gives '9 – 6 = . . .', and that the theorem will be true, makes the prediction easy: the completion will be whichever token means "three" (namely, 'X'). The reliability of such inferences (both ways) indicates that *this* relation between the tokens on the one hand and the numbers and operations on the other is *not* arbitrary—i.e., this interpretation somehow genuinely connects them.

Finally, and most important, interpreting is tantamount to "making sense of"; hence, if the system doesn't end by making sense (but, rather, makes nonsense), then the interpretation attempt has failed. Arithmetic salad does not make sense (whether clothed in the outer form of equations, or not); and that, primarily, is why random interpretation schemes don't really give *interpretations* at all. In the context of arithmetic, true equations make eminently good sense—hence the preferability of our second scheme. (An occasional lapse could be understood as meaningful though false; but constant, random falsehood is, in effect, impossible—because the tokens cease to make any sense at all.) So truth matters to interpretations not only because it provides a nonarbitrary choice among candidate schemes and because this choice reflects some relation between the system and what it is (interpreted to be) "about," but also, and most of all, because wild falsehood amounts to *nonsense*—the antithesis of meaning.

VIII. Interpretation and Pragmatics

In most activities involving meaningful tokens (other than logic and mathematics) truth is far from the only semantic property that matters. Take ordinary conversation, for example. In the first place, many speech acts—such as questions, commands, expletives, and even most banter and quips—are neither true nor false; so some other kind of appropriateness must be what matters. And even in the case of statements (which typically *are* true or false), much else is important besides just whether they are true. For instance, in conversation it is also important (usually) to stick to the topic, be polite, say only what is worth saying (not obvious, inane, redundant, etc.)—and, in general, to avoid making an ass of oneself. It is not clear to what extent such conditions should be called "semantic" (some authors prefer to call them "pragmatic"), but they are all relevant to the acceptability of an interpretation as soon as you get away from special cases like logic and mathematics.

In these cases we are driven back to the more general but also somewhat fuzzier notion of "making sense" as our criterion for the adequacy of interpretations. There is, to my knowledge, no satisfactory philosophical account of what it is to make sense; indeed, it is questionable whether a precise, explicit definition is even possible. Still, there is much to be said, and philosophers have worked out a variety of rough characterizations and prerequisites (sometimes referred to by the peculiar misnomer "principles of charity"). The truth of simple, uncontroversial declarative outputs (i.e., tokens interpreted as such) is, of course, one rough prerequisite on making sense in general; and a few philosophers (notably, Davidson, 1973b) are inclined to stick with that. But most would agree there are other considerations.

The most widely discussed, *rationality*, is loosely analogous to truth-preservation in mathematical systems. The idea is that "obvious consequences" of tokens in the current position should be relatively easy to evoke from the system (as outputs), or to get it to add to the position. In general, the point applies not only to logically valid inferences, but to common sense inferences of all kinds, including the formation of subsidiary goals and attitudes (given the facts, goals and attitudes already at hand) and also the ability to solve suitably simple "problems." Further, the system should have a tendency to root out tensions and incompatibilities among the tokens in its positions—e.g., by altering or eliminating one of the offending parties. It goes without saying that this notion is not very precisely defined; but it is equally clear that "rationality" in some such sense is an important factor in "making sense."

A second important factor is reliable interaction with the world via transducers. A *transducer* is a kind of automatic encoder or decoder which either reacts to the physical environment and adds tokens to the current position (an *input* transducer), or else reacts to certain tokens in the current position and produces physical behavior in the environment (an *output* transducer). So transducers are analogous to sense organs and motor systems in animals and people; and they become, in effect, part of the whole system, when it comes to determining whether (according to some interpretation) the system is making sense. Roughly, when an input transducer adds a token that is interpreted as a report, then (other things being equal) that report ought to be correct; and when an output transducer reacts to a token interpreted as a decision to do something, then (other things being equal) the behavior produced ought to be that action. For instance, if the token that regularly gets added in response to a rabbit running by were interpreted to mean "Lo, a flaming giraffe," then the system isn't making much sense—which is to say, the interpretation is probably defective. This is essentially Quine's (1960; ch. 2) criterion of preserving "stimulus meaning." Though he doesn't mention it, there is a corresponding condition on the reliability of output transducers.

A third condition on making sense is *conversational cooperativeness,* in more or less the sense introduced by Grice (1975)—assuming, of course, that the system is interpreted as "conversing" or communicating in some way. Suppose, for example, that you ask it what the capital of Illinois is (i.e., give it a token so interpreted); then "It is Springfield" or "I don't know" would be perfectly sensible replies, but "Easy on the mustard, please," or "Wow, 400 squirrels" would not. Even a false but relevant answer, like "It is Chicago," makes much more sense in context than some utterly irrelevant truth, such as "2+7 = 9." Answering the question one is asked is a very basic example of being cooperative; there are many subtler points as well, concerning how much information is given in the answer, the manner in which it is provided, how it pertains to the larger topic, whether it is rude, obvious, or funny, and so on. Cooperativeness is clearly a matter of degree, involving judgment and compromise; but if it is ever lacking altogether, a "conversation" quickly reduces to impossible nonsense.

A related consideration is what Austin (1970) called "felicity conditions" (compare also Searle's 1969 "constitutive rules"). Roughly, the idea is that one cannot or cannot "properly" make an unkeepable promise, threaten someone with something he or she wants anyway, give commands for which one lacks the authority, propose marriage to one's spouse, offer to sell (or buy) the planet Mars, and so on. That is, these "speech acts" or "performances" have various prerequisites or presuppositions; and if the prerequisites are not satisfied, there is something wrong with doing them. As with all of our conditions, a few such violations look merely foolish, or perhaps dishonest; but wholesale and flagrant disregard will yield an overall pattern of outputs which fails to make sense—and hence the interpretation will be unsatisfactory.

These last two points, more than the earlier ones, bring in the relevant "context," and indicate the importance of considering the outputs in relation to one another and in relation to the situation in which they are produced. Further work in this direction must confront issues like what is involved in the coherence of extended conversations, dramatic plots, and scholarly essays. Very little in the way of explicit theories or conditions has been proposed in this area—which is symptomatic of an impoverished philosophical literature on the problem of understanding and intelligibility in general. (For a brief overview of some of the difficulties, see Haugeland, 1979, and the works cited there.)

Interpreting an automatic formal system is finding a way of

construing its outputs (assigning them meanings) such that they consistently make reasonable sense in the light of the system's prior inputs and other outputs. In the special case of logical and mathematical systems, it suffices if the outputs are consistently true; and this can be guaranteed by having only true axioms and truth-preserving rules. In more ambitious systems, however, including any with aspirations to artificial intelligence, truth is not a sufficient condition on the output tokens "making sense"— many other considerations are important as well. Hence, there is no reason to believe that truth-preservingness is the only, or even the most important, requirement to be imposed on the system's rules. Unfortunately, the alternative—nonasininity-preservation, perhaps?—is not at all clear. And the foregoing motley list of amorphous "further conditions" holds out little promise of any quick or clean solution. I think that this problem constitutes one of the deepest challenges that cognitive science must face.

IX. Cognitive Science (Again)

The basic idea of cognitive science is that *intelligent beings are semantic engines*—in other words, automatic formal systems with interpretations under which they consistently make sense. We can now see why this includes psychology and artificial intelligence on a more or less equal footing: people and intelligent computers (if and when there are any) turn out to be merely different manifestations of the same underlying phenomenon. Moreover, with universal hardware, *any* semantic engine can in principle be formally imitated by a computer if only the right program can be found. And that will guarantee *semantic imitation* as well, since (given the appropriate formal behavior) the semantics is "taking care of itself" anyway. Thus we also see why, from this perspective, artificial intelligence can be regarded as psychology in a particularly pure and abstract form. The same fundamental structures are under investigation, but in AI, all the relevant parameters are under direct experimental control (in the programming), without any messy physiology or ethics to get in the way.

Of course, it is possible that this is all wrong. It might be that people just *aren't* semantic engines, or even that no semantic engine (in a robot, say) can be genuinely intelligent. There are two quite different strategies for arguing that cognitive science is basically misconceived. The first, or *hollow shell* strategy has the following form: no matter how well a (mere) semantic engine acts *as if* it understands, etc., it can't *really* understand anything, because it isn't (or hasn't got) "X" (for some "X"). In other words, a robot based on a semantic engine would still be a sham and a fake, no matter how "good" it got. The other, or *poor substitute*, strategy draws the line sooner: it denies that (mere) semantic engines are capable even of acting as if they understood—semantic engine robots are not going to get that good in the first place. The first strategy tends to be more conceptual and *a priori*, while the second depends more on experimental results. (Compare: No beverage made from coal tar would be wine, no matter what it tasted like; with: There's no way to turn coal tar into a beverage that tastes like wine.)

The most obvious candidate for "X" in the hollow shell strategy is *consciousness*; thus "No computer really understands anything, no matter how smart it *seems,* because it isn't conscious." Now it is true that cognitive science sheds virtually no light on the issue of what consciousness is (though see Dennett, 1978d, for a valiant effort); indeed, the term itself is almost a dirty word in the technical literature. So it's natural to suspect that something difficult and important is being left out. Unfortunately, nobody else has anything very specific or explanatory to say about consciousness either—it is just mysterious, regardless of your point of view. But that means that a cognitivist can say, "Look, none of us has much of an idea of what consciousness is; so how can we be so sure *either* that genuine understanding is impossible without it, *or* that semantic engines won't ever have it (e.g., when they are big and sophisticated enough)?" Those questions may seem intuitively perverse, but they are very difficult to answer.

A different candidate for "X" is what we might call *original intentionality.*[8] The idea is that a semantic engine's tokens only have meaning because we give it to them; their intentionality, like that of smoke signals and writing, is essentially borrowed, hence *derivative.* To put it bluntly: computers themselves don't mean anything by their tokens (any more than books do)—they only

8. "Intentionality" is a philosopher's term for being about something, or having a meaning.

mean what we say they do. Genuine understanding, on the other hand, is intentional "in its own right" and not derivatively from something else. But this raises a question similar to the last one: What does it take to have original intentionality (and how do we know computers can't have it)? If we set aside divine inspiration (and other magical answers), it seems that original intentionality must depend on whether the object has a suitable structure and/or dispositions, relative to the environment. But it is hard to see how these could fail to be suitable (whatever exactly that is) if the object (semantic engine *cum* robot) always *acts* intelligent, self-motivated, responsive to questions and challenges, and so on. A book, for instance, pays no attention to what "it" says—and that's (one reason) why we really do not think it is the *book* which is saying anything (but rather the author). A perfect robot, however, would seem to act on its opinions, defend them from attack, and modify them when confronted with counter-evidence—all of which would suggest that they really are the *robot's own* opinions.

A third candidate for "X" in the hollow shell strategy is *caring*. Here the intuition is that a system could not really *mean* anything unless it had a stake in what it was saying—unless its beliefs and goals mattered to it. Otherwise, it is just mouthing noises, or generating tokens mechanically. The popular picture of computers as cold (metallic, unfeeling) calculators motivates the view that they could never really *care* about anything, hence that they could never genuinely *mean* (or understand) anything on their own. But, of course, the legitimacy of this picture is just what we're inquiring about. If cognitive science is on the right track, then some semantic engines—starting with people—*can* care about things, be involved with them, have personalities, and so on. And, indeed, if we had a robot which *seemed* (in appropriate circumstances) to be sympathetic, disappointed, embarrassed, ambitious, offended, affectionate, and so on, it would be very difficult to claim that it was merely an unfeeling hunk of metal—especially if this very remark "hurt its feelings." Again, we need some further criterion or intuitive test for what it is to have the appropriate inner quality, if we are to justify saying that a semantic engine which merely *acts as if* it is intelligent (etc.) is a hollow shell.

The "poor substitute" strategy—which I, myself, think is much more likely to succeed—argues instead that semantic engines will never even *seem* to have the full range of common sense and values of people. The basic suggestion is that those areas in which computers excel (or can be expected eventually to excel) are all of a special sort, where the relevant considerations are comparatively few and well defined. This includes formal games (by definition) and also a number of other routine technical or micro-world tasks. But it is an open question whether the intelligence manifested in everyday life, not to mention art, invention, and discovery, is of essentially this same sort (though presumably more complicated). Cognitive science, in effect, is betting that it is; but the results are just not in yet. The above issues of consciousness, original intentionality, and caring can all be raised again in the poor substitute strategy, in a more empirical form: Does the system *in fact* act as if it had the relevant "X"? And if, so far, the answer is always "No," is there any pattern to the failures which might give us a clue to the deeper nature of the problems, or the ultimate outcome? These, it seems to me, are the most important questions, but they are beyond the scope of this introduction.

1

Computer Science as Empirical Inquiry:

Symbols and Search

ALLEN NEWELL
HERBERT A. SIMON

COMPUTER SCIENCE is the study of the phenomena surrounding computers. The founders of this society understood this very well when they called themselves the Association for Computing Machinery. The machine—not just the hardware, but the programmed living machine—is the organism we study.

This is the tenth Turing Lecture. The nine persons who preceded us on this platform have presented nine different views of computer science. For our organism, the machine, can be studied at many levels and from many sides. We are deeply honored to appear here today and to present yet another view, the one that has permeated the scientific work for which we have been cited. We wish to speak of computer science as empirical inquiry.

Our view is only one of many; the previous lectures make that clear. However, even taken together the lectures fail to cover the whole scope of our science. Many fundamental aspects of it have not been represented in these ten awards. And if the time ever arrives, surely not soon, when the compass has been boxed, when computer science has been discussed from every side, it will be time to start the cycle again. For the hare as lecturer will have to make an annual sprint to overtake the cumulation of small, incremental gains that the tortoise of scientific and technical development has achieved in his steady march. Each year will create a new gap and call for a new sprint, for in science there is no final word.

Computer science is an empirical discipline. We would have

called it an experimental science, but like astronomy, economics, and geology, some of its unique forms of observation and experience do not fit a narrow stereotype of the experimental method. Nonetheless, they are experiments. Each new machine that is built is an experiment. Actually constructing the machine poses a question to nature; and we listen for the answer by observing the machine in operation and analyzing it by all analytical and measurement means available. Each new program that is built is an experiment. It poses a question to nature, and its behavior offers clues to an answer. Neither machines nor programs are black boxes; they are artifacts that have been designed, both hardware and software, and we can open them up and look inside. We can relate their structure to their behavior and draw many lessons from a single experiment. We don't have to build 100 copies of, say, a theorem prover, to demonstrate statistically that it has not overcome the combinatorial explosion of search in the way hoped for. Inspection of the program in the light of a few runs reveals the flaw and lets us proceed to the next attempt.

We build computers and programs for many reasons. We build them to serve society and as tools for carrying out the economic tasks of society. But as basic scientists we build machines and programs as a way of discovering new phenomena and analyzing phenomena we already know about. Society often becomes confused about this, believing that computers and programs are to be constructed only for the economic use that can be made of them (or as intermediate items in a developmental sequence leading to such use). It needs to understand that the phenomena surrounding computers are deep and obscure, requiring much experimentation to assess their nature. It needs to understand that, as in any science, the gains that accrue from such experimentation and understanding pay off in the permanent acquisition of new techniques; and that it is these techniques that will create the instruments to help society in achieving its goals.

Our purpose here, however, is not to plead for understanding from an outside world. It is to examine one aspect of our science, the development of new basic understanding by empirical inquiry. This is best done by illustrations. We will be pardoned if, presuming upon the occasion, we choose our examples from the area of our own research. As will become apparent, these examples involve the whole development of artificial intelligence, especially in its early years. They rest on much more than our own personal contributions. And even where we have made direct contributions, this has been done in cooperation with others. Our collaborators have included especially Cliff Shaw, with whom we formed a team of three through the exciting period of the late fifties. But we have also worked with a great many colleagues and students at Carnegie-Mellon University.

Time permits taking up just two examples. The first is the development of the notion of a symbolic system. The second is the development of the notion of heuristic search. Both conceptions have deep significance for understanding how information is processed and how intelligence is achieved. However, they do not come close to exhausting the full scope of artificial intelligence, though they seem to us to be useful for exhibiting the nature of fundamental knowledge in this part of computer science.

I. Symbols and Physical Symbol Systems

One of the fundamental contributions to knowledge of computer science has been to explain, at a rather basic level, what symbols are. This explanation is a scientific proposition about Nature. It is empirically derived, with a long and gradual development.

Symbols lie at the root of intelligent action, which is, of course, the primary topic of artificial intelligence. For that matter, it is a primary question for all of computer science. For all information is processed by computers in the service of ends, and we measure the intelligence of a system by its ability to achieve stated ends in the face of variations, difficulties, and complexities posed by the task environment. This general investment of computer science in attaining intelligence is obscured when the tasks being accomplished are limited in scope, for then the full variations in the environment can be accurately foreseen. It becomes more obvious as we extend computers to more global, complex and knowledge-intensive tasks—as we attempt to make them our agents, capable of handling on their own the full contingencies of the natural world.

Our understanding of the system's requirements for intelligent action emerges slowly. It is composite, for no single elementary thing accounts for intelligence in all its manifestations. There is no "intelligence principle," just as there is no "vital principle" that conveys by its very nature the essence of life. But the lack of a simple *deus ex machina* does not imply that there are no structural requirements for intelligence. One such requirement is the ability to store and manipulate symbols. To put the scientific question, we may paraphrase the title of a famous paper by Warren McCulloch (1961): What is a symbol, that intelligence may use it, and intelligence, that it may use a symbol?

LAWS OF QUALITATIVE STRUCTURE

All sciences characterize the essential nature of the systems they study. These characterizations are invariably qualitative in nature, for they set the terms within which more detailed knowledge can be developed. Their essence can often be captured in very short, very general statements. One might judge these general laws, because of their limited specificity, as making relatively little contribution to the sum of a science, were it not for the historical evidence that shows them to be results of the greatest importance.

The Cell Doctrine in Biology. A good example of a law of qualitative structure is the cell doctrine in biology, which states that the basic building block of all living organisms is the cell. Cells come in a large variety of forms, though they all have a nucleus surrounded by protoplasm, the whole encased by a membrane. But this internal structure was not, historically, part of the specification of the cell doctrine; it was subsequent specificity developed by intensive investigation. The cell doctrine can be conveyed almost entirely by the statement we gave above, along with some vague notions about what size a cell can be. The impact of this law on biology, however, has been tremendous, and the lost motion in the field prior to its gradual acceptance was considerable.

Plate Tectonics in Geology. Geology provides an interesting example of a qualitative structure law, interesting because it has gained acceptance in the last decade and so its rise in status is still fresh in our memory. The theory of plate tectonics asserts that the surface of the globe is a collection of huge plates—a few dozen in all—which move (at geological speeds) against, over, and under each other into the center of the earth, where they lose their identity. The movements of the plates account for the shapes and relative locations of the continents and oceans, for the areas of volcanic and earthquake activity, for the deep sea ridges, and so on. With a few additional particulars as to speed and size, the essential theory has been specified. It was of course not accepted until it succeeded in explaining a number of details, all of which hung together (e.g. accounting for flora, fauna, and stratification agreements between West Africa and Northeast South America). The plate tectonics theory is highly qualitative. Now that it is accepted, the whole earth seems to offer evidence for it everywhere, for we see the world in its terms.

The Germ Theory of Disease. It is little more than a century since Pasteur enunciated the germ theory of disease, a law of qualitative structure that produced a revolution in medicine. The theory proposes that most diseases are caused by the presence and multiplication in the body of tiny single-celled living organisms, and that contagion consists in the transmission of these organisms from one host to another. A large part of the elaboration of the theory consisted in identifying the organisms associated with specific diseases, describing them, and tracing their life histories. The fact that the law has many exceptions—that many diseases are not produced by germs—does not detract from its importance. The law tells us to look for a particular kind of cause; it does not insist that we will always find it.

The Doctrine of Atomism. The doctrine of atomism offers an interesting contrast to the three laws of qualitative structure we have just described. As it emerged from the work of Dalton and his demonstrations that the chemicals combined in fixed proportions, the law provided a typical example of qualitative structure: the elements are composed of small, uniform particles, differing from one element to another. But because the underlying species of atoms are so simple and limited in their variety, quantitative theories were soon formulated which assimilated all the general structure in the original qualitative hypothesis. With cells, tectonic plates, and germs, the variety of structure is so great that the underlying qualitative principle remains distinct, and its contribution to the total theory clearly discernible.

Conclusion. Laws of qualitative structure are seen everywhere in science. Some of our greatest scientific discoveries are to be found among them. As the examples illustrate, they often set the terms on which a whole science operates.

PHYSICAL SYMBOL SYSTEMS

Let us return to the topic of symbols, and define a *physical symbol system*. The adjective "physical" denotes two important features: (1) Such systems clearly obey the laws of physics—they are realizable by engineered systems made of engineered components; (2) although our use of the term "symbol" prefigures our intended interpretation, it is not restricted to human symbol systems.

A physical symbol system consists of a set of entities, called symbols, which are physical patterns that can occur as components of another type of entity called an expression (or symbol structure). Thus a symbol structure is composed of a number of instances (or tokens) of symbols related in some physical way (such as one token being next to another). At any instant of time the system will contain a collection of these symbol structures. Besides these structures, the system also contains a collection of processes that operate on expressions to produce other expressions: processes of creation, modification, reproduction, and destruction. A physical symbol system is a machine that produces through time an evolving collection of symbol structures. Such a system exists in a world of objects wider than just these symbolic expressions themselves.

Two notions are central to this structure of expressions, symbols, and objects: designation and interpretation.

Designation. An expression designates an object if, given the expression, the system can either affect the object itself or behave in ways depending on the object.

In either case, access to the object via the expression has been obtained, which is the essence of designation.

Interpretation. The system can interpret an expression if the expression designates a process and if, given the expression, the system can carry out the process.[1]

1. *Editor's note:* This is a different notion of "interpretation" from that explained in the introduction.

Interpretation implies a special form of dependent action: given an expression, the system can perform the indicated process, which is to say, it can evoke and execute its own processes from expressions that designate them.

A system capable of designation and interpretation, in the sense just indicated, must also meet a number of additional requirements, of completeness and closure. We will have space only to mention these briefly; all of them are important and have far-reaching consequences.

(1) A symbol may be used to designate any expression whatsoever. That is, given a symbol, it is not prescribed a priori what expressions it can designate. This arbitrariness pertains only to symbols: the symbol tokens and their mutual relations determine what object is designated by a complex expression. (2) There exist expressions that designate every process of which the machine is capable. (3) There exist processes for creating any expression and for modifying any expression in arbitrary ways. (4) Expressions are stable; once created, they will continue to exist until explicitly modified or deleted. (5) The number of expressions that the system can hold is essentially unbounded.

The type of system we have just defined is not unfamiliar to computer scientists. It bears a strong family resemblance to all general purpose computers. If a symbol-manipulation language, such as LISP, is taken as defining a machine, then the kinship becomes truly brotherly. Our intent in laying out such a system is not to propose something new. Just the opposite: it is to show what is now known and hypothesized about systems that satisfy such a characterization.

We can now state a general scientific hypothesis—a law of qualitative structure for symbol systems:

The Physical Symbol System Hypothesis. A physical symbol system has the necessary and sufficient means for general intelligent action.

By "necessary" we mean that any system that exhibits general intelligence will prove upon analysis to be a physical symbol system. By "sufficient" we mean that any physical symbol system of sufficient size can be organized further to exhibit general intelligence. By "general intelligent action" we wish to indicate the same scope of intelligence as we see in human action: that in any real situation behavior appropriate to the ends of the system and adaptive to the demands of the environment can occur, within some limits of speed and complexity.

The Physical Symbol System Hypothesis clearly is a law of qualitative structure. It specifies a general class of systems within which one will find those capable of intelligent action.

This is an empirical hypothesis. We have defined a class of systems; we wish to ask whether that class accounts for a set of phenomena we find in the real world. Intelligent action is everywhere around us in the biological world, mostly in human behavior. It is a form of behavior we can recognize by its effects whether it is performed by humans or not. The hypothesis could indeed be false. Intelligent behavior is not so easy to produce that any system will exhibit it willy-nilly. Indeed, there are people whose analyses lead them to conclude either on philosophical or on scientific grounds that the hypothesis *is* false. Scientifically, one can attack or defend it only by bringing forth empirical evidence about the natural world.

We now need to trace the development of this hypothesis and look at the evidence for it.

DEVELOPMENT OF THE SYMBOL SYSTEM HYPOTHESIS

A physical symbol system is an instance of a universal machine. Thus the symbol system hypothesis implies that intelligence will be realized by a universal computer. However, the hypothesis goes far beyond the argument, often made on general grounds of physical determinism, that any computation that is realizable can be realized by a universal machine, provided that it is specified. For it asserts specifically that the intelligent machine is a symbol system, thus making a specific architectural assertion about the nature of intelligent systems. It is important to understand how this additional specificity arose.

Formal Logic. The roots of the hypothesis go back to the program of Frege and of Whitehead and Russell for formalizing logic: capturing the basic conceptual notions of mathematics in logic and putting the notions of proof and deduction on a secure footing. This effort culminated in mathematical logic—our familiar propositional, first-order, and higher-order logics. It developed a characteristic view, often referred to as the "symbol game." Logic, and by incorporation all of mathematics, was a game played with meaningless tokens according to certain purely syntactic rules. All meaning had been purged. One had a mechanical, though permissive (we would now say nondeterministic), system about which various things could be proved. Thus progress was first made by walking away from all that seemed relevant to meaning and human symbols. We could call this the stage of formal symbol manipulation.

This general attitude is well reflected in the development of information theory. It was pointed out time and again that Shannon had defined a system that was useful only for communication and selection, and which had nothing to do with meaning. Regrets were expressed that such a general name as "information theory" had been given to the field, and attempts were made to rechristen it as "the theory of selective information"—to no avail, of course.

Turing Machines and the Digital Computer. The development of the first digital computers and of automata theory, starting with Turing's own work in the '30s, can be treated together. They agree in their view of what is essential. Let us use Turing's own model, for it shows the features well.

A Turing machine consists of two memories: an unbounded tape and a finite state control. The tape holds data, i.e. the famous zeroes and ones. The machine has a very small set of proper operations—read, write, and scan operations—on the tape. The read operation is not a data operation, but provides conditional branching to a control state as a function of the data under the read head. As we all know, this model contains the essentials of all computers, in terms of what they can do, though other computers with different memories and operations might carry out the same computations with different requirements of space and time. In particular, the model of a Turing machine contains within it the notions both of what cannot be computed and of universal machines—computers that can do anything that can be done by any machine.

We should marvel that two of our deepest insights into information processing were achieved in the thirties, before modern computers came into being. It is a tribute to the genius of Alan Turing. It is also a tribute to the development of mathematical logic at the time, and testimony to the depth of computer science's obligation to it. Concurrently with Turing's work appeared the work of the logicians Emil Post and (independently) Alonzo Church. Starting from independent notions of logistic systems (Post productions and recursive functions, respectively), they arrived at analogous results on undecidability and universality—results that were soon shown to imply that all three systems were equivalent. Indeed, the convergence of all these attempts to define the most general class of information-processing systems provides some of the force of our conviction that we have captured the essentials of information processing in these models.

In none of these systems is there, on the surface, a concept of the symbol as something that *designates*. The data are regarded as just strings of zeroes and ones—indeed that data be inert is essential to the reduction of computation to physical process. The finite state control system was always viewed as a small controller, and logical games were played to see how small a state system could be used without destroying the universality of the machine. No games, as far as we can tell, were ever played to add new states dynamically to the finite control—to think of the control memory as holding the bulk of the system's knowledge. What was accomplished at this stage was half the principle of interpretation—showing that a machine could be run from a description. Thus this is the stage of automatic formal symbol manipulation.

The Stored Program Concept. With the development of the second generation of electronic machines in the mid-forties (after the Eniac) came the stored program concept. This was rightfully hailed as a milestone, both conceptually and practically. Programs now can be data, and can be operated on as data. This capability is, of course, already implicit in the model of Turing: the descriptions are on the very same tape as the data. Yet the idea was realized only when machines acquired enough memory to make it practicable to locate actual programs in some internal place. After all, the Eniac had only twenty registers.

The stored program concept embodies the second half of the interpretation principle, the part that says that the system's own data can be interpreted. But it does not yet contain the notion of designation—of the physical relation that underlies meaning.

List-Processing. The next step, taken in 1956, was list-processing. The contents of the data structures were now symbols, in the sense of our physical symbol system: patterns that designated, that had referents. Lists held addresses which permitted access to other lists—thus the notion of list structures. That this was a new view was demonstrated to us many times in the early days of list processing when colleagues would ask where the data were—that is, which list finally held the collections of bits that were the content of the system. They found it strange that there were no such bits, there were only symbols that designated yet other symbol structures.

List-processing is simultaneously three things in the development of computer science. (1) It is the creation of a genuine dynamic memory structure in a machine that had heretofore been perceived as having fixed structure. It added to our ensemble of operations those that built and modified structure in addition to those that replaced and changed content. (2) It was an early demonstration of the basic abstraction that a computer consists of a set of data types and a set of operations proper to these data types, so that a computational system should employ whatever data types are appropriate to the application, independent of the underlying machine. (3) List-processing produced a model of designation, thus defining symbol manipulation in the sense in which we use this concept in computer science today.

As often occurs, the practice of the time already anticipated all the elements of list-processing: addresses are obviously used to gain access, the drum machines used linked programs (so called one-plus-one addressing), and so on. But the conception of list-processing as an abstraction created a new world in which designation and dynamic symbolic structure were the defining characteristics. The embedding of the early list-processing systems in languages (the IPLs, LISP) is often decried as having been a barrier to the diffusion of list-processing techniques throughout programming practice; but it was the vehicle that held the abstraction together.

LISP. One more step is worth noting: McCarthy's creation of LISP in 1959–60 (McCarthy, 1960). It completed the act of abstraction, lifting list structures out of their embedding in concrete machines, creating a new formal system with S-expressions, which could be shown to be equivalent to the other universal schemes of computation.

Conclusion. That the concept of the designating symbol and symbol manipulation does not emerge until the mid-fifties does not mean that the earlier steps were either inessential or less important. The total concept is the join of computability, physical realizability (and by multiple technologies), universality, the symbolic representation of processes (i.e., interpretability), and, finally, symbolic structure and designation. Each of the steps provided an essential part of the whole.

The first step in this chain, authored by Turing, is theoretically motivated, but the others all have deep empirical roots. We have been led by the evolution of the computer itself. The stored program principle arose out of the experience with Eniac. List-processing arose out of the attempt to construct intelligent programs. It took its cue from the emergence of random access memories, which provided a clear physical realization of a designating symbol in the address. LISP arose out of the evolving experience with list-processing.

THE EVIDENCE

We come now to the evidence for the hypothesis that physical symbol systems are capable of intelligent action, and that general intelligent action calls for a physical symbol system. The hypothesis is an empirical generalization and not a theorem. We know of no way of demonstrating the connection between symbol systems and intelligence on purely logical grounds. Lacking such a demonstration, we must look at the facts. Our central aim, however, is not to review the evidence in detail, but to use the example before us to illustrate the proposition that computer science is a field of empirical inquiry. Hence, we will only indicate what kinds of evidence there are, and the general nature of the testing process.

The notion of physical symbol system had taken essentially its present form by the middle of the 1950's, and one can date from that time the growth of artificial intelligence as a coherent subfield of computer science. The twenty years of work since then has seen a continuous accumulation of empirical evidence of two main varieties. The first addresses itself to the *sufficiency* of physical symbol systems for producing intelligence, attempting to construct and test specific systems that have such a capability. The second kind of evidence addresses itself to the *necessity* of having a physical symbol system wherever intelligence is exhibited. It starts with Man, the intelligent system best known to us, and attempts to discover whether his cognitive activity can be explained as the working of a physical symbol system. There are other forms of evidence, which we will comment upon briefly later, but these two are the important ones. We will consider them in turn. The first is generally called artificial intelligence, the second, research in cognitive psychology.

Constructing Intelligent Systems. The basic paradigm for the initial testing of the germ theory of disease was: identify a disease, then look for the germ. An analogous paradigm has inspired much of the research in artificial intelligence: identify a task domain calling for intelligence, then construct a program for a digital computer that can handle tasks in that domain. The easy and well structured tasks were looked at first: puzzles and games, operations-research problems of scheduling and allocating resources, simple induction tasks. Scores, if not hundreds, of programs of these kinds have by now been constructed, each capable of some measure of intelligent action in the appropriate domain.

Of course intelligence is not an all-or-none matter, and there has been steady progress toward higher levels of performance in specific domains, as well as toward widening the range of those domains. Early chess programs, for example, were deemed successful if they could play the game legally and with some indication of purpose; a little later, they reached the level of human beginners; within ten or fifteen years, they began to compete with serious amateurs. Progress has been slow (and the total programming effort invested small) but continuous, and the paradigm of construct-and-test proceeds in a regular cycle—the whole research activity mimicking at a macroscopic level the basic generate-and-test cycle of many of the AI programs.

There is a steadily widening area within which intelligent action is attainable. From the original tasks, research has extended to building systems that handle and understand natural language in a variety of ways, systems for interpreting visual scenes, systems for hand-eye coordination, systems that design, systems that write computer programs, systems for speech understanding—the list is, if not endless, at least very long. If there are limits beyond which the hypothesis will not carry us, they have not yet become apparent. Up to the present, the rate of progress has been governed mainly by the rather modest quantity of scientific resources that have been applied and the inevitable requirement of a substantial system-building effort for each new major undertaking.

Much more has been going on, of course, than simply a piling up of examples of intelligent systems adapted to specific task domains. It would be surprising and unappealing if it turned out that the AI programs performing these diverse tasks had nothing in common beyond their being instances of physical symbol systems. Hence, there has been great interest in searching for mechanisms possessed of generality, and for common components among programs performing a variety of tasks. This search carries the theory beyond the initial symbol system hypothesis to a more complete characterization of the particular kinds of symbol systems that are effective in artificial intelligence. In the second section of this paper, we will discuss one example of a hypothesis at this second level of specificity: the heuristic search hypothesis.

The search for generality spawned a series of programs designed to separate out general problem-solving mechanisms from the requirements of particular task domains. The General Problem Solver (GPS) was perhaps the first of these; while among its descendants are such contemporary systems as PLANNER and CONNIVER. The search for common components has led to generalized schemes of representation for goals and plans, methods for constructing discrimination nets, procedures for the control of tree search, pattern-matching mechanisms, and language-parsing systems. Experiments are at present under way to find convenient devices for representing sequences of time and tense, movement, causality, and the like. More and more, it becomes possible to assemble large intelligent systems in a modular way from such basic components.

We can gain some perspective on what is going on by turning, again, to the analogy of the germ theory. If the first burst of research stimulated by that theory consisted largely in finding the germ to go with each disease, subsequent effort turned to learning what a germ was—to building on the basic qualitative law a new level of structure. In artificial intelligence, an initial burst of activity aimed at building intelligent programs for a wide variety of almost randomly selected tasks is giving way to more sharply targeted research aimed at understanding the common mechanisms of such systems.

The Modeling of Human Symbolic Behavior. The symbol system hypothesis implies that the symbolic behavior of man arises because he has the characteristics of a physical symbol system. Hence, the results of efforts to model human behavior with symbol systems become an important part of the evidence for the hypothesis, and research in artificial intelligence goes on in close collaboration with research in information processing psychology, as it is usually called.

The search for explanations of man's intelligent behavior in terms of symbol systems has had a large measure of success over the past twenty years; to the point where information-processing theory is the leading contemporary point of view in cognitive psychology. Especially in the areas of problem-solving, concept attainment, and long-term memory, symbol manipulation models now dominate the scene.

Research in information-processing psychology involves two main kinds of empirical activity. The first is the conduct of observations and experiments on human behavior in tasks requiring intelligence. The second, very similar to the parallel activity in artificial intelligence, is the programming of symbol systems to model the observed human behavior. The psychological observations and experiments lead to the formulation of hypotheses about the symbolic processes the subjects are using, and these are an important source of the ideas that go into the construction of the programs. Thus many of the ideas for the basic mechanisms of GPS were derived from careful analysis of the protocols that human subjects produced while thinking aloud during the performance of a problem-solving task.

The empirical character of computer science is nowhere more evident than in this alliance with psychology. Not only are psychological experiments required to test the veridicality of the simulation models as explanations of the human behavior, but out of the experiments come new ideas for the design and construction of physical-symbol systems.

Other Evidence. The principal body of evidence for the symbol-system hypothesis that we have not considered is negative evidence: the absence of specific competing hypotheses as to how intelligent activity might be accomplished—whether by man or by machine. Most attempts to build such hypotheses have taken place within the field of psychology. Here we have had a continuum of theories from the points of view usually labeled "behaviorism" to those usually labeled "Gestalt theory." Neither of these points of view stands as a real competitor to the symbol-system hypothesis, and for two reasons. First, neither behaviorism nor Gestalt theory has demonstrated, or even shown how to demonstrate, that the explanatory mechanisms it postulates are sufficient to account for intelligent behavior in complex tasks. Second, neither theory has been formulated with anything like the specificity of artificial programs. As a matter of fact, the alternative theories are so vague that it is not terribly difficult to give them information-processing interpretations, and thereby assimilate them to the symbol-system hypothesis.

CONCLUSION

We have tried to use the example of the Physical Symbol System Hypothesis to illustrate concretely that computer science is a scientific enterprise in the usual meaning of that term: it develops scientific hypotheses which it then seeks to verify by empirical inquiry. We had a second reason, however, for choosing this particular example to illustrate our point. The Physical Symbol System Hypothesis is itself a substantial scientific hypothesis of the kind that we earlier dubbed "laws of qualitative structure." It represents an important discovery of computer science, which if borne out by the empirical evidence, as in fact appears to be occurring, will have major continuing impact on the field.

We turn now to a second example, the role of search in intelligence. This topic, and the particular hypothesis about it that we shall examine, have also played a central role in computer science, in general, and artificial intelligence, in particular.

II. Heuristic Search

Knowing that physical symbol systems provide the matrix for intelligent action does not tell us how they accomplish this. Our second example of a law of qualitative structure in computer science addresses this latter question, asserting that symbol systems solve problems by using the processes of heuristic search. This generalization, like the previous one, rests on empirical evidence, and has not been derived formally from other premises. We shall see in a moment, however, that it does have some logical connection with the symbol-system hypothesis, and perhaps we can expect to formalize the connection at some time in the future. Until that time arrives, our story must again be one of empirical inquiry. We will describe what is known about heuristic search and review the empirical findings that show how it enables action to be intelligent. We begin by stating this law of qualitative structure, the Heuristic Search Hypothesis.

Heuristic Search Hypothesis. The solutions to problems are represented as symbol structures. A physical-symbol system exercises its intelligence in problem-solving by search—that is, by generating and progressively modifying symbol structures until it produces a solution structure.

Physical-symbol systems must use heuristic search to solve problems because such systems have limited processing resources; in a finite number of steps, and over a finite interval of time, they can execute only a finite number of processes. Of course that is not a very strong limitation, for all universal Turing machines suffer from it. We intend the limitation, however, in a stronger sense: we mean *practically* limited. We can conceive of systems that are not limited in a practical way but are capable, for example, of searching in parallel the nodes of an exponentially expanding tree at a constant rate for each unit advance in depth. We will not be concerned here with such systems, but with systems whose computing resources are scarce relative to the complexity of the situations with which they are confronted. The restriction will not exclude any real symbol systems, in computer or man, in the context of real tasks. The fact of limited resources allows us, for most purposes, to view a symbol system as though it were a serial, one-process-at-a-time device. If it can accomplish only a small amount of processing in any short time interval, then we might as well regard it as doing things one at a time. Thus "limited resource symbol system" and "serial symbol system" are practically synonymous. The problem of allocating a scarce resource from moment to moment can usually be treated, if the moment is short enough, as a problem of scheduling a serial machine.

PROBLEM SOLVING

Since ability to solve problems is generally taken as a prime indicator that a system has intelligence, it is natural that much of the history of artificial intelligence is taken up with attempts to build and understand problem-solving systems. Problem solving has been discussed by philosophers and psychologists for two millennia, in discourses dense with a feeling of mystery. If you think there is nothing problematic or mysterious about a symbol system solving problems, you are a child of today, whose views have been formed since mid-century. Plato (and, by his account, Socrates) found difficulty understanding even how problems could be *entertained*, much less how they could be solved. Let me remind you of how he posed the conundrum in the *Meno:*

> Meno: And how will you inquire, Socrates, into that which you know not? What will you put forth as the subject of inquiry? And if you find what you want, how will you ever know that this is what you did not know?

To deal with this puzzle, Plato invented his famous theory of recollection: when you think you are discovering or learning something, you are really just recalling what you already knew in a previous existence. If you find this explanation preposterous, there is a much simpler one available today, based upon our understanding of symbol systems. An approximate statement of it is:

> To state a problem is to designate (1) a *test* for a class of symbol structures (solutions of the problem), and (2) a *generator* of symbol structures (potential solutions). To solve a problem is to generate a structure, using (2), that satisfies the test of (1).

We have a problem if we know what we want to do (the test),

and if we don't know immediately how to do it (our generator does not immediately produce a symbol structure satisfying the test). A symbol system can state and solve problems (sometimes) because it can generate and test.

If that is all there is to problem-solving, why not simply generate at once an expression that satisfies the test? This is, in fact, what we do when we wish and dream. "If wishes were horses, beggars might ride." But outside the world of dreams, it isn't possible. To know how we would test something, once constructed, does not mean that we know how to construct it—that we have any generator for doing so.

For example, it is well known what it means to "solve" the problem of playing winning chess. A simple test exists for noticing winning positions, the test for checkmate of the enemy King. In the world of dreams one simply generates a strategy that leads to checkmate for all counter strategies of the opponent. Alas, no generator that will do this is known to existing symbol systems (man or machine). Instead, good moves in chess are sought by generating various alternatives, and painstakingly evaluating them with the use of approximate, and often erroneous, measures that are supposed to indicate the likelihood that a particular line of play is on the route to a winning position. Move generators there are; winning-move generators there are not.

Before there can be a move generator for a problem, there must be a problem space: a space of symbol structures in which problem situations, including the initial and goal situations, can be represented. Move generators are processes for modifying one situation in the problem space into another. The basic characteristics of physical symbol systems guarantee that they can represent problem spaces and that they possess move generators. How, in any concrete situation they synthesize a problem space and move generators appropriate to that situation is a question that is still very much on the frontier of artificial intelligence research.

The task that a symbol system is faced with, then, when it is presented with a problem and a problem space, is to use its limited processing resources to generate possible solutions, one after another, until it finds one that satisfies the problem-defining test. If the system had some control over the order in which potential solutions were generated, then it would be desirable to arrange this order of generation so that actual solutions would have a high likelihood of appearing early. A symbol system would exhibit intelligence to the extent that it succeeded in doing this. Intelligence for a system with limited processing resources consists in making wise choices of what to do next.

SEARCH IN PROBLEM-SOLVING

During the first decade or so of artificial intelligence research, the study of problem-solving was almost synonymous with the study of search processes. From our characterization of problems and problem solving, it is easy to see why this was so. In fact, it might be asked whether it could be otherwise. But before we try to answer that question, we must explore further the nature of search processes as it revealed itself during that decade of activity.

Extracting Information from the Problem Space. Consider a set of symbol structures, some small subset of which are solutions to a given problem. Suppose, further, that the solutions are distributed randomly through the entire set. By this we mean that no information exists that would enable any search generator to perform better than a random search. Then no symbol system could exhibit more intelligence (or less intelligence) than any other in solving the problem, although one might experience better luck than another.

A condition, then, for the appearance of intelligence is that the distribution of solutions be not entirely random, that the space of symbol structures exhibit at least some degree of order and pattern. A second condition is that pattern in the space of symbol structures be more or less detectible. A third condition is that the generator of potential solutions be able to behave differentially, depending on what pattern it detected. There must be information in the problem space, and the symbol system must be capable of extracting and using it. Let us look first at a very simple example, where the intelligence is easy to come by.

Consider the problem of solving a simple algebraic equation:

$$AX + B = CX + D$$

The test defines a solution as any expression of the form, $X = E$, such that $AE + B = CE + D$. Now one could use as generator any process that would produce numbers which could then be tested by substituting in the latter equation. We would not call this an intelligent generator.

Alternatively, one could use generators that would make use of the fact that the original equation can be modified—by adding or subtracting equal quantities from both sides, or multiplying or dividing both sides by the same quantity—without changing its solutions. But, of course, we can obtain even more information to guide the generator by comparing the original expression with the form of the solution, and making precisely those changes in the equation that leave its solution unchanged, while at the same time bringing it into the desired form. Such a generator could notice that there was an unwanted CX on the right-hand side of the original equation, subtract it from both sides, and collect terms again. It could then notice that there was an unwanted B on the left-hand side and subtract that. Finally, it could get rid of the unwanted coefficient $(A - C)$ on the left-hand side by dividing.

Thus by this procedure, which now exhibits considerable intelligence, the generator produces successive symbol structures, each obtained by modifying the previous one; and the modifications are aimed at reducing the differences between the form of the input structure and the form of the test expression, while maintaining the other conditions for a solution.

This simple example already illustrates many of the main mechanisms that are used by symbol systems for intelligent problem-solving. First, each successive expression is not generated independently, but is produced by modifying one produced previously. Second, the modifications are not haphazard, but depend upon two kinds of information. They depend on information that is constant over this whole class of algebra problems, and that is built into the structure of the generator itself: all modifications of expressions must leave the equation's solution unchanged. They also depend on information that changes at each step: detection of the differences in form that remain between the current expression and the desired expression. In effect, the generator incorporates some of the tests the solution must satisfy, so that expressions that don't meet these tests will never be generated. Using the first kind of information guarantees that only a tiny subset of all possible expressions is actually generated, but without losing the solution expression from this subset. Using the second kind of information arrives at the desired solution by a succession of approximations, employing a simple form of means-ends analysis to give direction to the search.

There is no mystery where the information that guided the search came from. We need not follow Plato in endowing the symbol system with a previous existence in which it already knew the solution. A moderately sophisticated generator-test system did the trick without invoking reincarnation.

Search Trees. The simple algebra problem may seem an unusual, even pathological, example of search. It is certainly not trial-and-error search, for though there were a few trials, there was no error. We are more accustomed to thinking of problem-solving search as generating lushly branching trees of partial solution possibilities which may grow to thousands, or even millions, of branches, before they yield a solution. Thus, if from each expression it produces, the generator creates B new branches, then the tree will grow as B^D, where D is its depth. The tree grown for the algebra problem had the peculiarity that its branchiness, B, equaled unity.

Programs that play chess typically grow broad search trees, amounting in some cases to a million branches or more. Although this example will serve to illustrate our points about tree search, we should note that the purpose of search in chess is not to generate proposed solutions, but to evaluate (test) them. One line of research into game-playing programs has been centrally concerned with improving the representation of the chess board, and the processes for making moves on it, so as to speed up search and make it possible to search larger trees. The rationale for this direction, of course, is that the deeper the dynamic search, the more accurate should be the evaluations at the end of it. On the other hand, there is good empirical evidence that the strongest human players, grandmasters, seldom explore trees of more than one hundred branches. This economy is achieved not so much by searching less deeply than do chess-playing programs, but by branching very sparsely and selectively at each node. This is only possible, without causing a deterioration of the evaluations, by having more of the selectivity built into the generator itself, so that it is able to select for generation only those branches which are very likely to yield important relevant information about the position.

The somewhat paradoxical-sounding conclusion to which this discussion leads is that search—successive generation of potential solution structures—is a fundamental aspect of a symbol system's exercise of intelligence in problem-solving but that amount of search is not a measure of the amount of intelligence being exhibited. What makes a problem a problem is not that a large amount of search is required for its solution, but that a large amount *would* be required if a requisite level of intelligence were not applied. When the symbolic system that is endeavoring to solve a problem knows enough about what to do, it simply proceeds directly towards its goal; but whenever its knowledge becomes inadequate, when it enters terra incognita, it is faced with the threat of going through large amounts of search before it finds its way again.

The potential for the exponential explosion of the search tree that is present in every scheme for generating problem solutions warns us against depending on the brute force of computers—even the biggest and fastest computers—as a compensation for the ignorance and unselectivity of their generators. The hope is still periodically ignited in some human breasts that a computer can be found that is fast enough, and that can be programmed cleverly enough, to play good chess by brute-force search. There is nothing known in theory about the game of chess that rules out this possibility. But empirical studies on the management of search in sizable trees with only modest results make this a much less promising direction than it was when chess was first chosen as an appropriate task for artificial intelligence. We must regard this as one of the important empirical findings of research with chess programs.

The Forms of Intelligence. The task of intelligence, then, is to avert the ever-present threat of the exponential explosion of search. How can this be accomplished? The first route, already illustrated by the algebra example and by chess programs that only generate "plausible" moves for further analysis, is to build selectivity into the generator: to generate only structures that show promise of being solutions or of being along the path toward solutions. The usual consequence of doing this is to decrease the rate of branching, not to prevent it entirely. Ultimate exponential explosion is not avoided—save in exceptionally highly structured situations like the algebra example—but only postponed. Hence, an intelligent system generally needs to supplement the selectivity of its solution generator with other information-using techniques to guide search.

Twenty years of experience with managing tree search in a variety of task environments has produced a small kit of general techniques which is part of the equipment of every researcher in artificial intelligence today. Since these techniques have been described in general works like that of Nilsson (1971), they can be summarized very briefly here.

In serial heuristic search, the basic question always is: What shall be done next? In tree search, that question, in turn, has two components: (1) from what node in the tree shall we search next, and (2) what direction shall we take from that node? Information helpful in answering the first question may be interpreted as measuring the relative distance of different nodes from the goal. Best-first search calls for searching next from the node that appears closest to the goal. Information helpful in answering the second question—in what direction to search—is often obtained, as in the algebra example, by detecting specific differences between the current nodal structure and the goal structure described by the test of a solution, and selecting actions that are relevant to reducing these particular kinds of differences. This is the technique known as means-ends analysis, which plays a central role in the structure of the General Problem Solver.

The importance of empirical studies as a source of general ideas in AI research can be demonstrated clearly by tracing the history, through large numbers of problem-solving programs, of these two central ideas: best-first search and means-ends analysis. Rudiments of best-first search were already present, though unnamed, in the Logic Theorist in 1955. The General Problem Solver, embodying means-ends analysis, appeared about 1957—but combined it with modified depth-first search rather than best-first search. Chess programs were generally wedded, for reasons of economy of memory, to depth-first search, supplemented after about 1958 by the powerful alpha-beta pruning procedure. Each of these techniques appears to have been reinvented a number of times, and it is hard to find general, task-independent, theoretical discussions of problem-solving in terms of these concepts until the middle or late 1960's. The amount of formal buttressing they have received from mathematical theory is still minuscule: some theorems about the reduction in search that can be secured from using the alpha-beta heuristic, a couple of theorems (reviewed by Nilsson, 1971) about shortest-path search, and some very recent theorems on best-first search with a probabilistic evaluation function.

"Weak" and "Strong" Methods. The techniques we have been discussing are dedicated to the control of exponential expansion rather than its prevention. For this reason, they have been properly called "weak methods"—methods to be used when the symbol system's knowledge or the amount of structure actually contained in the problem space are inadequate to permit search to be avoided entirely. It is instructive to contrast a highly structured situation, which can be formulated, say, as a lincar-programming problem, with the less structured situations of combinatorial problems like the traveling salesman problem or scheduling problems. ("Less structured" here refers to the insufficiency or non-existence of relevant theory about the structure of the problem space.)

In solving linear-programming problems, a substantial amount of computation may be required, but the search does not branch. Every step is a step along the way to a solution. In solving combinatorial problems or in proving theorems, tree search can seldom be avoided, and success depends on heuristic search methods of the sort we have been describing.

Not all streams of AI problem-solving research have followed the path we have been outlining. An example of a somewhat different point is provided by the work on theorem-proving systems. Here, ideas imported from mathematics and logic have had a strong influence on the direction of inquiry. For example, the use of heuristics was resisted when properties of completeness could not be proved (a bit ironic, since most interesting mathematical systems are known to be undecidable). Since completeness can seldom be proved for best-first search heuristics, or for many kinds of selective generators, the effect of this requirement was rather inhibiting. When theorem-proving programs were continually incapacitated by the combinatorial explosion of their search trees, thought began to be given to selective heuristics, which in many cases proved to be analogues of heuristics used in general problem-solving programs. The set-of-support heuristic, for example, is a form of working backward, adapted to the resolution theorem-proving environment.

A Summary of the Experience. We have now described the workings of our second law of qualitative structure, which asserts that physical-symbol systems solve problems by means of heuristic search. Beyond that, we have examined some subsidiary characteristics of heuristic search, in particular the threat that it always faces of exponential explosion of the search tree, and some of the means it uses to avert that threat. Opinions differ as to how effective heuristic search has been as a problem-solving mechanism—the opinions depending on what task domains are considered and what criterion of adequacy is adopted. Success can be guaranteed by setting aspiration levels low—or failure by setting them high. The evidence might be summed up about as follows: Few programs are solving problems at "expert" professional levels. Samuel's checker program and Feigenbaum and Lederberg's DENDRAL are perhaps the best-known exceptions, but one could point also to a number of heuristic search programs for such operations-research problem domains as scheduling and integer programming. In a number of domains, programs perform at the level of competent amateurs: chess, some theorem-proving domains, many kinds of games and puzzles. Human levels have not yet been nearly reached by programs that have a complex perceptual "front end": visual scene recognizers, speech understanders, robots that have to maneuver in real space and time. Nevertheless, impressive progress has been made, and a large body of experience assembled about these difficult tasks.

We do not have deep theoretical explanations for the particular pattern of performance that has emerged. On empirical grounds, however, we might draw two conclusions. First, from what has been learned about human expert performance in tasks like chess, it is likely that any system capable of matching that performance will have to have access, in its memories, to very large stores of semantic information. Second, some part of the human superiority in tasks with a large perceptual component can be attributed to the special-purpose built-in parallel-processing structure of the human eye and ear.

In any case, the quality of performance must necessarily depend on the characteristics both of the problem domains and of the symbol systems used to tackle them. For most real-life domains in which we are interested, the domain structure has so far not proved sufficiently simple to yield theorems about complexity, or to tell us, other than empirically, how large real-world problems are in relation to the abilities of our symbol systems to solve them. That situation may change, but until it does, we must rely upon empirical explorations, using the best problem solvers we know how to build, as a principal source of knowledge about the magnitude and characteristics of problem difficulty. Even in highly structured areas like linear programming, theory has been much more useful in strengthening the heuristics that underlie the most powerful solution algorithms than in providing a deep analysis of complexity.

INTELLIGENCE WITHOUT MUCH SEARCH

Our analysis of intelligence equated it with ability to extract and use information about the structure of the problem space, so as to enable a problem solution to be generated as quickly and directly as possible. New directions for improving the problem-solving capabilities of symbol systems can be equated, then, with new ways of extracting and using information. At least three such ways can be identified.

Nonlocal Use of Information. First, it has been noted by several investigators that information gathered in the course of tree search is usually only used *locally*, to help make decisions at the specific node where the information was generated. Information about a chess position, obtained by dynamic analysis of a subtree of continuations, is usually used to evaluate just that position, not to evaluate other positions that may contain many of the same features. Hence, the same facts have to be rediscovered repeatedly at different nodes of the search tree. Simply to take the information out of the context in which it arose and use it generally does not solve the problem, for the information may be valid only in a limited range of contexts. In recent years, a few exploratory efforts have been made to transport information from its context of origin to other appropriate contexts. While it is still too early to evaluate the power of this idea, or even exactly how it is to be achieved, it shows considerable promise. An important line of investigation that Berliner (1975) has been pursuing is to use causal analysis to determine the range over which a particular piece of information is valid. Thus if a weakness in a chess position can be traced back to the move that made it, then the same weakness can be expected in other positions descendant from the same move.

The HEARSAY speech understanding system has taken another approach to making information globally available. That system seeks to recognize speech strings by pursuing a parallel search at a number of different levels: phonemic, lexical, syntactic, and semantic. As each of these searches provides and evaluates hypotheses, it supplies the information it has gained to a common "blackboard" that can be read by all the sources. This shared information can be used, for example, to eliminate hypotheses, or even whole classes of hypotheses, that would otherwise have to be searched by one of the processes. Thus increasing our ability to use tree-search information nonlocally offers promise for raising the intelligence of problem-solving systems.

Semantic Recognition Systems. A second active possibility for raising intelligence is to supply the symbol system with a rich body of semantic information about the task domain it is dealing with. For example, empirical research on the skill of chess masters shows that a major source of the master's skill is stored information that enables him to recognize a large number of specific features and patterns of features on a chess board, and information that uses this recognition to propose actions appropriate to the features recognized. This general idea has, of course, been incorporated in chess programs almost from the beginning. What is new is the realization of the number of such patterns and associated information that may have to be stored for master-level play: something on the order of 50,000.

The possibility of substituting recognition for search arises because a particular, and especially a rare, pattern can contain an enormous amount of information, provided that it is closely linked to the structure of the problem space. When that structure is "irregular," and not subject to simple mathematical description, then knowledge of a large number of relevant patterns may be the key to intelligent behavior. Whether this is so in any particular task domain is a question more easily settled by empirical investigation than by theory. Our experience with symbol systems richly endowed with semantic information and pattern-recognizing capabilities for accessing it is still extremely limited.

The discussion above refers specifically to semantic information associated with a recognition system. Of course, there is also a whole large area of AI research on semantic information processing and the organization of semantic memories that falls outside the scope of the topics we are discussing in this paper.

Selecting Appropriate Representations. A third line of inquiry is concerned with the possibility that search can be reduced or avoided by selecting an appropriate problem space. A standard example that illustrates this possibility dramatically is the mutilated checkerboard problem. A standard 64-square checkerboard can be covered exactly with 32 tiles, each a 1 X 2 rectangle covering exactly two squares. Suppose, now, that we cut off squares at two diagonally opposite corners of the checkerboard, leaving a total of 62 squares. Can this mutilated board be covered exactly with 31 tiles? With (literally) heavenly patience, the impossibility of achieving such a covering can be demonstrated by trying all possible arrangements. The alternative, for those with less patience and more intelligence, is to observe that the two diagonally opposite corners of a checkerboard are of the same color. Hence, the mutilated checkerboard has two fewer squares of one color than of the other. But each tile covers one square of one color and one square of the other, and any set of tiles must cover the same number of squares of each color. Hence, there is no solution. How can a symbol system discover this simple inductive argument as an alternative to a hopeless attempt to solve the problem by search among all possible coverings? We would award a system that found the solution high marks for intelligence.

Perhaps, however, in posing this problem we are not escaping from search processes. We have simply displaced the search from a space of possible problem solutions to a space of possible representations. In any event, the whole process of moving from one representation to another, and of discovering and evaluating representations, is largely unexplored territory in the domain of problem-solving research. The laws of qualitative structure governing representations remain to be discovered. The search for them is almost sure to receive considerable attention in the coming decade.

CONCLUSION

That is our account of symbol systems and intelligence. It has been a long road from Plato's *Meno* to the present, but it is perhaps encouraging that most of the progress along that road has been made since the turn of the twentieth century, and a large fraction of it since the midpoint of the century. Thought was still wholly intangible and ineffable until modern formal logic interpreted it as the manipulation of formal tokens. And it seemed still to inhabit mainly the heaven of Platonic ideals, or the equally obscure spaces of the human mind, until computers taught us how symbols could be processed by machines. A. M. Turing made his great contributions at the mid-century crossroads of these developments that led from modern logic to the computer.

Physical Symbol Systems. The study of logic and computers has revealed to us that intelligence resides in physical-symbol systems. This is computer science's most basic law of qualitative structure.

Symbol systems are collections of patterns and processes, the latter being capable of producing, destroying, and modifying the former. The most important properties of patterns is that they can designate objects, processes, or other patterns, and that when they designate processes, they can be interpreted. Interpretation means carrying out the designated process. The two most significant classes of symbol systems with which we are acquainted are human beings and computers.

Our present understanding of symbol systems grew, as indicated earlier, through a sequence of stages. Formal logic familiarized us with symbols, treated syntactically, as the raw material of thought, and with the idea of manipulating them according to carefully defined formal processes. The Turing machine made the syntactic processing of symbols truly machine-like, and affirmed the potential universality of strictly defined symbol systems. The stored-program concept for computers reaffirmed the interpretability of symbols, already implicit in the Turing machine. List-processing brought to the forefront the denotational capacities of symbols, and defined symbol-processing in ways that allowed independence from the fixed structure of the underlying physical machine. By 1956 all of these concepts were available, together with hardware for implementing them. The study of the intelligence of symbol systems, the subject of artificial intelligence, could begin.

Heuristic Search. A second law of qualitative structure for AI is that symbol systems solve problems by generating potential solutions and testing them—that is, by searching. Solutions are usually sought by creating symbolic expressions and modifying them sequentially until they satisfy the conditions for a solution. Hence, symbol systems solve problems by searching. Since they have finite resources, the search cannot be carried out all at once, but must be sequential. It leaves behind it either a single path from starting point to goal or, if correction and backup are necessary, a whole tree of such paths.

Symbol systems cannot appear intelligent when they are surrounded by pure chaos. They exercise intelligence by extracting information from a problem domain and using that information to guide their search, avoiding wrong turns and circuitous bypaths. The problem domain must contain information—that is, some degree of order and structure—for the method to work. The paradox of the *Meno* is solved by the observation that information may be remembered, but new information may also be extracted from the domain that the symbols designate. In both cases, the ultimate source of the information is the task domain.

The Empirical Base. Research on artificial intelligence is concerned with how symbol systems must be organized in order to behave intelligently. Twenty years of work in the area has accumulated a considerable body of knowledge, enough to fill several books (it already has), and most of it in the form of rather concrete experience about the behavior of specific classes of symbol systems in specific task domains. Out of this experience, however, there have also emerged some generalizations, cutting across task domains and systems, about the general characteristics of intelligence and its methods of implementation.

We have tried to state some of these generalizations here. They are mostly qualitative rather than mathematical. They have more the flavor of geology or evolutionary biology than the flavor of theoretical physics. They are sufficiently strong to enable us today to design and build moderately intelligent systems for a considerable range of task domains, as well as to gain a rather deep understanding of how human intelligence works in many situations.

What Next? In our account we have mentioned open questions as well as settled ones; there are many of both. We see no abatement of the excitement of exploration that has surrounded this field over the past quarter century. Two resource limits will determine the rate of progress over the next such period. One is the amount of computing power that will be available. The second, and probably the more important, is the number of talented young computer scientists who will be attracted to this area of research as the most challenging they can tackle.

A. M. Turing concluded his famous paper "Computing Machinery and Intelligence" with the words:

We can only see a short distance ahead, but we can see plenty there that needs to be done.

Many of the things Turing saw in 1950 that needed to be done have been done, but the agenda is as full as ever. Perhaps we read too much into his simple statement above, but we like to think that in it Turing recognized the fundamental truth that all computer scientists instinctively know. For all physical-symbol systems, condemned as we are to serial search of the problem environment, the critical question is always: What to do next?

2

Complexity and the Study of Artificial and Human Intelligence

ZENON PYLYSHYN

THE PROCESS of understanding and expressing our understanding is analogous to the process of creating a work of art—such as a sculpture. In both cases there are three major elements: the imagination and tension in the creator, the nature of the tools (including the skills for using them), and the resistance offered by the materials. A sharp knife on soft wood calls for a very different process, and yields a very different result, from a massive chisel on granite. Similarly, a brilliant man tackling the world with only his eyes, ears, and the concepts his native tongue has given him will have different experiences, and will carve them up differently than will a person equipped with the tools of a technological culture—even though the world is in a sense the same.

Conceptual tools dominate periods of progress. Susanne Langer (1962) put it this way:

In every age, philosophical thinking exploits some dominant concepts and makes its greatest headway in solving problems conceived in terms of them. The seventeenth- and eighteenth-century philosophers construed knowledge, knower, and known in terms of sense data and their association. Descartes' self-examination gave classical psychology *the mind and its contents* as a starting point. Locke set up sensory immediacy as the new criterion of the real . . . Hobbes provided the genetic method of building up complex ideas from simple ones . . . and, in another quarter, still true to the Hobbesian method, Pavlov built intellect out of conditioned reflexes and Loeb built life out of tropisms.   (p. 54)

History may well record that around the middle of the twentieth century many classical problems of philosophy and psychology were transformed by a new (and not yet well understood) notion of mechanism, specifically in the form of a *computational mechanism*. Although this notion has many roots within philosophy and the foundations of mathematics (particularly in the work of Alonzo Church), the major milestone was probably the formalization of the notion of computation by Alan Turing (1937). Turing's work can be seen as the first study of cognitive activity fully abstracted in principle from both biological and phenomenological foundations. It provides a reference point for the scientific ideal of a mechanistic process, which can be understood without raising the specter of vital forces or elusive homunculi, but which at the same time is sufficiently rich to cover *every* informal notion of abstract mechanism. (This last claim—known as the Church-Turing thesis—is, of course, not provable; but it has withstood all attempts to find exceptions.) It would be difficult to overestimate the importance of this development for psychology. It represents the emergence of a new level of analysis, independent of physics yet mechanistic in spirit. It makes possible a science of structure and function divorced from material substance while avoiding any retreat to behavioristic peripheralism. Because it speaks the language of mental structures and internal processes, it can answer questions traditionally posed by psychologists.

Though Turing and others laid the foundations for this abstract study of cognition in the 30's and 40's, only in the last twenty years or so has it been articulated in a more specific and detailed form—one directly suitable to attacking the basic questions of cognitive psychology. This newer direction has grown with our understanding of computational processes and of the digital computer as a general symbol-processing system. It has led to the formation of a new intellectual discipline known as artificial intelligence (AI), which attempts to understand the nature of intelligence by *designing* mechanisms, in the form of computational systems, which exhibit it.

In spite of its apparent preoccupation with engineering, I

believe that the field of AI is coextensive with that of cognitive psychology. What I mean is: as intellectual disciplines (not applied technologies), both fields are concerned with the same problems and thus must ultimately be judged by the same criteria of success. The ultimate goal, in each case, is a better understanding of intelligence, and the relevant ground rules are those which govern any scientific enterprise. Though the meaning of intelligence and the canons of evidence may drift as the science progresses, the notion of intelligence will nevertheless continue to have meaning only in relation to human behavior and purposes, and evidence will continue to relate to that delicate balance between the rationally conceivable and the empirically demonstrable which characterizes evidence elsewhere in science.

Still, there are significant differences between the two disciplines, which derive from the priorities they attach to various constraints and the tolerances they have for various kinds of gaps and incompletenesses. In other words, they differ largely in the way they judge *partial* solutions to the problems of intelligence. In spite of their differences, however, I believe that AI is just the medicine that cognitive psychology needs at this stage in its development. My belief that research in artificial intelligence will provide the fruitful approach to understanding cognitive phenomena is based on the following observations:

1. The fertile interplay between theoretical superstructure and specific observations, which is the hallmark of mature sciences, has been absent in much of psychology. I will not speculate on why this is so, but only note among its consequences that psychology is splintered with micro-models—often so narrow that they are confined to a single experimental procedure. The discipline is largely example-driven, rather than guided by major theoretical systems. Hence, local puzzle-solving activities lack a convergent direction, and frequently degenerate into (in AI terms) a hill-climbing task dominated by local maxima. Such a piecemeal approach is ultimately hopeless, because, as Newell (1973b) has put it, "You can't play twenty questions with nature and win."

2. The second point is related. As poor cousin to physics, psychology is always very concerned with "rigor" and

"objectivity." But just as there are two sources of understanding, the empirical and the rational, so are there two *loci*
of rigor. One can be rigorous by operationally defining all of
one's constructs, and always sticking close to the experimental data. But one can also be *rigorous* by ensuring that
one's theoretical ideas are complete, consistent, and logically
sound. One can then try to capture one's intuitions and bring
everyday knowledge to bear on the development of theoretical
systems with some confidence that one's assumptions are
coherent, and with some means of exploring what they entail.
The point is that there are better and worse places for insisting on "rigor" in an evolving discipline. My own feeling is that
we already know such a tremendous amount about human
cognition, which we cannot begin to account for with our
mini-theories, that a more top-down, theory-driven strategy
(such as that characteristic of AI) would be more appropriate
at the present stage. One benefit of such an approach might
be to put us in position to ask better *empirical* questions.

3. My third observation is that there is a growing feeling, not
   only among those working in AI, but also among more
   enlightened experimental psychologists, that the study of
   intelligence cannot be decomposed along such traditional lines
   as, say, typical textbook chapters: sensation, perception,
   learning, memory, comprehension, reasoning, motivation, and
   so on. This is not to imply that we cannot study problems in
   these areas, but rather to suggest that categorizing them in
   such terms may not reveal (indeed, may cover up) the way in
   which they individually and collectively contribute to producing intelligent behavior. There is a growing suspicion that to
   understand the integration of cognitive activity we shall have
   to redraw the boundaries around such traditional categories
   as learning, comprehension, and memory.

What I propose to do is to examine some of the ways in which
the complexity associated with problems of intelligence can be
carved up. I am going to be very sketchy because I want to paint a
picture of the larger territory, bringing in some of the insights and
problems of AI to suggest alternative ways of casting questions
about intelligence. I will consider three general categories of

problems dealing with the nature of complexity: (1) the problem of the allocation of complexity—or the *organization* issue, (2) the problem of the allocation of responsibility—or the *control* issue, and (3) the problem of the allocation of constraints—or the *validation* issue.

Allocation of Complexity: The Organization Issue

Intelligent behavior is, like any complex phenomenon, the result of a great many contributing causes. So the question can arise: *Which* contributing cause shall we appeal to in explaining various aspects of the complexity? How we carve up this problem and how we attribute the sources of behavioral complexity can have dramatic consequences in the regularities we find and in the nature of the theories we construct. Consider the simple-minded scheme, shown in Figure 1, for subdividing the world into various possible sources of behavioral complexity.

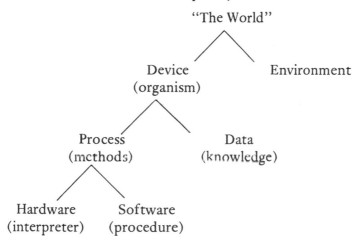

Figure 1

At each node, the complexity of the cause can be allocated to either branch (or apportioned between them). Newell and Simon (1972) have been instrumental in drawing our attention to the importance of recognizing that both the organism and the environment are essential sources of behavioral complexity. In his Compton Lectures, Simon (1969) gives a striking example of this sort of trade-off at the top node of Figure 1. The path taken by an ant walking across rugged terrain might be complex (and, we may suppose, not at all random). One possible explanation is that the ant is following a very complex and detailed internal program, which antecedently specifies its every step. But an alternative possibility is that the ant contains a very simple mechanism, which determines only how it will turn in response to changing slopes. In the first case, the complexity needed to explain the complex path is allocated to the organism (that is, to the structure of its program), whereas in the second case it is allocated to the environment (the topography). J. J. Gibson (1979) can also be read as arguing that the complexity of perceptual response should be attributed much more to complex environmental causes (and less to complexities in the organism) than is generally supposed. There are many difficulties with this view (cf. Fodor and Pylyshyn, in preparation), not the least of which is the problem of providing a plausible account of a noninferential mechanism that could mediate between the complex environment and the complex effect.

The process-data distinction, at the next node in Figure 1, is really very old; it is related to the universal noun-verb distinction in language, and to the function-argument distinction in mathematics and logic. It is concerned not with the intrinsic nature of a given symbol, but with the manner in which that symbol functions at some particular time. It is well known among computer scientists that there is a tradeoff between the complexity of data structures and the complexity of the processes that access them. Though this is not precisely understood in general, the history of artificial intelligence shows that advances (especially in problem-solving, computer graphics, and information retrieval) have frequently been associated with new data structure organizations. Sometimes difficult problems have been solved by designing new forms of data structure which are invariant under typical transformations that are applied in that particular problem domain, and thus need to be changed only when there is a major alteration in what is represented. For example, when "ring structures" are used to represent graphical information, the major structure is invariant under rotation, translation, change of scale, and attachment to other structures; only a change in the graph topology calls for a significant modification of the data strucutre. In other cases, such as problem solving, the task often reduces to finding a representation of the problem domain—discovering a "problem space"—in which simple procedures will solve the problem. (Here, "simple" can mean whatever is already available or is easily constructable from existing primitive operations.) In still other cases, as in language comprehension systems, one may want a data structure which, in effect, anticipates the most likely tasks the system will be called upon to perform, thus obviating the need for much deductive effort at later stages in the processing. The work of Schank (1979) can be viewed as based on this approach.

These all illustrate a principle which Moore and Newell (1974) call "natural intelligence," according to which, roughly, the dimension of problem difficulty is not uniform. The way in which the original problem is represented, plus the primitive operations available, define a class of problems that are trivial to the system: the solution can be "read off" the representation by the primitives. Problems that are not in this class, however, may require much more general and powerful methods. As Moore and Newell put it: "natural intelligence carries just a little way. To go further requires deliberate application of methods under the control of disciplined intention." Thus, especially for psychological theory, the way in which one partitions (the organism portion of) the intelligence problem into data and process is critical. The theory should factor out an appropriate broad class of "trivial" problems, solvable by "natural intelligence," from a class of more difficult problems, which must be approached with more general and deliberate problem-solving methods.[1]

Consider next the bottom node in Figure 1. Because the mapping between algorithms and one physical device (a computer) is very different from that between algorithms and another physical device (a brain), people are often reluctant to extend the same ontological

1. Devising systems that can generate appropriate representations, transform them into new ones, and deal with multiple representations is one of the major unsolved problems in AI. In particular, there is reason to believe it has been one of the stumbling blocks in the development of machine perception. In the latter case an attempt is made to compensate for weakness in methods for generating and transforming representations with more powerful problem-solving methods—an approach at variance with Moore and Newell's natural intelligence principle.

status to the algorithms in the two cases. I believe the difficulty is a cultural one and stems in part from an overly concrete view of computation. In the regress of procedures to interpret procedures to interpret procedures, etc., there eventually comes a point where (in the computer case) we have to stop talking about procedures and start talking about electronics. But, in fact, it is usually best to stop talking about procedures and interpreters much earlier—generally at the point below which the structures are not uniformly accessible to the programmer (such as at the level of LISP)—and call the rest the "virtual machine." This amounts to allocating more complexity to the hardware and less to the software; and it is good computer science practice. If we followed it routinely, the parallels between people and machines would be more apparent, for in each case we would have a device whose internal construction may in general be unspecified, but whose behavior can be exhibited and modified in rather similar ways at the relevant level of description—namely, the virtual machine level. In psychology, as in computer science, we need to distinguish between what, in computer terminology, is called the functional architecture and the actual software. Although this distinction is a pragmatic one in computer science, I have argued (Pylyshyn, 1980) that such a distinction is a matter of principle in psychology. To draw such a boundary is to specify the level at which the computer and mind may be compared literally—it specifies a level of aggregation appropriate for the notion of "strong equivalence" of processes. Making this distinction explicit also helps one to avoid the error, so common among critics of AI of comparing computers and minds at the level of bits and neurons, or even at the level of LISP functions.

If we take this approach, it becomes appropriate to ask about the nature of the human "functional architecture" or the architecture of the cognitive "virtual machine": what constraints it imposes on possible programs, what processes can be considered primitive, how it can be programmed, and so on. It is still an open question whether a single such level could suffice for characterizing all aspects of human intelligence. I defend (in Pylyshyn, 1980) the view that there is indeed a unique human virtual machine—defined in terms of the lowest level of function that must be explained by appeal to its having representations (goals and beliefs). No computational model can be constructed without making implicit assumptions about what the architecture is; thus placing constraints on such a function is of central concern in cognitive science. In fact, one might even take the point of view that discovering the nature of the functional architecture of the mind (or the nature of the "psychological programming language") ought to be one of the first tasks of the new discipline of cognitive science.

Allocation of Responsibility: The Control Issue

There is another closely related aspect of the organization of complex systems, which has become a focus of study in computer science yet has had very little impact in psychology. Let us start by introducing it in historical perspective.

A major breakthrough in understanding the nature of control was the articulation of the idea of feedback through the environment. Thus a certain relational balance was restored between a device or organism and its environment. Although only the device is credited with having a goal, the responsibility for its behavior is shared. At times when the environment is passive the initiative appears to come primarily from the device, while at other times the environment appears to intervene and the initiative seems to go in the opposite direction. However, the idea of control flowing or changing its locus did not become commonplace until the advent of computers. Here, the sequencing of instructions makes the notion of flow of control natural, and branch instructions make it equally natural to think of passing or sending control to some other place. When control-passing is combined with a primitive message-passing facility—at minimum, a reminder of where the control came from, so that it can be returned later—*subroutines* are born. And since subroutines can be nested—that is, they can themselves send control to still lower subroutines, and so on, with the assurance that it will eventually find its way back—the notion of a *hierarchy* of control also emerges. The subroutine notion was distilled by Miller, Gelanter, and Pribram (1960), who called it a test-operate-test-exit or TOTE unit and offered it to the psychological community as a basic unit of analysis to replace the ubiquitous reflex arc. It has been very influential in shaping psychologists' thinking about thinking.

There are a number of good reasons why a hierarchical system of control is such a powerful concept (for a discussion, see Simon,

1969). One of the most important is "partial decomposability" or "modularity" in the total system. By keeping the interactions between routine and subroutine simple (in terms both of when control is passed and of what messages are sent along with it), it becomes easier to think of each routine as a nearly independent subsystem; and that makes the whole system easier to add to, modify, and understand. Moreover, each routine in the hierarchy can be thought of as defining some (sub) goal, in an overall *goal-directed* system. Passing control to a subroutine amounts to activating a subgoal, and control is returned when that subgoal is consummated. So powerful an idea is this that its shortcomings were largely overlooked for many years.

As early as 1962, however, Allen Newell had pointed out some of the rigidity in such an organization. So long as each subroutine is a narrow "specialist," the minimal and rigidly prescribed communication between routine and subroutine works well: if it is a square root extractor, you can just hand it control and a number and say, "Come back here when you've done your thing with this number." But if the subroutine is not such a narrow specialist, it might help to be able to communicate each task in more flexible terms. Furthermore, it might help if the subroutine's progress could be monitored along the way, to prevent it from using up an unwarranted amount of time and resources (e.g., memory) on some relatively minor task or on a task that some other process might be in a position to determine was doomed to fail. Likewise, it would help if the subroutine could report its results more flexibly— especially if it could report what went wrong in cases where it has failed. How to convert these anthropomorphically stated desiderata into mechanical form and how to do so without swamping the system in a bureaucratic nightmare of control messages are two of the main design concerns in recent programming languages (e.g., PLANNER, CONNIVER, POPLER 1.5, QA4, and KRL; see Bobrow and Raphael, 1974).

Since differences in control structure can have implications for psychological theory as well as for AI, and since these implications are not always obvious, I will outline here some of the general aspects of the problem. I shall state these in terms of a notion of *locus of responsibility* for such actions as transferring control and passing messages. In particular, I want to make two distinctions:

(1) between *sending* control (where the initiative lies with the *old* locus), and *capturing* control (where the initiative lies with the *new* locus); and (2) between *directing* a message to one specified recipient, and *broadcasting* it to all routines or modules at once (that is, "to whom it may concern"). A variety of different control structures can be characterized on the basis of these two distinctions. For example, in the standard subroutine-hierarchy case, control is always *sent* (by the routine that already has it), and a message (containing parameters and a return address) is *directed* specifically to the routine that is being given control; and when the subgoal is achieved, control is *sent* back, along with a result message. In PLANNER-type languages, on the other hand, when a task needs to be done, a message describing the goal is broadcast, and control is then captured by some module designed to respond to that particular goal message (on the ground that it might plausibly be able to achieve that goal). After that, control is sent on to some other location—one that depends on how that particular execution terminated (e.g., on whether it was successful or not, or on what result it produced). In another kind of control scheme, called a "production system," messages are also broadcast, and control captured. But when the module (or "production") finishes, it again just broadcasts a message; only rarely is control sent to a specific locus. We will return to some of the implications of these choices in a moment; but first let us see how they show up in some simple examples, as well as in the design of certain computer systems.

Remembering often consists of arranging the environment to trigger the appropriate processes at the appropriate times. People used to tie knots in their handkerchiefs, or set up unusual situations to act as very general reminders (really, metareminders). While mnemonic cues, such as those used to improve one's memory, are usually content-oriented access keys, memories are often evoked by less specific signals from the environment. Such signals are more like interrupts, in that the initiative for a capture of control originates outside the currently active process—in fact, outside the organism. It might be useful to think of this allocation of responsibility to aspects of the environment as an even broader concept. There is a close parallel here with the allocation-of-complexity issue discussed earlier.

Consider a simple example. Suppose someone learns a set of household skills, such as cooking, setting the table, cleaning up, and so on. Suppose also that, in quite a different context, he learns that a certain plate in his home is a delicate and valued heirloom. How does he bring these two types of knowledge together so that all his usual actions on kitchenware are moderated by a "special case" warning where that dish is concerned? A possible but impractical answer is that when the person learns about the delicate dish, he modifies all his procedures that involve handling dishes (e.g., moving, washing, stacking) to test whether that particular dish is about to be handled, and branch accordingly. A slightly better way is to capitalize on the hierarchical structure of the procedures and identify a relevant primitive operation, such as grasping, and insert the test at that one point only. There are several problems with this solution. The organization rarely is strictly hierarchical. And, even if one could identify a single primitive module, this module may not always be accessible for modification. It may have become automated, or "compiled" into some larger module which is not decomposable, such as a MACROPS operator in the STRIPS programming system. This is extremely common in human skill learning, where larger units of skill become increasingly automated with practice. Furthermore, such an approach can result in complex primitive modules, which spend most of their time testing. Even in the simple-blocks world of Winograd's SHRDLU (Winograd, 1972), an examination of the running program shows that the robot spends a very large proportion of its effort checking to see if it is holding something. Since modules like "grasp" or "move" can be called in any situation, the system cannot be sure that SHRDLU is not holding something at the time; hence, the more primitive modules must keep checking.

A further improvement on these proposals might be achieved by declaring a special object type and putting all objects that could require special treatment into that type category. In that case only a single test is needed—to determine if the object is "special." If it is, special processing would be done on it; otherwise the normal procedure would continue. But even this is not satisfactory in general, since a single type will not determine where all the different tests ought to be inserted. On the other hand, increasing the number of types (e.g., delicate, hot, toxic) leads to either a proliferation of type-tests again or to the problem of adding new types. In fact, there are ways of dealing with the latter problem, which are adopted by so-called extensible programming systems, which I shall mention briefly below. For the present let me speak rather loosely and offer the following suggestion. Perhaps one ought to consider the responsibility for the special handling of the delicate dish to reside not with the organism but with the dish itself. In other words, some partial recognition of that object (which must, in any case, precede an action upon it) would have the status of an interupt rather than a test. The fundamental difference here is not in how these are implemented but rather in where the responsiblity lies—whether control is sent or captured.

Such anthropomorphic talk can be dangerous unless the details are filled out. In particular, there is no point in interrupting a process unless the system knows (a) what qualifies as a legitimate interrupt (a system which does not know this will be too distractible to complete any task), and (b) what to do after it has been interrupted. We shall return to consider several approaches to distributed responsibility. But first let me point out that although we have been discussing the allocation of responsibility to objects in the environment, the same issue is at stake at the next level down in Figure 1. Here there is a question about the allocation of responsibility to data rather than process. This means loosening the hierarchical authority relation common to most programs, and distributing authority in a more democratic manner, allowing for "local initiative." Attempts to work out a balance between process-directed and data-directed procedure invocation is a major concern in the design of control structures for computational systems.

The so-called extensible algebraic languages take a different approach, still retaining the distribution-of-responsibility idea. One of the problems to which such systems are addressed is that of adding new data types in a uniform manner. For example, suppose we had an algebraic language in which we had defined primitive operations on real numbers, and later wished to add a new data type—say, complex numbers. To go back and redefine all arithmetical operations to check for this new data type and apply the appropriate operations is, in general, impractical. Furthermore, it may involve some very difficult problems in cases where many already compiled functions (say, trigonometric functions) were constructed on the basis of the old arithmetical operations. One solution is to associate with the data type rather than with the arithmetic operators themselves, the responsibility of specifying how certain operators are to be interpreted for that data type. Thus the attempt to add something to X would, in effect, first find out what data type X is (which might be on X's property list), and then check the data type identifier for the procedural definition of addition for that data type. The procedure corresponding to the symbol '+' would be associated with X's data type, and not with '+' itself. This decentralization of responsibility makes it an easy matter to add new and unanticipated data types, and, of course, has implications for a broad class of problems—such as our "delicate dish" problem.

A natural extension of this diffusion of responsibility is found in the language ABSET (Elcock, McGregor, and Murray, 1971), where all responsibility for initiating procedures rests with the data. Data-directed or decentralized control schemes have been incorporated in many systems, including SMALLTALK (a proprietary computer language developed at Xerox), MERLIN (Moore and Newell, 1974), PLASMA (Hewett, 1977), KRL (Bobrow and Winograd, 1977). These examples and systems all illustrate some of the advantages of *decentralized* control, where the responsibility for initiating various procedures is *distributed* to the objects on which the procedures operate, instead of coming always from whatever procedure was executing previously.

As a final example, I want to discuss more fully a specific kind of system, which attempts to carry these ideas further and which is also, in my view, particularly well suited to psychological models. It is the "production system" formalism of Newell (1973c). A production system consists of two main parts: a communication area, called the *workspace,* and a set of condition-action pairs, called *productions.* If the condition side of a production is satisfied by the current contents of the workspace, then that production is said to be evoked, and the action on its action side is carried out. So the workspace is like a public bulletin board, and the productions are like simple-minded bureaucrats who mostly do nothing except look at the bulletin board; but each bureaucrat is looking for a certain pattern of "notices" on the board, and when it finds that pattern, it performs whatever its action is—which is usually just putting a notice of its own up (but some productions perform input or output operations for the overall system as their actions). In the original or "pure" version of production systems, there are no control transfer operations (called "go-to's" in conventional programming langauges) or subroutines in the strict sense—that is, no bureaucrat ever gives any orders, or delegates any authority, or even sends any messages to any other (particular) bureaucrat. All messages are broadcast, since the contents of the workspace are visible to all productions, and control is always captured by whatever production happens to have its conditions satisfied by the current workspace contents. The system is completely homogeneous, distributed, and modular. (We ignore technical details, like what to do when the conditions of several productions are satisfied at once.)

Even on the basis of this brief description, we can see that production systems have some attractive properties from a psychologist's point of view:

1. The system is responsive to a limited number of symbols at a time, which may be thought of as being in its focal attention. And it is completely data-directed, in the sense that nothing happens unless some symbols in the workspace initiate processing, by evoking a production.

2. Since symbols in the workspace can originate either from an environmental interrupt (as in our fragile-dish example) or from the action of some production, data-directed and environment-directed effects are combined—permitting a uniform treatment of what psychologists call stimulus-bound and stimulus-independent activity.

3. The primitive operation is *recognizing* that the symbols in the workspace satisfy some condition. Such recognitions can be made as elementary or as complex as desired, but choosing them is tantamount to selecting the primitive operations of the "virtual machine"—which for psychologists is, at least in part, an empirical issue.

4. Since production systems are completely data-directed, whenever they are used as models they must model *explicitly* the control structure of the process being modeled. That is,

since there is no hidden control apparatus (such as a push-down stack of return addresses), the flow of control must be handled by putting appropriate symbols *in the workspace* to evoke the relevant actions. These symbols then identify goals. A typical production system contains many goal-setting and goal-consummating productions. This has the interesting consequence that the contents of the workspace at any moment can be thought of as containing everything that occupies the system's attention—including all active goals (as well as the debris of recent processing).

5. Since production systems are highly modular, there is a uniform way of extending them, without making distributed alterations to the existing system. (It turns out, however, that production systems are difficult to program, because one must always bear in mind the communications via the workspace, and the actions of related productions.) Another benefit of this modularity is that individual productions tend to be meaningful components of the entire system, which may make it easier to give them psychological interpretations in terms of beliefs and goals.

6. Finally, since the workspace is the dynamic working memory of the system, it is assumed to be small (though perhaps not as small as Miller's magic number seven, since it contains goals and some bookkeeping symbols as well.) Thus, in order to attend to more aspects, it is necessary to trade off space for time. A natural approach is to assign a single symbol to designate a whole group of symbols, which can then be reconstructed from it whenever necessary. This fits quite well with psychological evidence for the mnemonic process called "chunking" (see Johnson, 1972); and Newell (1972) has used it in a model for Sternberg's high-speed memory-scan results (one of which we will describe later).

I have been examining some of the ways in which the strictly hierarchical organization of control is being challenged by the notion of dispersed responsibility. It is not yet clear whether a complete decentralization of authority is possible or desirable; and exactly how the central and distributed authorities should interact remains a difficult design problem. We can get a feeling

for some of the unresolved issues by considering some useful characteristics of social organizations, which do not have counterparts
in current computer systems. In social systems, for example, control is seldom given over completely to a local expert; when authority is delegated (say, in a corporation), the higher authority retains
the right to monitor progress, to reformulate goals as conditions
change, or even to stop the job before it's finished. There is no
good counterpart to monitoring in the computer case. The real
problem is not in the parallel-processing aspect, but simply in communicating enough relevant information to the monitor for it to
make a wise decision. A human boss and worker have much in
common, and they are able to communicate efficiently and accurately in brief, sketchy terms—relying heavily on their mutual
knowledge of the domain. Another option that a human authority
has is to obtain a commitment from the expert about the maxi-
mum time and cost for the job *before* giving the assignment. This
requires, among other things, a rather sophisticated meta-evaluation
capacity in the expert; and I know of no general approaches to
such meta-evaluation in computer systems (though all tree-pruning
techniques include something of the sort). Finally, the boss might
delegate a specifically limited authority—insisting, for instance, that
the expert get special permission before giving any further sub-
contracts, or before exceeding certain resource limits. Here again,
the boss has to know enough to make a wise decision when such
permission is requested, which, of course, repeats the problem of
providing enough relevant information—except that in this case
the information may have to be usable also at still higher levels in
the hierarchy if the permission requested exceeds even the boss's
authority.

Many of these difficulties reduce to the following three questions: how to enable flexible and effective communication among
modules, how to ensure that decisions are made in the context of
all relevant information, and how to withhold and release the making of decisions (including meta-decisions) at appropriate times. In
fact, these three questions are central to the whole control problem. The communication question raises the problem of appropriate ways of describing situations and plans. One way might be to
frame the description in a more abstract space, as suggested by
Sacerdoti (1973). The context question raises a host of problems

that many people are actively working on. The context mechanisms of CONNIVER and POPLER are directed at providing means for rendering various contexts visible to different processes. The third question, that of timing decisions, has also been the concern of a number of studies. The PLANNER distinction between if-added and if-needed procedures (sometimes called 'demon' and 'servant' procedures), ABSET's sequencer mechanism, and MERLIN's compile-when-used mechanisms are all efforts to deal with some aspect of this problem. The issue is of special concern to psychologists (e.g., Bransford and Johnson, 1972) who have experimentally demonstrated that many inferences are carried out in advance of being required for some particular task (e.g., at the time utterances are heard). Making decisions or executing procedures must sometimes be withheld until the appropriate context is available. Several proposals for dealing with such linguistic problems as referential opacity rely on this notion of withholding execution pending the appropriate context. For instance, Davies and Izard's (1972) discussion of language comprehension places considerable emphasis on the importance of withholding the evaluation of procedures which attempt to identify the referents of various parts of an utterance until the appropriate time. Thus there is a growing recognition among investigators interested in the problems of cognitive psychology that a variety of questions related to control must play a more prominent role.

Allocation of Constraints: The Validation Issue

The most frequent question that psychologists working in the computer simulation (or AI) tradition are asked goes something like this: "Maybe your program can perform the same task as people can (in some domain), but how do you know whether it does it in the same way that people do?" In this section I would like to discuss this question, and contrast the psychological and AI approaches. Before I do, however, I would like to point out that the question itself is not as well defined as is generally believed.

The question rests on the assumption that there is a clear distinction between process and product—between *what* an organism or device does, and *how* it does it. But to say that a computer performed the same task as a person, though perhaps in a different way, is not to claim that the machine behaved outwardly as some person did on some particular occasion. The claim is about a more abstract relation between the capabilities of the person and the machine in respect to some class of problems. It is not about some particular behavior, but about a class of potential behaviors—those which can be characterized as "doing a certain task," such as solving some problem. Now the point is that in characterizing this class of potential behavior—in saying *what* people can or will do—we are already saying something about *how* they do it. If "what people do"—in playing chess, say—could be satisfactorily described by listing their behaviors, then perhaps the distinction between the behavior and the process underlying it would be simple. But this is surely an unsatisfactory description of what they do. We would at least have to characterize the contingencies under which they did one thing rather than another and extrapolate to what they might do in related circumstances. But *this* kind of description must, in effect, take the form of a *procedure*, since it must characterize an extremely large class of moves (often an unbounded set). We can still ask whether there are not other procedural descriptions which better capture the behavioral regularities we observe; but we should recognize that such a description of *what* people do is at some level also a description of how people do it.

As a consequence, any AI system is at some level a psychological theory, simply because the description of the intelligent task to which it is addressed already is essentially a description of some psychological process. We would not call something "a description of intelligent behavior" if all it consisted of was a chronicle of what people did—for example, if it were a summary of the regularities in some corpus of observed behavior. A description of intelligent behavior has to go beyond mere reporting. It must, in Chomsky's (1964) terms, meet criteria of "descriptive adequacy," and not merely "observational adequacy." Such a description already incorporates theoretical commitments, in the sense that it necessarily involves stating generalizations about the behavior, and thus must use a theoretically augmented vocabulary. It asserts, for example, that a person does such-and-such in order to accomplish some goal, that certain conditions would result in the person taking certain action, etc. Such a description is not theoretically neutral.

Now, if this is so, then the statement that a person and a

machine do the same task (e.g., solve the same class of problems) but do it in different ways is, to some extent, self-contradictory. What the statement must mean is that there are differences between the processes in the human and in the machine which can be revealed by some types of observation, even though the two are indistinguishable with respect to some other types of observation. This is an important point, which I shall try to elaborate.

Whenever a class of evidence is admitted as relevant, constraints are placed on the processes that are considered theoretically adequate. In other words, the range of admissible systems or devices is reduced every time an additional constraint is applied. Thus if the only constraint we place on the process is that it solve the problem in finite time, then, providing the problem is mechanically solvable at all, there exist infinitely many Turing machines that will do it. But this, clearly, is not a strong enough constraint to be of interest. There is a wide choice of additional constraints, ranging all the way from efficiency and elegance to realizability in brain tissue. It is in the application of these additional constraints, and in the designers' tolerance for various kinds of partial solutions, that psychologists and AI people tend to diverge. This divergence is often simply one of personal preference or research strategy, but occasionally it appears to be deeper. In the remaining pages I will examine some of the constraints that are or can be imposed on systems.

As in our discussion of the allocation of complexity, constraints on a system can be either intrinsic or extrinsic. Moore and Newell (1974) list a number of constraints that are intrinsic to the "design issues which arise in the construction of understanding systems." These include constraints on how knowledge can be assimilated from the environment and represented internally (including the problems of partial knowledge, multiple representations, and the generation of new internal structures); on how represented knowledge can be accessed and used appropriately; on how the system accommodates the competing needs for flexibility and efficiency (such as the trade-offs between interpretation and compilation, input-time elaboration and retrieval-time inference, and uniformity of formalism versus data specificity); and, finally, on how the system handles errors (that is, is it brittle, in the sense that it either works or fails completely and halts, or can certain kinds of failures be accommodated with only a partial degradation in performance?). This is not the place to elaborate on any of these constraints, except to point out that there is a wide range of such issues, which function as primarily "rational" constraints on the design of intelligent systems in general. The more of these a system meets, the better *psychological* model it will be, other things being equal—which is not to deny that one can design an "idiot savant" system that meets many of these requirements yet is utterly unreasonable as a psychological model because of its failure to meet other important constraints.

In addition, there are a number of extrinsic constraints on systems, which determine their value as psychological models. In detail, these are limited mainly by the imagination of the experimental psychologist in ferreting them out, but we can identify several broad categories that will encompass most of them. I will begin with three types of evidence which bear fairly directly on the specific range of performances in question. I call these "intermediate state," "relative complexity," and "component analysis" evidence, respectively.

The ideas are easiest to present in terms of an example. Suppose someone claimed that an old-fashioned mechanical desk calculator is a model of human arithmetic skill. On what grounds would we counter this claim? First, the claim itself has to be made more specific. As Sellars (1963) pointed out, a model must always be accompanied by a "commentary," specifying how the object is to be interpreted *qua* model—which of its properties are relevant to the intended modeling function, and which are not. In this case, for instance, the color, weight, and size of the calculator are clearly irrelevant, whereas the numbers entered and the numbers output clearly are relevant. Then there is a grey area, which might or might not be relevant, such as how much time the computations take, and so on. But assuming we have some reasonable commentary, what kinds of reasons might we give for this being an inadequate model?

1. Suppose we give the model and some human subjects a pair of numbers to add, and we observe what intermediate states they go through in reaching the solution. For the calculator

this would be fairly easy (we might even slow it down or stop it periodically), and we might find first a state where some of the addend digits have been transformed, but none of the final digits yet determined, and then a state where some of the final digits (scattered throughout the sum) have been determined, but not the others, and then an end-state in which the remaining digits simultaneously reach the correct value. The corresponding observations on human subjects are much more difficult; the main method is the analysis of thinking-out-loud protocols, supplemented with some rational interpolation (see especially Newell and Simon, 1972). But despite its limitations, such evidence represents a unique and important constraint on models. In particular, a compelling case could be made that the human subjects do not go through intermediate states like those mentioned above for the calculator, and this is a powerful reason for being dissatisfied with the calculator as a model of human arithmetic skill.

2. Suppose we ranked various arithmetic problems in order of difficulty, both for the model and for human subjects. There are a variety of measures we might use, but two very simple ones are how long it takes to perform the computation, and the relative likelihood of making an error. For the model it might turn out that the difficulty of an addition is independent of the number of digits in the addends (up to some limit), and also of which digits they are—that is, 1+1 and 7986+57489 are equally difficult problems; and the difficulty of a multiplication depends only on the number of digits in the multiplier. For human subjects, on the other hand, the difficulty of additions (and even more so, of multiplications) depends both on the number of digits involved and on which particular digits they are (e.g., perhaps 0 and 1 might be easiest, 5 next easiest, and so on); and further variations are introduced by the number of "carries" required in an addition, and by the occurrence of zeros in the multiplier. Clearly, the two difficulty-rankings will not correspond very well to the range of skills allegedly modeled by the calculator, and this is another reason for being dissatisfied with the model.

3. If the problem can be resolved into a number of relatively independent subtasks, we can ask about how well the performance of these subtasks is modeled. One might argue, for example, that the differences between the human subjects and the calculator during addition were entirely due to the fact that the calculator adds all the columns simultaneously, whereas the people do them one at a time—but the individual column additions (the subtasks) are done "in the same way." Now, if this were so, it should be possible to show similar intermediate-state and relative-difficulty evidence for the performance of these subtasks. In fact, however, data on human addition of pairs of digits show (somewhat surprisingly) that the time required is not a constant but a function of the size of the smaller digit (see, e.g., Groen and Parkman, 1972). Componential analysis is a powerful means of validating and "fine tuning" models. In particular, the nature of the errors that people make, especially when pushed to the limits of their ability, can help to pinpoint the *loci* of processing difficulty—the "hard" subtasks. Newell and Simon (1972), in fact, have argued that selective stressing (that is, observing performance when the task must be carried out under certain adverse speed or memory-load conditions) is one of the most discriminating sources of evidence about human information processing.

As a concrete example of this use of selective stressing, consider Sternberg's (1967) discovery about memory mechanisms. If we teach a subject a short list of items—say, the digits 3, 7, and 8—and subsequently flash on a probe digit, say 7, then the amount of time it takes to say whether the probe digit was in the memorized set is a linear function of the number of items in the set. Because the slope of the line is usually less than 40 milliseconds per item—certainly not enough time to recite the digits to oneself—the question arises whether the search for a matching item is done on the basis of physical features of the presented probe. One way to test this is to present a degraded image of the probe, or one using a different script from the original memory-set presentation. If the search is on physical features, each individual comparison should take longer (we know this from independent studies) and so the slope should be greater. If, on the other hand, the probe is first converted to some internal symbolic form, then the intercept should be higher but the slope the same. Sternberg showed that the latter was clearly the case, thus neatly eliminating one possible mechanism. Newell (1970) gives a number of such examples to show that there are ways not only to apply global constraints, but in fact to carry out a detailed analysis of subprocesses, allowing one to constrain empirically even the fine structure of models.

These examples will suffice to give an idea of how general empirical constraints can be applied to validate processes as psychological models. Such constraints are applied routinely by investigators like Newell and Simon, who are determined that not only the gross behavior but also the detailed structures of computer systems must be taken seriously as psychological mechanisms.

In addition to the foregoing rather direct sorts of empirical constraint on the construction of adequate psychological models, there are several more general considerations that are worth mentioning. One is evidence regarding the malleability of behavior, including the system's ability to assimilate new information, to adjust to new environmental demands, and to learn by doing, as well as by being told or shown how. Another constraint enters when we consider how the system could possibly have developed—particularly in the growth of the individual, but also, to some extent, in the evolution of the species. Suppose we had accurate models for various developmental stages from infancy to adulthood; then we might want to know further how the transitions occur from stage to stage—what it is that changes, and what general developmental principles it follows. More to the point, should we try to understand the separate stages first, or is Piaget right that we can understand the stages themselves only in terms of their places in the developmental sequence? Finally, some general constraints may be found in the discoveries of neurophysiology and allied disciplines. Although the information-processing approach deliberately sets a level of analysis independent of specific material forms, it cannot entirely ignore physiological considerations—particularly as a source of evidence for potentially constraining the structure of the processes (although this source of constraint has been remarkably impotent in the past). For example, evidence from various pathologies (aphasias, agnosias, apraxias, and so on), as well as other evidence concerning the localization of certain functions, can bear on the problem of decomposing intelligence into partially independent component structures. Also, detailed analyses of some specialized subsystems (such as the visual system) may provide usable constraints on theories of intelligence; and, at the opposite extreme, research on split-brain patients could conceivably even shed new light on such deep philosophical problems as the nature of conscious experience and its relation to properties of cognitive processes.

Ultimately, the question of the nature of human intelligence may even involve us in a consideration of such *strong* constraints as how a mechanism could realize such functions within the real-time and real-space confines of the brain, how it can do this subject to such principles as captured roughly in Lashley's notions of "equipotential" and "mass action," and finally how subjective experience itself is mapped onto these mechanisms.

Needless to say, I have attempted to give not a *complete* list of all the kinds of intrinsic and extrinsic constraints on psychological models, but only a representative sample, which illustrates the great range and variety of relevant considerations. My basic point is that even granting the potential validity of *all* these sources of constraint, each research program will have to make some choices, in the form of setting relative priorities on meeting constraints of various kinds. If we apply only the minimal constraint of "computing the same input-output function," then indefinitely many Turing machines would be equally viable "models"; but if we try to apply all the constraints at once, there may be no stopping place, short of producing an entire human being. Hence, any system through which we are to understand intelligence has to be, at any stage, a compromise; and this leaves room for a wide variety of opinion on which sequence of approximations to pursue, and thus which kinds of incompleteness to tolerate along the way. Newell, for example, states his position as follows:

> I will, on balance, prefer to start with a grossly imperfect but complete model, hoping to improve it eventually, rather than start with an abstract but experimentally verified characterization, hoping to specify it further eventually. These may be looked at simply as different approximating sequences toward

the same scientific end. But they do dictate quite different approaches . . .   (1972; p. 375)

This position might be taken to characterize the AI or information-processing approach generally were it not for different ways of interpreting the phrases "imperfect but complete" and "abstract but experimentally verified." In stating his position, Newell was contrasting his approach with conventional theorizing on short-term memory and learning, in which abstract constructs like "imaginal mediators," "chunks," or "strategies" are operationally defined within an experimental paradigm. In such studies, little attention is paid to the details of any mechanisms capable of carrying out the required operations. The interest is not so much with the processes (though this term is frequently used) as with what are called "functional relations" among variables. In this approach, empirical regularities are exhibited by something akin to curve-fitting, rather than by designing mechanisms to do the task. Newell was concerned with "completeness," in the sense of spelling out just what mechanisms were involved, and how they worked, even at the price of an empirically imperfect fit.

He was not, however, trying to extend this completeness over a broad domain, such as perception or comprehension. The latter would be even more characteristic of AI endeavors, as opposed to typical psychological models. However, the kind of grossly imperfect mechanisms necessary to achieve some completeness over such broad domains are generally more than empirically minded psychologists can tolerate. This is, I believe, one of the main dimensions of tension between the AI and traditional psychological approaches to understanding intelligence (see, e.g., my discussion of commentators in Pylyshyn, 1978b).

Another illustration of this source of tension can be seen in terms of the differing attitudes that AI and psychology have toward the empirical constraints themselves. Returning to our calculator example, the AI-oriented person might object to the way in which we used "intermediate state" evidence in rejecting the calculator model on the grounds that our argument depended on assumptions about which intermediate states were the *relevant* ones to consider in the two cases. But these are not obvious a priori. There is a "grain" problem to be resolved first—or, to use

Newell and Simon's (1972) phrase, a question about the "level of aggregation" at which to compare human protocols and machine traces. Similar questions can come up in applying the "relative difficulty" constraint. If the difficulty of a task is ultimately to be understood in terms of the number of primitive operations required to perform it, then there is a question of which operations are to count as "primitive." Furthermore, what reasons are there for assuming that the number of primitive operations involved is reflected by the total time taken, or the relative frequencies of errors?

Lists of such questions and complications can be continued indefinitely. My point is only that the validation of models always involves meta-theoretical assumptions, and where there are broad differences in approach, one can expect to find different attitudes toward these assumptions. In my own view, this does not present any fundamental difficulty. Indeed, the situation is not significantly different from that in other scientific disciplines—except, perhaps, that we have not yet lived with the background assumptions of the information-processing approach long enough for them to have become embedded in our general scientific culture.

This brings me to a final point of contrast between AI and more traditional empirical psychology. Consider again the calculator example. An information-processing theorist, independent of any misgivings about the empirical constraints discussed above, will probably have a more serious objection to the model: it is simply *too narrow.* There is no reason to believe that mechanisms of the type found in the calculator would be of any use whatever to a system that understood English, perceived scenes, solved crossword puzzles, or performed any other intellectual tasks. Indeed, in the light of our earlier discussions about the allocation of complexity and the problem of control, there are good reasons to believe that such a model is fundamentally and irreparably limited. In particular, there is no suggestion in it of any incrementally expandable knowledge base; and without at least some hint, however "grossly imperfect," of an approach to the epistemological problem, the model is prevented at the outset from growing toward an intelligent mechanism. As Donald Michie (1971) put it, "we now have as a touchstone the realization that the central operations of intelligence are . . . transactions on a knowledge base." In view of this, it would be of little comfort even if the model met *all* the empirical constraints we examined. Though it might in some sense provide an "empirically adequate" model of arithmetical performance, it could in no way constitute a step toward understanding the broader problems of cognition.

This is a kind of incompleteness for which the AI community has developed a pronounced intolerance. Basically the problem is this: a system that is able to encompass some domain of evidence A may bear very little resemblance to a system that is able to encompass *both* domain A *and* some further domain of evidence B. If we have learned anything from the last decade of research in AI (take work in pattern recognition, for example), it is that continued progress is extremely sensitive to the way in which problems have been decomposed into strategic parcels. And, as I said at the beginning of this essay, traditional psychologists have opted for a type and size of parcel which many people, particularly in AI, are beginning to feel is fundamentally wrong-headed.

In closing let me summarize. There are many ways of approaching an understanding of intelligence. The empirical psychologist has traditionally preferred to take small steps, while standing on solid data. The rationalist or formalist (logician, linguist, etc.) also prefers to take small steps, but on a more abstract or intuitive footing. Although there have also been grand theoreticians (Freud, James, Piaget), who have ventured to take large steps, they have ultimately run up against the limits of the conceptual tools available to them—typically some sort of metaphor. What is needed is not only a dialectical relation among these various approaches, but also a new technical language with which to discipline and expand one's imagination. I believe that the notion of mechanism and of computational process, as it is being developed in the study of artificial intelligence, is the most promising idea yet to be enunciated for exploring these problems and bringing some convergence to the multiple strands of cognitive psychology.

Acknowledgment: I am grateful to John Haugeland for some suggestions on wording which have made this paper both briefer and more readable.

3

A Framework for Representing Knowledge

MARVIN MINSKY

1. *Frames*

IT SEEMS TO ME that the ingredients of most theories both in Artificial Intelligence and in Psychology have been on the whole too minute, local, and unstructured to account—either practically or phenomenologically—for the effectiveness of common-sense thought. The "chunks" of reasoning, language, memory, and perception ought to be larger and more structured; their factual and procedural contents must be more intimately connected in order to explain the apparent power and speed of mental activities.

Similar feelings seem to be emerging in several centers working on theories of intelligence. They take one form in the proposal of Papert and myself (1972) to divide knowledge into substructures, "micro-worlds." Another form is in the "problem-spaces" of Newell and Simon (1972), and yet another is in the new, large structures that theorists like Schank (1973), Abelson (1973), and Norman (1973) assign to linguistic objects. I see all these as moving away from the traditional attempts both by behavioristic psychologists and by logic-oriented students of Artificial Intelligence in trying to represent knowledge as collections of separate, simple fragments.

I try here to bring together several of these issues by pretending to have a unified, coherent theory. The paper raises more questions than it answers, and I have tried to note the theory's deficiencies.

Here is the essence of the theory: When one encounters a new situation (or makes a substantial change in one's view of the present problem), one selects from memory a structure called a *frame*. This is a remembered framework to be adapted to fit reality by changing details as necessary.

A *frame* is a data-structure for representing a stereotyped situation, like being in a certain kind of living room, or going to a child's birthday party. Attached to each frame are several kinds of information. Some of this information is about how to use the frame. Some is about what one can expect to happen next. Some is about what to do if these expectations are not confirmed.

We can think of a frame as a network of nodes and relations. The top levels of a frame are fixed, and represent things that are always true about the supposed situation. The lower levels have many *terminals*—slots that must be filled by specific instances or data. Each terminal can specify conditions its assignments must meet. (The assignments themselves are usually smaller subframes.) Simple conditions are specified by *markers* that might require a terminal assignment to be a person, an object of sufficient value, or a pointer to a subframe of a certain type. More complex conditions can specify relations among the things assigned to several terminals.

Collections of related frames are linked together into *frame-systems*. The effects of important actions are mirrored by *transformations* between the frames of a system. These are used to make certain kinds of calculations economical, to represent changes of emphasis and attention, and to account for the effectiveness of imagery.

For visual scene analysis, the different frames of a system describe the scene from different viewpoints, and the transformations between one frame and another represent the effects of moving from place to place. For nonvisual kinds of frames, the differences between the frames of a system can represent actions, cause-effect relations, or changes in conceptual viewpoint. *Different frames of a system share the same terminals;* this is the critical point that makes it possible to coordinate information gathered from different viewpoints.

Much of the phenomenological power of the theory hinges on the inclusion of expectations and other kinds of presumptions. *A frame's terminals are normally already filled with "default" assignments.* Thus a frame may contain a great many details whose supposition is not specifically warranted by the situation. These have many uses in representing general information, most likely cases, techniques for bypassing "logic," and ways to make useful generalizations.

The default assignments are attached loosely to their terminals, so that they can be easily displaced by new items that fit better the current situation. They thus can serve also as variables or as special cases for reasoning by example, or as textbook cases, and often make the use of logical quantifiers unnecessary.

The frame-systems are linked, in turn, by an *information retrieval network*. When a proposed frame cannot be made to fit reality—when we cannot find terminal assignments that suitably match its terminal marker conditions—this network provides a replacement frame. These interframe structures make possible other ways to represent knowledge about facts, analogies, and other information useful in understanding.

Once a frame is proposed to represent a situation, a *matching* process tries to assign values to each frame's terminals, consistent with the markers at each place. The matching process is partly controlled by information associated with the frame (which includes information about how to deal with surprises) and partly by knowledge about the system's current goals. There are important uses for the information, obtained when a matching process fails. I will discuss how it can be used to select an alternative frame that better suits the situation.

An apology: The schemes proposed herein are incomplete in many respects. First, I often propose representations without specifying the processes that will use them. Sometimes I only describe properties the structures should exhibit. I talk about markers and assignments as though it were obvious how they are attached and linked; it is not.

Besides the technical gaps, I will talk as though unaware of many problems related to "understanding" that really need much deeper analysis. I do not claim that the ideas proposed here are enough for a complete theory, only that the frame-system scheme may help explain a number of phenomena of human intelligence. The basic frame idea itself is not particularly original—it is in the tradition of the "schemata" of Bartlett and the "paradigms" of Kuhn; the idea of a frame-system is probably more novel. Winograd (1974) discusses the recent trend, in theories of AI, toward frame-like ideas.

In the body of the paper I discuss different kinds of reasoning by analogy, and ways to impose stereotypes on reality and jump to conclusions based on partial-similarity matching. These are basically uncertain methods. Why not use methods that are more logical and certain? Section 6 is a sort of Appendix which argues that traditional logic cannot deal very well with realistic, complicated problems because it is poorly suited to represent *approximations* to solutions—and these are absolutely vital.

> *Thinking always begins with suggestive but imperfect plans and images; these are progressively replaced by better—but usually still imperfect—ideas.*

1.3[1] ARTIFICIAL INTELLIGENCE AND HUMAN PROBLEM SOLVING

In this essay I draw no boundary between a theory of human thinking and a scheme for making an intelligent machine; no purpose would be served by separating them today, since neither domain has theories good enough to explain, or produce, enough mental capacity. There is, however, a difference in professional attitudes. Workers from psychology inherit stronger desires to minimize the variety of assumed mechanisms. I believe this leads to attempts to extract more performance from fewer "basic mechanisms" than is reasonable. Such theories especially neglect mechanisms of procedure control and explicit representations of processes. On the other side, workers in AI have perhaps focused too sharply on just such questions. Neither has given enough attention to the structure of knowledge, especially procedural knowledge.

It is understandable that psychologists are uncomfortable with complex proposals not based on well-established mechanisms, but I believe that parsimony is still inappropriate at this stage, valuable as it may be in later phases of every science. There is room in the anatomy and genetics of the brain for much more mechanism than anyone today is prepared to propose, and we should concentrate for a while longer on *sufficiency* and *efficiency* rather than on *necessity*.

---

1. *Editor's note:* Section numbers have been retained from the original, and hence are not always sequential in this abridged edition.

1.11 DEFAULT ASSIGNMENT

Although both seeing and imagining result in assignments to frame terminals, imagination leaves us wider choices of detail and variety of such assignments. I conjecture that frames are never stored in long-term memory with unassigned terminal values. Instead, what really happens is that frames are stored with weakly bound default assignments at every terminal! These manifest themselves as often-useful but sometimes counterproductive stereotypes.

Thus if I say, "John kicked the ball," you probably cannot think of a purely abstract ball, but must imagine characteristics of a vaguely particular ball; it probably has a certain default size, default color, default weight. Perhaps it is a descendant of one you first owned or were injured by. Perhaps it resembles your latest one. In any case your image lacks the sharpness of presence because the processes that inspect and operate upon the weakly bound default features are very likely to change, adapt, or detach them.

Such default assignments would have subtle, idiosyncratic influences on the paths an individual would tend to follow in making analogies, generalizations, and judgements, especially when the exterior influences on such choices are weak. Properly chosen, such stereotypes could serve as a storehouse of valuable heuristic plan-skeletons; badly selected, they could form paralyzing collections of irrational biases. Because of them one might expect, as reported by Freud, to detect evidences of early cognitive structures in free-association thinking.

2. Language, Understanding, and Scenarios

2.1 WORDS, SENTENCES AND MEANINGS

The device of images has several defects that are the price of its peculiar excellences. Two of these are perhaps the most important: the image, and particularly the visual image, is apt to go farther in the direction of the individualisation of situations than is biologically useful; and the principles of the combination of images have their own peculiarities and result in constructions which are relatively wild, jerky and irregular, compared with the straightforward unwinding of a habit, or with the somewhat orderly march of thought.

—F. C. Bartlett (1932)

The concepts of frame and default assignment seem helpful in discussing the phenomenology of "meaning." Chomsky (1957) points out that such a sentence as

(A) colorless green ideas sleep furiously

is treated very differently from the nonsentence

(B) furiously sleep ideas green colorless

and suggests that because both are "equally nonsensical," what is involved in the recognition of sentences must be quite different from what is involved in the appreciation of meanings.

There is no doubt that there are processes especially concerned with grammar. Since the meaning of an utterance is encoded as much in the positional and structural relations between the words as in the word choices themselves, there must be processes concerned with analyzing those relations in the course of building the structures that will more directly represent the meaning. What makes the words of (A) more effective and predictable than (B) in producing such a structure—putting aside the question of whether that structure should be called semantic or syntactic—is that the word-order relations in (A) exploit the (grammatical) conventions and rules people usually use to induce others to make assignments to terminals of structures. This is entirely consistent with theories of grammar. A generative grammar would be a summary description of the *exterior* appearance of those frame rules—or their associated processes—while the operators of transformational grammars seem similar enough to some of our frame transformations.

But one must also ask: to what degree does grammar have a separate identity in the actual working of a human mind? Perhaps the rejection of an utterance (either as nongrammatical, as nonsensical, or, most important, as *not understood*) indicates a more complex failure of the semantic process to arrive at any usable representation; I will argue now that the grammar-meaning distinction may illuminate two extremes of a continuum but obscures its all-important interior.

We certainly cannot assume that logical meaninglessness has a precise psychological counterpart. Sentence (A) can certainly generate an image! The dominant frame (in my case) is that of someone sleeping; the default system assigns a particular bed, and in it lies a mummy-like shape-frame with a translucent green color property. In this frame there is a terminal for the character of the sleep—restless, perhaps—and "furiously" seems somewhat inappropriate at that terminal, perhaps because the terminal does not like to accept anything so "intentional" for a sleeper. "Idea" is even more disturbing, because a person is expected, or at least something animate. I sense frustrated procedures trying to resolve these tensions and conflicts more properly, here or there, into the sleeping framework that has been evoked.

Utterance (B) does not get nearly so far because no subframe accepts any substantial fragment. As a result no larger frame finds anything to match its terminals, hence, finally, no top level "meaning" or "sentence" frame can organize the utterance as either meaningful or grammatical. By combining this "soft" theory with gradations of assignment tolerances, I imagine one could develop systems that degrade properly for sentences with poor grammar rather than none; if the smaller fragments—phrases and subclauses—satisfy subframes well enough, an image adequate for certain kinds of comprehension could be constructed anyway, even though some parts of the top level structure are not entirely satisfied. Thus we arrive at a qualitative theory of "grammatical": *if the top levels are satisfied but some lower terminals are not, we have a meaningless sentence; if the top is weak but the bottom solid, we can have an ungrammatical but meaningful utterance.*

I do not mean to suggest that sentences must evoke visual images. Some people do not admit to assigning a color to the ball in "he kicked the ball." But everyone admits (eventually) to having assumed, if not a size or color, at least some purpose, attitude, or other elements of an assumed scenario. When we go beyond vision, terminals and their default assignments can represent purposes and functions, not just colors, sizes and shapes.

2.6 SCENARIOS

Thinking . . . is biologically subsequent to the image-forming process. It is possible only when a way has been found of breaking up the 'massed' influence of past stimuli and situations, only when a device has already been discovered for conquering the sequential tyranny of past reactions. But though it is a later and a higher development, it does not supercede the method of images. It has its own drawbacks. Contrasted with imaging it loses something of vivacity, of vividness, of variety. Its prevailing instruments are words, and, not only because these are social, but also because in use they are necessarily strung out in sequence, they drop into habit reactions even more readily than images do. [With thinking] we run greater and greater risk of being caught up in generalities that may have little to do with actual concrete experience. If we fail to maintain the methods of thinking, we run the risks of becoming tied to individual instances and of being made sport of by the accidental circumstances belonging to these.

—F. C. Bartlett (1932)

We condense and conventionalize, in language and thought, complex situations and sequences into compact words and symbols. Some words can perhaps be "defined" in elegant, simple structures, but only a small part of the meaning of "trade" is captured by:

first frame	*second frame*
	$---\rightarrow$
A has X *B has Y*	*B has X* *A has Y*

Trading normally occurs in a social context of law, trust, and convention. Unless we also represent these other facts, most trade transactions will be almost meaningless. It is usually essential to know that each party usually wants both things but has to compromise. It is a happy but unusual circumstance in which each trader is glad to get rid of what he has. To represent trading strategies, one could insert the basic maneuvers right into the above frame-pair scenario: in order for A to make B want X more (or want Y less) we expect him to select one of the familiar tactics:

Offer more for Y.

Explain why X is so good.

Create favorable side-effect of B having X.

Disparage the competition.

Make B think C wants X.

These only scratch the surface. Trades usually occur within a scenario tied together by more than a simple chain of events each linked to the next. No single such scenario will do; when a clue about trading appears, it is essential to guess which of the different available scenarios is most likely to be useful.

Charniak's thesis (1972) studies questions about transactions that seem easy for people to comprehend yet obviously need rich default structures. We find in elementary school reading books such stories as:

Jane was invited to Jack's Birthday Party.
She wondered if he would like a kite.
She went to her room and shook her piggy bank.
It made no sound.

Most young readers understand that Jane wants money to buy Jack a kite for a present but that there is no money to pay for it in her piggy bank. Charniak proposes a variety of ways to facilitate such inferences—a "demon" for *present* that looks for things concerned with *money*, a demon for "piggy bank" which knows that shaking without sound means the bank is empty, etc. But although *present* now activates *money*, the reader may be surprised to find that neither of those words (nor any of their synonyms) occurs in the story. "Present" is certainly associated with "party" and "money" with "bank," but how are the longer chains built up? Here is another problem raised by Charniak. A friend tells Jane:

He already has a Kite.
He will make you take it back.

Take *which* kite back? We do not want Jane to return Jack's old kite. To determine the referent of the pronoun "it" requires understanding a lot about an assumed scenario. Clearly, "it" refers to the proposed *new* kite. How does one know this? (Note that we need not agree on any single explanation.) Generally, pronouns refer to recently mentioned things, but as this example shows, the referent depends on more than the local syntax.

Suppose for the moment we are already trying to instantiate a "buying a present" default subframe. Now, the word "it" alone is too small a fragment to deal with, but "take it back" could be a plausible unit to match a terminal of an appropriately elaborate *buying* scenario. Since that terminal would be constrained to agree with the assignment of "present" itself, we are assured of the correct meaning of *it* in "take X back." Automatically, the correct kite is selected. Of course, that terminal will have its own constraints as well; a subframe for the "take it back" idiom should know that "take X back" requires that:

X was recently purchased.
The return is to the place of purchase.
You must have your sales slip.
Etc.

If the current scenario does not contain a "take it back" terminal, then we have to find one that does and substitute it, maintaining as many prior assignments as possible. Notice that if things go well, the question of *it* being the old kite never even arises. *The sense of ambiguity arises only when a "near miss" mismatch is tried and rejected.*

Charniak's proposed solution to this problem is in the same spirit but emphasizes understanding that because Jack already has a kite, he may not want another one. He proposes a mechanism associated with "present":

(A) If we see that a person P might not like a present X, then look for X being returned to the store where it was bought.

(B) If we see this happening, or even being suggested, assert that the reason why is that P does not like X.

This statement of "advice" is intended by Charniak to be realized as a production-like entity to be added to the currently active data-base whenever a certain kind of context is encountered. Later, if its antecedent condition is satisfied, its action adds enough information about Jack and about the new kite to lead to a correct decision about the pronoun.

Charniak in effect proposes that the system should watch for certain kinds of events or situations and inject proposed reasons, motives, and explanations for them. The additional interconnections between the story elements are expected to help bridge the gaps that logic might find it hard to cross, because the additions are only "plausible" default explanations, assumed without corroborative assertions. By assuming (tentatively) "does not like X" when X is taken back, Charniak hopes to simulate much of ordinary "comprehension" of what is happening. We do not yet know how complex and various such plausible inferences must be to get a given level of performance, and the thesis does not answer this because it did not include a large simulation. Usually he proposes terminating the process by asserting the allegedly plausible motive without further analysis unless necessary. To understand why Jack might return the additional kite, it should usually be enough to assert that he does not like it. A deeper analysis might reveal that Jack would not really mind having two kites but he probably realizes that he will get only one present; his utility for two different presents is probably higher.

2.7 SCENARIOS AND "QUESTIONS"

The meaning of a child's birthday party is very poorly approximated by any dictionary definition like "a party assembled to celebrate a birthday," where a party would be defined, in turn, as "people assembled for a celebration." This lacks all the flavor of the culturally required activities. Children know that the "definition" should include more specifications, the particulars of which can normally be assumed by way of default assignments:

DRESS ------------------ *SUNDAY BEST.*

PRESENT --------------- *MUST PLEASE HOST.*
MUST BE BOUGHT AND GIFT-WRAPPED.

GAMES ------------------ *HIDE AND SEEK. PIN TAIL ON DONKEY.*

DECOR ------------------- *BALLOONS. FAVORS. CREPE-PAPER.*

PARTY-MEAL ------- *CAKE. ICE-CREAM. SODA. HOT DOGS.*

CAKE ------------------- *CANDLES. BLOW-OUT. WISH. SING BIRTHDAY SONG.*

ICE-CREAM ----------- *STANDARD THREE-FLAVOR.*

These ingredients for a typical American birthday party must be set into a larger structure. Extended events take place in one or more days. A Party takes place in a Day, of course, and occupies a substantial part of it, so we locate it in an appropriate day frame. A typical day has main events, such as

Get-up Dress Eat-1 Go-to-Work Eat-2

but a School-Day has more fixed detail:

Get-up Dress
  Eat-1 Go-to-School Be-in-School
    Home-Room Assembly English Math (arrgh)

       Eat-2   Science   Recess   Sport
       Go-Home   Play
       Eat-3   Homework   Go-To-Bed

Birthday parties obviously do not fit well into school-day frames. Any parent knows that the Party-Meal is bound to Eat-2 of its Day. I remember a child who did not seem to realize this. Absolutely stuffed after the Party-Meal, he asked when he would get Lunch.

Returning to Jane's problem with the kite, we first hear that she is invited to Jack's Birthday Party. Without this party scenario, or at least an invitation scenario, the second line seems rather mysterious:

She wondered if he would like a kite.

To explain one's rapid comprehension of this, I will make a somewhat radical proposal: *to represent explicitly, in the frame for a scenario structure, pointers to a collection of the most serious problems and questions commonly associated with it.* In fact we shall consider the idea that the frame terminals are exactly those questions. Thus, for the birthday party:

       Y must get P for X ------------ Choose P!
       X must like P -------------------- Will X like P?
         Buy P ---------------------------- Where to buy P?
         Get money to buy P ------- Where to get money?
         (Sub-question of the "present" frame?)
       Y must dress up -----------------What should Y wear?

Certainly these are one's first concerns, when one is invited to a party.

The reader is free to wonder, with the author, whether this solution is acceptable. The question, "Will X like P?" certainly matches "She wondered if he would like a kite?" and correctly assigns the kite to P. But is our world regular enough that such question sets could be precompiled to make this mechanism often work smoothly? I think the answer is mixed. We do indeed expect many such questions; we surely do not expect all of them. But surely "expertise" consists partly in not having to realize *ab initio* what are the outstanding problems and interactions in situations. Notice, for example, that there is *no* default assignment for the Present in our party-scenario frame. This mandates attention to that assignment problem and prepares us for a possible thematic concern. In any case, we probably need a more active mechanism for understanding *"wondered"* which can apply the information currently in the frame to produce an expectation of what Jane will think about.

The third line of our story, about shaking the bank, should also eventually match one of the present-frame questions, but the unstated connection between Money and Piggy-Bank is presumably represented in the piggy-bank frame, *not* the party frame, although once it is found, it will match our Get-Money question terminal. The primary functions and actions associated with piggy banks are Saving and Getting-Money-Out, and the latter has three principal methods:

1. Using a key. Most piggy banks don't offer this option.
2. Breaking it. Children hate this.
3. Shaking the money out, or using a thin slider.

In the fourth line does one know specifically that a *silent* Piggy Bank is empty, and hence out of money (I think, yes), or does one use general knowledge that a hard container which makes no noise when shaken is empty? I have found quite a number of people who prefer the latter. Logically the "general principle" would indeed suffice, but I feel that this misses the important point that a specific scenario of this character is engraved in every child's memory. The story is instantly intelligible to most readers. If more complex reasoning from general principles were required, this would not be so, and more readers would surely go astray. It is easy to find more complex problems:

A goat wandered into the yard where Jack was painting. The goat got the paint all over himself. When Mother saw the goat, she asked, "Jack, did you do *that?*"

There is no one word or line, which is the referent of "that." It seems to refer, as Charniak notes, to "cause the goat to be covered with paint." Charniak does not permit himself to make a specific proposal to handle this kind of problem, remarking only that his "demon" model would need a substantial extension to deal with such a poorly localized "thematic subject." Consider how much one has to know about our culture, to realize that *that* is not the *goat-in-the-yard* but the *goat-covered-with-paint.* Charniak's thesis —basically a study rather than a debugged system—discusses issues about the activation, operation, and dismissal of expectation and default-knowledge demons. Many of his ideas have been absorbed into this essay.

In spite of its tentative character, I will try to summarize this image of language understanding as somewhat parallel to seeing. The key words and ideas of a discourse evoke substantial thematic or scenario structures, drawn from memory with rich default assumptions. The individual statements of a discourse lead to temporary representations—which seem to correspond to what contemporary linguists call "deep structures"—which are then quickly rearranged or consumed in elaborating the growing scenario representation. In order of "scale," among the ingredients of such a structure there might be these kinds of levels:

Surface Syntactic Frames. Mainly verb and noun structures. Prepositional and word-order indicator conventions.

Surface Semantic Frames. Action-centered meanings of words. Qualifiers and relations concerning participants, instruments, trajectories and strategies, goals, consequences and side-effects.

Thematic Frames. Scenarios concerned with topics, activities, portraits, setting. Outstanding problems and strategies commonly connected with topic.

Narrative Frames. Skeleton forms for typical stories, explanations, and arguments. Conventions about foci, protagonists, plot forms, development, etc., designed to help a listener construct a new, instantiated Thematic Frame in his own mind.

A single sentence can assign terminals, attach subframes, apply a transformation, or cause a gross replacement of a high level frame when a proposed assignment no longer fits well enough. A pronoun is comprehensible only when general linguistic conventions, interacting with defaults and specific indicators, determine a terminal or subframe of the current scenario.

In *vision* the transformations usually have a simple grouplike structure, in *language* we expect more complex, less regular systems of frames. Nevertheless, because *time, cause,* and *action* are so important to us, we often use sequential transformation pairs that replace situations by their temporal or causal successors.

Because syntactic structural rules direct the selection and assembly of the transient sentence frames, research on linguistic structures should help us understand how our frame systems are constructed. One might look for such structures specifically associated with assigning terminals, selecting emphasis or attention viewpoints (transformations), inserting sentential structures into thematic structures, and changing gross thematic representations.

Finally, just as there are familiar "basic plots" for stories, there must be basic superframes for discourses, arguments, narratives, and so forth. As with sentences, we should expect to find special linguistic indicators for operations concerning these larger structures; we should move beyond the grammar of sentences to try to find and systematize the linguistic conventions that, operating across wider spans, must be involved with assembling and transforming scenarios and plans.

2.8 QUESTIONS, SYSTEMS, AND CASES

> Questions arise from a point of view—from something that helps to structure what is problematical, what is worth asking, and what constitutes an answer (or progress). It is not that the view determines reality, only what we accept from reality and how we structure it. I am realist enough to believe that in the long run reality gets its own chance to accept or reject our various views.
>
> —A. Newell (1973a)

Examination of linguistic discourse leads thus to a view of the frame concept in which the "terminals" serve to represent the questions most likely to arise in a situation. To make this important viewpoint more explicit, we will spell out this reinterpretation.

A Frame is a collection of questions to be asked about a hypothetical situation: it specifies issues to be raised and methods to be used in dealing with them.

The terminals of a frame correspond perhaps to what Schank (1973) calls "conceptual cases," although I do not think we should restrict them to as few types as Schank suggests. To understand a narrated or perceived action, one often feels compelled to ask such questions as

What caused it (agent)?
What was the purpose (intention)?
What are the consequences (side-effects)?
Whom does it affect (recipient)?
How is it done (instrument)?

The number of such "cases" or questions is problematical. While we would like to reduce meaning to a very few "primitive" concepts, perhaps in analogy to the situation in traditional linguistic analysis, I know of no reason to suppose that that goal can be achieved. My own inclination is to side with such workers as W. Martin (1974), who look toward very large collections of "primitives," annotated with comments about how they are related. Only time will tell which is better.

For entities other than actions one asks different questions; for thematic topics the questions may be much less localized, *e.g.*,

Why are they telling this to me?
How can I find out more about it?
How will it help with the "real problem"?

and so forth. In a "story" one asks what is the topic, what is the author's attitude, what is the main event, who are the protagonists, and so on. As each question is given a tentative answer, the corresponding subframes are attached and the questions they ask become active in turn.

The "markers" we proposed for vision-frames become more complex in this view. If we adopt for the moment Newell's larger sense of "view", it is not enough simply to ask a question; one must indicate how it is to be answered. Thus a terminal should also contain (or point to) suggestions and recommendations about how to find an assignment. Our "default" assignments then become the simplest special cases of such recommendations, and one certainly could have a hierarchy in which such proposals depend on features of the situation, perhaps along the lines of Wilks's (1973) "preference" structures.

For syntactic frames, the drive toward ritualistic completion of assignments is strong, but we are more flexible at the conceptual level. As Schank (1973a) says,

> People do not usually state all the parts of a given thought that they are trying to communicate because the speaker tries to be brief and leaves out assumed or unessential information [. . .]. The conceptual processor makes use of the unfilled slots to search for a given type of information in a sentence or a larger unit of discourse that will fill the needed slot.

Even in physical perception we have the same situation. A box will not present all of its sides at once to an observer, and although this is certainly not because it wants to be brief, the effect is the same; the processor is prepared to find out what the missing sides look like and (if the matter is urgent enough) to move around to find answers to such questions.

Frame-*Systems,* in this view, become choice-points corresponding (on the conceptual level) to the mutually exclusive choice "Systems" exploited by Winograd (1970). The different frames of a system represent different ways of using the same information, located at the common terminals. As in the grammatical situation, one has to choose one of them at a time. On the conceptual level this choice becomes: *what questions shall I ask about this situation?*

View-changing, as we shall argue, is a problem-solving technique important in representing, explaining, and predicting. In the rearrangements inherent in the frame-system representation (for example, of an action), we have a first approximation to Simmons' (1973) idea of "procedures which in some cases will change the contextual definitional structure to reflect the action of a verb."

Where do the "questions" come from? That is not in the scope of this paper, really, but we can be sure that the frame-makers (however they operate) must use some principles. The methods used to generate the questions ultimately shape each person's general intellectual style. People surely differ in details of preferences for asking "Why?", "How can I find out more?", "What's in it for me?", "How will this help with the current higher goals?", and so forth.

Similar issues about the style of *answering* must arise. In its simplest form the drive toward instantiating empty terminals would appear as a variety of hunger or discomfort, satisfied by any default or other assignment that does not conflict with a prohibition. In more complex cases we should perceive less animalistic strategies for acquiring deeper understandings.

It is tempting, then, to imagine varieties of frame-systems that span from simple template-filling structures to implementations of the "views" of Newell—with all their implications about coherent generators of issues with which to be concerned, ways to investigate them, and procedures for evaluating proposed solutions. But I feel uncomfortable about any superficially coherent synthesis in which one expects the same kind of theoretical framework to function well on many different levels of scale or concept. We should expect very different question-processing mechanisms to operate our low-level stereotypes and our most comprehensive strategic overviews.

3. Learning, Memory, and Paradigms

To the child, Nature gives various means of rectifying any mistakes he may commit respecting the salutary or hurtful qualities of the objects which surround him. On every occasion his judgements are corrected by experience; want and pain are the necessary consequences arising from false judgement; gratification and pleasure are produced by judging aright. Under such masters, we cannot fail but to become well informed; and we soon learn to reason justly, when want and pain are the necessary consequences of a contrary conduct.

In the study and practice of the sciences it is quite different: the false judgements we form neither affect our existence nor our welfare; and we are not forced by any physical necessity to correct them. Imagination, on the contrary, which is ever wandering beyond the bounds of truth, joined to self-love and that self-confidence we are so apt to indulge, prompt us to draw conclusions that are not immediately derived from facts.

—A. Lavoisier (1949)

How does one locate a frame to represent a new situation? Obviously, we cannot begin any complete theory outside the context of some proposed global scheme for the organization of knowledge in general. But if we imagine working within some bounded domain, we can discuss some important issues:

EXPECTATION: How to select an initial frame to meet some given conditions.

ELABORATION: How to select and assign subframes to represent additional details.

ALTERATION: How to find a frame to replace one that does not fit well enough.

NOVELTY: What to do if no acceptable frame can be found. Can we modify an old frame or must we build a new one?

LEARNING: What frames should be stored, or modified, as a result of the experience?

In popular culture, memory is seen as separate from the rest of thinking: but finding the right memory—it would be better to say: finding a *useful* memory—needs the same sorts of strategies used in other kinds of thinking!

We say someone is "clever" who is unusually good at quickly locating highly appropriate frames. His information-retrieval systems are better at making good hypotheses, formulating the conditions the new frame should meet, and exploiting knowledge gained in the "unsuccessful" part of the search. Finding the right memory is no less a problem than solving any other kind of puzzle! Because of this, a good retrieval mechanism can be based only in part upon basic "innate" mechanisms. It must also depend largely on (learned) knowledge about the structure of one's own knowledge! Our proposal will combine several elements—a Pattern Matching Process, a Clustering Theory, and a Similarity Network.

In seeing a room or understanding a story, one assembles a network of frames and subframes. Everything noticed or guessed, rightly or wrongly, is represented in this network. We have already suggested that an active frame cannot be maintained unless its terminal conditions are satisfied.

We now add the postulate that *all satisfied frames must be assigned to terminals of superior frames.* This applies, as a special case, to any substantial fragments of "data" that have been observed and represented.

Of course, there must be an exception! We must allow a certain number of items to be attached to something like a set of "short term memory" registers. But the intention is that very little can be remembered unless embedded in a suitable frame. This, at any rate, is the conceptual scheme; in certain domains we would, of course, admit other kinds of memory "hooks" and special sensory buffers.

3.1 REQUESTS TO MEMORY

We can now imagine the memory system as driven by two complementary needs. *On one side are items demanding to be properly represented by being embedded into larger frames; on the other side are incompletely filled frames demanding terminal assignments.* The rest of the system will try to placate these lobbyists, but not so much in accord with general principles as in accord with special knowledge and conditions imposed by the currently active goals.

When a frame encounters trouble—when an important condition cannot be satisfied—something must be done. We envision the following major kinds of accommodation to trouble:

MATCHING: When nothing more specific is found, we can attempt to use some "basic" associative memory mechanism. This will succeed by itself only in relatively simple situations, but should play a supporting role in the other tactics.

EXCUSE: An apparent misfit can often be excused or explained. A "chair" that meets all other conditions but is much too small could be a "toy."

ADVICE: The frame contains explicit knowledge about what to do about the trouble. Below, we describe an extensive, learned, "Similarity Network" in which to embed such knowledge.

SUMMARY: If a frame cannot be completed or replaced, one must give it up. But first one must construct a well-formulated complaint or summary to help whatever process next becomes responsible for reassigning the subframes left in limbo.

In my view, all four of these are vitally important. I discuss them in the following sections.

3.3 EXCUSES

We can think of a frame as describing an "ideal." If an ideal does not match reality because it is "basically" wrong, it must be replaced. *But it is in the nature of ideals that they are really elegant simplifications; their attractiveness derives from their simplicity, but their real power depends upon additional knowledge about interactions between them!* Accordingly we need not abandon an ideal because of a failure to instantiate it, provided one can explain the discrepancy in terms of such an interaction. Here are some examples in which such an "excuse" can save a failing match:

OCCLUSION: A table, in a certain view, should have four legs, but a chair might occlude one of them. One can look for things like T-joints and shadows to support such an excuse.

FUNCTIONAL VARIANT: A chair-leg is usually a stick, geometrically; but more important, it is *functionally* a support. Therefore, a strong center post, with an adequate base plate, should be an acceptable replacement for all the legs. Many objects are multiple purpose and need functional rather than physical descriptions.

BROKEN: A visually missing component could be explained as in fact physically missing, or it could be broken. Reality has a variety of ways to frustrate ideals.

PARASITIC CONTEXTS: An object that is just like a chair, except in size, could be (and probably is) a toy chair. The complaint "too small" could often be so interpreted in contexts with other things too small, children playing, peculiarly large "grain," and so forth.

In most of those examples, the kinds of knowledge to make the repair—and thus salvage the current frame—are "general" enough usually to be attached to the thematic context of a superior frame. In the remainder of this essay, I will concentrate on types of more sharply localized knowledge that would naturally be attached to a frame itself, for recommending its own replacement.

3.5 CLUSTERS, CLASSES, AND A GEOGRAPHIC ANALOGY

Though a discussion of *some* of the attributes shared by a *number* of games or chairs or leaves often helps us to learn how to employ the corresponding term, there is no set of characteristics that is simultaneously applicable to all members of the class and to them alone. Instead, confronted with a previously unobserved activity, we apply the term 'game' because what we are seeing bears a close 'family resemblance' to a number of the activities we have previously learned to call by that name. For Wittgenstein, in short, games, chairs, and leaves are natural families, each constituted by a network of overlapping and crisscross resemblances. The existence of such a network sufficiently accounts for our success in identifying the corresponding object or activity.

—T. Kuhn (1970)

To make the Similarity Network act more "complete," consider the following analogy. In a city, any person should be able to visit any other; but we do not build a special road between each pair of houses; we place a group of houses on a "block." We do not connect roads between each pair of blocks, but have them share streets. We do not connect each town to every other, but construct main routes, connecting the centers of larger groups. Within such an organization, each member has direct links to some other individuals at his own "level," mainly to nearby, highly similar ones; but each individual has also at least a few links to "distinguished" members of higher level groups. The result is that there is usually a rather short sequence between any two individuals, if one can but find it.

To locate something in such a structure, one uses a hierarchy like the one implicit in a mail address. Everyone knows something about the largest categories, in that he knows where the major cities are. An inhabitant of a city knows the nearby towns, and people in the towns know the nearby villages. No person knows all the individual routes between pairs of houses; but, for a particular friend, one may know a special route to his home in a nearby town that is better than going to the city and back. *Directories* factor the problem, basing paths on standard routes between major nodes in the network. Personal shortcuts can bypass major nodes and go straight between familiar locations. Although the standard routes are usually not quite the very best possible, our stratified transport and communication services connect everything together reasonably well, with comparatively few connections.

At each level, the aggregates usually have distinguished foci or *capitals*. These serve as elements for clustering at the next level of aggregation. There is no nonstop airplane service between New Haven and San Jose because it is more efficient overall to share the trunk route between New York and San Francisco, which are the capitals at that level of aggregation.

As our memory networks grow, we can expect similar aggregations of the destinations of our similarity pointers. Our decisions about what we consider to be primary or trunk difference features and which are considered subsidiary will have large effects on our abilities. Such decisions eventually accumulate to become epistemological commitments about the conceptual cities of our mental universe.

The nonrandom convergences and divergences of the similarity pointers, for each difference *d,* thus tend to structure our conceptual world around

(1) the aggregation into *d*-clusters
(2) the selection of *d*-capitals

Note that it is perfectly all right to have *several capitals in a cluster,* so that there need be no one attribute common to them all. The "crisscross resemblances" of Wittgenstein are then consequences of the local connections in our similarity network, which are surely adequate to explain how we can feel as though we know what a chair or a game is—yet cannot always define it in a logical way as an element in some class-hierarchy or by any other kind of compact, formal, declarative rule. The apparent coherence of the conceptual aggregates need not reflect explicit definitions, but can emerge from the success-directed sharpening of the difference-describing processes.

The selection of capitals corresponds to selecting stereotypes or typical elements whose default assignments are unusually useful. There are many forms of chairs, for example, and one should choose carefully the chair-description frames that are to be the major capitals of chair-land. These are used for rapid matching and assigning priorities to the various differences. The lower priority features of the cluster center then serve either as default properties of the chair types or, if more realism is required, as dispatch pointers to the local chair villages and towns. Difference pointers could be "functional" as well as geometric. Thus after rejecting a first try at "chair," one might try the functional idea of "something one can sit on" to explain an unconventional form. This requires a deeper analysis in terms of forces and strengths. Of course, that analysis would fail to capture toy chairs, or chairs of such ornamental delicacy that their actual use would be unthinkable. These would be better handled by the method of excuses, in which one would bypass the usual geometrical or functional explanations in favor of responding to contexts involving art or play.

It is important to re-emphasize that there is no reason to restrict the memory structure to a single hierarchy; the notions of "level" of aggregation need not coincide for different kinds of differences. The *d*-capitals can exist, not only by explicit declarations, but also implicitly by their focal locations in the structure defined by convergent *d*-pointers. (In the Newell-Simon GPS framework, the "differences" are ordered into a fixed hierarchy. By making the priorities depend on the goal, the same memories could be made to serve more purposes; the resulting problem-solver would lose the elegance of a single, simple-ordered measure of "progress," but that is the price of moving from a first-order theory.)

Finally, we should point out that we do not need to invoke any mysterious additional mechanism for *creating* the clustering structure. Developmentally, one would assume, the earliest frames would tend to become the capitals of their later relatives, unless this is firmly prevented by experience, because each time the use of one stereotype is reasonably successful, its centrality is reinforced by another pointer from somewhere else. Otherwise, *the acquisition of new centers is in large measure forced upon us from the outside: by the words available in one's language; by the behavior of objects in one's environment; by what one is told by one's teachers, family, and general culture.* Of course, at each step the structure of the previous structure dominates the acquisition of the later. But in any case such forms and clusters should emerge from the interactions between the world and almost any memory-using mechanism; it would require more explanation were they *not* found!

3.6 ANALOGIES AND ALTERNATIVE DESCRIPTIONS

We have discussed the use of different frames of the same system to describe the same situation in different ways: for change of position in vision and for change of emphasis in language. Sometimes, in "problem-solving" we use two or more descriptions in a more complex way to construct an analogy or to apply two radically *different* kinds of analysis to the same situation. *For hard problems, one "problem space" is usually not enough!*

Suppose your car battery runs down. You believe that there is an electricity shortage and blame the generator.

The generator can be represented as a mechanical system: the rotor has a pulley wheel driven by a belt from the engine. Is the belt tight enough? Is it even there? The output, seen mechanically, is a cable to the battery or whatever. Is it intact? Are the bolts tight? Are the brushes pressing on the commutator?

Seen electrically, the generator is described differently. The rotor is seen as a flux-linking coil, rather than as a rotating device. The brushes and commutator are seen as electrical switches. The output is current along a pair of conductors leading from the brushes through control circuits to the battery.

We thus represent the situation in two quite different frame-systems. In one, the armature is a mechanical rotor with pulley; in the other, it is a conductor in a changing magnetic field. The same —or analogous—elements share terminals of different frames, and the frame-transformations apply only to some of them.

The differences between the two frames are substantial. The entire mechanical chassis of the car plays the simple role, in the electrical frame, of one of the battery connections. The diagnostician has to use both representations. A failure of current to flow often means that an intended conductor is not acting like one. For this case, the basic transformation between the frames depends on the fact that electrical continuity is in general equivalent to firm mechanical attachment. Therefore, any conduction disparity revealed by electrical measurements should make us look for a corresponding disparity in the mechanical frame. In fact, since "repair" in this universe is synonymous with "mechanical repair," the diagnosis *must* end in the mechanical frame. Eventually, we might locate a defective mechanical junction and discover a loose connection, corrosion, wear, or whatever.

Why have two separate frames, rather than one integrated structure to represent the generator? I believe that in such a complex problem, one can never cope with many details at once. At each moment one must work within a reasonably simple framework. I contend that any problem that a person can solve at all is worked out at each moment in a small context and that the key operations in problem-solving are concerned with finding or constructing these working environments.

Indeed, finding an electrical fault requires moving between at least three frames: a visual one along with the electrical and mechanical frames. If electrical evidence suggests a loose mechanical connection, one needs a visual frame to guide one's self to the mechanical fault.

Are there general methods for constructing adequate frames? The answer is both yes and no! There are some often-useful strategies for adapting old frames to new purposes; but I should emphasize that humans certainly have no magical way to solve *all* hard problems! One must not fall into what Papert calls the Superhuman-Human Fallacy and require a theory of human behavior to explain even things that people cannot really do!

One cannot expect to have a frame exactly right for any problem or expect always to be able to invent one. But we do have a good deal to work with, and it is important to remember the contribution of one's culture in assessing the complexity of problems people seem to solve. *The experienced mechanic need not routinely invent;* he already has engine representations in terms of ignition, lubrication, cooling, timing, fuel mixing, transmission, compression, and so forth. Cooling, for example, is already subdivided into fluid circulation, air flow, thermostasis, etc. Most "ordinary" problems are presumably solved by systematic use of the analogies provided by the transformations between pairs of these structures. The huge network of knowledge, acquired from school, books, apprenticeship, or whatever is interlinked by difference and relevancy pointers. No doubt the culture imparts a good deal of this structure by its conventional *use of the same words* in explanations of different views of a subject.

3.8 FRAMES AND PARADIGMS

> Until that scholastic paradigm [the medieval 'impetus' theory] was invented, there were no pendulums, but only swinging stones, for scientists to see. Pendulums were brought into the world by something very like a paradigm-induced gestalt switch.
>
> Do we, however, really need to describe what separates Galileo from Aristotle, or Lavoisier from Priestly, as a transformation of vision? Did these men really *see* different things when *looking at* the same sorts of objects? Is there any legitimate sense in which we can say they pursued their research in different worlds?
>
> [I am] acutely aware of the difficulties created by saying that when Aristotle and Galileo looked at swinging stones, the first saw constrained fall, the second a pendulum. Nevertheless, I am convinced that we must learn to make sense of sentences that at least resemble these.
>
> —T. Kuhn (1970)

According to Kuhn's model of scientific evolution, normal science proceeds by using established descriptive schemes. Major changes result from new paradigms, new ways of describing things that lead to new methods and techniques. Eventually there is a redefining of "normal."

Now while Kuhn prefers to apply his own very effective redescription paradigm at the level of major scientific revolutions, it seems to me that the same idea applies as well to the microcosm of everyday thinking. Indeed, in that last sentence quoted, we see that Kuhn is seriously considering that the paradigms play a substantive rather than metaphorical role in visual perception, just as we have proposed for frames.

Whenever our customary viewpoints do not work well, whenever we fail to find effective frame systems in memory, we must construct new ones that bring out the right features. Presumably, the most usual way to do this is to build some sort of pair-system from two or more old ones and then edit or debug it to suit the circumstances. How might this be done? It is tempting to formulate the requirements, and then solve the construction problem.

But that is certainly not the usual course of ordinary thinking! Neither are requirements formulated all at once, nor is the new system constructed entirely by deliberate preplanning. Instead we recognize unsatisfied requirements, one by one, as deficiencies or "bugs," in the course of a sequence of modifications made to an unsatisfactory representation.

I think Papert (1972; see also Minsky, 1970) is correct in believing that the ability to diagnose and modify one's own procedures is a collection of specific and important "skills." *Debugging,* a fundamentally important component of intelligence, has its own special techniques and procedures. Every normal person is pretty good at them; or otherwise he would not have learned to see and talk! Although this essay is already speculative, I would like to point here to the theses of Goldstein (1974) and Sussman (1973) about the explicit use of *knowledge about debugging* in learning symbolic representations. They build new procedures to satisfy multiple requirements by such elementary but powerful techniques as:

1. Make a crude first attempt by the first order method of simply putting together procedures that *separately* achieve the individual goals.

2. If something goes wrong, try to characterize one of the defects as a *specific* (and undesirable) kind of interaction between two procedures.

3. Apply a debugging technique that, according to a record in memory, is good at repairing that *specific kind* of interaction.

4. Summarize the experience, to add to the "debugging techniques library" in memory.

These might seem simple-minded, but if the new problem is not too radically different from the old ones, they have a good chance to work, especially if one picks out the right first-order approximations. If the new problem *is* radically different, one should not expect *any* learning theory to work well. Without a structured cognitive map—without the "near misses" of Winston or a cultural supply of good training sequences of problems, we should not expect radically new paradigms to appear magically whenever we need them.

What are "kinds of interactions," and what are "debugging techniques?" The simplest, perhaps, are those in which the result of achieving a first goal interferes with some condition prerequisite for achieving a second goal. The simplest repair is to reinsert that prerequisite as a new condition. There are examples in which this technique alone cannot succeed because a prerequisite for the second goal is incompatible with the first. Sussman presents a more sophisticated diagnosis and repair method that recognizes this and exchanges the order of the goals. Goldstein considers related problems in a multiple description context.

If asked about important future lines of research on Artificial or Natural Intelligence, I would point to the interactions between these ideas and the problems of using multiple representations to deal with the same situation from several viewpoints. To carry out such a study, we need better ideas about interactions among the transformed relationships. Here the frame-system idea by itself begins to show limitations. Fitting together new representations from parts of old ones is clearly a complex process itself, and one that could be solved within the framework of our theory (if at all) only by an intricate bootstrapping. This, too, is surely a special skill with its own techniques. I consider it a crucial component of a theory of intelligence.

We must not expect complete success in the above enterprise; there is a difficulty, as Newell (1973) notes in a larger context:

'Elsewhere' is another view—possibly from philosophy—or other 'elsewheres' as well, since the views of man are multiple. Each view has its own questions. Separate views speak mostly past each other. Occasionally, of course, they speak to the same issue and then comparison is possible, but not often and not on demand.

6. Appendix: Criticism of the Logistic Approach

If one tries to describe processes of genuine thinking in terms of formal traditional logic, the result is often unsatisfactory; one has, then, a series of correct operations, but the sense of the process and what was vital, force-ful, creative in it seems somehow to have evaporated in the formulations.
—M. Wertheimer (1959)

I here explain why I think more "logical" approaches will not work. There have been serious attempts, from as far back as Aristotle, to represent common sense reasoning by a "logistic" system—that is, one that makes a complete separation between

(1) "propositions" that embody specific information, and

(2) "syllogisms" or general laws of proper inference.

No one has been able successfully to confront such a system with a realistically large set of propositions. I think such attempts will continue to fail, because of the character of logistic in general rather than from defects of particular formalisms. (Most recent attempts have used variants of "first order predicate logic," but I do not think *that* is the problem.)

A typical attempt to simulate common-sense thinking by logistic systems begins in a microworld of limited complication. At one end are high-level goals such as "I want to get from my house to the Airport." At the other end we start with many small items—the *axioms*—like "The car is in the garage," "One does not go outside undressed," "To get to a place one should (on the whole) move in its direction," etc. To make the system work, one designs heuristic search procedures to "prove" the desired goal, or to produce a list of actions that will achieve it.

I will not recount the history of attempts to make both ends meet—but merely summarize my impression: in simple cases one can get such systems to "perform," but as we approach reality, the obstacles become overwhelming. The problem of finding suitable axioms—the problem of "stating the facts" in terms of always-correct, logical assumptions—is very much harder than is generally believed.

FORMALIZING THE REQUIRED KNOWLEDGE: Just constructing a knowledge base is a major intellectual research problem. Whether one's goal is logistic or not, we still know far too little about the contents and structure of common-sense knowledge. A "minimal" common-sense system must "know" something about cause-and-effect, time, purpose, locality, process, and types of knowledge. It also needs ways to acquire, represent, and use such knowledge. We need a serious epistemological research effort in this area. The essays of McCarthy (1969) and Sandewall (1970) are steps in that direction. I have no easy plan for this large enterprise; but the magnitude of the task will certainly depend strongly on the representations chosen, and I think that "Logistic" is already making trouble.

RELEVANCY: The problem of selecting relevance from excessive variety is a key issue! A modern epistemology will not resemble the old ones! Computational concepts are necessary and novel. Perhaps the better part of knowledge is not propositional in character, but interpropositional. For each "fact" one needs meta-facts about how it is to be used and when it should not be used. In McCarthy's "Airport" paradigm we see ways to deal with some interactions between "situations, actions, and causal laws" within a restricted microworld of things and actions. But though the system can make deductions implied by its axioms, it cannot be told when it should or should not make such deductions.

For example, one might want to tell the system to "not cross the road if a car is coming." But one cannot demand that the system "prove" no car is coming, for there will not usually be any such proof. In PLANNER, one can direct an *attempt* to prove that a car IS coming, and if the (limited) deduction attempt ends with "failure," one can act. This cannot be done in a pure logistic system. "Look right, look left" is a first approximation. But if one tells the system the real truth about speeds, blind driveways, probabilities of racing cars whipping around the corner, proof becomes impractical. If it reads in a physics book that intense fields perturb light rays, should it fear that a mad scientist has built an invisible car? We need to represent "usually"! Eventually it must understand the trade-off between mortality and accomplishment, for one can do nothing if paralyzed by fear.

MONOTONICITY: Even if we formulate relevancy restrictions, logistic systems have a problem in using them. In any logistic system, all the axioms are necessarily "permissive"—they all help to permit new inferences to be drawn. Each added axiom means more theorems; none can disappear. There simply is no direct way to add information to tell such a system about kinds of conclusions that should *not* be drawn! To put it simply: if we adopt enough axioms to deduce what we need, we deduce far too simply: if we adapt enough axioms to deduce what we need, we deduce far too many other things. But if we try to change this by adding axioms about relevancy, we still produce all the unwanted theorems, plus annoying statements about their irrelevancy.

Because Logicians are not concerned with systems that will later be enlarged, they can design axioms that permit only the conclusions they want. In the development of Intelligence the situation is different. One has to learn which features of situations are important and which kinds of deductions are not to be regarded seriously. The usual reaction to the "liar's paradox" is, after a while, to laugh. The conclusion is not to reject an axiom, but to reject the deduction itself! This raises another issue:

PROCEDURE-CONTROLLING KNOWLEDGE: The separation between axioms and deduction makes it impractical to include classificational knowledge about propositions. Nor can we include knowledge about management of deduction. A paradigm problem is that of axiomatizing everyday concepts of approximation or nearness. One would like nearness to be transitive:

(A near B) and (B near C) ==> (A near C)

but unrestricted application of this rule would make everything near everything else. One can try technical tricks like

(A near *1 B) AND (B near *1 C) ==> (A near *2 C)

and admit only (say) five grades of near *1, near *2, near *3, etc. One might invent analog quantities or parameters. But one cannot (in a Logistic system) decide to make a new kind of "axiom" to prevent applying transitivity after (say) three chained uses, conditionally, unless there is a "good excuse." I do not mean to propose a particular solution to the transitivity of nearness. (To my knowledge, no one has made a creditable proposal about it.) My complaint is that because of acceptance of Logistic, no one has freely explored this kind of procedural restriction.

COMBINATORIAL PROBLEMS: I see no reason to expect these systems to escape combinatorial explosions when given richer knowledge-bases. Although we see encouraging demonstrations in microworlds, from time to time, it is common in AI research to encounter high-grade performance on hard puzzles—given just enough information to solve the problem—but this does not often lead to good performance in larger domains.

CONSISTENCY and COMPLETENESS: A human thinker reviews plans and goal-lists as he works, revising his knowledge and policies about using it. One can program some of this into the theorem-proving program itself—but one really wants also to represent it directly, in a natural way, in the declarative corpus—for use in further introspection. Why then do workers try to make Logistic systems do the job? A valid reason is that the systems have an attractive simple elegance; if they worked, this would be fine. An invalid reason is more often offered: that such systems have a mathematical virtue because they are

(1) Complete—"All true statements can be proven"; and
(2) Consistent—"No false statements can be proven."

It seems not often realized that Completeness is no rare prize. It is a trivial consequence of any exhaustive search procedure, and any system can be "completed" by adjoining to it any other complete system and interlacing the computational steps. Consistency is more refined; it requires one's axioms to imply no contradictions. But I do not believe that consistency is necessary or even desirable in a developing intelligent system. No one is ever completely consistent. What is important is how one handles paradox or conflict, how one learns from mistakes, how one turns aside from suspected inconsistencies.

Because of this kind of misconception, Godel's Incompleteness Theorem has stimulated much foolishness about alleged differences between machines and men. No one seems to have noted its more "logical" interpretation: that enforcing consistency produces limitations. Of course there will be differences between humans (who are demonstrably inconsistent) and machines whose designers have imposed consistency. But it is not inherent in machines that they be programmed only with consistent logical systems. Those "philosophical" discussions all make these quite unnecessary assumptions! (I regard the recent demonstration of the consistency of modern set-theory, thus, as indicating that set-theory is probably inadequate for our purposes—not as reassuring evidence that set-theory is safe to use!)

A famous mathematician, warned that his proof would lead to a paradox if he took one more logical step, replied "Ah, but I shall not take that step." He was completely serious. A large part of ordinary (or even mathematical) knowledge resembles that in dangerous professions: When are certain actions unwise? When are certain approximations safe to use? When do various measures yield sensible estimates? Which self-referent statements are permissible if not carried too far? Concepts like "nearness" are too valuable to give up just because no one can exhibit satisfactory axioms for them. To summarize:

1. "Logical" reasoning is not flexible enough to serve as a basis for thinking: I prefer to think of it as a collection of heuristic methods, effective only when applied to starkly simplified schematic plans. The Consistency that Logic absolutely demands is not otherwise usually available—*and probably not even desirable!*—because consistent systems are likely to be too weak.

2. I doubt the feasibility of representing ordinary knowledge effectively in the form of many small, independently true propositions.

3. The strategy of complete separation of specific knowledge from general rules of inference is much too radical. We need more direct ways for linking fragments of knowledge to advice about *how* they are to be used.

4. It was long believed that it was crucial to make all knowledge

accessible to deduction in the form of declarative statements; but this seems less urgent as we learn ways to manipulate structural and procedural descriptions.

I do not mean to suggest that "thinking" can proceed very far without something like "reasoning." We certainly need (and use) something like syllogistic deduction; but I expect mechanisms for doing such things to emerge in any case from processes for "matching" and "instantiation" required for other functions. Traditional formal logic is a technical tool for discussing either *everything that can be deduced from some data* or *whether a certain consequence can be so deduced;* it cannot discuss at all what *ought* to be deduced under ordinary circumstances. Like the abstract theory of Syntax, formal Logic without a powerful procedural semantics cannot deal with meaningful situations.

I cannot state strongly enough my conviction that the preoccupation with Consistency, so valuable for Mathematical Logic, has been incredibly destructive to those working on models of mind. At the popular level it has produced a weird conception of the potential capabilities of machines in general. At the "logical" level it has blocked efforts to represent ordinary knowledge, by presenting an unreachable image of a corpus of context-free "truths" that can stand almost by themselves. And at the intellect-modeling level it has blocked the fundamental realization that *thinking begins first with suggestive but defective plans and images that are slowly (if ever) refined and replaced by better ones.*

4

Artificial Intelligence:

A Personal View

DAVID MARR

ARTIFICIAL INTELLIGENCE is the study of complex information-processing problems that often have their roots in some aspect of biological information processing. The goal of the subject is to identify interesting and solvable information-processing problems, and solve them.

The solution to an information-processing problem divides naturally into two parts. In the first, the underlying nature of a particular computation is characterized, and its basis in the physical world is understood. One can think of this part as an abstract formulation of *what* is being computed and *why*, and I shall refer to it as the "theory" of a computation. The second part consists of particular algorithms for implementing a computation, and so it specifies *how*. The choice of algorithm usually depends upon the hardware in which the process is to run, and there may be many algorithms that implement the same computation. The theory of a computation, on the other hand, depends only on the nature of the problem to which it is a solution. Jardine and Sibson (1971) decomposed the subject of cluster analysis in precisely this way, using the term "method" to denote what I call the theory of a computation.

To make the distinction clear, let us take the case of Fourier analysis. The (computational) theory of the Fourier transform is well understood, and is expressed independently of the particular way in which it is computed. There are, however, several algorithms for implementing a Fourier transform—the Fast Fourier transform

(Cooley and Tukey, 1965), which is a serial algorithm, and the parallel "spatial" algorithms that are based on the mechanisms of coherent optics. All these algorithms carry out the same computation, and the choice of which one to use depends upon the available hardware. In passing, we also note that the distinction between serial and parallel resides at the algorithm level and is not a deep property of a computation.

Strictly speaking then, a *result* in AI consists of the isolation of a particular information-processing problem, the formulation of a computational theory for it, the construction of an algorithm that implements it, and a practical demonstration that the algorithm is successful. The important point here, and it is what makes progress possible, is that once a computational theory has been established for a particular problem, it never has to be done again, and in this respect a result in AI behaves like a result in mathematics or any of the hard natural sciences. Some judgment has to be applied when deciding whether the computational theory for a problem has been formulated adequately: the statement "take the opponent's king" defines the goal of chess, but it is hardly an adequate characterization of the computational problem of doing it.[1] The kind of judgment that is needed seems to be similar to that which decides whether a result in mathematics amounts to a substantial new theorem, and I do not feel uncomfortable about having to leave the basis of such judgments unspecified.[2]

This view of what constitutes a result in AI is probably acceptable to most scientists. Chomsky's (1965) notion of a "competence" theory for English syntax is precisely what I mean by a computational theory for that problem. Both have the quality of being little concerned with the gory details of algorithms that

1. One computational theory that in principle can solve chess is exhaustive search. The real interest lies, however, in formulating the pieces of computation that we apply to the game. One presumably wants a computational theory that has a general application, together with a demonstration that it happens to be applicable to some class of games of chess, and evidence that we play games in this class.

2. New algorithms for implementing a known computational theory may subsequently be devised without throwing substantial new light upon the theory, just as S. Winograd's (1976) Very Fast Fourier Transform sheds no new light on the nature of Fourier analysis.

must be run to express the competence (i.e., to implement the computation). That is not to say that devising suitable algorithms will be easy, but it is to say that before one can devise them, one has to know what exactly they are supposed to be doing, and this information is captured by the computational theory. When a problem decomposes in this way, I shall refer to it as having a *Type 1* theory.

The fly in the ointment is that while many problems of biological information processing have a Type 1 theory, there is no reason why they should all have. This can happen when a problem is solved by the simultaneous action of a considerable number of processes, *whose interaction is its own simplest description,* and I shall refer to such a situation as a *Type 2* theory.[3] One promising candidate for a Type 2 theory is the problem of predicting how a protein will fold. A large number of influences act on a large polypeptide chain as it flaps and flails in a medium. At each moment only a few of the possible interactions will be important, but the importance of those few is decisive. Attempts to construct a simplified theory must ignore some interactions; but if most interactions are crucial at some stage during the folding, a simplified theory will prove inadequate. Interestingly, the most promising studies of protein folding are currently those that take a brute force approach, setting up a rather detailed model of the amino acids, the geometry associated with their sequence, hydrophobic interactions with the circumambient fluid, random thermal perturbations, etc., and letting the whole set of processes run until a stable configuration is achieved (Levitt and Warshel, 1975).

The principal difficulty in AI is that one can never be sure whether a problem has a Type I theory. If one is found, well and good; but failure to find one does not mean that it does not exist. Most AI programs have hitherto amounted to Type 2 theories, and the danger with such theories is that they can bury crucial decisions, which in the end provide the key to the correct Type 1

3. The underlying point here is that there is often a natural modularity in physics (e.g., under normal conditions, electrical interactions are independent of gravitational interactions), but some processes involve several at the same time and with roughly equal importance, like protein folding. Thus the Type 1–Type 2 distinction is not a pure dichotomy, and there is a spectrum of possibilities between them.

decomposition of the problem, beneath the mound of small administrative decisions that are inevitable whenever a concrete program is designed. This phenomenon makes research in AI difficult to pursue and difficult to judge. If one shows that a given information-processing problem is solved by a particular, neatly circumscribed computational theory, then that is a secure result. If, on the other hand, one produces a large and clumsy set of processes that solves a problem, one cannot always be sure that there is not a simple underlying computational theory for one or more related problems whose formulation has somehow been lost in the fog. With any candidate for a Type 2 theory, much greater importance is attached to the performance of the program. Since its only possible virtue might be that it works, it is interesting only if it does. Often, a piece of AI research has resulted in a large program without much of a theory, which commits it to a Type 2 result, but that program either performs too poorly to be impressive or (worse still) has not even been implemented. Such pieces of research have to be judged very harshly, because their lasting contribution is negligible.

Thus we see that as AI pursues its study of information-processing problems, two types of solution are likely to emerge. In one there is a clean underlying theory in the traditional sense. Examples of this from vision are Horn's (1975) method for obtaining shape from shading; the notion of the primal sketch as a representation of the intensity changes and local geometry of an image (Marr, 1976); Ullman's (1976) method for detecting light sources; Binford's (1971) generalized cylinder representation, on which Marr and Nishihara's (1977) theory of the internal representation and manipulation of 3-D structures was based; a recent theory of stereo vision (Marr, 1974; Marr and Poggio, 1976);[4] and Poggio and Reichardt's (1976) analysis of the visual orienting behavior of the housefly. One characteristic of these results is that they often lie at a relatively low level in the overall canvas of intellectual functions, a level often dismissed with contempt by

4. The notion of cooperative computation, or relaxation-labeling (Zucker, 1976), is a notion at the algorithm level. It suggests a way of implementing certain computations but does not address the problem of what should be implemented, which seems to be the real issue for vision no less than elsewhere.

those who purport to study "higher, more central" problems of intelligence. Our reply to such criticism is that low-level problems probably do represent the easier kind, but that is precisely the reason for studying them first. When we have solved a few more, the questions that arise in studying the deeper ones will be clearer to us.

But even relatively clean Type 1 theories such as these involve Type 2 theories as well. For example, Marr and Nishihara's 3-D representation theory asserts that the deep underlying structure is based on a distributed, object-centered coordinate system that can be thought of as a stick figure, and that this representation is explicitly manipulated during the analysis of an image. Such a theory would be little more than speculation unless it could also be shown that such a description may be computed from an image and can be manipulated in the required way. To do so involves several intermediate theories, for some of which there is hope of eventual Type 1 status, but others look intractably to be of Type 2. For example, a Type 1 theory now exists for part of the problem of determining the appropriate local coordinate system from the contours formed in an object's image (Marr, 1977), but it may be impossible to derive a Type 1 theory for the basic grouping processes that operate on the primal sketch to help separate figure from ground. The figure-ground "problem" may not be a single problem, being instead a mixture of several subproblems which combine to achieve figural separation, just as the different molecular interactions combine to cause a protein to fold. There is, in fact, no reason why a solution to the figure-ground problem should be derivable from a single underlying theory. The reason is that it needs to contain a procedural representation of many facts about images that derive ultimately via evolution from the cohesion and continuity of matter in the physical world. Many kinds of knowledge and different techniques are involved; one just has to sort them out one by one. As each is added, the performance of the whole improves, and the complexity of the images that can be handled increases.

We have already seen that to search for a Type 2 theory for a problem may be dangerous if in fact it has a Type 1 theory. This danger is most acute in premature assaults on a high-level problem, for which few or none of the concepts that underlie its eventual

Type 1 theory have yet been developed, and the consequence is a complete failure to formulate correctly the problems that are, in fact, involved. But it is equally important to realize that the opposite danger exists lower down. For example, in our current theory of visual processing, the notion of the primal sketch seems respectable enough, but one might have doubts about the aesthetics of the grouping processes that decode it. There are many of them; their details are somewhat messy; and seemingly arbitrary preferences occur (e.g., for vertical or horizontal organizations). A clear example of a Type 2 theory is our assertion that texture-vision discriminations rest on these grouping processes and first-order discriminations applied to the information held in primal sketch of the image (Marr, 1976). As such, it is less attractive than Julesz's (1975) clean (Type 1) theory that textured regions are discriminable only if there is a difference in the first or second-order statistics of their intensity arrays. But as Julesz himself found, there exist patterns with different second-order statistics that are nevertheless indiscriminable; and one can in fact view our own work as attempting to define precisely what characteristics of the second-order statistical structure cause discriminability (see Schatz, 1977, in preparation).

This inevitably forces us to relinquish the beauty of Julesz's concise theory, but I feel that one should not be too distressed by the need at this level of investigation to explore rather messy and untidy details. We already know that separate modules must exist for computing other aspects of visual information—motion, stereoscopy, fluorescence, color—and there is no reason why they should all be based on a single theory. Indeed, one would a priori expect the opposite: as evolution progressed, new modules came into existence that could cope with yet more aspects of the data, and as a result kept the animal alive in ever more widely ranging circumstances. The only important constraint is that the system as a whole should be roughly modular, so that new facilities can be added easily.

So, especially at the more peripheral stages of sensory information processing, and perhaps also more centrally, one should not give up if one fails to find a Type 1 theory—there may not be one. More importantly, even if there were, there would be no reason why that theory should bear much relation to the theory of more central phenomena. In vision, for example, the theory that says 3-D representations are based on stick-figure coordinate systems and shows how to manipulate them is independent of the theory of the primal sketch, or for that matter of most other stages en route from the image to that representation. In particular, it is especially dangerous to suppose that an approximate theory of a peripheral process has any significance for higher-level operations. For example, because Julesz's second-order statistics idea is so clean and so neatly fits much data, that one might be tempted to ask whether the idea of second-order interactions is in some way central to higher processes. In doing so one should bear in mind that the true explanation of visual-texture discrimination may be quite different in nature even if the theory is very often a correct predictor of performance.

The reason for making this point at such length is that it bears upon another issue, namely the type of theory that the grammar of natural language might have. The purpose of human language is presumably to transform a data structure that is not inherently one-dimensional into one-dimensional form for transmission as a sequential utterance, thereafter to be retranslated into some rough copy of the original in the head of the listener. Viewed in this light, it becomes entirely possible that there may exist no Type 1 theory of English syntax of the type that transformational grammar attempts to define—that its constraints resemble wired-in conventions about useful ways of executing this tedious but vital operation, rather than deep principles about the nature of intel ligence. An abstract theory of syntax may be an illusion, approximating what really happens only in the sense that Julesz's second order statistics theory approximates the behavior of the set of processes that implement texture vision and which, in the final analysis, are all the theory there is. In other words, the grammar of natural language may have a theory of Type 2 rather than of Type 1.

Even if a biological information-processing problem has only a Type 2 theory, it may be possible to infer more from a solution to it than the solution itself. This comes about because at some point in the implementation of a set of processes, design constraints attached to the machine in which they will run start to affect the structure of the implementation. This observation adds a different perspective to the two types of research carried out by linguists and by members of the artificial intelligence community. If the theory of syntax is really of Type 2, any important implications about the CNS are likely to come from details of the way in which its constituent processes are implemented, and these are often explorable only by implementing them.

Implications of this View

If one accepts this view of AI research, one is led to judge its achievements according to rather clear criteria. What information-processing problem has been isolated? Has a clean theory been developed for solving it, and if so how good are the arguments that support it? If no clean theory has been given, what is the evidence that favors a set-of-processes solution or suggests that no single clean theory exists for it, and how well does the proposed set of mechanisms work? For very advanced problems like story-understanding, current research is often purely exploratory. That is to say, in these areas our knowledge is so poor that we cannot even begin to formulate the appropriate questions, let alone solve them. It is important to realize that this is an inevitable phase of any human endeavor, personally risky (almost surely no exploring pioneer will himself succeed in finding a useful question), but a necessary precursor of eventual success.

Most of the history of AI (now fully 16 years old) has consisted of exploratory studies. Some of the best-known are Slagle's (1963) symbolic integration program, Weizenbaum's (1965) Eliza program, Evans' (1968) analogy program, Raphael's (1968) SIR, Quillian's (1968) semantic nets and Winograd's (1972) SHRDLU. All these programs have (in retrospect) the property that they are either too simple to be interesting Type 1 theories, or very complex yet perform too poorly to be taken seriously as a Type 2 theory. Perhaps the only really successful Type 2 theory to emerge in the early phase of AI was Waltz's (1972) program. Yet many things have been learned from these experiences—mostly negative things (the first twenty obvious ideas about how intelligence might work are too simple or wrong) but including several positive things. The MACSYMA algebraic manipulation system (Moses, 1974) is undeniably successful and useful, and it had its roots in programs like Slagle's. The mistakes made in the field lay not in having carried out such studies—they formed an essential part of its development—but mainly in failures of judgment about their value, since it is now clear that few of the early studies themselves formulated any solvable problems. Part of the reason for these internal failures of judgment lay in external pressures for early results from the field, but this is not the place to discuss what in the end are political matters.

Yet, I submit, one would err to judge these failures of judgment harshly. They are merely the inevitable consequence of a necessary enthusiasm, based on a view of the long-term importance of the field that seems to me correct. All important fields of human endeavor start with a personal commitment based on faith rather than on results. AI is just one more example. Only a crabbed and unadventurous spirit will hold it against us.

Current Trends

Exploratory studies are important. Many people in the field expect that, deep in the heart of our understanding of intelligence, there will lie at least one and probably several important principles about how to organize and represent knowledge that in some sense captures what is important about the *general* nature of our intellectual abilities. An optimist might see the glimmer of such prinicples in programs like those of Sussman and Stallman (1975), of Marr and Nishihara (1977), in the overall attitudes to central problems set out by Minsky (1974), and possibly in some of Schank's (1973b, 1975c) work, although I sometimes feel that he failed to draw out the important points. Although still somewhat cloudy, the ideas that seem to be emerging (and which owe much to the early exploratory studies) are:

(1) That the "chunks" of reasoning, language, memory, and perception ought to be larger than most recent theories in psychology have allowed (Minsky, 1974). They must also be very flexible—at least as flexible as Marr and Nishihara's stick-figure 3-D models, and probably more. Straightforward mechanisms that are suggested by the terms "frame" and "terminal" are certainly too inflexible.

(2) That the perception of an event or of an object must include the simultaneous computation of several different descrip-

tions of it, which capture diverse aspects of the use, purpose, or circumstances of the event or object.

(3) That the various descriptions described in (2) include coarse versions as well as fine ones. These coarse descriptions are a vital link in choosing the appropriate overall scenarios demanded by (1), and in establishing correctly the roles played by the objects and actions that caused those scenarios to be chosen.

An example will help to make these points clear. If one reads

(A) The fly buzzed irritatingly on the window-pane.
(B) John picked up the newspaper.

the immediate inference is that John's intentions toward the fly are fundamentally malicious. If he had picked up the telephone, the inference would be less secure. It is generally agreed that an "insect-damaging" scenario is somehow deployed during the reading of these sentences, being suggested in its coarsest form by the fly buzzing irritatingly. Such a scenario will contain a reference to something that can squash an insect on a brittle surface—a description that fits a newspaper but not a telephone. We might therefore conclude that when the newspaper is mentioned (or, in the case of vision, seen), is it described not only internally as a newspaper and some rough 3-D description of its shape and axes set up, but also as a light, flexible object with area. Because sentence (B) might have continued "and sat down to read," the newspaper may also be being described as reading matter; similarly, as a combustible article, and so forth. Since one does not usually know in advance what aspect of an object or action is important, it follows that most of the time a given object will give rise to several different coarse internal descriptions. Similarly for actions. It may be important to note that the description of fly-swatting or reading or fire-lighting does not have to be attached to the newspaper; merely that a description of the newspaper is available that will match its role in each scenario.

The important thing about Schank's "primitive actions" seems to me not the fact that there happens to be a certain small number of them, nor the idea that every act is expressed solely by reduction to them (which I cannot believe at all), nor even the idea that the scenarios to which they are attached contain all the answers for the present situation (that is where the missing flexibility comes in). The importance of a primitive, coarse catalogue of events and objects lies in the role such coarse descriptions play in the ultimate access and construction of perhaps exquisitely tailored specific scenarios, rather in the way that a general 3-D animal model in Marr and Nishihara's theory can finish up as a very specific Cheshire Cat, after due interaction between the image and information stored in the primitive model. What after sentence (A) existed as little more than a malicious intent toward the innocent fly becomes, with the additional information about the newspaper, a very specific case of fly-squashing.

Marr and Nishihara have labeled the problem of providing multiple-descriptions for the newspaper its "reference-window problem." Exactly how it is best done, and exactly what descriptions should accompany different words or perceived objects, is not yet known. These insights are the result of exploratory studies, and the problems to which they lead have yet to be precisely formulated, let alone satisfactorily solved. But it is now certain that some problems of this kind do exist and are important; and it seems likely that a fairly respectable theory of them will eventually emerge.

Mimicry versus Exploration

Finally, I would like to draw one more distinction that seems to be important when choosing a research problem, or when judging the value of completed work. The problem is that studies—particularly of natural language understanding, problem-solving, or the structure of memory—can easily degenerate into the writing of programs that do no more than mimic in an unenlightening way some small aspect of human performance. Weizenbaum (1976) now judges his program Eliza to belong to this category, and I have never seen any reason to disagree. More controversially, I would also criticize on the same grounds Newell and Simon's work on production systems, and some of Norman and Rummelhart's (1974) work on long-term memory.

The reason is this. If one believes that the aim of information-processing studies is to formulate and understand particular information-processing problems, then it is the structure of those problems that is central, not the mechanisms through which they are implemented. Therefore, the first thing to do is to find problems that we can solve well, find out how to solve them, and examine our performance in the light of that understanding. The most fruitful source of such problems is operations that we perform well, fluently (and hence unconsciously), since it is difficult to see how reliability could be achieved if there were no sound underlying method. On the other hand, problem-solving research has tended to concentrate on problems that we understand well intellectually but perform poorly on, like mental arithmetic and criptarithmetic or on problems like geometry theorem-proving, or games like chess, in which human skills seem to rest on a huge base of knowledge and expertise. I argue that these are exceptionally good grounds for *not* studying how we carry out such tasks yet. I have no doubt that when we do mental arithmetic we are doing *something* well, but it is not arithmetic, and we seem far from understanding even one component of what that something is. Let us therefore concentrate on the simpler problems first, for there we have some hope of genuine advancement.

If one ignores this stricture, one is left in the end with unlikely looking mechanisms whose only recommendation is that they cannot do something we cannot do. Production systems seem to me to fit this description quite well. Even taken on their own terms as mechanisms, they leave a lot to be desired. As a programming language they are poorly designed and hard to use, and I cannot believe that the human brain could possibly be burdened with such poor implementation decisions at so basic a level.

A parallel may perhaps be drawn between production systems for students of problem-solving and Fourier analysis for visual neurophysiologists. Simple operations on a spatial frequency representation of an image can mimic several interesting visual phenomena that seem to be exhibited by our visual systems. These include the detection of repetition, certain visual illusions, the notion of separate linearly adding channels, separation of overall shape from fine local detail, and a simple expression of size invariance. The reason why the spatial frequency domain is ignored by image analysts is that it is virtually useless for the main job of vision—building up a description of what is there from the intensity array. The intuition that visual physiologists lack, and which is so important, is for how this may be done. A production system exhibits several interesting ideas—the absence of explicit subroutine calls, a blackboard communication channel, and some notion of a short-term memory. But just because production systems display these side effects (as Fourier analysis "displays" some visual illusions) does not mean that they have anything to do with what is really going on. My own guess would be, for example, that the fact that short-term memory can act as a storage register is probably the least important of its functions. I expect that there are several "intellectual reflexes" that operate on items held there, about which nothing is yet known and which will eventually be held to be the crucial things about it because they perform central functions like opening up an item's reference window. Studying our performance in close relation to production systems seems to me a waste of time, because it amounts to studying a mechanism, not a problem, and can therefore lead to no Type 1 results. The mechanisms that such research is trying to penetrate will be unraveled by studying problems, just as vision research is progressing because it is the *problem* of vision that is being attacked, not neural visual mechanisms.

A reflexion of the same criticism can be made of Norman and Rummelhart's work, where they studied the way information seems to be organized in long-term memory. Again, the danger is that questions are not asked in relation to a clear information-processing problem. Instead, they are asked and answers proposed in terms of a mechanism—in this case, it is called an "active structural network," and it is so simple and general as to be devoid of theoretical substance. They may be able to say that such and such an "association" seems to exist, but they cannot say of what the association consists, nor that it has to be so because to solve problem X (which we can solve) you *need* a memory organized in such-and-such a way; and that if one has it, certain apparent "associations" occur as side effects. Experimental psychology can do a valuable job in discovering facts that need explaining, including those about long-term memory, and the work of Shepard (1975), Rosch (1976, 1977), and Warrington (1975), for example, seems to me very successful at this; but like experimental neurophysiology, experimental psychology will not be able to explain those facts unless information-processing research has identified and solved the appropriate problems X.[5] It seems to me that finding such problems X, and solving them, is what AI should be trying to do.

Acknowledgment: Although I take full responsibility for the purely personal views set out here, any virtues that they may have are due in part to many conversations with Drew McDermott. This report describes work done at the Artificial Intelligence Laboratory of the Massachusetts Institute of Technology. Support for the Laboratory's artificial intelligence research is provided in part by the Advanced Research Projects Agency of the Department of Defense under Office of Naval Research contract number N00014–75–C–0643.

5. In the present state of the art, it seems wisest to concentrate on problems that probably have Type 1 solutions, rather than on those that are almost certainly of Type 2.

5
Artificial Intelligence Meets Natural Stupidity

DREW MCDERMOTT

AS A FIELD, artificial intelligence has always been on the border of respectability, and therefore on the border of crackpottery. Many critics (Dreyfus, 1972; Lighthill, 1973) have urged that we are over the border. We have been very defensive toward this charge, drawing ourselves up with dignity when it is made and folding the cloak of Science about us. On the other hand, in private we have been justifiably proud of our willingness to explore weird ideas, because pursuing them is the only way to make progress.

Unfortunately, the necessity for speculation has combined with the culture of the hacker in computer science (Weizenbaum, 1976) to cripple our self-discipline. In a young field, self-discipline is not necessarily a virtue, but we are not getting any younger. In the past few years, our tolerance of sloppy thinking has led us to repeat many mistakes over and over. If we are to retain any credibility, this should stop.

This paper is an effort to ridicule some of these mistakes. Almost everyone I know should find himself the target at some point or other; if you don't, you are encouraged to write up your own favorite fault. The three described here I suffer from myself. I hope self-ridicule will be a complete catharsis, but I doubt it. Bad tendencies can be very deep-rooted. Remember, though, if we can't criticize ourselves, someone else will save us the trouble.

Wishful Mnemonics

A major source of simple-mindedness in AI programs is the use of mnemonics like "UNDERSTAND" or "GOAL" to refer to programs and data structures. This practice has been inherited from more traditional programming applications, in which it is liberating and enlightening to be able to refer to program structures by their purposes. Indeed, part of the thrust of the structured programming movement is to program entirely in terms of purposes at one level before implementing them by the most convenient of the (presumably many) alternative lower-level constructs.

However, in AI our programs to a great degree are problems rather than solutions. If a researcher tries to write an "understanding" program, it isn't because he has thought of a better way of implementing this well-understood task, but because he thinks he can come closer to writing the *first* implementation. If he calls the main loop of his program "UNDERSTAND", he is (until proven innocent) merely begging the question. He may mislead a lot of people, most prominently himself, and enrage a lot of others.

What he should do instead is refer to this main loop as "G0034", and see if he can *convince* himself or anyone else that G0034 implements some part of understanding. Or he could give it a name that reveals its intrinsic properties, like NODE-NET-INTERSECTION-FINDER, it being the substance of his theory that finding intersections in networks of nodes constitutes understanding. If Quillian (1969) had called his program the "Teachable Language Node Net Intersection Finder", he would have saved us some reading (except for those of us fanatic about finding the part on teachability).

Many instructive examples of wishful mnemonics by AI researchers come to mind once you see the point. Remember GPS? (Ernst and Newell, 1969.) By now, "GPS" is a colorless term denoting a particularly stupid program to solve puzzles. But it originally meant "General Problem Solver", which caused everybody a lot of needless excitement and distraction. It should have been called LFGNS—"Local-Feature-Guided Network Searcher".

Compare the mnemonics in Planner (Hewitt, 1972) with those in Conniver (Sussman and McDermott, 1972):

Planner	*Conniver*
GOAL	FETCH & TRY-NEXT
CONSEQUENT	IF-NEEDED
ANTECEDENT	IF-ADDED
THEOREM	METHOD
ASSERT	ADD

It is so much harder to write programs using the terms on the right! When you say (GOAL . . .), you can just feel the enormous power at your fingertips. It is, of course, an illusion.

Of course, Conniver has some glaring wishful primitives, too. Calling "multiple data bases" CONTEXTS was dumb. It implies that, say, sentence understanding in context is really easy in this system.

LISP's mnemonics are excellent in this regard (Levin *et al*, 1965). What if atomic symbols had been called "concepts", or CONS had been called ASSOCIATE? As it is, the programmer has no debts to pay to the system. He can build whatever he likes. There are some minor faults; "property lists" are a little risky; but by now the term is sanitized.

Resolution theorists have been pretty good about wishful mnemonics. They thrive on hitherto meaningless words like RESOLVE and PARAMODULATE, which can only have their humble, technical meaning. There are actually quite few pretensions in the resolution literature (Robinson, 1965). Unfortunately, at the top of their intellectual edifice stands the word "deduction". This is very wishful, but not entirely their fault. The logicians who first misused the term (e.g., in the "deduction" theorem) didn't have our problems; pure resolution theorists don't either. Unfortunately, too many AI researchers took them at their word and assumed that deduction, like payroll processing, had been tamed.

Of course, as in many such cases, the only consequence in the long run was that "deduction" changed in meaning, to become something narrow, technical, and not a little sordid.

As AI progresses (at least in terms of money spent), this malady gets worse. We have lived so long with the conviction that robots are possible, even just around the corner, that we can't help hastening their arrival with magic incantations. Winograd (1971) explored some of the complexity of language in sophisticated detail; and now everyone takes "natural-language interfaces" for granted, though none has been written. Charniak (1972) pointed out some approaches to understanding stories, and now the OWL interpreter includes a "story-understanding module". (And, God help us, a top-level "ego loop" (Sunguroff, 1975)).

Some symptoms of this disease are embarrassingly obvious once the epidemic is exposed. We should avoid, for example, labeling any part of our programs an "understander". It is the job of the text accompanying the program to examine carefully how much understanding is present, how it got there, and what its limits are.

But even seemingly harmless mnemonics should be handled gingerly. Let me explore as an example the ubiquitous "IS-A link", which has mesmerized workers in this field for years (Quillian, 1968; Fahlman, 1975; Winograd, 1975). I shall take examples from Fahlman's treatment, but what I say is criticism of calling the thing "IS-A", not his work in particular.

An IS-A link joins two nodes in a "semantic net" (a by-now emasculated misnomer), thus:

DOG
↑
| IS-A
|
FIDO

which is presumably meant to express "Fido is a dog". However, the *intrinsic* description of this link is "indicator-value pair inheritance link." That is, if the piece of network

            HAS-AS-PART
DOG -------------------→ TAIL
↑
| IS-A
|
FIDO

is present, then implicitly, "Fido has [a] tail" is present as well. Here HAS-AS-PART is the indicator, TAIL the value.

Most readers will think it extreme to object to calling this IS-A. Indeed, a self-disciplined researcher will be safe. But many people have fallen into the following IS-A traps:

Often, a programmer will shut his mind to other interpretations
of IS-A, or conclude that IS-A is a very simple concept. Then he
begins to write nonsensical networks like

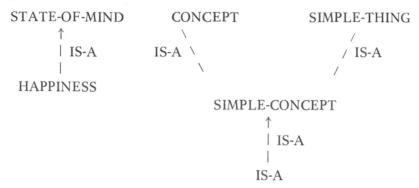

STATE-OF-MIND   CONCEPT   SIMPLE-THING
    ↑   \   /
  | IS-A   IS-A \   / IS-A
  | \   /
HAPPINESS

                  SIMPLE-CONCEPT
                       ↑
                     | IS-A
                     |
                   IS-A

or suspiciously wishful networks like

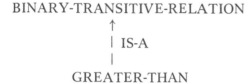

BINARY-TRANSITIVE-RELATION
        ↑
      | IS-A
      |
    GREATER-THAN

This is an illustration of "contagious wishfulness": because one
piece of a system is labeled impressively, the things it interacts
with inherit grandiosity. A program called "THINK" is likely
inexorably to acquire data structures called "THOUGHTS"

A good test for the disciplined programmer is to try using
gensyms in key places and see if he still admires his system. For
example, if STATE-OF-MIND is renamed G1073, we might have:

G1073
  ↑
 | INHERITS-INDICATORS
 |
HAPPINESS

which looks much more dubious.

Concepts borrowed from human language must shake off a lot
of surface-structure dust before they become clear. (See the next
section of this paper.) "Is" is a complicated word, syntactically
obscure. We use it with great facility, but we don't understand it

well enough to appeal to it for clarification of anything. If we want to call attention to the "property inheritance" use, why not just *say* INHERITS-INDICATORS? Then, if we wish, we can prove from a completed system that this captures a large part of what "is a" means.

Another error is the temptation to write networks like this:

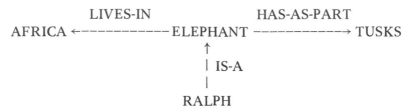

```
              LIVES-IN                HAS-AS-PART
AFRICA ←------------ ELEPHANT ------------→ TUSKS
                        ↑
                        | IS-A
                        |
                     RALPH
```

which people do all the time. It is clear to them that Ralph lives in Africa, the same Africa as all the other elephants, but his tusks are his own. But the network doesn't say this. Woods (1975) discusses errors like this in detail.

People reason circularly about concepts like IS-A. Even if originally they were fully aware they were just naming INHERITS-INDICATORS with a short, friendly mnemonic, they later use the mnemonic to conclude things about "is a." For example, it has been proposed that a first cut at representing "Nixon is a Hitler" is:

```
HITLER
  ↑
  | IS-A
  |
NIXON
```

It worked for Fido and Dog, didn't it? But we just can't take stuff out of the IS-A concept that we never put in. I find this diagram worse than useless.

Lest this all seem merely amusing, meditate on the fate of those who have tampered with words before. The behaviorists ruined words like "behavior", "response", and, especially, "learning". They now play happily in a dream world, internally consistent but lost to science. And think about this: if "mechanical translation" had been called "word-by-word text manipulation", the people doing it might still be getting government money.

Unnatural Language

In this section I wish to rail against a pervasive sloppiness in our thinking: the tendency to see in natural language a natural source of problems and solutions. Many researchers tend to talk as if an internal knowledge representation ought to be closely related to the "corresponding" English sentences; and that operations on the structure should resemble human conversation or "word problems". Because the fault here is a disregard for logic, it will be hard for my criticism to be logical and clear. Examples will help.

A crucial problem in internal representation is effective naming of entities. Although every entity can be given a primary name of some kind, much information about it will be derived from knowledge about roles it plays. If two persons marry and have children, they play the role of parents in whatever data structure encodes knowledge of the family. Information about them (such as, "parents are older than their children") will be in terms of PARENT-1 and PARENT-2 (or "mother" and "father" if they are of opposite sexes). The naming problem is to ensure that information about PARENT-1 is applied to the primary name G0073 when it is discovered that G0073 shares a family with G0308.

The "natural-language fallacy" appears here in the urge to identify the naming problem with the problem of resolving references in English-language discourse. Although the two problems must at some remote intersection meet, it seems to me to be a waste of time to focus on their similarities. Yet it is hard to avoid the feeling that our ability to understand "the mother" to mean "Maria" is the same as the internal function of "binding" PARENT-1 to G0073. But it can't be.

The uses of reference in discourse are not the same as those of naming in internal representation. A good reason to have differing referential expressions in natural language is to pick out an object to talk about with the least amount of breath. After all, the speaker already knows exactly what he wants to refer to; if he says, "the left arm of the chair" in one place, "the arm" in another, and "it" in a third, it isn't because he thinks of this object in three different ways. But internally, this is exactly the reason for having multiple names. Different canonical data structures with different names for the constituent entities come to be instantiated to refer to the same thing in different ways. The internal user of such a structure must be careful to avoid seeing two things where one is meant.

In discourse, a speaker will introduce a hand and easily refer to "the finger". Frame theorists and other notation-developers find it marvelous that their system practically gives them "the finger" automatically as a piece of the data structure for "hand". As far as I can see, doing this automatically is the worst way of doing it. First, of course, there are four or five fingers, each with its own name, so "the finger" will be ambiguous. Second, a phrase like "the finger" can be used in so many ways that an automatic evaluation to FINGER 109 will be wasteful at best. There are idioms to worry about, as in, "He raised his hand and gave me the finger". (Are we to conclude that the "default finger in the hand frame" is the middle finger?) But even ignoring them, there are many contexts where "the" just doesn't mean what we would like it to. For example, "He removed his glove and I saw the finger was missing". This is like, "The barn burned to the ground five years ago and was completely rebuilt". There are logics in which the same BARN 1051 can have different denotations in different time periods, but do we really want this clumsiness in the heart of our internal representation?

It seems much smarter to put knowledge about translation from natural language to internal representation in the natural language processor, not in the internal representation. I am using "in" loosely; my intent is to condemn an approach that translates language very superficially (using a little syntax and morphology) and hands it to the data base in that form. Instead, the language routine must draw on knowledge about all parts of the sentence in translating "the finger". Its output must be a directly useful internal representation, probably as remote as possible from being "English-like".

These problems stem from a picture of a program constructed of cooperating modules that "talk to" each other. While this may be a reasonable metaphor in some ways, anyone who has actually written such a program knows that "talking" is a very poor model of the communication. Yet many researchers (most extremely Stansfield, 1975, and Hawkinson, 1975) find English to be the ideal notation in which to encode messages. They are aware that message-passing channels are the most frustrating bottleneck through which intelligence must pass, so they wish their way into the solution: let the modules speak in human tongues! Let them use metaphor, allusion, hints, polite requests, pleading, flattery, bribes, and patriotic exhortations to their fellow modules!

It is hard to say where they have gone wronger, in underestimating language or overestimating computer programs. Language is only occasionally a medium of communication of information; even when it is, the ratio of information to packaging is low. The problem of a language speaker is to get the directed attention of an unprepared hearer and slide some information into his mind in a very short time. Since the major time sink is moving his mouth, the language sacrifices everything else to brevity, forcing the hearer to do much quick thinking to compensate. Furthermore, since the speaker doesn't quite know the organization of his hearer's mind, his phrasing of information and packaging must, except for the most stereotyped conversations, be an artwork of suggestiveness and insight.

Communication between computer programs is under completely different constraints. At the current stage of research, it is ridiculous to focus on anything but raw communication of information; we are unable to identify where more devious, Freudian intercourse might occur. Packaging and encoding of the information are usually already done. Ambiguity is avoidable. Even brevity is unimportant (at least for speed), since a huge structure can be transmitted by passing an internal name or pointer to it shared by sender and receiver. Instead, the whole problem is getting the hearer to notice what it has been told. (Not "understand", but "notice". To appeal to understanding at this low level will doom us to tail-chasing failure.) The new structure handed to the receiver should give it "permission" to make progress on its problem. If the sender could give more detailed instructions, it could just execute them itself. Unfortunately, the latitude this leaves the receiver is wasted if it is too "narrow-minded" to see what it has received. (The 1962 paper by Newell on these topics is still the best.)

Everyone who has written a large AI program will know what I am talking about. In this communication effort, the naming problem can be irritating, since the sender must make sure the receiver understands its terms. But there are so many approaches to solving the problem (for example, by passing translation tables around), which are not open to conversing humans, that it recedes quickly into the background. The frustrations lie elsewhere.

Reference is not the only "unnatural language" problem. A related one is the feeble analysis of concepts like "the" and "a" by most AI researchers. There is a natural inclination to let "the" flag a definite description and "a" an existential quantifier (or occasionally a description). Except for *Dick, Jane, and Sally,* and some of Bertrand Russell's work, this approach is not even an approximation.

First the typical noun phrase is not directly translated into the internal representation at all, and does not wind up as an object name. For example, "Despite the peripatetic nature of American students and their families . . . there remain wide gaps and serious misconceptions in our understanding of other peoples and cultures". (*Media and Methods, 11,* No. 2 (1974), 43). Translating this sentence (whose meaning is transparent) is problematic in the extreme. The author means to allude to the fact that Americans travel a lot, as a way of getting around to the claim that they don't travel enough or well enough. Why? We don't know yet why people talk this way. But translation methods that worked on "the big red block" will never succeed on "the . . . nature of American students".

Second, the difference between "the" and "a" is not the difference between "definite" and "indefinite", except vacuously. For example, what is the difference in meaning between

"Due to the decrease in the American birthrate in the 1960's, our schools are underutilized".

"Due to a decrease in the American birthrate in the 1960's, our schools are underutilized".

In most respects, they "mean" exactly the same thing, since there can have been only one decrease in the birthrate in the 1960's, and each sentence presupposes that it occurred. But in one the author is assuming we know it already; in the other, he is more casual about whether we do or not. We have no theory at all about what difference this difference makes.

It is unfortunate that a logical back seepage has caused people to see words like "the", "a", "all", "or", "and", etc. as being embellished or ambiguous versions of "iota", "∃", "∀", "∨", and "∧". To cure yourself of this, try examining two pages of a book for ten-year olds, translating the story as you go into an internal representation. (I found Kenny, 1963, pp. 14–15 useful.) If you can do this without difficulty, your case is hopeless.

The obsession with natural language seems to have caused the feeling that the human use of language is a royal road to the cognitive psyche. I find this analogous to preoccupation with imagery as a way of studying vision. Most AI researchers react with amusement to proposals to explain vision in terms of stored images, reducing the physical eye to the mind's eye. But many of the same people notice themselves talking to themselves in English, and conclude that English is very close to the language of thought.

Clearly, there must be some other notation, different in principle from natural language, or we will have done for the ear what imagery theory does for the eye. No matter how fascinating the structure of consciousness is, it is dangerous to gaze too long into its depths. The puzzles we find there can be solved only by sneaking up on them from behind. As of now, we have no idea at all why people experience their thoughts the way they do, in pictures and words. It will probably turn out to be quite different, even simpler, than what we think now, once we understand why and how people experience their thoughts at all.

In the meantime, for many people, natural language has become the preferred means of stating problems for programs to solve. For example, research that began as a study of visual recognition becomes a study of how people come up with an animal that is white, has hooves, and has one horn in the middle of its head. People can do this (and get "unicorn"), but the fact that they can obviously has nothing to do with visual recognition. In visual recognition, the main problems are guessing that you're looking at an animal in the first place, deciding that thing is a horn and that it belongs to the head, deciding whether to look for hooves, etc. The problem as stated in natural language is just not the same. (For example, the difficulties raised by the fact that I omitted presence or absence of wings from my description are different from the corresponding visual problems.)

Linguists have, I think, suffered from this self-misdirection for years. The standard experimental tool of modern linguistics is the eliciting of judgments of grammaticality from native speakers. Although anyone can learn how to make such judgments fairly quickly, it is plainly not a skill that has anything to do with ability to speak English. The real parser in your head is not supposed to report on its inputs' degree of grammaticality; indeed, normally it doesn't "report" at all in a way accessible to verbalization. It just tries to aid understanding of what it hears as best it can. So the grammaticality judgment task is completely artificial. It doesn't correspond to something people normally do.

Linguists, of course, have a place in their ontology for these judgments. They are a direct road to the seat of linguistic "competence". AI people find this notion dubious. They would be just as suspicious if someone claimed that a good way to measure "visual recognition competence" was to measure the ability of a subject to guess where the cubes were in a scene presented to him as an English description of intensity contours. ("A big steep one in the corner, impetuous but not overbearing".)

Eventually, though, we all trick ourselves into thinking that the statement of a problem in natural language is natural. One form of this self-delusion that I have had difficulty avoiding is the "information-retrieval fixation". It dates from Winograd's (1971) analysis of questions like, "Do I like any pyramids?" as a simple PLANNER program like (THAND (THGOAL (LIKE WINO-GRAD ?X)) (THGOAL (IS PYRAMID ?X))). This was entirely justified in the context he was dealing with, but clearly a stopgap. Nonetheless, nowadays, when someone invents a representation or deduction algorithm, he almost always illustrates it with examples like this, couched either in natural language or a simple translation like (THAND . . .).

This tight coupling of internal and external problem statements if taken seriously, reduces the chance of progress on representation and retrieval problems. If a researcher tries to think of his problem as natural-language question answering, he is hurt by the requirement that the answers be the results of straightforward data-base queries. Real discourse is almost never of the literal-minded information-retrieval variety. In real discourse, the context leading up to a question sets the stage for it, and usually affects its meaning considerably. But, since the researcher is not really studying language, he cannot use the natural-language context. The only version of natural language he can have in mind must exclude this example of a conversation between two programmers on a system with six-letter file names:

"Where is the function TRY-NEXT defined?"
"In the file TRYNXT >". (pronounced TRY-NEXT)
"How do you spell 'TRY-NEXT'?"
"Omit the e".

Such contextual and intentional effects are distracting at best for the designer of a data base; presumably they are normally helpful to humans.

The other course is to concentrate on handling the query after it has been translated into (THAND . . .), but if this formula is still thought of as a direct translation of an English question, the approach ignores whatever framework a system might use to focus its computational attention. Generally a program builds or prunes its data structure as it goes, organizing it in such a way that most queries worth making at all can be handled with reasonable efficiency. Just picking the THAND problem out of the blue throws this organization away. This is what happens with the naive natural-language information-retrieval paradigm. A researcher who designs his retrieval algorithm around the case of a completely unmotivated formal query is likely to become preoccupied with problems like the efficient intersection of lists of likable objects and pyramids. (Nevins, 1974, Fahlman, 1975.) In the design of programs whose knowledge is organized around problems, such issues are not nearly so important.

Someone must still work on the context-free English query problem, but there is no reason to expect it to be the same as the data-base retrieval problem. Besides, it might turn out that natural language is not the best notation for information-retrieval requests. Perhaps we should postpone trying to get computers to speak English, and try programming librarians in PL/1!

In this section I have been harsh toward AI's tendency to over-simplify or overglorify natural language, but don't think that my opinion is that research in this area is futile. Indeed, probably because I am an academic verbalizer, I feel that understanding natural language is the most fascinating and important research goal we have in the long run. But it deserves more attention from a theoretical point of view before we rush off and throw together "natural-language" interfaces to programs with inadequate depth. We should do more studies of what language is for, and we should develop complex programs with a need to talk, before we put the two together.

"**Only a Preliminary Version of the Program was Actually Implemented"

A common idiocy in AI research is to suppose that having identified the shortcomings of Version I of a program is equivalent to having written Version II. (McDermott, 1974a, Sussman, 1975, Goldstein, 1974.) Naturally, the sincere researcher doesn't think of his actions this way. From my own experience, the course of a piece of research is like this:

Having identified a problem, the ambitious researcher stumbles one day upon a really good idea that neatly solves several related subproblems of it at once. (Sometimes the solution actually comes before the problem is identified.) The idea is formally pretty and seems to mesh smoothly with the way a rational program ought to think. Let us call it "sidetracking control structure" for concreteness. The researcher immediately implements an elegant program embodying automatic sidetracking, with an eye toward applying it to his original problem. As always, implementation takes much longer than expected, but matters are basically tidy.

However, as he develops and debugs this piece of code, he becomes aware that there are several theoretical holes in his design and that it doesn't work. It doesn't work for good and respectable reasons, most of them depending on the fact that the solution to the problem requires more than one good idea. But, having got a framework, he becomes more and more convinced that those small but numerous holes are where the good ideas are to fit. He may even be right.

Here, however, he begins to lose his grip. Implementing Version I, whose shortcomings are all too obvious, was exhausting; it made him feel grubby for nothing. (Not at all like the TECO macros he took time out for along the way!) He feels as though he's paid his dues; now he can join the theoreticians. What's more, he *should.*

Implementation details will make his thesis dull. The people want *epistemology*.

Simultaneously, he enjoys the contradictory feeling that the implementation of Version II would be easy. He has reams of notes on the holes in Version I and how to fill them. When he surveys them, he feels their master. Though a stranger to the trees, he can talk with confidence about the forest. Indeed, that is precisely what he does in his final document. It is full of allusions to a program he seems to be claiming to have written. Only in a cautious footnote does he say, "the program was never actually finished", or, "a preliminary version of the program was actually written".

This final report can have interesting quirks. It is likely to be titled *A Side-Tracking Control Structure Approach to Pornographic Question-Answering,* because the author's fondness for sidetracking never quite left him. However, sidetracking is the only part of the solution he really understands, so he is likely to be quite diffident about it. He feels much better about the multitude of patch mechanisms which he describes. He designed them as solutions, not problems; he wisely avoided implementing them and spoiling the illusion, so he can talk at length about how each one neatly ties up a loose end of sidetracking.

The final report usually pleases most people (more people than it should), impressing them but leaving them a little hungover. They are likely to be taken with sidetracking, especially if a theorem about it is proved, but the overall approach to the real problem lacks definition. Performance and promise run together like the colors of a sunset. The happy feeling is kindled in the reader that indefinite progress has already started. On the other hand, they usually know the author's approach won't solve everything; he avoids claiming this. So the document fails to stimulate or challenge; it merely feeds the addict's desire for reassurance that AI is not standing still, and raises his tolerance a little.

This muddle finally hurts those following in the researcher's path. Long after he has his Ph.D. or his tenure, inquiring students will be put off by the document he has left behind. He seems to have solved everything already, so the report says, yet there is no tangible evidence of it besides the report itself. No one really wants to take up the problem again, even though the original research is essentially a partial success or even a failure! If a student decides sidetracking is a good idea, and wants to study it, people will assume he is "merely implementing" an already fully designed program. (No Ph.D. for that!) He would be willing or even eager to start from a smoothly running Version II and write Version III, incorporating a new theoretical idea like Syntactic Network Data Bases, but there is no Version II. Even a Version I would help, but it isn't really working very well and its author has no desire for it to be publicized.

Of course, the student can turn his back on sidetracking, and develop an entirely new approach to Pornographic Question-Answering. But this will only antagonize people. They thought they understood sidetracking; they had convinced themselves it could be made to work. Disagreeing will only confuse them. Besides, it probably could have been made to work. If only its inventor had left it an open question!

This inflationary spiral can't go on forever. After five theses have been written, each promising with fuzzy grandeur a different solution to a problem, people will begin to doubt that the problem has any solution at all. Five theses, each building on the previous one, might have been enough to solve it completely.

The solution is obvious: insist that people report on Version I (or possibly "I½"). If a thorough report on a mere actual implementation were required, or even *allowed*, as a Ph.D. thesis, progress would appear slower, but it would be real.

Furthermore, the program should be user-engineered enough and debugged enough so that it can be run by people besides its author. What people want to know about such a program is how far they can diverge from the examples given in the thesis before it fails. Think of their awe when they discover that the hardest cases it handles weren't even mentioned! (Nowadays, the cases mentioned are, at the very best, the *only* ones the program handles.)

When a program does fail, it should tell the explorer why it failed by behavior more illuminating than, e.g., going into an infinite loop. Often a program will begin to degrade in time or accuracy before it fails. The program should print out statistics showing its opinion of how hard it had to work ("90,265 side-tracks"), so the user will not have to guess from page faults or console time. If he wishes to investigate further, a clearly written, up-to-date source program should be available for him to run interpretively, trace, etc. (More documentation should not be necessary.) In any other branch of computer science, these things are taken for granted.

My proposal is that thesis research, or any other two-year effort, should be organized as follows:

As before, a new problem, or *old problem with partial solution*, should be chosen. The part of the problem where most progress could be made (a conceptual "inner loop") should be thought about hardest. Good ideas developed here should appear in a research proposal.

The first half of the time allotted thereafter should be applied to writing Version $n+1$, where n is the version number you started with (0 for virgin problems). (Substantial rewriting of Version n should be anticipated.) The second half should be devoted to writing the report and improving Version $n+1$ with enough breadth, clean code, and new user features to make it useful to the next person that needs it.

The research report will then describe the improvements made to Version n, good ideas implemented, and total progress made in solving the original problem. Suggestions for further improvements should be included, in the future subjunctive tense.

The standard for such research should be a partial success, but AI as a field is starving for a few carefully documented failures. Anyone can think of several theses that could be improved stylistically and substantively by being rephrased as reports on failures. I can learn more by just being told why a technique won't work than by being made to read between the lines.

Benediction

This paper has focussed on three methodological and substantive issues over which we have stumbled. Anyone can think of more. I chose these because I am more guilty of them than other mistakes, which I am prone to lose my sense of humor about, such as:

1. The insistence of AI people that an action is a change of state of the world or a world model, and that thinking about actions amounts to stringing state changes together to

accomplish a big state change. This seems to me not an oversimplification, but a false start. How many of your actions can be characterized as state changes, or are even performed to effect state changes? How many of a program's actions in problem solving? (Not the actions it strings together, but the actions it *takes*, like "trying short strings first", or "assuming the block is where it's supposed to be".)

2. The notion that a semantic network is a network. In lucid moments, network hackers realize that lines drawn between nodes stand for pointers, that almost everything in an AI program is a pointer, and that any list structure could be drawn as a network, the choice of what to call node and what to call link being arbitrary. Their lucid moments are few.

3. The notion that a semantic network is semantic.

4. Any indulgence in the "procedural-declarative" controversy. Anyone who hasn't figured this "controversy" out yet should be considered to have missed his chance, and be banned from talking about it. Notice that at Carnegie-Mellon they haven't worried too much about this dispute, and haven't suffered at all. The first half of Moore and Newell (1974) has a list of much better issues to think about.

5. The idea that because *you* can see your way through a problem space, your program can: the "wishful control structure" problem. The second half of Moore and Newell (1974) is a great example.

In this paper I have criticized AI researchers very harshly. Let me express my faith that people in other fields would, on inspection, be found to suffer from equally bad faults. Most AI workers are responsible people who are aware of the pitfalls of a difficult field and produce good work in spite of them. However, to say anything good about anyone is beyond the scope of this paper.

Acknowledgment: I thank the AI Lab Playroom crowd for constructive play.

6

From Micro-Worlds to Knowledge Representation:

AI at an Impasse

HUBERT L. DREYFUS

SINCE THE COMPLETION, nearly a decade ago, of the first edition of *What Computers Can't Do* (Dreyfus, 1972), there has been considerable change and development in artificial intelligence research. None of this more recent work leads me to relax my overall skepticism, but it does call for new and detailed discussion. In this article I review and examine a representative sample of AI as it has developed in the seventies. The work discussed falls into two categories, which can be assigned to the first and second halves of the decade, respectively.

The Early Seventies: Micro-Worlds

Inasmuch as it was the most impressive new achievement at the time, we begin with Winograd's (1972) natural language understanding program: SHRDLU. SHRDLU simulates a robot arm which can move a set of variously shaped blocks, and allows a person to engage in a dialogue with the computer—asking questions, making statements, and issuing commands about this simple world of movable blocks. The program is an integrated system which makes use of syntax, semantics, and facts about blocks. It is thus, as Winograd cautiously claims, "a computer program which 'understands' language in a limited domain, by including a model of the subject being talked about and a context of discourse" (1973). Furthermore, this program explores the new idea of representing this knowledge in the form of procedures. The resulting dialogue is strikingly natural. Here is a sample. (The sentences in capital letters are computer print-out. The parentheses contain Winograd's comments.)

1. pick up a big red block.

    OK.

    (The system answers "OK" when it carries out a command. In order to pick up the red block, it had to clear it off by finding a space for the green one and moving the green one away.)

2. grasp the pyramid.

    I DON'T UNDERSTAND WHICH PYRAMID YOU MEAN.

    (There are three pyramids in the scene, so the program does nothing.)

3. find a block which is taller than the one you are holding and put it into the box.

    (The system has to figure out what is meant by "one" and "it", as well as using deduction to decide which block it is holding.)

    BY "IT", I ASSUME YOU MEAN THE BLOCK WHICH IS TALLER THAN THE ONE I AM HOLDING.

    (Printed out to keep us informed.)

    OK.

    (The hand has to set down the red block to pick up the taller blue one.)

4. what does the box contain?

    THE BLUE PYRAMID AND THE BLUE BLOCK.

5. what is the pyramid supported by?

    (Earlier the system responded to "the pyramid" by saying, "I don't understand which pyramid you mean". Now, it assumes that we mean the one just mentioned.)

    THE BOX.

    . . .

9. can the table pick up blocks?

    NO.

(The semantic rules make this a nonsensical question which therefore must be false.)

10. can a pyramid be supported by a block?

 YES.

 (The deductive system finds an actual example, so it knows this is possible.)

11. can a pyramid support a pyramid?

 I DON'T KNOW.

 (The question makes sense, but there is no example in the scene, so there is no easy way to tell without being able to examine the robot's programs.)

12. stack up two pyramids.

 I CAN'T.

 (The robot tries and fails.)

13. the blue pyramid is mine.

 I UNDERSTAND.

 (This datum is added to the data base.)

14. I own blocks which are not red, but I don't own anything which supports a pyramid.

 I UNDERSTAND.

 (Two new theorems are created for proving things about "owning".)

15. do I own the box?

 NO.   (Winograd, 1972; pp. 8–11)

If being a major advance means being more general than its predecessors, then SHRDLU, since it no longer depends for its analysis of language on external constraints of the sort essential to Bobrow's STUDENT, is a major achievement. Winograd himself points out the superiority of his program over earlier language understanding programs.

A program may succeed by carefully choosing the problem it will attack, so that some simple special-purpose solution will work. ELIZA (Weizenbaum, 1964) and STUDENT (Bobrow, 1967) are examples of programs which give impressive performances owing to a severe and careful restriction of the kind of understanding they try to achieve. If a model is to be of broader significance, it must be designed to cover a large range of the things we mean when we talk of understanding. The principles should derive from an attempt to deal with the basic cognitive structures.   (1973; p. 167)

If, however, "a major advance" means that a step has been made in dealing with the basic cognitive structures needed to cover everyday understanding—that, thanks to SHRDLU, there is now reason to be optimistic about the possibility of AI—then no progress at all can be claimed. To justify this negative judgment we must first find out how the optimists of the early seventies were able to convince themselves that with SHRDLU AI was at last on the right track. Workers in AI were certainly not trying to cover up the fact that it was SHRDLU's restricted domain which made apparent understanding possible. They even had a name for Winograd's method of restricting the domain of discourse. He was dealing with a *micro-world.* And in a 1970 internal memo at M.I.T., Minsky and Papert frankly note:

Each model—or "micro-world" as we shall call it—is very schematic; it talks about a fairyland in which things are so simplified that almost every statement about them would be literally false if asserted about the real world.   (p. 39)

But they immediately add:

Nevertheless, we feel that they [the micro-worlds] are so important that we are assigning a large portion of our effort toward developing a collection of these micro-worlds and finding how to use the suggestive and predictive powers of the models without being overcome by their incompatibility with literal truth.

Given the admittedly artificial and arbitrary character of micro-worlds, why do Papert and Minsky think they provide a promising line of research?

To find an answer we must follow Minsky and Papert's perceptive remarks on narrative, and their less than perceptive conclusions:

In a familiar fable, the wily Fox tricks the vain Crow into

dropping the meat by asking it to sing. The usual test of understanding is the ability of the child to answer questions like: "Did the Fox think the Crow had a lovely voice?" The topic is sometimes classified as "natural language manipulation" or as "deductive logic", etc. These descriptions are badly chosen. For the real problem is not to understand English; it is to *understand* at all. To see this more clearly, observe that nothing is gained by presenting the story in simplified syntax: CROW ON TREE. CROW HAS MEAT. FOX SAYS "YOU HAVE A LOVELY VOICE. PLEASE SING." FOX GOBBLES MEAT. The difficulty in getting a machine to give the right answer does not at all depend on "disambiguating" the words (at least, not in the usual primitive sense of selecting one "meaning" out of a discrete set of "meanings"). And neither does the difficulty lie in the need for unusually powerful logical apparatus. The main problem is that no one has constructed the elements of a body of knowledge about such matters that is adequate for understanding the story. Let us see what is involved.

To begin with, there is never a unique solution to such problems, so we do not ask what the Understander *must* know. But he will surely gain by having the concept of FLATTERY. To provide this knowledge, we imagine a "micro-theory" of flattery—an extendible collection of facts or procedures that describe conditions under which one might expect to find flattery, what forms it takes, what its consequences are, and so on. How complex this theory is depends on what is presupposed. Thus it would be very difficult to describe flattery to our Understander if he (or it) does not already know that statements can be made for purposes other than to convey literally correct, factual information. It would be almost impossibly difficult if he does not even have some concept like PURPOSE or INTENTION.   (1970; pp. 42–44)

The surprising move here is the conclusion that there could be a circumscribed "micro-theory" of flattery—somehow intelligible apart from the rest of human life—while at the same time the account shows an understanding of flattery opening out into the rest of our everyday world, with its understanding of purposes and intentions.

What characterizes the period of the early seventies, and makes SHRDLU seem an advance toward general intelligence, is the very concept of a micro-world—a domain which can be analyzed in isolation. This concept implies that although each area of discourse seems to open out into the rest of human activities, its endless ramifications are only apparent and will soon converge on a self-contained set of facts and relations. For example, in discussing the micro-world of bargaining, Papert and Minsky consider what a child needs to know to understand the following fragment of conversation:

> Janet: "That isn't a very good ball you have. Give it to me and I'll give you my lollipop. (p. 48)

And remark:

> We conjecture that, eventually, the required micro-theories can be made reasonably compact and easily stated (or, by the same token, *learned*) once we have found an adequate set of structural primitives for them. When one begins to catalogue what one needs for just a little of Janet's story, it seems at first to be endless:

Time	Things	Words
Space	People	Thoughts

Talking: Explaining. Asking. Ordering. Persuading. Pretending
Social relations: Giving. Buying. Bargaining. Begging. Asking.
                  Presents. Stealing . . .
Playing: Real and Unreal. Pretending
Owning: Part of. Belong to. Master of. Captor of
Eating: How does one compare the values of foods with the
       values of toys?
Liking: good. bad. useful. pretty. conformity
Living: Girl. Awake. Eats. Plays
Intention: Want. Plan. Plot. Goal. Cause. Result. Prevent
Emotions: Moods. Dispositions. Conventional expressions
States: asleep. angry. at home
Properties: grown-up. red-haired. called "Janet"
Story: Narrator. Plot. Principal actors
People: Children. Bystanders
Places: Houses. Outside

Angry: State
        caused by: Insult
                        deprivation
                        assault
                        disobedience
                        frustration
                        spontaneous
Results: not cooperative
        lower threshold
        aggression
        loud voice
        irrational
        revenge
Etc.   (pp. 50–52)

They conclude:

> But [the list] is not endless. It is only large, and one needs
> a large set of concepts to organize it. After a while one will find
> it getting harder to add new concepts, and the new ones will
> begin to seem less indispensable.   (p. 52)

This totally unjustified belief that the seemingly endless reference to other human practices will converge so that simple microworlds can be studied in relative isolation reflects a naive transfer to AI of methods that have succeeded in the natural sciences. Winograd characteristically describes his work in terms borrowed from physical science:

> We are concerned with developing a formalism, or "representation," with which to describe . . . knowledge. We seek the "atoms" and "particles" of which it is built, and the "forces" that act on it.   (Winograd, 1976; p. 9)

It is true that physical theories about the universe can be built up by studying relatively simple and isolated systems and then making the model gradually more complex and integrating it with other domains of phenomena. This is possible because all the phenomena are presumably the result of the lawlike relations of a set of basic elements, what Papert and Minsky call "structural primitives." This belief in local success and gradual generalization was clearly also Winograd's hope at the time he developed SHRDLU:

> The justification for our particular use of concepts in this system is that it is thereby enabled to engage in dialogs that simulate in many ways the behavior of a human language user. For a wider field of discourse, the conceptual structure would have to be expanded in its details, and perhaps in some aspects of its overall organization.   (Winograd, 1972; p. 26)

Thus, for example, it might seem that one could "expand" SHRDLU's concept of owning, since in the above sample conversation SHRDLU seems to have a very simple "micro-theory" of owning blocks. But as Simon points out in an excellent analysis of SHRDLU's limitations, the program does not understand owning at all, because it cannot deal with meanings. It has merely been given a set of primitives and their possible relationships. As Simon puts it:

> The SHRDLU system deals with problems in a single blocks world, with a fixed representation. When it is instructed to "pick up a big red block", it needs only to associate the term "pick up" with a procedure for carrying out that process; identify, by applying appropriate tests associated with "big", "red", and "block", the argument for the procedure and use its problem-solving capabilities to carry out the procedure. In saying "it needs only", it is not my intention to demean the capabilities of SHRDLU. It is precisely because the program possesses stored programs expressing the intensions of the terms used in inquiries and instructions that its interpretation of those inquiries and instructions is relatively straightforward.
> (Simon, 1977; p. 1062)

In understanding, on the other hand,

> the problem-understanding sub-system will have a more complicated task than just mapping the input language onto the intentions stored in a lexicon. It will also have to create a representation for the information it receives, and create meanings for the terms that are consistent with the representation." (p. 1063).

So, for example, in the conversation concerning owning:

> although SHRDLU's answer to the question is quite correct,

the system cannot be said to understand the meaning of "own" in any but a sophistic sense. SHRDLU's test of whether something is owned is simply whether it is tagged "owned". There is no intensional test of ownership, hence SHRDLU knows what it owns, but doesn't understand what it is to own something. SHRDLU would understand what it meant to own a box if it could, say, test its ownership by recalling how it had gained possession of the box, or by checking its possession of a receipt in payment for it; could respond differently to requests to move a box it owned from requests to move one it didn't own; and, in general, could perform those tests and actions that are generally associated with the determination and exercise of ownership in our law and culture. (p. 1064)

Moreover, even if it satisfied all these conditions, it still wouldn't understand, unless it also understood that it (SHRDLU) couldn't own anything, since it isn't a part of the community in which owning makes sense. Given our cultural practices which constitute owning, a computer cannot own something any more than a table can.

This discussion of owning suggests that, just as it is misleading to call a program UNDERSTAND when the problem is to find out what understanding is (cf. McDermott, 1976, p. 4; this volume, p. 144), it is likewise misleading to call a set of facts and procedures concerning blocks a micro-*world* when what is really at stake is the understanding of what a world is. A set of interrelated facts may constitute a *universe*, a domain, a group, etc., but it does not constitute a *world*, for a world is an organized body of objects, purposes, skills, and practices in terms of which human activities have meaning or make sense. It follows that although there is a children's world in which, among other things, there are blocks, there is no such thing as a blocks world. Or, to put this as a critique of Winograd, one cannot equate, as he does, a program which deals with "a tiny bit of the world," with a program which deals with a "mini-world" (Winograd, 1974; p. 20).

In our everyday life we are, indeed, involved in such various "sub-worlds" as the world of the theater, of business, or of mathematics, but each of these is a "mode" of our shared everyday world.[1]

1. This view is worked out further in Heidegger (1972); see especially p. 93 and all of section 18.

That is, sub-worlds are not related like isolable physical systems to larger systems they *compose;* rather they are local elaboarations of a whole which they *presuppose.* If micro-worlds *were* sub-worlds, one would not have to extend and combine them to reach the everyday world, because the everyday world would have to be included already. Since, however, micro-worlds are *not* worlds, there is no way they can be combined and extended to the world of everyday life. As a result of failing to ask what a world is, five years of stagnation in AI was mistaken for progress.

A second major application of the micro-world technique was in computer vision. Already in 1968, Adolfo Guzman's SEE program could analyze two-dimensional projections of complicated three-dimensional "scenes," consisting of piles of polyhedra. Even this early program correctly analyzed certain classes of scenes which people find difficult to figure out; but it had serious limitations. In 1972, David Waltz generalized Guzman's methods, and produced a much more powerful vision system. Together, these programs provide a case study not only in how much can be achieved with the micro-worlds approach, but also in the kind of generalization that is possible within that approach—and, by implication, the kind that isn't.

Guzman's program analyzes scenes involving cubes and other such rectilinear solids by merging regions into bodies using evidence from the vertices. Each vertex suggests that two or more of the regions around it belong together, depending on whether the vertex is shaped like an L, an arrow, a T, a K, an X, a fork, a peak, or an upside-down peak. With these eight primitives and commonsense rules for their use, Guzman's program did quite well. But it had certain weaknesses. According to Winston, "The program could not handle shadows, and it did poorly if there were holes in objects or missing lines in the drawing" (1975; p. 8). Waltz then generalized Guzman's work and showed that by introducing three more such primitives, a computer can be programmed to decide if a particular line in a drawing is a shadow, a crack, an obscuring edge, or an internal seam in a way analogous to the   solution of sets of algebraic equations. As Winston later sums up the change:

Previously it was believed that only a program with a complicated

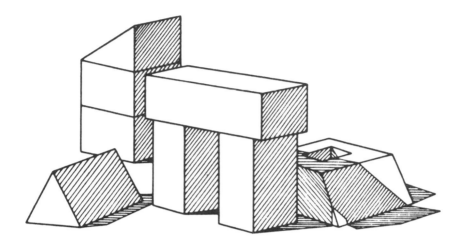

Figure 1.

control structure and lots of explicit reasoning power could hope to analyze scenes like that in figure [1]. Now we know that understanding the constraints the real world imposes on how boundaries, concave and convex interiors, shadows, and cracks can come together at junctions is enough to make things much simpler. A table which contains a list of the few thousand physically possible ways that line types can come together accompanied by a simple matching program are all that is required. Scene analysis is translated into a problem resembling a jigsaw puzzle or a set of linear equations. No deep problem solving effort is required; it is just a matter of executing a very simple constraint-dependent, iterative process that successively throws away incompatible line arrangment combinations.

(1976; pp. 77–78)

This is just the kind of mathematical generalization within a domain that one might expect in micro-worlds where the rule-governed relation of the primitives (in this case the set of vertices) are under some external constraint (in this case the laws of geometry and optics). What one would not expect is that the special-purpose heuristics which depend on corners for segregating rectilinear objects could in any way be generalized so as to make possible the recognition of other sorts of objects. And, indeed, none of Guzman's or Waltz's techniques, since they rely on the intersection of straight lines, have any use in analyzing a scene involving curved objects. What one gains in narrowing a domain, one loses in breadth of significance. Winston's evaluation covers up this lesson.

> It is wrong to think of Waltz's work as only a statement of the epistemology of line drawings of polyhedra. Instead I think it is an elegant case study of a paradigm we can expect to see again and again, and as such, it is a strong metaphoric tool for guiding our thinking, not only in vision but also in the study of other systems involving intelligence. (1975; p. 8)

But in a later grant proposal he acknowledges that:

> To understand the real world, we must have a different set of primitives from the relatively simple line trackers suitable and sufficient for the blocks world. (1976; p. 39)

Waltz's work is a paradigm of the kind of generalization one can strive for *within* a micro-world all right, but for that very reason it provides no way of thinking about general intelligent systems.

The nongeneralizable character of the programs so far discussed makes them engineering feats, not steps toward generally intelligent systems, and they are, therefore, not at all promising as contributions to psychology. Yet Winston includes Waltz's work in his claim that "making machines see is an important way to understand how we animals see" (1975; p. 2), and Winograd makes similar claims for the psychological relevance of his work:

> The gain from developing AI is not primarily in the usefulness of the programs we create, but in the set of concepts we develop, and the ways in which we can apply them to understanding human intelligence. (1976; p. 3)

These comments suggest that in the early seventies an interesting change was taking place at M.I.T. In previous papers Minsky and his co-workers sharply distinguished themselves from workers in Cognitive Simulation, such as Simon, who presented their programs as psychological theories, insisting that the M.I.T. programs were "an attempt to build intelligent machines without any prejudice toward making the system . . . humanoid" (Minsky, 1969; p. 7). Now in their book *Artificial Intelligence,* a summary of work done at M.I.T. during the period 1967–72, Minsky and Papert (1973) present the M.I.T. research as a contribution to psychology. They first introduce the notion of a symbolic description:

> What do we mean by "description"? We do not mean to suggest that our descriptions must be made of strings of ordinary language words (although they might be). The simplest kind of description is a structure in which some features of a situation are represented by single ("primitive") symbols, and relations between those features are represented by other symbols—or by other features of the way the description is put together.
>
> (p. 11)

They then defend the role of symbolic descriptions in a psychological account of intelligent behavior by a constant polemic against behaviorism and gestalt theory which have opposed the use of formal models of the mind.

One can detect, underlying this change, the effect of the proliferation of micro-worlds, with their reliance on symbolic descriptions, and the disturbing failure to produce even the hint of a system with the flexibility of a six-month-old child. Instead of concluding from this frustrating situation that the special-purpose techniques which work in context-free, gamelike, micro-worlds may in no way resemble general-purpose human and animal intelligence, the AI workers seem to have taken the less embarrassing if less plausible tack of suggesting that even if they could not succeed in building intelligent systems, the *ad hoc* symbolic descriptions successful in micro-world analysis could be justified as a valuable contribution to psychology.

Such a line, however, since it involves a stronger claim than the old slogan that as long as the machine was intelligent it did not matter at all whether it performed in a humanoid way, runs the obvious risk of refutation by empirical evidence. An information-processing model must be a formal symbolic structure, however, so Minsky and Papert, making a virtue of necessity, revive the implausible intellectualist position according to which concrete perception is assimilated to the rule-governed symbolic descriptions used in abstract thought:

> The Gestaltists look for simple and fundamental principles about how perception is organized, and then attempt to show how symbolic reasoning can be seen as following the same principles, while we construct a complex theory of how knowledge is applied to solve intellectual problems and then attempt to show how the symbolic description that is what one "sees" is constructed according to similar processes.   (1973; p. 34)

Some recent work in psychology, however, points exactly in the opposite direction. Rather than showing that perception can be analyzed in terms of formal features, Erich Goldmeier's (1972) extention of early Gestalt work on the perception of similarity of simple perceptual figures—arising in part in response to "the frustrating efforts to teach pattern recognition to [computers]" (p. 1)—has revealed sophisticated distinctions between figure and ground, matter and form, essential and accidental aspects, norms and distortions, etc., which he shows cannot be accounted for in terms of any known formal features of the phenomenal figures. They can, however, according to Goldmeier, perhaps be explained on the neurological level, where the importance of Prägnanz—i.e., singularly salient shapes and orientations—suggests underlying physical phenomena such as "regions of resonance" (p. 128) in the brain.

Of course, it is still possible that the Gestaltists went too far in trying to assimilate thought to the same sort of concrete, holistic, processes they found necessary to account for perception. Thus, even though the exponents of symbolic descriptions have no account of perceptual processes, they might be right that the mechanism of everyday thinking and learning consists in constructing a formal description of the world and transforming this representation in a rule-governed way. Such a formal model of everyday learning and categorization is proposed by Winston in his 1970 thesis, "Learning Structural Descriptions from Examples" (see Winston, 1975). Given a set of positive and negative instances, Winston's self-proclaimed "classic" program can, for example, use a descriptive repertoire to construct a formal description of the class of arches. Since Winston's program (along with those of Winograd and Guzman) is often mentioned as a major success of the micro-worlds technique, we must examine it in detail.

This program, too, illustrates the possibilities and essential limitations of micro-worlds. Is it the basis of a plausible general approach to learning? Winston thinks so:

> Although this may seem like a very special kind of learning, I think the implications are far ranging, because I believe that learning by examples, learning by being told, learning by imitation, learning by reinforcement and other forms are much like one another. In the literature on learning there is frequently an unstated assumption that these various forms are fundamentally different. But I think the classical boundaries between the various kinds of learning will disappear once superficially different kinds of learning are understood in terms of processes that construct and manipulate descriptions. (1975; p. 185)

Yet Winston's program works only if the "student" is saved the trouble of what Charles Sanders Peirce called abduction, by being "told" a set of context-free features and relations—in this case a list of possible spatial relationships of blocks such as "left-of," "standing," "above," and "supported by"—from which to build up a description of an arch. Minsky and Papert presuppose this preselection when they say that "to eliminate objects which seem atypical . . . the program lists all relationships exhibited by more than half of the candidates in the set" (1973; p. 56). Lurking behind this claim is the supposition that there are only a finite number of relevant features; but without preselected features all objects share an indefinitely large number of relationships. The work of discriminating, selecting, and weighting a limited number of relevant features is the result of repeated experience and is the first stage of learning. But since in Winston's work the programmer selects and preweights the primitives, his program gives us no idea how a computer could make this selection and assign these weights. Thus the Winston program, like every micro-world program, works only because it has excluded from its task domain the very ability it is supposed to explain.

If not a theory of learning, is Winston's program at least a plausible theory of categorization? Consider again the arch example. Once it has been given what Winston disarmingly calls a "good description" (p. 158) and carefully chosen examples, the program does conclude that an arch is a structure in which a prismatic body is supported by two upright blocks that do not touch each other. But, since arches function in various ways in our everyday activity, there is no reason to suppose that these are the necessary and sufficient conditions for being an arch, or that there are any such defining features. Some prominent characteristics shared by most everyday arches are "helping to support something while leaving an important open space under it," or "being the sort of thing one can walk under and through at the same time." How does Winston propose to capture such contextual characteristics in terms of the context-free features required by his formal representation?

Winston admits that having two supports and a flat top does not begin to capture even the geometrical structure of arches. So he proposes "generalizing the machine's descriptive ability to acts and properties required by those acts" (p. 194) by adding a functional predicate, "something to walk through" (p. 193). But it is not at all clear how a functional predicate which refers to implicit knowledge of the bodily skill of walking through is to be formalized. Indeed, Winston himself provides a *reductio ad absurdum* of this facile appeal to formal functional predicates:

> To a human, an arch may be something to walk through, as well as an appropriate alignment of bricks. And certainly, a flat rock serves as a table to a hungry person, although far removed from the image the word table usually calls to mind. But the machine does not yet know anything of walking or eating, so the programs discussed here handle only some of the physical aspects of these human notions. There is no inherent obstacle forbidding the machine to enjoy functional understanding. It is a matter of generalizing the machine's descriptive ability to acts and properties required by those acts. Then chains of pointers can link TABLE to FOOD as well as to the physical image

of a table, and the machine will be perfectly happy to draw up its chair to a flat rock with the human given that there is something on that table which it wishes to eat.   (pp. 193–194)

Progress on recognition of arches, tables, etc., must, it seems, either wait until we have captured in an abstract symbolic description much of what human beings implicitly know about walking and eating simply by having a body, or else until computers no longer have to be told what it is to walk and eat, because they have human bodies and appetites themselves!

Despite these seemingly insurmountable obstacles Winston boasts that "there will be no contentment with [concept learning] machines that only do as well as humans" (p. 160). But it is not surprising that Winston's work is nine years old and there has been little progress in machine learning, induction, or concept formation. In their account Minsky and Papert (1973) admit that "we are still far from knowing how to design a powerful yet subtle and sensitive inductive learning program" (p. 56). What is surprising is that they add: "but the schemata developed in Winston's work should take us a substantial part of the way." The lack of progress since Winston's work was published, plus the use of predigested weighted primitives from which to produce its rigid, restricted, and largely irrelevant descriptions, makes it hard to understand in what way the program is a substantial step.

Moreover, if Winston claims to "shed some light on [the question:] How do we recognize examples of various concepts?" (1975; p. 157), his theory of concepts as definitions must, like any psychological theory, be subject to empirical test. It so happens that contrary to Winston's claims, recent evidence collected and analyzed by Eleanor Rosch on just this subject shows that human beings are not aware of classifying objects as instances of abstract rules but rather group objects as more or less distant from an imagined paradigm. This does not exclude the possibility of unconscious processing, but it does highlight the fact that there is no empirical evidence at all for Winston's formal model. As Rosch puts it:

Many experiments have shown that categories appear to be coded in the mind neither by means of lists of each individual member of the category, nor by means of a list of formal criteria necessary and sufficient for category membership, but, rather, in terms of a prototype of a typical category member. The most cognitively economical code for a category is, in fact, a *concrete image* of an average category member. (1977; p. 30)

One paradigm, it seems, is worth a thousand rules. As we shall soon see, one of the characteristics of the next phase of work in AI is to try to take account of the implications of Rosch's research.

Meanwhile, what can we conclude concerning AI's contribution to the science of psychology? No one can deny Minsky and Papert's claim that "Computer Science has brought a flood of . . . ideas, well defined and experimentally implemented, for thinking about thinking" (1973; p. 25). But all of these ideas can be boiled down to ways of constructing and manipulating symbolic descriptions, and, as we have seen, the notion that human cognition can be explained in terms of formal representations does not seem at all obvious in the face of actual research on perception, and everyday concept formation. Even Minsky and Papert show a commendable new modesty. They as much as admit that AI is still at the stage of astrology, and that the much heralded breakthrough still lies in the future:

Just as astronomy succeeded astrology, following Kepler's discovery of planetary regularities, the discoveries of these many principles in empirical explorations on intellectual processes in machines should lead to a science, eventually.   (1973; p. 25)

Happily, "should" has replaced "will" in their predictions. Indeed, this period's contribution to psychology suggests an even more modest hope: As more psychologists like Goldmeier are frustrated by the limitations of formal computer models, and others turn to investigating the function of images as opposed to symbolic representations, the strikingly limited success of AI may come to be seen as an important disconfirmation of the information processing approach.

Before concluding our discussion of this research phase, it should be noted that some problem domains are (nearly enough) micro-worlds already; so they lend themselves to AI techniques without the need for artificial restrictions, and, by the same token, nongeneralizability is not the same kind of Waterloo. Game playing, particularly chess, is the most conspicuous example. Though some extravagant early predictions were not fulfilled, large computers now play fairly high caliber chess, and small machines that play creditable amateur games are being marketed as toys. But game players are not the only examples; excellent programs have been written for analyzing certain kinds of mass spectroscopy data (Feigenbaum, 1977), and for assisting in the diagnosis and treatment of some diseases (Shortliffe, 1976). Such work is both impressive and important; but it shouldn't give the *wrong* impression. In each case, it succeeds because (and to the extent that) the relevant domain is well circumscribed in advance, with all the significant facts, questions, and/or options already laid out, and related by a comparatively small set of explicit rules—in short, because it's a micro-world. This is not to belittle either the difficulty or the value of spelling out such domains, or designing programs which perform well in them. But we should not see them as any closer to the achievement of genuine artificial intelligence than we do the "blocks-world" programs. In principle, interpreting mass spectrograms or batteries of specific symptoms has as little to do with the general intelligence of physicists and physicians, as disentangling vertices in projections of polyhedra does with vision. The real, theoretical problems for AI lie elsewhere.

The Later Seventies: Knowledge Representation

In roughly the latter half of the decade, the problem of how to structure and retrieve information, in situations where *anything* might be relevant, has come to the fore as the "knowledge representation problem." Of course, the representation of knowledge was always a central problem for work in AI, but earlier periods were characterized by an attempt to repress it by seeing how much could be done with as little knowledge as possible. Now, the difficulties are being faced. As Roger Schank of Yale recently remarked:

Researchers are starting to understand that tour-de-forces in programming are interesting but non-extendable . . . the AI people recognize that how people use and represent knowledge is the key issue in the field.   (1977; pp. 1007–1008)

Papert and Goldstein explain the problem:

> It is worthwhile to observe here that the goals of a knowledge-based approach to AI are closely akin to those which motivated Piaget to call . . . himself an "epistemologist" rather than a psychologist. The common theme is the view that the process of intelligence is determined by the knowledge held by the subject. The deep and primary questions are to understand the operations and data structures involved.   (1975; p. 7)

Another memorandum illustrates how ignoring the background knowledge can come back to haunt one of AI's greatest tricks in the form of nongeneralizability:

> Many problems arise in experiments on machine intelligence because things obvious to any person are not represented in any program. One can pull with a string, but one cannot push with one. One cannot push with a thin wire, either. A taut inextensible cord will break under a very small lateral force. Pushing something affects first its speed, only indirectly its position! Simple facts like these caused serious problems when Charniak attempted to extend Bobrow's "Student" program to more realistic applications, and they have not been faced up to until now.   (Papert and Minsky, 1973; p. 77)

The most interesting current research is directed toward the underlying problem of developing new, flexible, complex data types which will allow the representation of background knowledge in large, more structured units.

In 1972, drawing on Husserl's phenomenological analysis, I pointed out that it was a major weakness of AI that no programs made use of expectations (see pp. 241f and 250, in the 1979 edition). Instead of modeling intelligence as a passive receiving of context-free facts into a structure of already stored data, Husserl thinks of intelligence as a context-determined, goal-directed activity—as a *search* for anticipated facts. For him the noema, or mental representation of any type of object, provides a context or "inner horizon" of expectations or "predelineations" for structuring the incoming data: a "rule governing *possible* other consciousness of [the object] as identical—possible, as exemplifying essentially predelineated types" (Husserl, 1960; p. 53). As I explained in chapter 7:

We perceive a house, for example, as more than a façade—as having some sort of back—some inner horizon. We respond to this whole object first and then, as we get to know the object better, fill in the details as to inside and back.   (1979; p. 241)

The noema is thus a symbolic description of all the features which can be expected with certainty in exploring a certain type of object—features which remain "inviolably the same: as long as the objectivity remains intended as *this* one and of this kind" (p. 51) —plus "predelineations" of those properties which are possible but not necessary features of this type of object.

Then, in 1974, Minsky proposed a new data structure remarkably similar to Husserl's for representing everyday knowledge:

A frame is a data-structure for representing a stereotyped situation, like being in a certain kind of living room, or going to a child's birthday party. . . .

We can think of a frame as a network of nodes and relations. The "top levels" of a frame are fixed, and represent things that are always true about the supposed situation. The lower levels have many *terminals*—"slots" that must be filled by specific instances or data. Each terminal can specify conditions its assignments must meet. . . .

Much of the phenomenological power of the theory hinges on the inclusion of expectations and other kinds of presumptions. A frame's terminals are normally already filled with "default" assignments.   (pp. 1–2/ 96)[2]

In Minsky's model of a frame, the "top level" is a developed version of what in Husserl's terminology "remains inviolably the same" in the representation, and Husserl's predelineations have been made precise as "default assignments"—additional features that can normally be expected. The result is a step forward in AI techniques from a passive model of information processing to one which tries to take account of the context of the interactions between a knower and his world. Husserl thought of his method of transcendental-phenomenological constitution, i.e., "explicating" the noema for all types of objects, as the beginning of progress

2. *Editor's note:* numbers after the slash refer to pages in this volume.

toward philosophy as a rigorous science, and Patrick Winston has hailed Minsky's proposal as "the ancestor of a wave of progress in AI" (1975; p. 16). But Husserl's project ran into serious trouble and there are signs that Minsky's may too.

During twenty years of trying to spell out the components of the noema of everyday objects, Husserl found that he had to include more and more of what he called the "outer horizon," a subject's total knowledge of the world:

> To be sure, even the tasks that present themselves when we take single types of objects as restricted clues prove to be extremely complicated and always lead to extensive disciplines when we penetrate more deeply. That is the case, for example, with a transcendental theory of the constitution of a spatial object (to say nothing of a Nature) as such, of psycho-physical being and humanity as such, cultures as such.   (1960; pp. 54–55)

He sadly concluded at the age of seventy-five that he was "a perpetual beginner" and that phenomenology was an "infinite task"—and even that may be too optimistic. His successor, Heidegger, pointed out that since the outer horizon or background of cultural practices was the condition of the possibility of determining relevant facts and features and thus prerequisite for structuring the inner horizon, as long as the cultural context had not been clarified the proposed analysis of the inner horizon of the *noema* could not even claim progress.

There are hints in the frame paper that Minsky has embarked on the same misguided "infinite task" that eventually overwhelmed Husserl:

> Just constructing a knowledge base is a major intellectual research problem. . . . We still know far too little about the contents and structure of common-sense knowledge. A "minimal" common-sense system must "know" something about cause-effect, time, purpose, locality, process, and types of knowledge. . . . We need a serious epistemological research effort in this area.   (p. 74/ 124)

Minsky's naïveté and faith are astonishing. Philosophers from Plato to Husserl, who uncovered all these problems and more, have carried on serious epistemological research in this area for two thousand years without notable success. Moreover, the list Minsky includes in this passage deals only with natural objects, and their positions and interactions. As Husserl saw, intelligent behavior also presupposes a background of cultural practices and institutions. Observations in the frame paper such as: "Trading normally occurs in a social context of law, trust, and convention. Unless we also represent these other facts, most trade transactions will be almost meaningless" (p. 34/ 102) show that Minsky has understood this too. But Minsky seems oblivious to the hand-waving optimism of his proposal that programmers rush in where philosophers such as Heidegger fear to tread, and simply make explicit the totality of human practices which pervade our lives as water encompasses the life of a fish.

To make this essential point clear, it helps to take an example used by Minsky and look at what is involved in understanding a piece of everyday equipment as simple as a chair. No piece of equipment makes sense by itself. The physical object which is a chair can be defined in isolation as a collection of atoms, or of wood or metal components, but such a description will not enable us to pick out chairs. What makes an object a *chair* is its function, and what makes possible its role as equipment for sitting is its place in a total practical context. This presupposes certain facts about human beings (fatigue, the ways the body bends), and a network of other culturally determined equipment (tables, floors, lamps) and skills (eating, writing, going to conferences, giving lectures, etc.). Chairs would not be equipment for sitting if our knees bent backwards like those of flamingos, or if we had no tables, as in traditional Japan or the Australian bush.

Anyone in our culture understands such things as how to sit on kitchen chairs, swivel chairs, folding chairs; and in arm chairs, rocking chairs, deck chairs, barber's chairs, sedan chairs, dentist's chairs, basket chairs, reclining chairs, wheel chairs, sling chairs, and beanbag chairs—as well as how to get out of them again. This ability presupposes a repertoire of bodily skills which may well be indefinitely large, since there seems to be an indefinitely large variety of chairs and of successful (graceful, comfortable, secure, poised, etc.) ways to sit in them. Moreover, understanding chairs also includes social skills such as being able to sit appropriately (sedately, demurely, naturally, casually, sloppily, provocatively, etc.) at dinners, interviews, desk jobs, lectures, auditions, concerts (intimate enough for there to be chairs rather than seats), and in waiting rooms, living rooms, bedrooms, courts, libraries, and bars (of the sort sporting chairs, not stools).

In the light of this amazing capacity, Minsky's remarks on chairs in his frame paper seem more like a review of the difficulties than even a hint of how AI could begin to deal with our common sense understanding in this area:

> There are many forms of chairs, for example, and one should choose carefully the chair-description frames that are to be the major capitals of chair-land. These are used for rapid matching and assigning priorities to the various differences. The lower priority *features* of the *cluster* center then serve . . . as properties of the chair *types* . . .   (p. 52/ 117; emphasis added)

There is no argument why we should expect to find elementary context-free *features* characterizing a chair *type,* nor any suggestion as to what these features might be. They certainly cannot be legs, back, seat, etc., since these are not context-free characteristics defined apart from chairs which then "cluster" in a chair representation, but, rather, legs, back, etc. come in all shapes and variety and can only be recognized as *aspects* of already recognized chairs. Minsky continues:

> Difference pointers could be "functional" as well as geometric. Thus, after rejecting a first try at "chair" one might try the functional idea of "something one can sit on" to explain an unconventional form.   (p. 52/ 117)

But, as we already saw in our discussion of Winston's concept-learning program, a function so defined is not abstractable from human embodied know-how and cultural practices. A functional description such as "something one can sit on" treated merely as an additional context-free descriptor cannot even distinguish conventional chairs from saddles, thrones, and toilets. Minsky concludes:

> Of course, that analysis would fail to capture toy chairs, or chairs of such ornamental delicacy that their actual use would be unthinkable. These would be better handled by the method

of excuses, in which one would bypass the usual geometrical or functional explanation in favor of responding to *contexts* involving *art* or *play*.   (p. 52/ 117; emphasis added)

This is what is required all right, but by what elementary features are *these* contexts to be recognized? There is no reason at all to suppose that one can avoid the difficulty of formally representing our knowledge of chairs by abstractly representing even more holistic, concrete, culturally determined, and loosely organized human practices such as art and play.

Minsky in his frame article claims that: "the frame idea . . . is in the tradition of . . . the 'paradigms' of Kuhn" (p. 3/ 97), so it is appropriate to ask whether a theory of formal representation such as Minsky's, even if it can't account for everyday objects like chairs, can do justice to Thomas Kuhn's analysis of the role of paradigms in the practice of science. Such a comparison might seem more promising than testing the ability of frames to account for our everyday understanding, since science is a theoretical enterprise which deals with context-free data whose lawlike relations can in principle be grasped by any sufficiently powerful "pure-intellect," whether human, Martian, digital, or divine.

Paradigms, like frames, serve to set up expectations. As Kuhn notes: "In the absence of a paradigm or some candidate for paradigm, all the facts that could possibly pertain to the development of a given science are likely to seem equally relevant" (Kuhn, 1970; p. 15). Minsky interprets as follows:

> According to Kuhn's model of scientific evolution 'normal' science proceeds by using established *descriptive schemes.* Major changes result from new 'paradigms', new ways of describing things. . . . Whenever our customary viewpoints do not work well, whenever we fail to find effective frame systems in memory, we must construct new ones that bring out the right *features.*   (p. 58/ 121; emphasis added)

But what Minsky leaves out is precisely Kuhn's claim that a paradigm or exemplar is *not* an *abstract explicit descriptive scheme* utilizing formal *features,* but rather a shared *concrete* case, which dispenses with features altogether:

The practice of normal science depends on the ability, acquired from exemplars, to group objects and situations into similarity sets which are primitive in the sense that the grouping is done without an answer to the question, "Similar with respect to what?" (Kuhn, 1970; p. 200)

Thus, although it is the job of scientists to find abstractable, exact, symbolic descriptions, and *the subject matter of science* consists of such formal accounts, the *thinking* of scientists themselves does not seem to be amenable to this sort of analysis. Kuhn explicitly repudiates any formal reconstruction which claims that the scientists must be using symbolic descriptions.

I have in mind a manner of knowing which is misconstrued if reconstructed in terms of rules that are first abstracted from exemplars and thereafter function in their stead. (p. 192)

Indeed, Kuhn sees his book as raising just those questions which Minsky refuses to face:

Why is the *concrete* scientific achievement, as a locus of professional commitment, prior to the various concepts, laws, theories, and points of view that may be *abstracted* from it? In what sense is the shared paradigm a fundamental unit for the student of scientific development, a unit that *cannot* be fully reduced to logically *atomic components* which might function in its stead? (p. 11; emphasis added)

Although research based on frames cannot deal with this question and so cannot account for commonsense or scientific knowledge, the frame idea did bring the problem of how to represent our everyday knowledge into the open in AI. Moreover, it provided a model so vague and suggestive that it could be developed in several different directions. Two alternatives immediately presented themselves: either to use frames as part of a special-purpose micro-world analysis dealing with commonsense knowledge as if everyday activity took place in preanalyzed specific domains, or else to try to use frame structures in "a no-tricks basic study" of the open-ended character of everyday know-how. Of the two most influential current schools in AI, Roger Schank and his students at Yale have tried the first approach. Winograd, Bobrow, and their research group at Stanford and Xerox, the second.

Schank's version of frames are called "scripts," Scripts encode the essential steps involved in stereotypical social activities. Schank uses them to enable a computer to "understand" simple stories. Like the micro-world builders, Schank believes he can start with isolated stereotypical situations described in terms of primitive actions and gradually work up from there to all of human life.

To carry out this project, Schank invented an event description language consisting of eleven primitive acts such as: ATRANS—the transfer of an abstract relationship such as possession, ownership, or control; PTRANS—the transfer of physical location of an object; INGEST—the taking of an object by an animal into the inner workings of that animal, etc. (Schank, 1975a; p. 39); and from these primitives he builds gamelike scenarios which enable his program to fill in gaps and pronoun reference in stories.

Such primitive acts, of course, make sense only when the context is already interpreted in a specific piece of discourse. Their artificiality can easily be seen if we compare one of Schank's context-free primitive acts to real-life actions. Take PTRANS, the transfer of physical location of an object. At first it seems an interpretation-free fact if ever there was one. After all, either an object moves or it doesn't. But in real life things are not so simple; even what counts as physical motion depends on our purposes. If someone is standing still in a moving elevator on a moving ocean liner, is his going from A to B deck a PTRANS? What about when he is just sitting on B deck? Are we all PTRANSing around the sun? Clearly the answer depends on the situation in which the question is asked.

Such primitives can be used, however, to describe fixed situations or scripts once the relevant purposes have already been agreed upon. Schank's definition of a script emphasizes its predetermined, bounded, gamelike character:

We define a script as a *predetermined* causal chain of conceptualizations that describe the *normal sequence of things* in a familiar situation. Thus there is a restaurant script, a birthday-party script, a football game script, a classroom script, and so on. Each script has in it a *minimum number of players* and objects that assume certain roles within the script . . . [E]ach *primitive* action given stands for the most important *element* in a *standard set* of actions.   (1975b; p. 131; emphasis added)

His illustration of the restaurant script spells out in terms of primitive actions the rules of the restaurant game:

Script: restaurant
Roles: customer; waitress; chef; cashier
Reason: to get food so as to go down in hunger and up in pleasure

Scene 1 entering
PTRANS—go into restaurant
MBUILD—find table
PTRANS—go to table
MOVE—sit down

Scene 2 ordering
ATRANS—receive menu
ATTEND—look at it
MBUILD—decide on order
MTRANS—tell order to waitress

Scene 3 eating
ATRANS—receive food
INGEST—eat food

Scene 4 exiting
MTRANS—ask for check
ATRANS—give tip to waitress
PTRANS—go to cashier
ATRANS—give money to cashier
PTRANS—go out of restaurant   (1975b; p. 131)

No doubt many of our social activities are stereotyped, and there is nothing in principle misguided in trying to work out primitives and rules for a restaurant game, the way the rules of Monopoly are meant to capture a simplified version of the typical moves in the real estate business. But Schank claims that he can use this approach to understand stories about *actual* restaurant-going—that in effect he can treat the sub-world of restaurant going as if it were an isolated micro-world. To do this, however, he must artificially limit the possibilities: for, as one might suspect, no matter how stereotyped, going to the restaurant is not a self-contained game but a highly variable set of behaviors which open out into the rest of human activity. What "normally" happens when one goes to a restaurant can be preselected and formalized by the programmer as default assignments, but the background has been left out so that a program using such a script cannot be said to understand going to a restaurant at all. This can easily be seen by imagining a situation that deviates from the norm. What if when one tries to order he finds that the item in question is not available, or before paying he finds that the bill is added up wrongly? Of course, Schank would answer that he could build these normal ways restaurant-going breaks down into his script. But there are always *abnormal* ways everyday activities can break down: the juke box might be too noisy, there might be too many flies on the counter, or as in the film *Annie Hall,* in a New York delicatessen one's girl friend might order a pastrami sandwich on white bread with mayonnaise. When we understand going to a restaurant we understand how to cope with even these abnormal possibilities because going to a restaurant is part of our everyday activities of going into buildings, getting things we want, interacting with people, etc.

To deal with this sort of objection Schank has added some general rules for coping with unexpected disruptions. The general idea is that in a story "it is usual for non-standard occurrences to be explicitly mentioned" (Schank and Abelson, 1977; p. 51); so the program can spot the abnormal events and understand the subsequent events as ways of coping with them. But here we can see that dealing with stories allows Schank to bypass the basic problem, since it is the *author's* understanding of the situation which enables him to decide which events are disruptive enough to mention.

This *ad hoc* way of dealing with the abnormal can always be revealed by asking further questions, for the program has not understood a restaurant story the way people in our culture do, until it can answer such simple questions as: When the waitress came to the table, did she wear clothes? Did she walk forward or backward? Did the customer eat his food with his mouth or his ear? If the program answers, "I don't know," we feel that all of its right answers were tricks or lucky guesses and that it has not understood anything of our everyday restaurant behavior.[3] The point here, and throughout, is not that there are subtle things human beings can do and recognize which are beyond the low-level understanding of present programs, but that in any area there are simple taken-for-granted responses central to human understanding, lacking which a computer program cannot be said to have any understanding at all. Schank's claim, then, that "the paths of a script are the possibilities that are extant in a situation" (1975b; p. 132) is insidiously misleading. Either it means that the script accounts for the possibilities in the restaurant game defined by Schank, in which case it is true but uninteresting; or he is claiming that he can account for the possibilities in an everyday restaurant situation which is impressive but, by Schank's own admission, false.

Real short stories pose a further problem for Schank's approach. In a script what the primitive actions and facts are is determined beforehand, but in a short story *what counts as the relevant facts depends on the story itself.* For example, a story that describes a bus trip contains in its script that the passenger thanks the driver (a Schank example). But the fact that the passenger thanked the driver would not be important in a story in which the passenger simply took the bus as a part of a longer journey, while it might be crucially important if the story concerned a misanthrope who had never thanked anyone before, or a very law-abiding young man who had courageously broken the prohibition against speaking to drivers in order to speak to the attractive woman driving the bus. Overlooking this point, Schank claimed at a recent meeting that his program, which can

---

3. This is John Searle's way of formulating this important point. In a talk at the University of California at Berkeley (October 19, 1977), Schank agreed with Searle that to understand a visit to a restaurant, the computer needs more than a script; it needs to know everything that people know. He added that he is unhappy that as it stands his program cannot distinguish "degrees of weirdness." Indeed, for the program it is equally "weird" for the restaurant to be out of food as it is for the customer to respond by devouring the chef. Thus Schank seems to agree that without some understanding of degree of deviation from the norm, the program does not understand a story even when in that story events follow a completely normal stereotyped script. It follows that although scripts capture a necessary condition of everyday understanding, they do not provide a sufficient condition.

extract death statistics from newspaper accident reports, had answered my challenge that a computer would count as intelligent only if it could summarize a short story.[4] But Schank's newspaper program cannot provide a clue concerning judgments of what to include in a story summary because it works only where relevance and significance have been predetermined, and thereby avoids dealing with the world built up in a story in terms of which judgments of relevance and importance are made.

Nothing could ever call into question Schank's basic assumption that all human practice and know-how is represented in the mind as a system of beliefs constructed from context-free primitive actions and facts, but there are signs of trouble. Schank does admit that an individual's "belief system" cannot be fully elicited from him; although he never doubts that it exists and that it could in principle be represented in his formalism. He is therefore led to the desperate idea of a program which could learn about everything from restaurants to life themes the way people do. In one of his papers he concludes:

> We hope to be able to build a program that can learn, as a child does, how to do what we have described in this paper instead of being spoon-fed the tremendous information necessary.
>
> (1972; pp. 553–554)

In any case, Schank's appeal to learning is at best another evasion. Developmental psychology has shown that children's learning does not consist merely in acquiring more and more information about specific routine situations by adding new primitives and combining old ones as Schank's view would lead one to expect. Rather, learning of specific details takes place on a background of shared practices which seem to be picked up in everyday interactions not as facts and beliefs but as bodily skills for coping with the world. Any learning presupposes this background of implicit know-how which gives significance to details. Since Schank admits that he cannot see how this background can be made explicit so as to be given to a computer, and since the

---

4. At the Society for Interdisciplinary Study of the Mind, Symposium for Philosophy and Computer Technology, State University College, New Paltz, N.Y., March 1977.

background is presupposed for the kind of script learning Schank has in mind, it seems that his project of using preanalyzed primitives to capture common sense understanding is doomed.

A more plausible, even if in the last analysis perhaps no more promising, approach would be to use the new theoretical power of frames or stereotypes to dispense with the need to preanalyze everyday situations in terms of a set of primitive features whose *relevance is independent of context.* This approach starts with the recognition that in everyday communication " 'Meaning' is multi-dimensional, formalizable only in terms of the entire complex of goals and knowledge [of the world] being applied by both the producer and understander" (Winograd, 1976b; p. 262). This knowledge, of course, is assumed to be "A body of specific beliefs (expressed as symbol structures . . .) making up the person's 'model of the world' " (p. 268). Given these assumptions, Terry Winograd and his co-workers are developing a new knowledge representation language (KRL), which they hope will enable programmers to capture these beliefs in symbolic descriptions of multidimensional prototypical objects whose *relevant aspects are a function of their context.*

Prototypes would be structured so that any sort of description from proper names to procedures for recognizing an example could be used to fill in any one of the nodes or slots that are attached to a prototype. This allows representations to be defined in terms of each other, and results in what the authors call "a *wholistic* as opposed to *reductionistic* view of representation" (Bobrow and Winograd, 1977; p. 7). For example, since any description could be part of any other, chairs could be described as having aspects such as seats and backs, and seats and backs in turn could be described in terms of their function in chairs. Furthermore, each prototypical object or situation could be described from many different perspectives. Thus nothing need be defined in terms of its necessary and sufficient features in the way Winston and traditional philosophers have proposed, but rather, following Rosch's research on prototypes, objects would be classified as more or less resembling certain prototypical descriptions.

Winograd illustrates this idea by using the traditional philosophers' favorite example:

The word "bachelor" has been used in many discussions of semantics, since (save for obscure meanings involving aquatic mammals and medieval chivalry) it seems to have a formally tractable meaning which can be paraphrased "an adult human male who has never been married". . . . In the realistic use of the word, there are many problems which are not as simply stated and formalized. Consider the following exchange:

Host: I'm having a big party next weekend. Do you know any nice bachelors I could invite?

Friend: Yes, I know this fellow X.

The problem is to decide, given the facts below, for which values of X the response would be a reasonable answer in light of the normal meaning of the word "bachelor". A simple test is to ask for which ones the host might fairly complain "You lied. You said X was a bachelor.":

A: Arthur has been living happily with Alice for the last five years. They have a two year old daughter and have never officially married.

B: Bruce was going to be drafted, so he arranged with his friend Barbara to have a justice of the peace marry them so he would be exempt. They have never lived together. He dates a number of women, and plans to have the marriage annulled as soon as he finds someone he wants to marry.

C: Charlie is 17 years old. He lives at home with his parents and is in high school.

D: David is 17 years old. He left home at 13, started a small business, and is now a successful young entrepreneur leading a playboy's life style in his penthouse apartment.

E: Eli and Edgar are homosexual lovers who have been living together for many years.

F: Faisal is allowed by the law of his native Abu Dhabi to have three wives. He currently has two and is interested in meeting another potential fiancee.

G: Father Gregory is the bishop of the Catholic cathedral at Groton upon Thames.

[This] cast of characters could be extended indefinitely, and in each case there are problems in deciding whether the word "bachelor" could appropriately be applied. In normal use, a word does not convey a clearly definable combination of primitive propositions, but evokes an *exemplar* which possesses a number of properties. This exemplar is not a specific individual in the experience of the language user, but is more abstract, representing a conflation of typical properties. A prototypical bachelor can be described as:

1. a person
2. a male
3. an adult
4. not currently officially married
5. not in a marriage-like living situation
6. potentially marriageable
7. leading a bachelor-like life style
8. not having been married previously
9. having an intention, at least temporarily, not to marry
10. . . .

Each of the men described above fits some but not all of these characterizations. Except for narrow legalistic contexts, there is no significant sense in which a subset of the characteristics can be singled out as the "central meaning" of the word. In fact, among native English speakers there is little agreement about whether someone who has been previously married can properly be called a "bachelor" and fairly good agreement that it should not apply to someone who is not potentially marriageable (e.g. has taken a vow of celibacy).

Not only is this list [of properties] open-ended, but the individual terms are themselves not definable in terms of primitive notions. In reducing the meaning of 'bachelor' to a formula involving 'adult' or 'potentially marriageable', one is led into describing these in terms of exemplars as well. 'Adult' cannot be defined in terms of years of age for any but technical legal purposes and in fact even in this restricted sense, it is defined differently for different aspects of the law. Phrases such as 'marriage-like living situation' and 'bachelor-like life style' reflect directly in their syntactic form the intention to convey stereotyped exemplars rather than formal definitions.

(Winograd, 1976b; pp. 276–278)

Obviously if KRL succeeds in enabling AI researchers to use such prototypes to write flexible programs, such a language will be a major breakthrough and will avoid the *ad hoc* character of the "solutions" typical of micro-world programs. Indeed, the future of AI depends on some such work as that begun with the development of KRL. But there are problems with this approach. Winograd's analysis has the important consequence that in comparing two prototypes, what counts as a match and thus what counts as the relevant aspects which justify the match will be a result of the program's understanding of the current context.

> The result of a matching process is not a simple true/false answer. It can be stated in its most general form as: "Given the set of alternatives which I am currently considering . . . and looking in order at those stored structures which are most accessible in the *current context,* here is the best match, here is the degree to which it seems to hold, and here are the specific detailed places where match was not found. . . ."
> The selection of the order in which sub-structures of the description will be compared is a function of their current accessibility, which depends both on the form in which they are stored and the *current context.*
>
> (1976b; p. 281–282; emphasis added)

This raises four increasingly grave difficulties. First, for there to be "a class of cognitive 'matching' processes which operate on the descriptions (symbol structures) available for two entities, looking for correspondences and differences" (p. 280), there must be a finite set of prototypes to be matched. To take Winograd's example:

> A single object or event can be described with respect to several prototypes, with further specifications from the perspective of each. The fact that last week *Rusty flew to San Francisco* would be expressed by describing the event as a typical instance of *Travel* with the mode specified as *Airplane*, destination *San Francisco,* etc. It might also be described as a *Visit* with the actor being *Rusty*, the friends a particular group of people, the interaction warm, etc.   (Bobrow and Winograd, 1977; p. 8)

But *etc.* covers what might, without predigestion for a specific purpose, be a hopeless proliferation. The same flight might also be a test flight, a check of crew performance, a stopover, a mistake, a golden opportunity, not to mention a visit to brother, sister, thesis adviser, guru, etc., etc., etc. Before the program can function at all the total set of possible alternatives must be pre-selected by the programmer.

Second, the matching makes sense only *after* the current candidates for comparison have been found. In chess, for example, positions can be compared only after the chess master calls to mind past positions the current board positions might plausibly resemble. And (as in the chess case) the discovery of the relevant candidates which make the matching of aspects possible requires experience and intuitive association.

The only way a KRL-based program (which must use symbolic descriptions) could proceed, in chess or anywhere else, would be to guess some frame on the basis of what was already "understood" by the program, and then see if that frame's features could be matched to some current description. If not, the program would have to backtrack and try another prototype until it found one into whose slots or default terminals the incoming data could be fitted. This seems an altogether implausible and inefficient model of how we perform, and only rarely occurs in our conscious life. Of course, cognitive scientists could answer the above objection by maintaining, in spite of the implausibility, that we try out the various prototypes very quickly and are simply not aware of the frantic shuffling of hypotheses going on in our unconscious. But, in fact, most would still agree with Winograd's (1974) assessment that the frame selection problem remains unsolved:

> The problem of choosing the frames to try is another very open area. There is a selection problem, since we cannot take all of our possible frames for different kinds of events and match them against what is going on. (p. 80)

There is, moreover, a third and more basic question which may pose an in-principle problem for any formal holistic account in which the significance of any fact, indeed what counts as a fact, always depends on context. Winograd stresses the critical importance of context:

The results of human reasoning are *context dependent,* the

structure of memory includes not only the long-term storage organization (what do I know?) but also a current context (what is in focus at the moment?). We believe that this is an important feature of human thought, not an inconvenient limitation.   (Bobrow and Winograd, 1977; p. 32)

He further notes that "the problem is to find a formal way of talking about . . . current attention focus and goals" (1976b; p. 283). Yet he gives no formal account of how a computer program written in KRL could determine the current context.

Winograd's work does contain suggestive claims, such as his remark that "the procedural approach formalizes notions like 'current context' . . . and 'attention focus' in terms of the processes by which cognitive state changes as a person comprehends or produces utterances" (pp. 287–288). There are also occasional parenthetical references to "current goals, focus of attention, set of words recently heard, etc." (p. 282). But reference to recent words has proven useless as a way of determining what the current context is, and reference to current goals and focus of attention is vague and perhaps even question-begging. If a human being's current goal is, say, to find a chair to sit on, his current focus might be on recognizing whether he is in a living room or a warehouse. He will also have short-range goals like finding the walls, longer-range goals like finding the light switch, middle-range goals like wanting to write or rest; and what counts as satisfying these goals will in turn depend on his ultimate goals and interpretation of himself as, say, a writer, or merely as easily exhausted and deserving comfort. So Winograd's appeal to "current goals and focus" covers too much to be useful in determining what specific situation the program is in.

To be consistent, Winograd would have to treat each type of situation the computer could be in as an object with *its* prototypical description; then in recognizing a specific situation, the situation or context in which *that* situation was encountered would determine which foci, goals, etc. were relevant. But where would such a regress stop? Human beings, of course, don't have this problem. They are, as Heidegger puts it, already in a situation, which they constantly revise. If we look at it genetically, this is no mystery. We can see that human beings are gradually trained into their cultural situation on the basis of their embodied precultural situation, in a way no programmer using KRL is trying to capture. But for this very reason a program in KRL is not always-already-in-a-situation. Even if it represents all human knowledge in its stereotypes, including all possible types of human situations, it represents them from the outside like a Martian or a god. It isn't situated in any one of them, and it may be impossible to program it to behave as if it were.

This leads to my fourth and final question. Is the know-how that enables human beings constantly to sense what specific situation they are in the sort of know-how that can be represented as a kind of knowledge in *any* knowledge representation language no matter how ingenious and complex? It seems that our sense of our situation is determined by our changing moods, by our current concerns and projects, by our long-range self-interpretation and probably also by our sensory-motor skills for coping with objects and people—skills we develop by practice without ever having to represent to ourselves our body as an object, our culture as a set of beliefs, and our propensities as situation—action rules. All these uniquely human capacities provide a "richness" or a "thickness" to our way of being-in-the-world and thus seem to play an essential role in situatedness, which in turn underlies all intelligent behavior.

There is no reason to suppose that moods, mattering, and embodied skills can be captured in any formal web of belief, and except for Kenneth Colby, whose view is not accepted by the rest of the AI community, no current work assumes that they can. Rather, all AI workers and cognitive psychologists are committed, more or less lucidly, to the view that such noncognitive aspects of the mind can simply be ignored. This belief that a significant part of what counts as intelligent behavior can be captured in purely cognitive structures defines cognitive science and is a version of what I call the psychological assumption (Dreyfus, 1979; ch. 4). Winograd makes it explicit:

> AI is the general study of those aspects of cognition which are common to all physical symbol systems, including humans and computers.   (see Schank et al., 1977; p. 1008)[5]

5. He means "physical symbol system" in Newell and Simon's sense; see this volume, Chapter 1.

But this definition merely delimits the field; it in no way shows there is anything to study, let alone guarantees the project's success.

Seen in this light, Winograd's grounds for optimism contradict his own basic assumptions. On the one hand, he sees that a lot of what goes on in human minds cannot be programmed, so he only hopes to program a significant part:

> [C]ognitive science . . . does not rest on an assumption that the analysis of mind as a physical symbol system provides a *complete* understanding of human thought. . . . For the paradigm to be of value, it is only necessary that there be *some significant aspects* of thought and language which can be profitably understood through analogy with other symbol systems we know how to construct.   (1976b; p. 264)

On the other hand, he sees that human intelligence is "holistic" and that meaning depends on "the entire complex of goals and knowledge." What our discussion suggests is that all aspects of human thought, including nonformal aspects like moods, sensory-motor skills, and long-range self-interpretations, are so interrelated that one cannot substitute an abstractable web of explicit beliefs for the whole cloth of our concrete everyday practices.

What lends plausibility to the cognitivist position is the conviction that such a web of beliefs must finally fold back on itself and be complete, since we can know only a finite number of facts and procedures describable in a finite number of sentences. But since facts are discriminated and language is used only in a context, the argument that the web of belief must in principle be completely formalizable does not show that such a belief system can account for intelligent behavior. This would be true only if the context could also be captured in the web of facts and procedures. But if the context is determined by moods, concerns, and skills, then the fact that our beliefs can in principle be completely represented does not show that representations are sufficient to account for cognition. Indeed, if nonrepresentable capacities play an essential role in situatedness, and the situation is presupposed by all intelligent behavior, then the "aspects of cognition which are common to all physical symbol systems" will not be able to account for any cognitive *performance* at all.

In the end the very idea of a holistic information processing model in which the relevance of the facts depends on the context may involve a contradiction. To recognize any context one must have already selected from the indefinite number of possibly discriminable features the possibly relevant ones, but such a selection can be made only after the context has already been recognized as similar to an already analyzed one. The holist thus faces a vicious circle: relevance presupposes similarity and similarity presupposes relevance. The only way to avoid this loop is to be always-already-in-a-situation without representing it so that the problem of the priority of context and features does not arise, or else to return to the reductionist project of preanalyzing all situations in terms of a fixed set of possibly relevant primitives—a project which has its own practical problems, as our analysis of Schank's work has shown, and, as we shall see in the conclusion, may have its own internal contradiction as well.

Whether this is, indeed, an in-principle obstacle to Winograd's approach only further research will tell. Winograd himself is admirably cautious in his claims:

> If the procedural approach is successful, it will eventually be possible to describe the mechanisms at such a level of detail that there will be a verifiable fit with many aspects of detailed human performance . . . but we are nowhere near having explanations which cover language processing as a whole, including meaning.   (1976b; p. 297)

If problems do arise because of the necessity in any formalism of isolating beliefs from the rest of human activity, Winograd will no doubt have the courage to analyze and profit from the discovery. In the meantime everyone interested in the philosophical project of cognitive science will be watching to see if Winograd and company can produce a moodless, disembodied, concernless, already adult surrogate for our slowly acquired situated understanding.

Conclusion

Given the fundamental supposition of the information processing approach that all that is relevant to intelligent behavior can be formalized in a structured description, all problems must appear to be merely problems of complexity. Bobrow and Winograd put this final faith very clearly at the end of their description of KRL:

> The system is complex, and will continue to get more so in the near future. . . . [W]e do not expect that it will ever be reduced to a very small set of mechanisms. Human thought, we believe, is the product of the interaction of a fairly large set of inter-dependent processes. Any representation language which is to be used in modeling thought or achieving "intelligent" performance will have to have an extensive and varied repertoire of mechanisms.   (Bobrow and Winograd, 1977; p. 43)

Underlying this mechanistic assumption is an even deeper assumption which has gradually become clear during the past ten years of research. During this period AI researchers have consistently run up against the problem of representing everyday context. Work during the first five years (1967–1972) demonstrated the futility of trying to evade the importance of everyday context by creating artificial gamelike contexts preanalyzed in terms of a list of fixed-relevance features. More recent work has thus been forced to deal directly with the background of common-sense know-how which guides our changing sense of what counts as the relevant facts. Faced with this necessity researchers have implicitly tried to treat the broadest context or background as an object with its own set of preselected descriptive features. This assumption, that the background can be treated as just another object to be represented in the same sort of structured description in which everyday objects are represented, is essential to our whole philosophical tradition. Following Heidegger, who is the first to have identified and criticized this assumption, I will call it the metaphysical assumption.

The obvious question to ask in conclusion is: Is there any evidence besides the persistent difficulties and history of unfulfilled promises in AI for believing that the metaphysical assumption is unjustified? It may be that no argument can be given against it, since facts put forth to show that the background of practices is unrepresentable are in that very act shown to be the sort of facts which *can* be represented. Still, I will attempt to lay out the argument which underlies my antiformalist, and, therefore, antimechanist convictions.

My thesis, which owes a lot to Wittgenstein (1953), is that whenever human behavior is analyzed in terms of rules, these rules must always contain a *ceteris paribus* condition, i.e., they apply "everything else being equal," and what "everything else" and "equal" mean in any specific situation can never be fully spelled out without a regress. Moreover, this *ceteris paribus* condition is not merely an annoyance which shows that the analysis is not yet complete and might be what Husserl called an "infinite task." Rather the *ceteris paribus* condition points to a background of practices which are the condition of the possibility of all rulelike activity. In explaining our actions we must always sooner or later fall back on our everyday practices and simply say "this is what we do" or "that's what it is to be a human being." Thus in the last analysis all intelligibility and all intelligent behavior must be traced back to our sense of what we *are*, which is, according to this argument, necessarily, on pain of regress, something we can never explicitly *know*.

Still, to this dilemma the AI researchers might plausibly respond: "Whatever the background of shared interests, feelings, and practices necessary for understanding specific situations, that knowledge *must* somehow be represented in the human beings who have that understanding. And how else could such knowledge be represented but in some explicit data structure?" Indeed, the kind of computer programming accepted by all workers in AI would require such a data structure, and so would philosophers who hold that all knowledge must be explicitly represented in our minds, but there are two alternatives which would avoid the contradictions inherent in the information-processing model by avoiding the idea that everything we know must be in the form of some explicit symbolic representation.

One response, shared by existential phenomenologists such as Merleau-Ponty and ordinary language philosophers such as Wittgenstein, is to say that such "knowledge" of human interests and practices need not be represented at all. Just as it seems plausible that I can learn to swim by practicing until I develop the necessary patterns of responses, without representing my body and muscular movements in some data structure, so too what I "know" about the cultural practices which enables me to recognize and act in specific situations has been gradually acquired through training in which no one ever did or could, again on pain of regress, make explicit what was being learned.

Another possible account would allow a place for representations, at least in special cases where I have to stop and reflect, but such a position would stress that these are usually nonformal representations, more like images, by means of which I explore what I *am,* not what I *know.* We thus appeal to *concrete* representations (images or memories) based on our own experience without having to make explicit the strict rules and their spelled out *ceteris paribus* conditions required by *abstract* symbolic representations.

The idea that feelings, memories, and images *must* be the conscious tip of an unconscious framelike data structure runs up against both *prima facie* evidence and the problem of explicating the *ceteris paribus* conditions. Moreover, the formalist assumption is not supported by one shred of scientific evidence from neurophysiology or psychology, or from the past successes of AI, whose repeated failures required appeal to the metaphysical assumption in the first place.

AI's current difficulties, moreover, become intelligible in the light of this alternative view. The proposed formal representation of the background of practices in symbolic descriptions, whether in terms of situation-free primitives or more sophisticated data structures whose building blocks can be descriptions of situations, would, indeed, look more and more complex and intractable if minds were not physical symbol systems. If belief structures are the result of abstraction from the concrete practical context rather than the true building blocks of our world, it is no wonder the formalist finds himself stuck with the view that they are endlessly explicatable. On my view the organization of world knowledge provides the largest stumbling block to AI precisely because the programmer is forced to treat the world as an object, and our know-how as knowledge.

Looking back over the past ten years of AI research we might say that the basic point which has emerged is that *since intelligence must be situated it cannot be separated from the rest of human life.* The persistent denial of this seemingly obvious point cannot, however, be laid at the door of AI. It starts with Plato's separation of the intellect or rational soul from the body with its skills, emotions, and appetites. Aristotle continued this unlikely dichotomy when he separated the theoretical from the practical, and defined man as a rational animal—as if one could separate man's rationality from his animal needs and desires. If one thinks of the importance of the sensory-motor skills in the development of our ability to recognize and cope with objects, or of the role of needs and desires in structuring all social situations, or finally of the whole cultural background of human self-interpretation involved in our simply knowing how to pick out and use chairs, the idea that we can simply ignore this know-how while formalizing our intellectual understanding as a complex system of facts and rules is highly implausible.

Great artists have always sensed the truth, stubbornly denied by both philosophers and technologists, that the basis of human intelligence cannot be isolated and explicitly understood. In *Moby-Dick* Melville writes of the tattooed savage, Queequeg, that he had "written out on his body a complete theory of the heavens and the earth, and a mystical treatise on the art of attaining truth; so that Queequeg in his own proper person was a riddle to unfold, a wondrous work in one volume; but whose mysteries not even he himself could read" (1952; p. 477). Yeats puts it even more succinctly: "I have found what I wanted—to put it in a phrase, I say, 'Man can embody the truth, but he cannot know it'."

Acknowledgement: I am grateful to John Haugeland for editorial suggestions on transforming this from a book introduction into an independent article.

7
Reductionism and the Nature of Psychology

HILARY PUTNAM

1. Reduction

A DOCTRINE to which most philosophers of science sub-
scribe (and to which I subscribed for many years) is the doctrine
that the laws of such "higher-level" sciences as psychology and
sociology are reducible to the laws of lower-level sciences—biology,
chemistry, ultimately to the laws of elementary particle physics.
Acceptance of this doctrine is generally identified with belief in
"The Unity of Science" (with capitals), and rejection of it with
belief in vitalism, or psychism, or, anyway, something *bad.*

In this paper I want to argue that this doctrine is wrong. In
later sections, I shall specifically discuss the Turing machine
model of the mind—and the conception of psychology associated
with reductionism and with the Turing machine model. I want to
argue that while materialism is right, and while it is true that the
only method for gaining knowledge of anything is to rely on testing
ideas in practice (and evaluating the results of the tests scientifically), acceptance of these doctrines need not lead to reductionism.

I shall begin with a logical point and then apply it to the special
case of psychology. The logical point is that from the fact that the
behavior of a system can be *deduced* from its description as a
system of elementary particles, it does not follow that it can be
explained from that description. Let us look at an example and
then see why this is so.

My example will be a system of two macroscopic objects, a

board in which there are two holes, a square hole one inch across and a round hole one inch in diameter, and a square peg, a fraction less than one inch across. The fact to be explained is: The peg goes through the square hole, and it does not go through the round hole.

One explanation is that the peg is approximately rigid under transportation and the board is approximately rigid. The peg goes through the hole that is large enough and not through the hole that is too small. Notice that the microstructure of the board and the peg is irrelevant to this explanation. All that is necessary is that, whatever the microstructure may be, it be compatible with the fact that the board and the peg are approximately rigid objects.

Suppose, however, we describe the board as a cloud of elementary particles (for simplicity, we will assume these are Newtonian elementary particles) and imagine ourselves given the position and velocity at some arbitrary time t_0 of each one. We then describe the peg in a similar way. (Say the board is "cloud B" and the peg is "cloud A".) Suppose we describe the round hole as "region 1" and the square hole as "region 2". Let us say that by a heroic feat of calculation we succeed in proving that "cloud A" will pass through "region 2" but not through "region 1". Have we explained anything?

It seems to me that whatever the pragmatic constraints on explanation may or may not be, one constraint is surely this: The relevant features of a situation should be brought out by an explanation and not buried in a mass of irrelevant information. By this criterion, it seems clear that the first explanation—which points out that the two macro-objects are approximately rigid and that one of the two holes is big enough for the peg and the other is not—*explains* why "cloud A" passes through "region 2" and never through "region 1", while the second—the deduction of the fact to be explained from the positions and velocities of the elementary particles, their electrical attractions and repulsions, etc.—fails to *explain.*

If this seems counterintuitive, it is for two reasons, I think. (1) We have been taught that to *deduce* a phenomenon in this way is to *explain* it. But this is ridiculous on the face of it. Suppose I deduce a fact F from G and I, where G is a genuine explanation and I is something irrelevant. Is G and I an *explanation* of F?

Normally we would answer. "No. Only the part G is an explanation". Now, suppose I subject the statement G and I to logical transformations so as to produce a statement H that is mathematically equivalent to G and I (possibly in a complicated way), but such that the information G is, practically speaking, virtually impossible to recover from H. Then on any reasonable standard the resulting statement H is *not* an explanation of F; but F is deducible from H. I think that the description of the peg and board in terms of the positions and velocities of the elementary particles, their electrical attractions and repulsions, etc., is such a statement H: The relevant information, that the peg and the board are approximately rigid, and the relative sizes of the holes and the peg are buried in this information, but in a useless way (practically speaking). (2) We forget that explanation is not *transitive*. The microstructure of the board and peg may explain why the board and the peg are rigid, and the rigidity is part of the explanation of the fact that the peg passes through one hole and not the other, but it does not follow that the microstructure, so to speak "raw"— as an assemblage of positions, velocities, etc.—explains the fact that the peg passes through one hole and not the other. Even if the microstructure is not presented "raw", in this sense, but the information is *organized* so as to give a *revealing* account of the rigidity of the macro-objects, a revealing explanation of the rigidity of the macro-objects is not an explanation of something which is explained by that rigidity. If I want to know why the peg passes through one hole and not the other in a normal context (e.g., I already know that these macro-objects are rigid), then the fact that one hole is bigger than the peg all around and the other isn't is a complete explanation. That the peg and the board consist of atoms arranged in a certain way, and that atoms arranged in that way form a rigid body, etc., might also be an explanation— although one which gives me information (*why* the board and the peg are rigid) I didn't ask for. But at least the relevant information—the rigidity of the board and the peg, and the relation of the sizes and shapes of the holes and the pegs—are still *explicit*. That the peg and the board consist of atoms arranged in a certain way *by itself* does *not* explain why the peg goes through one hole and not the other, even if it explains something which in turn explains that.

The relation between (1) and (2) is this: An explanation of an explanation (a "parent" of an explanation, so to speak), generally contains information I, which is irrelevant to what we want to explain, and in addition it contains the information which *is* relevant, if at all, in a form that may be impossible to recognize. For this reason a parent of an explanation is generally not an explanation.

What follows is that certain systems can have behaviors to which their microstructure is *largely* irrelevant. For example, a great many facts about rigid bodies can obviously be explained just from their *rigidity* and the principles of geometry, as in the example just given, without at all going into why those bodies are rigid. A more interesting case is the one in which the higher-level organizational facts on which an explanation turns themselves depend on *more* than the micro-structure of the body under consideration. This, I shall argue, is the typical case in the domain of social phenomena.

For an example, consider the explanation of social phenomena. Marx in his analysis of capitalism uses certain facts about human beings—for example, that they have to eat in order to live, and they have to produce in order to eat. He discusses how, under certain conditions, human production can lead to the institution of *exchange,* and how that exchange in turn leads to a new form of production, production of commodities. He discusses how production of commodities for exchange can lead to production of commodities for profit, to wage labor and capital.

Assume that something like this is right. How much is the microstructure of human beings relevant? The case is similar to the first example in that the *specifics* or the microstructure are irrelevant: What is relevant is, so to speak, an organizational result of microstructure. In the first case the relevant organizational result was rigidity: In the present case, the relevant organizational result is intelligent beings able to modify both the forces of production and the relations of production to satisfy both their basic biological needs and those needs which result from the relations of production they develop. To explain how the microstructure of the human brain and nervous system accounts for this intelligence would be a great feat for *biology;* it might or might not have relevance for political economy.

But there is an important difference between the two examples.

Given the micro-structure of the peg and the board, one *can* deduce the rigidity. But given the micro-structure of the brain and the nervous system, one cannot deduce that *capitalist* production relations will exist. The same creatures can exist in precapitalist commodity production, or in feudalism, or in socialism, or in other ways. The laws of capitalist society cannot be deduced from the laws of physics plus the description of the human brain: They depend on "boundary conditions" which are *accidental* from the point of view of physics but essential to the description of a situation as "capitalism". In short, the laws of capitalism have a certain *autonomy* vis-à-vis the laws of physics: They have a physical *basis* (men have to eat), but they cannot be deduced from the laws of physics. They are compatible with the laws of physics; but so are the laws of socialism and of feudalism.

This same autonomy of the higher-level science appears already at the level of biology. The laws that collectively make up the theory of evolution are not deducible from the laws of physics and chemistry; from the latter laws it does not even follow that one living thing will live for five seconds, let alone that living things will live long enough to evolve. Evolution *depends on* a result of microstructure (variation in genotype); but it also depends on conditions (presence of oxygen, etc.) which are *accidental* from the point of view of physics and chemistry. The laws of the higher-level discipline are deducible from the laws of the lower-level discipline together with "auxiliary hypotheses" which are *accidental from the point of view of the lower-level discipline*. And *most of the structure at the level of physics is irrelevant from the point of view of the higher-level discipline;* only certain *features* of that structure (variation in genotype, or rigidity, or production for profit are relevant), and these are specified by the higher-level discipline, not the lower-level one.

The alternative, mechanism *or* vitalism, is a false alternative. The laws of human sociology and psychology, for example, have a basis in the material organization of persons and things, but they also have the autonomy just described vis-à-vis the laws of physics and chemistry.

The reductionist way of looking at science both springs from and reinforces a specific set of ideas about the social sciences. Thus human biology is relatively unchanging. If the laws of psychology are deducible from the laws of biology and (also unchanging) reductive definitions, then it follows that the laws of psychology are also unchanging. Thus the idea of an unchanging human nature—a set of structured psychological laws, dependent on biology but independent of sociology—is presupposed at the outset. Also, each science in the familiar sequence—physics, chemistry, biology, psychology, sociology—is supposed to reduce to the one below (and ultimately to physics). Thus sociology is supposed to reduce to psychology which in turn reduces to biology via the theory of the brain and nervous system. This assumes a definite attitude toward sociology, the attitude of methodological individualism. (In conventional economics, for example, the standard attitude is that the market is shaped by the desires and preferences of individual people; no conceptual apparatus even exists for investigating the ways in which the desires and preferences of individuals are shaped by the economic institutions.)

Besides supporting the idea of an unchanging human nature and methodological individualism, there is another and more subtle role that reductionism plays in one's outlook. This role may be illustrated by the effect of reductionism on biology departments: When Crick and Watson made their famous discoveries, many biology departments fired some or all of their naturalists! Of course, this was a crude mistake. Even from an extreme reductionist point of view, the possibility of explaining the behavior of species via DNA mechanisms "in principle" is very different from being able to do it in practice. Firing someone who has a lot of knowledge about the habits of, say, bats, because someone else has a lot of knowledge about DNA is a big mistake. Moreover, as we saw above, you *can't* explain the behavior of bats, or whatever species, *just* in terms of DNA mechanisms—you have to know the "boundary conditions". That a given structure enables an organism to fly, for example, is a function not just of its strength, etc., but also of the density of the earth's atmosphere. And DNA mechanisms represent the wrong level of organization of the data—what one wants to know about the bat, for example, is that it has mechanisms for producing supersonic sounds, and mechanisms for "triangulating" on its own reflected sounds ("echolocating").

The point is that reductionism comes on as a doctrine that breeds respect for science and the scientific method. In fact, what it breeds is physics worship coupled with neglect of the "higher-level" sciences. Infatuation with what is supposedly possible "in principle" goes with indifference to *practice* and to the actual structure of practice.

I don't mean to ascribe to reductionists the doctrine that the "higher-level" laws could be arrived at in the first place by deduction from the "lower-level" laws. Reductionist philosophers would very likely have said that firing the naturalist was a misapplication of their doctrines, and that neglect of direct investigation at "the level of sociology" would also be a misapplication of their doctrine. What I think goes on is this: Their claim that higher-level laws are deducible from lower-level laws and *therefore* higher-level laws are *explainable* by lower-level laws involves a mistake (in fact, two mistakes). It involves neglect of the *structure* of the higher-level explanations which reductionists never talk about at all, and it involves neglect of the fact that *more than one* higher-level structure can be realized by the lower-level entities (so that what the higher-level laws are cannot be deduced from *just* the laws obeyed by the "lower-level" entities). Neglect of the "higher-level" sciences themselves seems to me to be the inevitable corollary of neglecting the structure of the explanations in those sciences.

2. Turing Machines

In previous papers (1960; 1965; 1967), I have argued for the hypothesis that (1) a whole human being is a Turing machine, and (2) that psychological states of a human being are Turing machine states or disjunctions of Turing machine states. In this section I want to argue that this point of view was essentially wrong, and that I was too much in the grip of the reductionist outlook just described.

Let me begin with a technical difficulty. A *state* of a Turing machine is described in such a way that the machine can be in exactly one state at a time. Moreover, memory and learning are not represented in the Turing machine model as acquisition of new states, but as acquisition of new information printed on the machine's tape. Thus if human beings have any states at all which resemble Turing machine states, those states must (1) be states the human can be in at any time, independently of learning and memory; and (2) be *total* instantaneous states of the human being—states which determine, together with learning and memory, what the next state will be, as well as totally specifying the present condition of the human being ("totally" from the standpoint of psychological theory, that means).

These characteristics already establish that *no* psychological state in any customary sense can be a Turing machine state.[1] Take a particular kind of pain to be a "psychological state". If I *am* a Turing machine, then my present "state" must determine not only whether I am having that particular kind of pain, but also whether I am about to say "three", whether I am hearing a shrill whine, etc. So the psychological state in question (the pain) is not the same as my "state" in the sense of *machine state,* although it is possible (so far) that my machine state *determines* my psychological state. Moreover, *no* psychological theory would pretend that having a pain of a particular kind, being about to say "three", or hearing a shrill whine, etc. all belong to *one* psychological state, although there could well be a machine state characterized by the fact that I was in it only when simultaneously having that pain, being about to say "three", hearing a shrill whine, etc. So, even if I am a Turing machine, my machine states are *not* the same as my psychological states. My description *qua* Turing machine (machine table) and my description *qua* human being (*via* a psychological theory) are descriptions at two totally different levels of organization.

So far it is still possible that a psychological state is a large disjunction (practically speaking, an almost infinite disjunction) of machine states, although no *single* machine state is a psychological state. But this is very unlikely when we move away from states like "pain" (which are almost *biological*) to states like "jealousy" or "love" or "competitiveness". Being jealous is certainly not an *instantaneous* state, and it depends on a great deal of information and on many learned facts and habits. But Turing machine states are instantaneous and are independent of learning and memory. That is, learning and memory may cause a Turing machine to go into a state, but the identity of the state does not depend on

1. For an exposition of Turing machines, see Davis (1958); there is also an attractive little monograph by Trachtenbrot on the subject.

learning and memory, whereas, no matter what state I am in, identifying that state as "being jealous of X's regard for Y" involves specifying that I have learned that X and Y are persons and a good deal about social relations among persons. Thus jealousy can neither be a machine state nor a disjunction of machine states.

One might attempt to modify the theory by saying that being jealous equals either being in State A and having tape c_1 *or* being in State A and having tape c_2 *or* . . . being in State B and having tape d_1 *or* being in State B and having tape d_2 *or* . . . being in State Z and having tape y_1 . . . or being in State Z and having tape y_n — i.e., define a psychological state as a disjunction, the individual disjuncts being not Turing machine states, as before, but conjunctions of a machine state and a tape (i.e., a total description of the content of the memory bank). Besides the fact that such a description would be literally infinite, the theory is now without content, for the original purpose was to use the machine table as a model of a psychological theory, whereas it is now clear that the machine table description, although different from the description at the elementary particle level, is as removed from the description *via* a psychological theory as the physico-chemical description is.

I now want to make a different point about the Turing machine model. The laws of psychology, if there *are* "laws of psychology", need not even be *compatible* with the Turing machine model, or with the physico-chemical description, except in a very attenuated sense. And I don't have in mind any version of psychism.

As an example, consider the laws stated by Hull in his famous theory of rote learning. Those laws specify an analytical relationship between *continuous* variables. Since a Turing machine is wholly discrete, those laws are formally incompatible with the Turing machine model. Yet they could perfectly well be correct.

The reader may at this point feel annoyed, and want to retort: Hull's laws, if "correct", are correct only with a certain accuracy, to a certain approximation. And the *exact* law has to be compatible with the Turing machine model, if I am a Turing machine, or with the laws of physics, if materialism is true. But there are two separate and distinct elements to this retort. (1) Hull's laws are "correct" only to a certain accuracy. True. And the statement "Hull's laws are correct to within measurement error" is perfectly compatible with the Turing machine model, with the physicalist model, etc. It is in this attenuated sense that the laws of any higher-level discipline have to be compatible with the laws of physics: It has to be compatible with the laws of physics that the higher-level laws could be true *to within the required accuracy.* But the *model* associated with the higher-level laws need not *at all* be compatible with the model associated with the lower-level laws. Another way of putting the same point is this. Let L be the higher-level laws as normally stated in psychology texts (or texts of political economy, or whatever). Let L* be the statement "L is approximately correct". Then it is only L* that has to be compatible with the laws of physics, not L. (2) The *exact* law has to be compatible with the Turing machine model (or anyway the laws of physics). False. There need not *be* any "exact" law—any law *more* exact than Hull's—at the psychological level. *In each individual case of rote learning,* the exact *description* of what happened has to be compatible with the laws of physics. But the best statement one can make in the general case, at the psychological level of organization, may well be that Hull's laws are correct to within random errors whose explanation is beneath the level of *psychology.*

The general picture, it seems to me, is this: Each science describes a set of structures in a somewhat idealized way. It is sometimes believed that a non-idealized description, an "exact" description, is possible "in principle" at the level of physics; be that as it may, there is not the slightest reason to believe that it is possible at the level of psychology or sociology. The difference is this: If a model of a physical structure is not perfect, we can argue that it is the business of *physics* to account for the inaccuracies. But if a model of a social structure is not perfect, if there are unsystematic errors in its application, the business of accounting for those errors may or may not be the business of *social science.* If a model of, say, memory in functional terms (e.g., a flow chart for an algorithm) fails to account for certain memory losses, that may be because a better psychological theory of memory (different flow chart) is called for, or because on certain occasions memory losses are to be accounted for by biology (an accident in the brain, say) rather than by psychology.

If this picture is correct, then "oversimplified" models may well be the best possible at the "higher" levels. And the relationship to physics is just this: It is compatible with physics that the "good" models on the higher levels should be *approximately* realized by systems having the physical constitution that human beings actually have.

At this point, I should like to discuss an argument proposed by Hubert Dreyfus. Dreyfus believes that the functional organization of the brain is not correctly represented by the model of a digital computer. As an alternative he has suggested that the brain may function more like an *analog* computer (or a complicated system of analog computers). One kind of analog computer mentioned by Dreyfus is the following: Construct a map of the railway system of the U.S. made out of *string* (the strings represent the railroad lines, the knots represent the junctions). Then to find the shortest path between any two junctions—say, Miami and Las Vegas—just pick up the map by the two corresponding knots and pull the two knots away from each other until a string between them becomes straight. That string will represent the shortest path.

When Dreyfus advanced this in conversation, I rejected it on the following grounds: I said that the physical analog computer (the map) really was a digital computer, or could be treated as one, on the grounds that (1) matter is atomic; (2) one could treat the molecules of which the string consists as gears which are capable of assuming a discrete number of positions vis-à-vis adjacent molecules. Of course, this only says that the analog computer can be well approximated by a system which is digital. What I overlooked is that the atomic structure of the string is *irrelevant* to the working of the analog computer. Worse, I had to invent a microstructure which is just as fictitious as the idealization of a continuous string of constant length (the idea of treating molecules as gears) in order to carry through the re-description of the analog device as a digital device. The difference between my idealization (strings of gears) and the classical idealization (continuous strings) is that the classical idealization is relevant to the functioning of the device *as* an analog computer (the device works *because* the strings *are—approximately—*continuous strings), while my idealization is *irrelevant* to the description of the system on *any* level.

3. Psychology

The previous considerations show that the Turing machine model need not be taken seriously as a model of the functional organization of the brain. Of course, the brain has digital elements—the yes-no firing of the neurons—but whether the larger organization is correctly represented by something like a flow chart for an algorithm or by something quite different we have no way of knowing right now. And Hull's model for rote learning suggests that some brain processes are best conceptualized in terms of continuous rather than discrete variables.

In the first section of this paper we argued that psychology need not be deducible from the laws describing the functional organization of the human brain, and in the previous section we used a psychological state (jealousy) to illustrate that the Turing machine model *cannot* be correct as a paradigm for psychological theory.

In short, there are two different questions which have got confused in the literature: (1) Is the Turing machine model correct as a model for the functional organization of the human brain? and (2) Is the Turing machine model correct as a model for psychological theory? Only on the reductionist assumption that psychology *is* the description of the functional organization of the brain, or something very close to it, can these two questions be identified.

Our answer to these two questions so far is that (1) there is little evidence that the Turring machine model is correct as a model of the functional organization of the brain; and (2) the Turing machine model *cannot* be correct as a model for psychological theory—i.e., psychological states are not machine states nor are they disjunctions of machine states. But what *is* the nature of psychological states?

The idea of a fixed repertoire of emotions, attitudes, etc., independent of culture is easily seen to be questionable. An attitude that we are very familiar with, for example, is the particular kind of arrogance that one person feels toward other people "because" he does mental work and they do manual work. (The reason I put "because" in shudder quotes is that really the causality is much more complicated—he feels arrogant because his society has successfully won him and millions of other people to the idea that the worker is superior to the extent his work differs from the work of a common laborer and resembles that of a manager, perhaps, or because it has won him and millions of other people to the idea that certain kinds of work are inherently above most people—"they couldn't understand"—etc.). An attitude we find it almost *impossible* to imagine is the following: One person feeling superior to others because the first person cleans latrines and the others do not. This is not the case because people who clean latrines are innately inferior, not because latrine-cleaning is inherently degrading. Given the right social setting, this attitude which we cannot now imagine would be commonplace. Not only the particular attitudes and emotions we feel are culture-bound, but so are the *connections*. For example, in our society, arrogance of mental workers is associated with extreme competitiveness; but in a different society it might be associated with the attitude that one is above competing, while being no less arrogant. This might be a reflection of the difference between living in a society based on competition and living in a society based on a feudal hierarchy.

Anthropological literature is replete with examples that support the idea that emotions and attitudes are culture-dependent. For example, there have existed and still exist cultures in which private property and the division of labor are unknown. An Arunha cannot imagine the precise attitude with which Marie Antoinette said "Let them eat cake", nor the precise attitude of Richard Herrnstein toward the "residue" of low I.Q. people which, he says, is being "precipitated", nor the precise attitude which made me and thousands of other philosophers feel tremendous admiration toward John Austin for distinguishing "Three Ways of Spilling Ink" ("intentionally", "deliberately", and "on purpose"). Nor can we imagine many of the attitudes which Arunha feel, and which are bound up with *their* culture and religion.

This suggests the following thesis: Psychology is as underdetermined by biology as it is by elementary particle physics, and people's psychology is partly a reflection of deeply entrenched societal beliefs. One advantage of this position is that it permits one to deny that there is a fixed human nature at the level of psychology, without denying that *homo sapiens* is a natural kind at the level of *biology.* Marx's thesis that there is no fixed "human nature" which people have under all forms of social organization was not a thesis about "nature versus nurture."

[Because of its length, Section 4 has been omitted from this edition. It is a discussion of the social and political biases built into the concept of intelligence, including the technical concept of IQ.]

5. Psychology Again

If these reflections are right, then it is worthwhile re-examining the nature of psychology. Reductionism asserts that psychology is deducible from the functional organization of the brain. The foregoing remarks suggest that psychology is strongly determined by sociology. Which is right?

The answer, I suspect, is that it depends on what you mean by psychology. Chomsky remarks that "so far as we know, animals learn according to a genetically determined program." While scientific knowledge reflects the development of a *socially* determined program for learning, there can be little doubt that the possible forms of socially determined programs must in some ways be conditioned by the "genetically determined program" and presuppose the existence of this program in the individual members of the society. The determination of the truth of this hypothesis and the spelling out of the details are the tasks of cognitive psychology. Nothing said here is meant to downgrade the importance of that task, or to downgrade the importance of determining the functional organization of the brain. Some parts of psychology are extremely close to biology—Hull's work on rote learning, much of the work on reinforcement, and so on. It is no accident that in my own reductionist papers the example of a psychological state was usually "pain", a state that is strongly biologically marked. On the other hand, if one thinks of the parts of psychology that philosophers and clinical psychologists tend to talk about—psychological theories of aggression, for instance, or theories of intelligence, or theories of sexuality, then it seems to me that one is thinking of the parts of psychology which study mainly societal beliefs and their effects in individual behavior.

That these two sides of psychology are not distinguished very clearly is itself an effect of reductionism. If they were, one might have noticed that none of the literature on intelligence in the past seventy-five years has anything in the slightest to do with illuminating the nature and structure of human cognitive capacity.

8

Intentional Systems

DANIEL C. DENNETT

I WISH TO EXAMINE the concept of a system whose behavior can be—at least sometimes—explained and predicted by relying on ascriptions to the system of beliefs and desires (and hopes, fears, intentions, hunches, . . .). I will call such systems *intentional systems,* and such explanations and predictions intentional explanations and predictions, in virtue of the intentionality of the idioms of belief and desire (and hope, fear, intention, hunch, . . .).

I used to insist on capitalizing "intentional" wherever I meant to be using Brentano's notion of *intentionality,* in order to distinguish this technical term from its cousin, e.g., "an intentional shove", but the technical term is now in much greater currency, and since almost everyone else who uses the term seems content to risk this confusion, I have decided, with some trepidation, to abandon my typographical eccentricity. But let the uninitiated reader beware: "intentional" as it occurs here is *not* the familiar term of layman's English.[1] For me, as for many recent authors, intentionality is primarily a feature of linguistic entities—idioms, contexts—and for my purposes here we can be satisfied that an idiom is intentional if substitution of codesignative terms does not preserve truth or if the "objects" of the idiom are not capturable in the usual way by quantifiers. I discuss this in more detail in *Content and Consciousness* (1969).

1. For a lucid introduction to the concept and its history, see Chisholm (1967).

I

The first point to make about intentional systems[2] as I have just defined them is that a particular thing is an intentional system only in relation to the strategies of someone who is trying to explain and predict its behavior. What this amounts to can best be brought out by example. Consider the case of a chess-playing computer, and the different strategies or stances one might adopt as its opponent in trying to predict its moves. There are three different stances of interest to us. First there is the *design stance.* If one knows exactly how the computer is designed (including the impermanent part of its design: its program), one can predict its designed response to any move one makes by following the computation instructions of the program. One's prediction will come true provided only that the computer performs as designed—that is, without breakdown. Different varieties of design-stance predictions can be discerned, but all of them are alike in relying on the notion of *function,* which is purpose-relative or teleological. That is, a design of a system breaks it up into larger or smaller functional parts, and design-stance predictions are generated by assuming that each functional part will function properly. For instance, the radio engineer's schematic wiring diagrams have symbols for each resistor, capacitor, transistor, etc.—*each with its task to perform*—and he can give a design-stance prediction of the behavior of a circuit by assuming that each element performs its task. Thus one can make design-stance predictions of the computer's response at several different levels of abstraction, depending on whether one's design treats as smallest functional elements strategy-generators and consequence-testers, multipliers and dividers, or transistors and switches. (It should be noted that not all diagrams or pictures are designs in this sense, for a diagram may carry no information about the functions—intended or observed—of the elements it depcits.)

We generally adopt the design stance when making predictions

2. The term "intentional system" occurs in Charles Taylor's *The Explanation of Behaviour* (1964), p. 62, where its use suggests it is co-extensive with the term as I use it, but Taylor does not develop the notion in depth. See, however, his pp. 58 ff. For an introduction to the concept of an intentional system with fewer philosophical presuppositions, see Dennett (1973, 1976).

about the behavior of mechanical objects, e.g., "As the typewriter carriage approaches the margin, a bell will ring (provided the machine is in working order)," and more simply, "Strike the match and it will light." We also often adopt this stance in predictions involving natural objects: "Heavy pruning will stimulate denser foliage and stronger limbs." The essential feature of the design stance is that we make predictions solely from knowledge or assumptions about the system's functional design, irrespective of the physical constitution or condition of the innards of the particular object.

Second, there is what we may call the *physical stance.* From this stance our predictions are based on the actual physical state of the particular object, and are worked out by applying whatever knowledge we have of the laws of nature. It is from this stance alone that we can predict the malfunction of systems (unless, as sometimes happens these days, a system is *designed* to malfunction after a certain time, in which case malfunctioning in one sense becomes a part of its proper functioning). Instances of predictions from the physical stance are common enough: "If you turn on the switch, you'll get a nasty shock," and, "When the snows come, that branch will break right off." One seldom adopts the physical stance in dealing with a computer just because the number of critical variables in the physical constitution of a computer would overwhelm the most prodigious calculator. Significantly, the physical stance is generally reserved for instances of breakdown, where the condition preventing normal operation is generalized and easily locatable, e.g., "Nothing will happen when you type in your questions, because it isn't plugged in," or, "It won't work with all that flood water in it." Attempting to give a physical account or prediction of the chess-playing computer would be a pointless and herculean labor, but it would work in principle. One could predict the response it would make in a chess game by tracing out the effects of the input energies all the way through the computer until once more type was pressed against paper and a response was printed. (Because of the digital nature of computers, quantum-level indeterminacies, if such there be, will cancel out rather than accumulate, unless of course a radium "randomizer" or other amplifier of quantum effects is built into the computer.)

The best chess-playing computers these days are practically

inaccessible to prediction from either the design stance or the physical stance; they have become too complex for even their own designers to view from the design stance. A man's best hope of defeating such a machine in a chess match is to predict its responses by figuring out as best he can what the best or most rational move would be, given the rules and goals of chess. That is, one assumes not only (1) that the machine will function as designed, but (2) that the design is optimal as well, that the computer will "choose" the most rational move. Predictions made on these assumptions may well fail if either assumption proves unwarranted in the particular case, but still this *means* of prediction may impress us as the most fruitful one to adopt in dealing with a particular system. Put another way, when one can no longer hope to beat the machine by utilizing one's knowledge of physics or programming to anticipate its responses, one may still be able to avoid defeat by treating the machine rather like an intelligent human opponent.

We must look more closely at this strategy. A prediction relying on the assumption of the system's rationality is relative to a number of things. First, rationality here so far means nothing more than optimal design relative to a goal or optimally weighted hierarchy of goals (checkmate, winning pieces, defense, etc., in the case of chess) and a set of constraints (the rules and starting position). Prediction itself is, moreover, relative to the nature and extent of the information the system has at the time about the field of endeavor. The question one asks in framing a prediction of this sort is: What is the most rational thing for the computer to do, given goals $x,y,z, \ldots$, constraints $a,b,c, \ldots$ and information (including misinformation, if any) about the present state of affairs $p,q,r, \ldots$? In predicting the computer's response to my chess move, my assessment of the computer's most rational move may depend, for instance, not only on my assumption that the computer has information about the present disposition of all the pieces, but also on whether I believe the computer has information about my inability to see four moves ahead, the relative powers of knights and bishops, and my weakness for knight-bishop exchanges. In the end I may not be able to frame a very good prediction, if I am unable to determine with any accuracy what information and goals the computer has, or if the information and goals I take to be given do not dictate any one best move, or if I simply am not so good as the computer is at generating an optimal move from this given. Such predictions then are very precarious; not only are they relative to a set of postulates about goals, constraints, and information, and not only do they hinge on determining an optimal response in situations where we may have no clear criteria for what is optimal, but also they are vulnerable to short-circuit falsifications that are in principle unpredictable from this stance. Just as design-stance predictions are vulnerable to malfunctions (by depending on the assumption of no malfunction), so these predictions are vulnerable to design weaknesses and lapses (by depending on the assumption of optimal design). It is a measure of the success of contemporary program designers that these precarious predictions turn out to be true with enough regularity to make the method useful.

The dénouement of this extended example should now be obvious: this third stance, with its assumption of rationality, is the *intentional stance;* the predictions one makes from it are intentional predictions; one is viewing the computer as an intentional system. One predicts behavior in such a case by ascribing to the system *the possession of certain information* and supposing it to be *directed by certain goals,* and then by working out the most reasonable or appropriate action on the basis of these ascriptions and suppositions. It is a small step to calling the information possessed the computer's *beliefs,* its goals and subgoals its *desires.* What I mean by saying that this is a small step, is that the notion of possession of information or misinformation is just as intentional a notion as that of belief. The "possession" at issue is hardly the bland and innocent notion of storage one might suppose; it is, and must be, "epistemic possession"—an analogue of belief. Consider: the Frenchman who possesses the *Encyclopedia Britannica* but who knows no English might be said to "possess" the information in it, but if there is such a sense of possession, it is not strong enough to serve as the sort of possession the computer must be supposed to enjoy, relative to the information it *uses* in "choosing" a chess move. In a similar way, the goals of a goal-directed computer must be specified intentionally, just like desires.

Lingering doubts about whether the chess-playing computer *really* has beliefs and desires are misplaced; for the definition of intentional systems I have given does not say that intentional systems *really* have beliefs and desires, but that one can explain and predict their behavior by *ascribing* beliefs and desires to them, and whether one calls what one ascribes to the computer beliefs or belief-analogues or information complexes or intentional whatnots makes no difference to the nature of the calculation one makes on the basis of the ascriptions. One will arrive at the same predictions whether one forthrightly thinks in terms of the computer's beliefs and desires, or in terms of the computer's information-store and goal-specifications. The inescapable and interesting fact is that for the best chess-playing computers of today, intentional explanation and prediction of their behavior is not only common, but works when no other sort of prediction of their behavior is manageable. We do quite successfully treat these computers as intentional systems, and we do this independently of any considerations about what substance they are composed of, their origin, their position or lack of position in the community of moral agents, their consciousness or self-consciousness, or the determinacy or indeterminacy of their operations. The decision to adopt the strategy is pragmatic, and is not intrinsically right or wrong. One can always refuse to adopt the intentional stance toward the computer, and accept its checkmates. One can switch stances at will without involving oneself in any inconsistencies or inhumanities, adopting the intentional stance in one's role as opponent, the design stance in one's role as redesigner, and the physical stance in one's role as repairman.

This celebration of our chess-playing computer is not intended to imply that it is a completely adequate model or simulation of Mind, or intelligent human or animal activity; nor am I saying that the attitude we adopt toward this computer is precisely the same that we adopt toward a creature we deem to be conscious and rational. All that has been claimed is that on occasion, a purely physical system can be so complex, and yet so organized, that we find it convenient, explanatory, pragmatically necessary for prediction, to treat it as if it had beliefs and desires and was rational. The chess-playing computer is just that, a machine for playing chess, which no man or animal is; and hence its "rationality" is pinched and artificial.

Perhaps we could straightforwardly expand the chess-playing computer into a more faithful model of human rationality, and perhaps not. I prefer to pursue a more fundamental line of inquiry first.

When should we expect the tactic of adopting the intentional stance to pay off? Whenever we have reason to suppose the assumption of optimal design is warranted, and doubt the practicality of prediction from the design or physical stance. Suppose we travel to a distant planet and find it inhabited by things moving about its surface, multiplying, decaying, apparently reacting to events in the environment, but otherwise as unlike human beings as you please. Can we make intentional predictions and explanations of their behavior? If we have reason to suppose that a process of natural selection has been in effect, then we can be assured that the populations we observe have been selected in virtue of their design: they will respond to at least some of the more common event-types in this environment in ways that are normally appropriate—that is, conducive to propagation of the species.[3] Once we have tentatively identified the perils and succors of the environment (relative to the constitution of the inhabitants, not ours), we shall be able to estimate which goals and which weighting of goals will be optimal relative to the creatures' *needs* (for survival and propagation), which sorts of information about the environment will be *useful* in guiding goal-directed activity, and which activities will be appropriate given the environmental circumstances. Having doped out these conditions (which will always be subject to revision) we can proceed at once to ascribe beliefs and desires to the creatures. Their behavior will "manifest" their beliefs by being seen as the actions which, given the creatures' desires, would be appropriate to such beliefs as would be appropriate to the environmental stimulation. Desires, in turn, will be "manifested" in behavior as those appropriate desires (given the needs of the creature) to which the actions of the creature would be appropriate, given the creature's beliefs. The circularity of these interlocking specifications is no accident. Ascriptions of beliefs and desires must be interdependent, and the only points of anchorage are the demonstrable needs for survival,

---

3. Note that what is *directly* selected, the gene, is a diagram and not a design; it is selected, however, because it happens to ensure that its bearer has a certain (functional) design. This was pointed out to me by Woodruff.

the regularities of behavior, and the assumption, grounded in faith in natural selection, of optimal design. Once one has ascribed beliefs and desires, however, one can at once set about predicting behavior on their basis, and if evolution has done its job—as it must over the long run—our predictions will be reliable enough to be useful.

It might at first seem that this tactic unjustifiably imposes human categories and attributes (belief, desire, and so forth) on these alien entities. It is a sort of anthropomorphizing, to be sure, but it is conceptually innocent anthropomorphizing. We do not have to suppose these creatures share with us any peculiarly human inclinations, attitudes, hopes, foibles, pleasures, or outlooks; their actions may not include running, jumping, hiding, eating, sleeping, listening, or copulating. All we transport from our world to theirs are the categories of rationality, perception (information input by some "sense" modality or modalities—perhaps radar or cosmic radiation), and action. The question of whether we can expect them to share any of our beliefs or desires is tricky, but there are a few points that can be made at this time; in virtue of their rationality they can be supposed to share our belief in logical truths,[4] and we cannot suppose that they normally desire their own destruction, for instance.

II

When one deals with a system—be it man, machine, or alien creature—by explaining and predicting its behavior by citing its beliefs and desires, one has what might be called a "theory of behavior" for the system. Let us see how such intentional theories of behavior relate to other putative theories of behavior.

One fact so obvious that it is easily overlooked is that our "common-sense" explanations and predictions of the behavior of both men and animals are intentional. We start by assuming rationality. We do not *expect* new acquaintances to react irrationally to particular topics or eventualities, but when they do we learn to adjust our strategies accordingly, just as, with a chess-

---

4. Cf. Quine's argument about the necessity of "discovering" our logical connectives in any language we can translate, in *Word and Object* (1960), section 13. More will be said below in defense of this.

playing computer, one sets out with a high regard for its rationality and adjusts one's estimate downward wherever performance reveals flaws. The presumption of rationality is so strongly entrenched in our inference habits that when our predictions prove false, we at first cast about for adjustments in the information-possession conditions (he must not have heard, he must not know English, he must not have seen x, been aware that y, etc.) or goal weightings, before questioning the rationality of the system as a whole. In extreme cases personalities may prove to be so unpredictable from the intentional stance that we abandon it, and if we have accumulated a lot of evidence in the meanwhile about the nature of response patterns in the individual, we may find that a species of design stance can be effectively adopted. This is the fundamentally different attitude we occasionally adopt toward the insane. To watch an asylum attendant manipulate an obsessively countersuggestive patient, for instance, is to watch something radically unlike normal interpersonal relations.

Our prediction of animal behavior by "common sense" is also intentional. Whether or not sentimental folk go overboard when they talk to their dogs or fill their cats' heads with schemes and worries, even the most hardboiled among us predict animals' behavior intentionally. If we observe a mouse in a situation where it can see a cat waiting at one mousehole and cheese at another, we know which way the mouse will go, providing it is not deranged; our prediction is not based on our familiarity with maze-experiments or any assumptions about the sort of special training the mouse has been through. We suppose the mouse can see the cat and the cheese, and hence has beliefs (belief-analogues, intentional whatnots) to the effect that there is a cat to the left, cheese to the right, and we ascribe to the mouse also the desire to eat the cheese and the desire to avoid the cat (subsumed, appropriately enough, under the more general desires to eat and to avoid peril); so we predict that the mouse will do what is appropriate to such beliefs and desires, namely, go to the right in order to get the cheese and avoid the cat. Whatever academic allegiances or theoretical predilections we may have, we would be astonished if, in the general run, mice and other animals falsified such intentional predictions of their behavior. Indeed, experimental psychologists of every school would have a hard time devising experimental situations to support their various theories without the help of their intentional expectations of how the test animals will respond to circumstances.

Earlier I alleged that even creatures from another planet would share with us our beliefs in logical truths; light can be shed on this claim by asking whether mice and other animals, in virtue of being intentional systems, also believe the truths of logic. There is something bizarre in the picture of a dog or mouse cogitating a list of tautologies, but we can avoid that picture. The assumption that something is an intentional system is the assumption that it is rational; that is, one gets nowhere with the assumption that entity *x* has beliefs *p,q,r,* . . . unless one also supposes that *x* believes what follows from *p,q,r,* . . . ; otherwise there is no way of ruling out the prediction that *x* will, in the face of its beliefs *p,q,r,* . . . do something utterly stupid, and, if we cannot rule out *that* prediction, we will have acquired no predictive power at all. So whether or not the animal is said to *believe* the *truths* of logic, it must be supposed to *follow* the *rules* of logic. Surely our mouse follows or believes in *modus ponens,* for we ascribed to it the beliefs: (a) *there is a cat to the left,* and (b) *if there is a cat to the left, I had better not go left,* and our prediction relied on the mouse's ability to get to the conclusion. In general there is a trade-off between rules and truths; we can suppose *x* to have an inference rule taking *A* to *B* or we can give *x* the belief in the "theorem": *if A then B.* As far as our predictions are concerned, we are free to ascribe to the mouse either a few inference rules and belief in many logical propositions, or many inference rules and few if any logical beliefs.[5] We can even take a patently nonlogical belief like (b) and recast it as an inference rule taking (a) to the desired conclusion.

Will all logical truths appear among the beliefs of any intentional system? If the system were ideally or perfectly rational, all logical truths would appear, but any actual intentional system will be imperfect, and so not all logical truths must be ascribed as beliefs

5. Accepting the argument of Lewis Carroll, in "What the Tortoise Said to Achilles" (1895; reprinted in Copi and Gould, 1964), we cannot allow all the rules for a system to be replaced by beliefs, for this would generate an infinite and unproductive nesting of distinct beliefs about what can be inferred from what.

to any system. Moreover, not all the inference rules of an actual intentional system may be valid; not all its inference-licensing beliefs may be truths of logic. Experience may indicate where the shortcomings lie in any particular system. If we found an imperfectly rational creature whose allegiance to *modus ponens,* say, varied with the subject matter, we could characterize that by excluding *modus ponens* as a rule and ascribing in its stead a set of nonlogical inference rules covering the *modus ponens* step for each subject matter where the rule was followed. Not surprisingly, as we discover more and more imperfections (as we banish more and more logical truths from the creature's beliefs), our efforts at intentional prediction become more and more cumbersome and undecidable, for we can no longer count on the beliefs, desires, and actions going together that *ought* to go together. Eventually we end up, following this process, by predicting from the design stance; we end up, that is, dropping the assumption of rationality.[6]

This migration from common-sense intentional explanations and predictions to more reliable design-stance explanations and predictions that is forced on us when we discover that our subjects are imperfectly rational is, independently of any such discovery, the proper direction for theory builders to take whenever possible. In the end, we want to be able to explain the intelligence of man, or beast, in terms of his design, and this in turn in terms of the natural selection of this design; so whenever we stop in our explanations at the intentional level we have left over an unexplained instance of intelligence or rationality. This comes out vividly if we look at theory building from the vantage point of economics.

Any time a theory builder proposes to call any event, state, structure, etc., in any system (say the brain of an organism) a *signal* or *message* or *command* or otherwise endows it with content, he *takes out a loan* of intelligence. He implicitly posits along with his signals, messages, or commands, something that can serve as a signal-*reader,* message-*understander,* or *commander,* else

6. This paragraph owes much to discussion with John Vickers, whose paper "Judgment and Belief" (1969) goes beyond the remarks here by considering the problems of the relative strength or weighting of beliefs and desires.

his "signals" will be for naught, will decay unreceived, uncomprehended. This loan must be repaid eventually by finding and analyzing away these readers or comprehenders; for, failing this, the theory will have among its elements unanalyzed man-analogues endowed with enough intelligence to read the signals, etc., and thus the theory will *postpone* answering the major question: what makes for intelligence? The intentionality of all such talk of signals and commands reminds us that rationality is being taken for granted, and in this way shows us where a theory is incomplete. It is this feature that, to my mind, puts a premium on the yet unfinished task of devising a rigorous definition of intentionality, for if we can lay claim to a purely formal criterion of intentional discourse, we will have what amounts to a medium of exchange for assessing theories of behavior. Intentionality *abstracts* from the inessential details of the various forms intelligence-loans can take (e.g., signal-readers, volition-emitters, librarians in the corridors of memory, egos and superegos) and serves as a reliable means of detecting exactly where a theory is *in the red* relative to the task of explaining intelligence; wherever a theory relies on a formulation bearing the logical marks of intentionality, there a little man is concealed.

This insufficiency of intentional explanation from the point of view of psychology has been widely felt and as widely misconceived. The most influential misgivings, expressed in the behaviorism of Skinner and Quine, can be succinctly characterized in terms of our economic metaphor. Skinner's and Quine's adamant prohibitions of intentional idioms at all levels of theory is the analogue of rock-ribbed New England conservatism: no deficit spending when building a theory! In Quine's case, the abhorrence of loans is due mainly to his fear that they can never be repaid, whereas Skinner stresses rather that what is borrowed is worthless to begin with. Skinner's suspicion is that intentionally couched claims are empirically vacuous, in the sense that they are altogether too easy to accommodate to the data, like the *virtus dormitiva* Molière's doctor ascribes to the sleeping powder. Questions can be begged on a temporary basis, however, permitting a mode of prediction and explanation not totally vacuous. Consider the following intentional prediction: if I were to ask a thousand American mathematicians how much seven times five is, more than nine hundred would respond by saying that it was thirty-five. (I have allowed for a few to mis-hear my question, a few others to be obstreperous, a few to make slips of the tongue.) If you doubt the prediction, you can test it; I would bet good money on it. It seems to have empirical content because it can, in a fashion, be tested, and yet it is unsatisfactory as a prediction of an empirical theory of psychology. It works, of course, because of the contingent, empirical—but evolution-guaranteed—fact that men in general are well enough designed both to get the answer right and to want to get it right. It will hold with as few exceptions for any group of Martians with whom we are able to converse, for it is not a prediction just of *human* psychology, but of the "psychology" of intentional systems generally.

Deciding on the basis of available empirical evidence that something is a piece of copper or a lichen permits one to make predictions based on the empirical theories dealing with copper and lichens, but deciding on the basis of available evidence that something is (may be treated as) an intentional system permits predictions having a normative or logical basis rather than an empirical one, and hence the success of an intentional prediction, based as it is on no particular picture of the system's design, cannot be construed to confirm or disconfirm any particular pictures of the system's design.

Skinner's reaction to this has been to try to frame predictions purely in non-intentional language, by predicting bodily responses to physical stimuli, but to date this has not provided him with the alternative mode of prediction and explanation he has sought, as perhaps an extremely cursory review can indicate. To provide a setting for nonintentional prediction of behavior, he invented the Skinner box, in which the rewarded behavior of the occupant—say, a rat—is a highly restricted and stereotypic bodily motion—usually pressing a bar with the front paws.

The claim that is then made is that once the animal has been trained, a law-like relationship is discovered to hold between non-intentionally characterized events: controlling stimuli and bar-pressing responses. A regularity is discovered to hold, to be sure, but the fact that it is between non-intentionally defined events is due to a property of the Skinner box and not of the occupant. For let us turn our prediction about mathematicians into a

Skinnerian prediction: strap a mathematician in a Skinner box so he can move only his head; display in front of him a card on which appear the marks: "How much is seven times five?"; move into the range of his head-motions two buttons, over one of which is the mark "35" and over the other "34"; place electrodes on the soles of his feet and give him a few quick shocks; the controlling stimulus is then to be the sound: "Answer now!" I predict that in a statistically significant number of cases, even *before* training trials to condition the man to press button "35" with his forehead, he will do this when given the controlling stimulus. Is this a satisfactory scientific prediction just because it eschews the intentional vocabulary? No, it is an intentional prediction disguised by so restricting the environment that only one bodily motion is available to fulfill the intentional *action* that anyone would prescribe as appropriate to the circumstances of perception, belief, desire. That it is action, not merely motion, that is predicted can also be seen in the case of subjects less intelligent than mathematicians. Suppose a mouse were trained, in a Skinner box with a food reward, to take exactly four steps forward and press a bar with its nose; if Skinner's laws truly held between stimuli and responses defined in terms of bodily motion, were we to move the bar an inch farther away, so four steps did not reach it, Skinner would have to predict that the mouse would jab its nose into the empty air rather than take a fifth step.

A variation of Skinnerian theory designed to meet this objection acknowledges that the trained response one predicts is not truly captured in a description of skeletal motion alone, but rather in a description of an environmental effect achieved: the bar going down, the "35" button being depressed. This will also not do. Suppose we could in fact train a man or animal to achieve an environmental effect, as this theory proposes. Suppose, for instance, we train a man to push a button under the longer of two displays, such as drawings or simple designs, that is, we reward him when he pushes the button under the longer of two pictures of pencils, or cigars, etc. The miraculous consequence of this theory, were it correct, would be that if, after training him on simple views, we were to present him with the Müller-Lyer arrow-head illusion, he would be immune to it, for *ex hypothesi* he has been trained to achieve an *actual* environmental effect (choosing the display that *is* longer), not a *perceived* or *believed* environmental effect (choosing the display that *seems* longer). The reliable prediction, again, is the intentional one.[7]

Skinner's experimental design is supposed to eliminate the intentional, but it merely masks it. Skinner's non-intentional predictions work to the extent they do, not because Skinner has truly found nonintentional behavioral laws, but because the highly reliable intentional predictions underlying his experimental situations (the rat desires food and believes it will get food by pressing the bar—something for which it has been given good evidence—so it will press the bar) are disguised by leaving virtually no room in the environment for more than one bodily motion to be the appropriate action and by leaving virtually no room in the environment for discrepancy to arise between the subject's beliefs and the reality.

Where, then, should we look for a satisfactory theory of behavior? Intentional theory is vacuous as psychology because it presupposes and does not explain rationality or intelligence. The apparent successes of Skinnerian behaviorism, however, rely on hidden intentional predictions. Skinner is right in recognizing that intentionality can be no *foundation* for psychology, and right also to look for purely mechanistic regularities in the activities of his subjects, but there is little reason to suppose they will lie on the surface in gross behavior—except, as we have seen, when we put an artificial straitjacket on an intentional regularity. Rather, we will find whatever mechanistic regularities there are in the functioning of internal systems whose design approaches the optimal (relative to some ends). In seeking knowledge of internal design our most promising tactic is to take out intelligence-loans, endow peripheral and internal events with content, and then look for mechanisms that will function appropriately with such "messages" so that we can pay back the loans. This tactic is hardly untried. Research in artificial intelligence, which has produced, among other things, the chess-playing computer, proceeds by working from an intentionally characterized problem (how to get the computer to consider the right sorts of information, make the right decisions)

7. R. L. Gregory (1966, p. 137) reports that pigeons and fish given just this training are, not surprisingly, susceptible to visual illusions of length.

to a design-stance solution—an approximation of optimal design. Psychophysicists and neurophysiologists who routinely describe events in terms of the transmission of information within the nervous system are similarly borrowing intentional capital—even if they are often inclined to ignore or disavow their debts.

Finally, it should not be supposed that, just because intentional theory is vacuous as psychology, in virtue of its assumption of rationality, it is vacuous from all points of view. Game theory, for example, is inescapably intentional,[8] but as a formal normative theory and not a psychology this is nothing amiss. Game-theoretical predictions applied to human subjects achieve their accuracy in virtue of the evolutionary guarantee that man is well designed as a game player, a special case of rationality. Similarly, economics, the social science of greatest predictive power today, is not a psychological theory and presupposes what psychology must explain. Economic explanation and prediction is intentional (although some is disguised) and succeeds to the extent that it does because individual men are in general good approximations of the optimal operator in the marketplace.

III

The concept of an intentional system is a relatively uncluttered and unmetaphysical notion, abstracted as it is from questions of the composition, constitution, consciousness, morality, or divinity of the entities falling under it. Thus, for example, it is much easier to decide whether a machine can be an intentional system than it is to decide whether a machine can *really* think, or be conscious, or morally responsible. This simplicity makes it ideal as a source of order and organization in philosophical analyses of "mental" concepts. Whatever else a person might be—embodied mind or soul, self-conscious moral agent, "emergent" form of intelligence— he is an intentional system, and whatever follows just from being an intentional system is thus true of a person. It is interesting to see just how much of what we hold to be the case about persons or their minds follows directly from their being intentional systems. To revert for a moment to the economic metaphor, the

8. Hintikka notes in passing that game theory is like his epistemic logic in assuming rationality: *Knowledge and Belief* (1962, p. 38).

guiding or challenging question that defines work in the philosophy of mind is this: are there mental treasures that cannot be purchased with intentional coin? If not, a considerable unification of science can be foreseen in outline. Of special importance for such an examination is the subclass of intentional systems that have language, that can communicate; for these provide a framework for a theory of consciousness. In *Content and Consciousness,* part II, and in *Brainstorms,* parts III and IV, I have attempted to elaborate such a theory; here I would like to consider its implications for the analysis of the concept of belief. What will be true of human believers just in virtue of their being intentional systems with the capacity to communicate?

Just as not all intentional systems currently known to us can fly or swim, so not all intentional systems can talk, but those which can do this raise special problems and opportunities when we come to ascribe beliefs and desires to them. That is a massive understatement; without the talking intentional systems, of course, there would be no ascribing beliefs, no theorizing, no assuming rationality, no predicting. The capacity for language is without doubt the crowning achievement of evolution, an achievement that feeds on itself to produce ever more versatile and subtle rational systems, but still it can be looked at as an adaptation which is subject to the same conditions of environmental utility as any other behavioral talent. When it is looked at in this way several striking facts emerge. One of the most pervasive features of evolutionary histories is the interdependence of distinct organs and capacities in a species. Advanced eyes and other distance receptors are of no utility to an organism unless it develops advanced means of locomotion; the talents of a predator will not accrue to a species that does not evolve a carnivore's digestive system. The capacities of belief and communication have prerequisites of their own. We have already seen that there is no point in ascribing beliefs to a system unless the beliefs ascribed are in general appropriate to the environment, and the system responds appropriately to the beliefs. An eccentric expression of this would be: the capacity to believe would have no survival value unless it were a capacity to believe truths. What is eccentric and potentially misleading about this is that it hints at the picture of a species "trying on" a faculty giving rise to beliefs most of which were false, having its inutility demonstrated, and abandoning it. A species might "experiment" by mutation in any number of inefficacious systems, but none of these systems would deserve to be called belief systems precisely because of their defects, their nonrationality, and hence a false belief system is a conceptual impossibility. To borrow an example from a short story by MacDonald Harris, a soluble fish is an evolutionary impossibility, but a system for false beliefs cannot even be given a coherent description. The same evolutionary bias in favor of truth prunes the capacity to communicate as it develops; a capacity for false communication would not be a capacity for communication at all, but just an emission proclivity of no systematic value to the species. The faculty of communication would not gain ground in evolution unless it was by and large the faculty of transmitting true beliefs, which means only: the faculty of altering other members of the species in the direction of more optimal design.

This provides a foundation for explaining a feature of belief that philosophers have recently been at some pains to account for. (see, e.g., Griffiths, 1962–63, and Mayo, 1964). The concept of belief seems to have a normative cast to it that is most difficult to capture. One way of putting it might be that an avowal like "I believe that p" seems to imply in some fashion: "One ought to believe that p." This way of putting it has flaws, however, for we must then account for the fact that "I believe that p" seems to have normative force that "He believes that p", said of me, does not. Moreover, saying that one ought to believe this or that suggests that belief is voluntary, a view with notorious difficulties. (see, e.g., Price, 1954). So long as one tries to capture the normative element by expressing it in the form of moral or pragmatic injunctions to believers, such as "one ought to believe the truth" and "one ought to act in accordance with one's beliefs", dilemmas arise. How, for instance, is one to follow the advice to believe the truth? Could one abandon one's sloppy habit of believing falsehoods? If the advice is taken to mean: believe only what you have convincing evidence for, it is the vacuous advice: believe only what you believe to be true. If alternatively it is taken to mean: believe only what is in fact the truth, it is an injunction we are powerless to obey.

The normative element of belief finds its home not in such

injunctions but in the preconditions for the ascription of belief, what Phillips Griffiths calls "the general conditions for the possibility of application of the concept". For the concept of belief to find application, two conditions, we have seen, must be met: (1) In general, normally, more often than not, if x believes p, p is true. (2) In general, normally, more often than not, if x avows that p, he believes p [and, by (1), p is true]. Were these conditions not met, we would not have rational, communicating systems; we would not have believers or belief-avowers. The norm for belief is evidential well-foundedness (assuring truth in the long run), and the norm for avowal of belief is accuracy (which includes sincerity). These two norms determine pragmatic implications of our utterances. If I assert that p (or that I believe that p—it makes no difference), I assume the burden of defending my assertion on two fronts: I can be asked for evidence for the truth of p, and I can be asked for behavioral evidence that I do in fact believe p. (cf. Collins, 1969). I do not need to examine my own behavior in order to be in a position to avow my belief that p, but if my sincerity or self-knowledge is challenged, this is where I must turn to defend my assertion. But again, challenges on either point must be the exception rather than the rule if belief is to have a place among our concepts.

Another way of looking at the importance of this predominance of the normal is to consider the well-known circle of implications between beliefs and desires (or intentions) that prevent non-intentional behavioral definitions of intentional terms. A man's standing under a tree is a behavioral indicator of his belief that it is raining, but only on the assumption that he desires to stay dry, and if we then look for evidence that he wants to stay dry, his standing under the tree will do, but only on the assumption that he believes the tree will shelter him; if we ask him if he believes the tree will shelter him, his positive response is confirming evidence only on the assumption that he desires to tell us the truth, and so forth *ad infinitum*. It is this apparently vicious circle that turned Quine against the intentional (and foiled Tolman's efforts at operational definition of intentional terms), but if it is true that in any particular case a man's saying that p is evidence of his belief only conditionally, we can be assured that in the long run and in general the circle is broken; a man's assertions are, unconditionally, indicative of his beliefs, as are his actions in general. We get around the "privacy" of beliefs and desires by recognizing that in general anyone's beliefs and desires must be those he "ought to have" given the circumstances.

These two interdependent norms of belief, one favoring the truth and rationality of belief, the other favoring accuracy of avowal, normally complement each other, but on occasion can give rise to conflict. This is the "problem of incorrigibility". If rationality is the mother of intention, we still must wean intentional systems from the criteria that give them life, and set them up on their own. Less figuratively, if we are to make use of the concept of an intentional system in particular instances, at some point we must cease *testing* the assumption of the system's rationality, adopt the intentional stance, and grant without further ado that the system is qualified for beliefs and desires. For mute animals—and chess-playing computers—this manifests itself in a tolerance for less than optimal performance. We continue to ascribe beliefs to the mouse, and explain its actions in terms of them, after we have tricked it into some stupid belief. This tolerance has its limits of course, and the less felicitous the behavior—especially the less adaptable the behavior—the more hedged are our ascriptions. For instance, we are inclined to say of the duckling that "imprints" on the first moving thing it sees upon emerging from its shell that it "believes" the thing is its mother, whom it follows around, but we emphasize the scare-quotes around "believes". For intentional systems that can communicate—persons for instance—the tolerance takes the form of the convention that a man is incorrigible or a special authority about his own beliefs. This convention is "justified" by the fact that evolution does guarantee that our second norm is followed. What better source could there be of a system's beliefs than its avowals? Conflict arises, however, whenever a person falls short of perfect rationality, and avows beliefs that either are strongly disconfirmed by the available empirical evidence or are self-contradictory or contradict other avowals he has made. If we lean on the myth that a man is perfectly rational, we must find his avowals less than authoritative: "You *can't* mean—understand—what you're saying!"; if we lean on his "right" as a speaking intentional system to have his word accepted, we grant him an irrational set of beliefs. Neither position provides a stable resting place; for, as we saw earlier, intentional explanation and prediction cannot be accommodated either to breakdown or to less than optimal design, so there is no coherent intentional description of such an impasse.[9]

Can any other considerations be brought to bear in such an instance to provide us with justification for one ascription of beliefs rather than another? Where should one look for such considerations? The phenomenologist will be inclined to suppose that individual introspection will provide us a sort of data not available to the outsider adopting the intentional stance; but how would such data get used? Let the introspector amass as much inside information as you please; he must then communicate it to us, and what are we to make of his communications? We can suppose that they are incorrigible (barring corrigible verbal errors, slips of the tongue, and so forth), but we do not need phenomenology to give us that option, for it amounts to the decision to lean on the accuracy-of-avowal norm at the expense of the rationality norm. If, alternatively, we demand certain standards of consistency and rationality of his utterances before we accept them as authoritative, what standards will we adopt? If we demand perfect rationality, we have simply flown to the other norm at the expense of the norm of accuracy of avowal. If we try to fix minimum standards at something less than perfection, what will guide our choice? Not phenomenological data, for the choice we make will determine what is to count as phenomenological data. Not neurophysiological data either, for whether we interpret a bit of neural structure to be endowed with a particular belief content hinges on our having granted that the neural system under examination has met the standards of rationality for being an intentional system, an assumption jeopardized by the impasse we are trying to resolve. That is, one might have a theory about an individual's

9. Hintikka takes this bull by the horns. His epistemic logic is acknowledged to hold only for the ideally rational believer; were we to apply this logic to persons in the actual world in other than a normative way, thus making its implications *authoritative* about actual belief, the authority of persons would have to go by the board. Thus his rule A.CBB* (*Knowledge and Belief*, pp. 24–26), roughly that if one believes *p*, then one believes that one believes *p*, cannot be understood, as it is tempting to suppose, as a version of the incorrigibility thesis.

neurology that permitted one to "read off" or predict the propositions to which he would assent, but whether one's theory had uncovered his *beliefs*, or merely a set of assent-inducers, would depend on how consistent, reasonable, true we found the set of propositions.

John Vickers has suggested to me a way of looking at this question. Consider a set T of transformations that take beliefs into beliefs. The problem is to determine the set T_s for each intentional system S, so that if we know that S believes p, we will be able to determine other things that S believes by seeing what the transformations of p are for T_s. If S were ideally rational, every valid transformation would be in T_s; S would believe every logical consequence of every belief (and, ideally, S would have no false beliefs). Now we know that no actual intentional system will be ideally rational; so we must suppose any actual system will have a T with less in it. But we also know that, to qualify as an intentional system at all, S must have a T with some integrity; T cannot be empty. What rationale could we have, however, for fixing some set between the extremes and calling it *the* set for belief (for S, for earthlings, or for ten-year-old girls)? This is another way of asking whether we could replace Hintikka's normative theory of belief with an empirical theory of belief, and, if so, what evidence we would use. "Actually," one is tempted to say, "people do believe contradictions on occasion, as their utterances demonstrate; so any adequate logic of belief or analysis of the concept of belief must accommodate this fact." But any attempt to *legitimize* human fallibility in a theory of belief by fixing a permissible level of error would be like adding one more rule to chess: an Official Tolerance Rule to the effect that any game of chess containing no more than k moves that are illegal relative to the other rules of the game is a legal game of chess. Suppose we discovered that, in a particular large population of poor chess-players, each game on average contained three illegal moves undetected by either opponent. Would we claim that these people *actually* play a different game from ours, a game with an Official Tolerance Rule with k fixed at 3? This would be to confuse the norm they follow with what gets by in their world. We could claim in a similar vein that people *actually* believe, say, all synonymous or intentionally isomorphic consequences of their beliefs, but not all their logical consequences, but of course the occasions when a man resists assenting to a logical consequence of some avowal of his are unstable cases; he comes in for criticism and cannot appeal in his own defense to any canon absolving him from believing nonsynonymous consequences. If one wants to get away from norms and predict and explain the "actual, empirical" behavior of the poor chess-players, one stops talking of their *chess moves* and starts talking of their proclivities to move pieces of wood or ivory about on checkered boards; if one wants to predict and explain the "actual, empirical" behavior of believers, one must similarly cease talking of belief, and descend to the design stance or physical stance for one's account.

The concept of an intentional system explicated in these pages is made to bear a heavy load. It has been used here to form a bridge connecting the intentional domain (which includes our "common-sense" world of persons and actions, game theory, and the "neural signals" of the biologist) to the non-intentional domain of the physical sciences. That is a lot to expect of one concept, but nothing less than Brentano himself expected when, in a day of less fragmented science, he proposed intentionality as the mark that sunders the universe in the most fundamental way: dividing the mental from the physical.

Acknowledgment: I am indebted to Peter Woodruff for making extensive improvements in this article prior to its initial publication. Since it appeared, I have found anticipations and developments of similar or supporting themes in a variety of writers, most notably Hempel (1962); Cohen (1950–51, 1955–56); Williams (1970); and Lewis (1974).

9

The Nature and Plausibility of Cognitivism

JOHN HAUGELAND

COGNITIVISM in psychology and philosophy is roughly the position that intelligent behavior can (only) be explained by appeal to internal "cognitive processes," that is, rational thought in a very broad sense. Sections 1 to 5 attempt to explicate in detail the nature of the scientific enterprise that this intuition has inspired. That enterprise is distinctive in at least three ways: It relies on a style of explanation which is different from that of mathematical physics, in such a way that it is not basically concerned with quantitative equational laws; the states and processes with which it deals are interpreted, in the sense that they are regarded as meaningful or representational; and it is not committed to reductionism, but is open to reduction in a form different from that encountered in other sciences. Spelling these points out makes it clear that the Cognitivist study of the mind can be rigorous and empirical, despite its unprecedented theoretical form. The philosophical explication has another advantage as well: It provides a much needed framework for articulating questions about whether the Cognitivist approach is right or wrong. The last three sections take that advantage of the account, and address several such questions, pro and con.

1. Systematic explanation

From time to time, the ills of psychology are laid to a misguided effort to emulate physics and chemistry. Whether the study of people is inherently "humanistic" and "soft" (Hudson, 1972), or whether states described in terms of their significance necessarily escape the net of physical law (Davidson, 1970, 1973a), the implication is that psychology cannot live up to the standards of rigorous science, and perhaps cannot be a science at all. But science itself often leaves behind efforts to say what it can and cannot be. The Cognitive approach to psychology offers, I think, a science of a distinctive form, and thereby sidesteps many philosophical objections—including those born of a dazzled preoccupation with physics. In my first five sections I will try to characterize that form.

Science in general is an endeavor to understand what occurs in the world; hence explanation, which is essentially a means to understanding, has a pivotal importance. Scientific explanations differ from common sense explanations at least in being more explicit, more precise, more general, and more deliberately integrated with one another. Without attempting a full analysis, we can notice several broad characteristics which all scientific explanations share. They depend on specifying a range of features which are exhibited in, or definable for, a variety of concrete situations. They depend on knowing or hypothesizing certain regularities or relationships which always obtain in situations exhibiting the specified features. And they depend on our being able to see (understand), for particular cases, that since the specified features are deployed together in way X, the known regularities or relationships guarantee that Y. We then say that Y has been *explained* through an appeal to (or in terms of) the general regularities and the particular deployment of the features. The regularities and deployment appealed to have been presupposed by the explanation, and not themselves explained—though either might be explained, in turn, through appeal to further presuppositions.

Philosophers have coined the term *deductive-nomological* for explanations in which the presupposed regularities are formulated as laws (Greek: *nomos*), and for which the guarantee that Y will occur is formulated as a deductive argument from the laws plus statements describing the deployment X (Hempel and Oppenheim, 1949). It can be maintained that all scientific explanations are deductive-nomological, though in many cases that requires a counter-intuitive strain on the notion of "law." So to avoid confusion I will introduce some more restricted terminology, and at the same time illustrate several different ways in which the foregoing schematic remarks get fleshed out.

The most familiar scientific explanations come from classical mechanics. The situational features on which they depend include masses, inertial moments, distances, angles, durations, velocities, energies, and so on—all of which are quantitative, measurable parameters. The known regularities or relationships are expressed as equations (algebraic, vectorial, differential, etc.) relating the values of the various parameters in any given situation—e.g., $F = ma = dp/dt$. Usually some of the equations are designated laws and the others definitions, but there's a well known trade-off in which are which. Equations are conveniently manipulable and combinable in ways that preserve equality; that is, other equations can be mathematically derived from them. The standard form of an explanation in mechanics is such a derivation, given specified deployments of masses, forces, and what have you (see Newton's derivations of Kepler's laws). It is the derived equational relationships which are explained (or sometimes the actual values of some of the parameters so related, determined by plugging in the known values of others).

I use *derivational-nomological* for this special case form of deductive-nomological explanation—where the distinction of the special case is that the presupposed regularities are expressed as equational relationships among quantitative parameters, and the deduction is a mathematical derivation of other such equations (and then, perhaps, computing some of the values). Besides mechanics, fields as diverse as optics, thermodynamics, and macroeconomics commonly involve derivational-nomological explanations.

But what is important here is that there are other forms or styles of explanation, even in advanced sciences. I will delineate (only) two such distinct styles, though I will not claim that the distinctions are sharp. The claim is rather that interesting differences can be characterized among prime examples, despite the fact that intermediate cases blur the boundaries. Only one of these further styles is relevant to cognitive psychology; I delineate them both because they are superficially similar, and easily confused. Thus explicitly distinguishing them permits a closer focus on the one we want. These distinctions are independent of anything peculiar to psychology, and I will draw them that way first, to keep separate issues as clear as possible.

Imagine explaining to someone how a fiber optics bundle can take any image that is projected on one end and transmit it to the other end. I think most people would come to understand the phenomenon, given the following points. (If I am right, then readers unfamiliar with fiber optics should nevertheless be able to follow the example): (i) the bundles are composed of many long thin fibers, which are closely packed side by side, and arranged in such a way that each one remains in the same position relative to the others along the whole length of the bundle; (ii) each fiber is a leak-proof conduit for light—that is, whatever light goes in one end of a fiber comes out the other end of the same fiber; (iii) a projected image can be regarded as an array of closely packed dots of light, differing in brightness and color; and (iv) since each end of each fiber is like a dot, projecting an image on one end of the bundle will make the other end light up with dots of the same brightness and color in the same relative positions—thus preserving the image.

Clearly that was not a derivational-nomological explanation. One could, with effort, recast it as a logical deduction, but I think it would lose more prespicacity than it would gain (diagrams would help much more). If we do not try to force it into a preconceived mold of scientific explanations, several distinctive aspects stand out as noteworthy. First, what is explained is a disposition or ability of a kind of object (compare Cummins, 1975). Second, the explanation makes appeals (presuppositions) of two basic sorts: that the kind of object in question has a certain form or structure (compare Putnam, 1975b, 1973), and that whatever is formed or structured in that way has certain dispositions or abilities. (The object is a bundle of "parallel" fibers, and each fiber is able to conduct light without leaking.) Third, any object structured in the presupposed way, out of things with the presupposed abilities, would have the overall ability being explained. That is, it doesn't matter how or why the fibers are arranged as they are, or how or why they conduct light; these are simply presupposed, and they are sufficient to explain the ability to transmit images.

I call explanations of this style *morphological*, where the distinguishing marks of the style are that an ability is explained through appeal to a specified structure and to specified abilities of whatever is so structured. (These specifications implicitly determine the "kind" of object to which the explanation applies). In science, morphological explanations are often called "models" (which in this sense amount to specifications of structure), but that term is both too broad and too narrow for our purposes: Logicians have a different use for it, and few would call the fiber optics account a model.

On the other hand, the account of how DNA can replicate itself *is* called a model—the double-helix model—and it is morphological. Simplistically put, the structure is two adjacent strands of sites, with each site uniquely mated to a complementary one in the other strand. And the sites have the ability to split up with their mates and latch onto an exactly similar new one, selected from a supply which happens to be floating around loose. This process starts at one end of the double strand, and by the time it reaches the other end there are two double strands, each an exact replica of the original. At the opposite extreme of sophistication, an explanation of how cups are able to hold coffee is also morphological. The specified structure is little more than shape, and the specified abilities of what is so structured amount to rigidity, insolubility, and the like.

Now consider a case that is subtly but importantly different: an explanation of how an automobile engine works. As with morphological explanations, this one appeals to a specified structure, and to specified abilities or dispositions of what is so structured. But in addition, and so important as to dominate the account, it requires specification of a complexly organized pattern of interdependent interactions. The various parts of an engine do many different things, so to speak "working together" or "cooperating" in an organized way, to produce an effect quite unlike what any of them could do alone.

I reserve the term *systematic* for explanations of this style, where the distinction from morphological explanation is the additional element of organized cooperative interaction. Strictly, it is again an ability or disposition which gets explained, but the ordinary expression "how it works" often gives a richer feel for what's at stake. A consequence of this definition is that objects with abilities that get systematically explained must be composed of distinct parts, because specifying interactions is crucial to the explanation, and interactions require distinct interactors. Let a *system* be any object with an ability that is explained systematically, and *functional components* be the distinct parts whose interactions are cited in the explanation. In a system, the specified structure is essentially the arrangement of functional components such that they will interact as specified; and the specified abilities of the components are almost entirely the abilities to so interact, in the environment created by their neighboring components. Note that what counts as a system, and as its functional components, is relative to what explanation is being offered. Other examples of systems (realtive to the obvious explanations) are radios, common mousetraps, and (disregarding some messiness) many portions of complex organisms.

Fiber optics bundles and DNA molecules are deceptively similar to systems, because they have clearly distinct components, each of which contributes to the overall ability by performing its own little assigned "job." But the jobs are not interdependent; it is not through cooperative interaction that the image transmission or replication is achieved, but only an orderly summation of the two cents' worth from each separate fiber or site. In an engine, the carburetor, distributor, spark plugs, and so forth, do not each deliver a portion of the engine's turning, in the way that each site or fiber contributes a portion of the replication or image. The job metaphor can be expanded to further illustrate the difference. In old fashioned plantation harvesting, each laborer picked a portion of the crop (say one row), and when each was done, it was all done. But at a bureaucratic corporation like General Motors, comparatively few workers actually assemble automobiles; the others make parts, maintain the factories, come up with new designs, write paychecks, and so on. All of these tasks are prerequisite to continued production, but only indirectly, through a complex pattern of interdependencies. A system is like a bureaucratic corporation, with components playing many different roles, most contributing to the final outcome only indirectly, via the organized interactions.

I have described three different styles of explanation, each of which can be scientifically rigorous and respectable. They are all abstract or formal, in that they all abstract certain features and regularities from a variety of concrete situations, and then show

how the resulting forms make certain properties or events intelligible in all such situations. But they differ notably in the nature of the abstract forms they specify, at least in clear cases. Only the derivational-nomological style puts an explicit emphasis on equations of the sort that we usually associate with scientific laws. But I shall claim that only the systematic style is directly relevant to cognitive psychology. Thus the charge of slavishly imitating mathematical physics does not apply to Cognitivism, and it doesn't matter that quantitative equational laws of behavior seem to be few and far between. Many of the points I have made have been made before (Cummins, 1975; Putnam, 1973; Dennett, 1971; Simon, 1969; Fodor, 1965), but no one, to my knowledge, has previously distinguished morphological and systematic explanation. The importance of that distinction will emerge in section 4.

2. Systematic Reduction

Traditional philosophical concerns for the unity of science and for the metaphysical doctrine of materialism (i.e., that everything is "ultimately just" matter in motion) customarily lead to questions about scientific reduction. Psychological concepts and theories are prime targets for such questions because they are not, at first glance, materialistic. This is not the place for a full discussion of the problem of reduction, but my position about the nature of Cognitivism will have several specific implications which should be pointed out. Some of these derive from the suggestion that Cognitivist explanation is systematic, and those can be considered independently of issues peculiar to psychology.

An aspect common to all the explanations discussed in the last section (indeed, to all explanations) is that they presuppose some things in the course of explaining others. More particularly, they presuppose certain specified general regularities, which are appealed to, but not themselves explained. But such regularities often can be explained, by appeal to others which are more "basic." Such further explanation is *reduction,* though obviously it counts as reduction only relative to the explanations whose presupposed regularities are being explained. This is a fairly broad definition of reduction, and includes cases which aren't very exciting in form. Thus Newton's derivation of Kepler's laws counts as a reduction of Kepler's explanations of planetary positions.

A more famous reduction in classical physics and one with a more interesting form was that of thermodynamics to statistical mechanics. In outline, the values of the parameters occurring in the equations of thermodynamic theory were found (or hypothesized) to correlate with quantities definable statistically in terms of the mechanical parameters of groups of atoms. For example, the absolute temperature of a region was found to be proportional to the average kinetic energy of the atoms in that region. Such correlations are expressed in specific equations called "bridge equations." It then turned out that the laws of thermodynamics could be mathematically derived from the laws of mechanics, some plausible statistical assumptions, and these bridge equations. The effect was to explain the regularities which were presupposed by thermodynamic explanations—in other words, to reduce thermodynamics.

Reductive explanations which explain the equational laws presupposed by derivational-nomological explanations I call *nomological reductions.* Note that the definition refers to the style of explanation being reduced, not to the style of the reducing explanation. The reduction of thermodynamics is often cited as a paradigm of scientific reduction, as if all others should have a similar structure. But a moment's reflection shows that this structure only makes sense if the explanation being reduced is derivational-nomological; otherwise there would be no equational laws to derive, and probably no quantitative parameters to occur in bridge equations.

The regularities presupposed by morphological and systematic explanations are mainly the specified dispositions or abilities of whatever is structured in the specified way. Hence, *morphological* and *systematic reductions* (which are pretty similar) are explanations of those abilities. Such reducing explanations can themselves be of various styles. Thus an explanation of how thin glass fibers can be light conduits would be, I think, borderline between morphological and derivational-nomological. But the explanation of how DNA sites can do the things appealed to in the replication explanation is very complex and, for all I know, is systematic.

In explaining a system, almost all the abilities presupposed are abilities of individual components to interact with certain neighboring components in specified ways. Since intricate, interdependent organization is the hallmark of systems, the abilities demanded of individual components are often enough themselves rather sophisticated and specialized. Conversely, since systems typically have abilities strikingly different from those of any of their separate components, systematic organization is a common source of sophisticated and specialized abilities. These considerations together suggest that very elaborate systems could be expected to have smaller systems as functional components. And frequently they do—sometimes with numerous *levels* of systems within systems. For example, the distributor system of a car is a component in the (larger) ignition system, which, in turn, is a component in the complete engine system. Such a multilevel structure of nested systems is a *systematic hierarchy*. (See Simon, 1969, for further discussion of hierarchical organization.)

So a systematic reduction of the highest system in a systematic hierarchy would involve systematic explanations of the specified interactive abilities of its functional components; and perhaps likewise for reductions of those, and so on. Only at the lowest level would systematic reductions be a different style of explanation (typically morphological; compare the explanation of a crankshaft or piston to that of a coffee cup). Since any scientific reduction is also a scientific explanation, it will explicitly presuppose certain regularities, which can be enquired after in turn. At any given time, however, some regularities will not be explainable. Modern wisdom has it that in the golden age these will include only the "fundamental" laws of physics, all others being reducible to them (perhaps through many stages of reduction). A sequence of reductions taking the presuppositions of an explanation all the way to physics is a *complete reduction.* A complete reduction of pscyhology is one of the traditional dreams of unified science.

A common misconception is that reductions supplant the explanations they reduce—that is, render them superfluous. This is not so. Consider the fiber optics reduction. There could be any number of different explanations for why different kinds of fibers can conduct light; thus glass threads, with variable index of refraction versus radius, would call for a different explanation than hollow silver tubes. But those are irrelevant to the explanation of how the bundle transmits images. The latter takes light conduction in the fibers for granted and goes on to tell us something new.

This something new would be lost if we settled exclusively for explanations of light conductivity; and on the other hand, it would not be lost (given the original morphological explanation) even if light conductivity were totally inexplicable. The two explanations are independent, even though one is of the presuppositions of the other (compare Putnam, 1973).

The main point of this section has been that reductions, like explanations, are not all alike. Hence, the reduction of thermodynamics cannot serve as a universal paradigm, despite its ubiquitous use as an example. In particular, if I am right that Cognitivist explanation is systematic, then any reduction of Cognitivism would be systematic reduction (a point to be taken up further in section 5). This means at least that Cognitivists are not interested in "psycho-physical bridge" equations (*pace* Fodor, 1974), nor are they worried if none is possible (*pace* Davidson, 1970).

3. Intentional Interpretation

Because the study of the mind presents special scientific difficulties all of its own, I have so far mentioned psychology only incidentally. At the heart of these special difficulties is the problem of "significance" or "meaningfulness." Large portions of human behavior, preeminently linguistic behavior, are meaningful on the face of it, and a larger portion still is "rational" or "intelligent" in a way that involves significance at least indirectly. Yet meaningfulness is a slippery notion to pin down empirically, and there are conceptual difficulties in connecting "meanings" with the physical order of cause and effect. So serious are the problems that some investigators have even tried to study behavior entirely without regard to its significance—but their achievements have been narrow and limited. Cognitivism, on the other hand, gives the meanings of various states and processes a central importance. In this section, I will show how that can be compatible with the rigorous demands of empirical science.

I take my cue from the pioneering work of Quine, and the refinements it has inspired (Quine, 1960; Davidson, 1970, 1973b; Harman, 1973; compare Sellars, 1963, chap. 11; Dennett, 1971; and McCarthy, 1979). Quine's original concern was the translation of utterances in totally alien languages; since Cognitivism's topic is broader, we generalize "translation" to "intentional interpretation" and "utterance" to "quasilinguistic representation." These now must be explicated.

Suppose we come upon an unfamiliar object—a "black box"—which someone tells us plays chess. What evidence would it take to convince us that the claim was empirically justified? It is neither necessary nor sufficient that it produce tokens of symbols in some standard chess notation (let alone, physically move the pieces of a chess set). It is not sufficient because the object might produce standard symbols but only in a random order. And it is not necessary, because the object might play brilliant chess, but represent moves in some oddball notation.

So it is up to the person who claims that it plays chess to tell us how it represents moves. More particularly, we must know what in its behavior to count as its making a move, and how to tell what move that is. Further, we must know what effects on it count as opponents' moves, and how to tell what moves they count as. Succinctly: we must know what its inputs and outputs are, and how to interpret them. Note that the inputs and outputs must be of some antecedently recognizable or identifiable types, and the interpretations of them must be according to some antecedently specifiable regular scheme; otherwise, we will suspect that the "interpretation" is being made up along the way, so as to make things come out right.

Of course, simply specifying the interpretation does not convince us that the object really plays chess. For that we would need to watch it play a few games—perhaps with several opponents, so we're sure there's no trick. What will count as success in this test? First, each output that the object produces must turn out, under the specified interpretation, to be a legal move for the board position as it stands at that time. Second, depending on how strictly we distinguish blundering from playing, the moves must be to some extent plausible (the hypothesis is only that it plays, not that it plays well). If the object passes this test in a sufficient variety of cases, we will be empirically convinced that it is indeed a chess player.

Further, when the object passes the test, the original interpretation scheme is shown to be not merely gratuitous. This is important because, in themselves, interpretation schemes are a dime a dozen. With a little ingenuity, one can stipulate all kinds of bizarre "meanings" for the behavior of all kinds of objects; and insofar as they are just stipulations, there can be no empirical argument about whether one is any better than another. How would you test, for example, the claims that producing marks shaped like "Q-B2" represented ("meant"): (i) one (or another) particular chess move, (ii) the solution of a logic problem, or (iii) a scurrilous remark about the Queen of England and the Bishop of Canterbury? Nothing observable about those marks in themselves favors one rendition over another. But one can further observe when and where the marks are produced, in relation to others produced by the same object, and in relation to the object's inputs. If those relationships form a pattern, such that under one interpretation the observed outputs consistently "make reasonable sense" in the context of the other observed inputs and outputs, while under another interpretation they don't, then the first interpretation scheme as a whole is observably "better" (more convincing) than the second. In our example, the pattern amounts to playing legal and plausible chess games, time after time. None (or at most very few) of the countless other conceivable interpretations of the same marks would make such sense of the observed pattern, so the given interpretation is empirically preferable.

The problem now is to generalize the points made about this specific example. I believe there are principled limits to how precisely such a generalization can be stated; but let us proceed with a few definitions, relying on intuitions and examples to keep them clear.

1. A set of types is *uniquely determinable* relative to a specified range of phenomena iff:

    i. for almost every phenomenon in that range one can unequivocally determine whether it is a token (instance) of one of the types, and if so, which one; and
    ii. no phenomenon is ever a token of more than one type.

(Compare Goodman, 1968, Ch. 4; Quine, 1960, section 18.)

2. An *articulated typology* (relative to a range of phenomena) is an ordered pair of uniquely determinable sets of types such that:

    i. tokens of types in the second set (=*complete types*) are composed of one or more token of types in the first set (=*simple types*); and

ii. no token of a simple type ever actually occurs in the specified range of phenomena except as a component of a complete type.

For example, suppose a sheet of paper has a chess game recorded on it in standard notation (and has no other markings but doodles). Then relative to the marks on that page, the alphameric characters of chess notation are the simple types of an articulated typology, and the sequences of characters that would canonically represent moves (plus odds and ends) are the complete types. Note that definitions of complete types may include specifications of the order in which they are composed of simple types, and that in general this order need not be merely serial.

3. An *intentional interpretation* of an articulated typology is:

i. a regular general scheme for determining what any token of a complete type means or represents, such that:
ii. the determination is made entirely in terms of:
   a. how it is composed of tokens of simple types; and
   b. some stipulations about ("definitions" of) the simple types.

("Intentional" is a philosopher's term for "meaningful" or "representational.")

4. A *quasilinguistic representation* is a token of a complete type from an intentionally interpreted articulated typology.

(Compare "structured description," Pylyshyn, 1978a). Obviously, the identity of a quasilinguistic representation is relative to the specified typology and interpretation, and hence also to a specified range of phenomena. The complete types in the chess notation typology are quasilinguistic representations (of moves), relative to the chess interpretation.

I am unable to define either "mean" or "represent," nor say in general what kinds of stipulations about simple types (3-ii-b, earlier) are appropriate. In practice, however, it is not hard to give clear intentional interpretations; there are two common ways of doing it. The first is translation into some language or notation that we, the interpreters, already understand. Thus a manual might be provided for translating some strange chess notation into the standard one. The second is giving an "intended interpretation," in roughly the logicians' sense. Thus, a function can be defined from a subset of the simple types onto some domain—say, chess pieces and board squares; then the meanings of tokens of complete types (e.g., what moves they represent) are specified recursively in terms of this function, plus the roles of other simple types (such as punctuation) characterized implicitly by the recursion.

Definitions 1 to 4 were all preparatory for the following:

5. An object is interpreted as an *intentional black box* (an IBB) just in case:

  i. an intentionally interpreted articulated typology is specified relative to the causal influences of its environment on it—resulting quasilinguistic representations being *inputs;*
  ii. likewise for *outputs,* relative to its causal influences on its environment; and
  iii. it is shown empirically that under the interpretations the actual outputs consistently make reasonable sense in the context (pattern) of actual prior inputs and other actual outputs.

One important complication with this should be spelled out explicitly. Since the inputs and outputs "make sense" in virtue of a *pattern* they exhibit—a pattern that is extended in time—an IBB interpretation can also attribute enduring intentional "states" (and changes therein) to an object. For instance, a blind chess player (person or machine) must keep track of, or "remember" the current position, updating it after each move; and any player will continuously "know" the rules, "desire" to win, and so on. In some cases, an input/output pattern can be so complicated that no sense can be made of it at all without attributing a rich (though slowly varying) "inner life" of beliefs and desires. It is important to realize, however, that this is "inner" only in the sense of an interpolation in the (external) input/output pattern—nothing is being said about the actual innards of the object.

Sometimes it will be convenient to use the term 'IBB' on the assumption that such an interpretation can be given, even though the specifics are not known. The chess player example with which this section began is an IBB; so are adding machines logic problem solvers, automated disease diagnosers, and (applying the definitions fairly flexibly) normal people.

There are three problems with this definition that need immediate comment. First, "making reasonable sense" under an interpretation is not defined—and I doubt that it can be. Again, however, it is seldom hard to recognize in practice. Often, explicit conditions can be stated for making sense about certain problem domains or subject matters; these I call *cogency conditions.* For the chess player, the cogency condition was outputting legal and plausible moves in the context created by the previous moves. For interpreting an object as an adding machine, the condition is giving correct sums of the inputs; for a disease diagnostician it is giving good diagnoses relative to the symptoms provided. Various authors have tried to give completely general cogency conditions for interpreting creatures as language users (Wilson, 1959; Quine, 1960, chap. 2; Lewis, 1974; Grandy, 1973; Davidson, 1973b). For reasons beyond the scope of this discussion, I don't think any of these succeed. But it doesn't matter much in actual field or laboratory work, because by and large everyone can agree on what does and doesn't make sense.

Second, if one is knee-jerk liberal about what makes reasonable sense, then all kinds of objects can be trivially interpreted as IBBs. Thus a flipped coin might be interpreted as a yes-no decision maker for complex issues tapped on it in Morse code (and compare McCarthy, 1979, *re* thermostats). I will assume that such cases can be ignored.

Third, and most serious, the requirement that inputs and outputs be quasilinguistic representations appears to rule out many perceptions and actions. In at least some cases, this problem can be handled indirectly. Suppose an alleged chess player used no notation at all, but had a TV camera aimed at the board and a mechanical arm which physically moved the pieces. The problem of showing that this device indeed plays chess is essentially the same as before: It must consistently make legal and plausible moves. This succeeds, I think, because we can give quasilinguistic descriptions of what it "looks" at and what it does, such that if they were the inputs and outputs, the object would count as an IBB. In such cases we can enlarge our interpretation and say that the object perceives and acts "under those descriptions" (sees that . . . , intends that . . . , etc.), and regard the descriptions as inputs and outputs. Where this strategy won't work, my definition won't apply.

In this section I have addressed the question how meaningfulness or significance can be dealt with empirically. In brief, the idea is that although meaningfulness is not an intrinsic property of behavior that can be observed or measured, it is a characteristic that can be attributed in an empirically justified interpretation, if the behavior is part of an overall pattern that "makes sense" (e.g., by satisfying specified cogency conditions). In effect, the *relationships* among the inputs and outputs are the only relevant observational data; their intrinsic properties are entirely beside the point, so long as the relationships obtain. But the fact that they have some characteristics or other, independent of the interpretation (that is, they are causal interactions with the environment), means that there is no mystery about how states with significance "connect" with the rest of nature (Davidson, 1970). The upshot is that a psychological theory need not in principle ignore meaningfulness in order to maintain its credentials as empirical and scientific.

4. Information Processing Systems

The last section showed only that there is an empirically legitimate way to talk about significances in scientific theories. It did not say anything about what kind of scientific account might deal with phenomena in terms of their meanings. To put it another way, we saw only how the notion of IBB could make good empirical sense, not how anything could be *explained*. Yet an IBB always manages to produce reasonable outputs, given its inputs; and that's a fairly remarkable ability, which cries out for explanation. There may be many ways to explain such an ability, but two in particular are relevant to Cognitivism. One will be the subject of this section, and the other of the next.

If one can systematically explain how an IBB works, without "de-interpreting" it, it is an *information processing system* (an IPS). By "without de-interpreting," I mean explaining its input/output ability in terms of how it would be characterized under the intentional interpretation, regardless of whatever other descriptions might be available for the same input and output behavior. For example, if our chess player is an IPS, that means there is a systematic explanation of how it manages to come up with legal and plausible moves as such, regardless of how it manages to press certain type bars against paper, light certain lights, or do whatever it does that gets interpreted as those moves.

In a systematic explanation, the ability in question is understood as resulting from the organized, cooperative interactions of various distinct functional components, plus their separate abilities. Further, whatever result it is that the object is able to yield (in this case the IBB outputs), is typically delivered directly by some one or few of the functional components. Now, since we're not de-interpreting, those few components which directly deliver the outputs of the IPS must have among their presupposed abilities the ability to produce the outputs as interpreted. But if attributing this ability to those components is to make good empirical sense, then they must be IBBs themselves. Hence the effects on them by their functional neighbors in the system (the interactions appealed to in the explanation) must be their IBB inputs, which means that they too are dealt with as interpreted. But since these inputs are at the same time the effects delivered by other components, those other components must be able to deliver effects (outputs) under an interpretation. Consequently, they also—and by the same argument, all the functional components of an IPS—must be IBBs.

Moreover, all the interpretations of the component IBBs must be, in a sense, the same as that of the overall IBB (= the IPS). The sense is that they must all pertain to the same subject matter or problem. This actually follows from the preceding argument, but an example will make it obvious. Assuming that the chess playing IBB is an IPS, we would expect its component IBBs to generate possible moves, evaluate board positions, decide which lines of play to investigate further, or some such. These not only all have to do with chess, but in any given case they all have to do with the same partially finished game of chess. By contrast, components interpreted as generating football plays, evaluating jockeys, or deciding to pull trump could have no part in explaining how a chess player works.

Still, the sense in which the interpretations have to be the same is limited. First, of course, the types which get interpreted can vary throughout; they might be keyboard characters in one case, electric pulses in another, and so forth. More important, the internal "discourse" among component IBBs can be in a richer "vocabulary" than that used in the overall inputs and outputs. Thus, chess player inputs and outputs include little more than announcements of actual moves, but the components might be engaged in setting goals, weighing options, deciding which pieces are especially valuable, and so on. Even so, they all still pertain to the chess game, which is the important point. (The importance will become clearer in section 5).

It is natural in a certain way to seek a systematic explanation of an IBB's input/output ability. Seeing this is to appreciate one of the essential motivations of Cognitivism. The relevant ability of an IBB is to produce reasonable outputs relative to whatever inputs it happens to get from within a wide range of possibilities. In a broad sense of the term, we can think of the actual inputs as posing "problems," which the IBB is then able to solve. Now only certain outputs would count as reasonable solutions to any given problem, and those are the ones for which some kind of reasonable argument or rationale can be given. (Cogency conditions are typically spelled out as a relevant rationale for certain outputs as opposed to others, given the inputs). An argument or rationale for a solution to a problem amounts to a decomposition of the problem into easier subproblems, plus an account of how all the subsolutions combine to yield a solution of the overall problem. (How "easy" the subproblems have to be is, of course, relative to the context in which the rationale is required). The point is that the separate IBB components of the IPS can be regarded as solving the easier subproblems, and their interactions as providing the combination necessary for coming up with the overall solution. The interactions in general must be organized and "cooperative" (i.e., systematic) because rational considerations and relationships generally "combine" in complexly interdependent and interlocking ways. (This is why the systematic/morphological distinction is important.)

So, the interacting components of an IPS "work out," in effect, an explicit rationale for whatever output they collectively produce. And that's the explanation for how they manage to come up with reasonable outputs; they, so to speak, "reason it through." This also is the fundamental idea of cognitive psychology: intelligent behavior is to be explained by appeal to internal "cognitive processes"—meaning, essentially, processes interpretable as working out a rationale. Cognitivism, then, can be summed up in a slogan: the mind is to be understood as an IPS.[1]

This suggestion stands on two innovative cornerstones, compared to older notions about what psychology should look like as a science. The first is that psychological explanation should be systematic, not derivational-nomological; hence, that psychology is not primarily interested in quantitative, equational laws, and that psychological theories will not look much like those in physics. The second is that intentional interpretation gives an empirically legitimate (testable) way of talking and theorizing about phenomena regarded as meaningful; hence, that psychology does not have to choose between the supposedly disreputable method of introspection, and a crippling confinement to purely behavioral description. Together they add up to an exciting and promising new approach to the study of the mind.

5. Intentional Reduction

The abilities of component IBBs are merely presupposed by an IPS explanation. That explanation can be systematically reduced—in the sense of section 2—by turning one's attention to explaining those component abilities. If it happens that the components are themsevles IPSs, then reduction can proceed a step by appealing to

1. For readers familiar with the work of Quine, I would like to clear up what I think is a common misunderstanding. Quine is a Behaviorist of sorts, and he sometimes seems to defend that on the basis of his doctrine of the indeterminacy of translation (Quine, 1960, chap. 2). Thus, it's natural to suppose that Cognitivism is as opposed to the latter doctrine as it is to Behaviorism. It isn't. In the terminology of this paper, Quine's claim is the following: For any IBB, there are many different intentional interpretations of the same input/output typologies, which are all equally "good" by any empirical tests; that is, they are all such that the outputs consistently make reasonable sense in context. Hence, one's "translation" of the inputs and outputs is empirically indeterminate, at least among these options. Now, it might seem that if the IBB were an IPS, and if one knew what it was "thinking" (its internal cognitive processes), then one could determine what its outputs really meant, and thereby undercut the indeterminacy. But if Quine is right in his original claim (and I take no stand on that), then it applies to the interpretations of the component IBBs as well. Thus the indeterminacy, rather than being undercut, is just carried inward; in Quine's terms, all the translations are "relative to a translation manual." That would no more rule out Cognitivism than it would linguistics.

the organized interactions and abilities of still smaller component IBBs, and so on. An extension of the argument in the last section shows that all the IBB components at all the levels in such a hierarchy must be interpreted as having the same subject matter; for example, all their inputs and outputs pertain to the same game of chess, or whatever.

Obviously, then, a complete reduction down to physics (or electronics or physiology) would have to involve some further kind of step; that is, eventually the abilities of component IBBs would have to be explained in some other way than as IPSs. By definition, IPS explanation does not involve de-interpretation. Explanation of an IBB's input/output ability that does involve de-interpretation I call explanation by *instantiation*. We shall see that instantiation has two importantly distinct forms.

An object of the sort computer engineers call an "and-gate" is a simple IBB. It has two or more input wires, and a complete input type is (for example) a distribution of positive and negative voltages among these wires. It has one output wire, and is constructed electronically to put a positive voltage in this wire if and only if all the input voltages are positive; otherwise it puts out a negative voltage. Now the cogency condition for a proposition conjoiner is that it give the truth-value "true" if and only if all the conjoined propositions are true; otherwise it gives "false." Since this truth function for "and" is isomorphic to the electrical behavior of the object (taking positive voltage as "true," and negative as "false"), the object can be interpreted as an and-gate.

But to explain how the object manages to satisfy the prescribed cogency conditions, one would not look for component IBBs interpretable as "reasoning the problem through." Rather, one would de-interpret and explain the electrical behavior in terms of the electric circuitry and components. The electrical circuit might well be a system, but it would not be an IPS. Since the first step of the explanation is de-interpretation, it is an explanation by instantiation; I call it *physical instantiation* because the remainder of it is expressed in physical terms.

Not all instantiations, however, are physical instantiations. For example, computer-based chess players are generally written in a programming language called LISP, in which the inputs and outputs of program components are interpreted as operations on complex lists. So interpreted, these components are IBBs, but their subject matter is not chess. What happens, however, is that the input/output constraints (cogency conditions) on the lowest level components in the chess related hierarchy are isomorphic to the constraints on IBBs built up in LISP.[2] Thus, the required abilities of bottom-level chessplayer components can be explained by de-interpreting (or re-interpreting) them as IBBs solving problems about list-structures—IBBs which can then be understood as IPS's working through the rationale for the LISP problem. This, too, is reduction by instantiation, but I call it *intentional instantiation*, because the redescribed ability is still an IBB ability, just about a different subject matter.

Actually, in a complete reduction of a fancy computer program, there can be several stages of intentional instantiation. Thus, LISP languages are generally written (compiled) in still more basic languages—say, ones in which the only IBB abilities are number-crunching and inequality testing (the conditional branch). The last intentional instantiation is in a primitive "machine language," so-called because that is the one which is finally reduced by physical instantiation. The real genius of computer science has been to design ever more sophisticated languages which can be compiled or intentionally instantiated in cruder existing languages. If it weren't for intentional instantiation, machines built of flip-flops and the like would hardly be candidates for artificial intelligence.

It is easy to confuse the maneuver of explaining an IBB by intentional instantiation with that of explaining it as an IPS. The essential difference is the re-interpretation—or, intuitively, the change in subject matter. Since I have already used "change of level" to describe the move from IPS to its separate components, I will use "change of *dimension*" to describe the move of de-/re-interpretation involved in an instantiation. One can think of the

---

2. Strictly, the required relation between the two sets of constraints is weaker than isomorphism. It suffices if every input/output pattern which would satisfy the explained constraints on the lower dimension would also satisfy the cogency conditions on the interpretation being reduced (the constraints on the upper dimension). This amounts to saying that the instantiation can explain more than the IBB ability in question—e.g., not only how it manages to play chess, but also why it always neglects certain options.

many dimensions in a sophisticated "system" as forming a hierarchy, but dimension hierarchies should not be confused with the earlier level hierarchies. There can be different level hierarchies on different dimensions, but they are "orthogonal" rather than sequential. That is, it's a mistake to think of the lowest level on one dimension as a higher level than the highest level on a lower dimension. Thus, an and-gate is not a higher level component than a disk memory; they are components on different dimensions, and hence incomparable as to level.

In this section, I have outlined what a reduction of cognitive psychology to the relevant physical dimension theory would look like. I have not argued that Cognitivism *per se* is committed to such reducibility. It would be theoretically consistent to maintain that at some bottom level the presupposed IBB abilities were simply not explainable (much as physics cannot explain its fundamental laws). Nevertheless, I suspect that many investigators would strongly resist such a suggestion, and would feel their work was not done until the reduction was complete.

6. Fallacious Supporting Arguments

In sections 1 through 5, I have given a general characterization of the Cognitivist approach to psychology, and its possible reduction. In so doing, I have shown how it is innovatively different from earlier approaches more captivated by the image of physics, and how it can be unimpeachably rigorous and empirical all the same. However, it seems to me that the eventual success of this program, for all its attractiveness, is still very much in doubt. In the remaining three sections, I hope to make clear my reasons for caution—taking as much advantage as possible from the explicit characterization just completed. I will begin in this section by pointing out the flaws in two seductive general arguments to the effect that some Cognitivist theory or other *must* be right.

The first argument is directed more specifically at the systematicity cornerstone, though as we have seen, the two cornerstone innovations go hand in hand (see the end of section 4). It goes like this: we know that the nervous system is composed of numerous distinct and highly organized "functional components" —namely neurons; and (assuming materialism) there is every reason to believe that the human IBB is somehow instantiated in the nervous system. So, all that remains to be found are how the neurons are grouped into higher level components, how the first instantiation proceeds, how the lowest components on that dimension are grouped into higher components, what the next instantiation is, and so on. That is, we need only "build back up" the intentional and systematic reductions described in sections 2 and 5, until we reach the overall IBB. That's an enormous task, of course, but since we know there are organized components at the bottom, we know in principle it can be done.

Formally this argument is circular; the reductions mentioned in describing the "building back up" presuppose the very systematicity that the argument is supposed to prove. But the idea behind the reasoning is so attractive that it is tempting to think that the circularity is an artifact of the formulation, and that a better version could be found. To see that this is not so, we must expose in detail the real basis of the formal circularity.

As we observed in section 1, scientific explanation is essentially a route to understanding; and the understanding is achieved in part through specifying certain features and regularities that are common to the range of situations where that kind of explanation applies. The demands of rigor and explicitness that distinguish some explanations as scientific require that the features and regularities specified "encompass" or "encapsulate" every consideration that is relevant to understanding the phenomenon being explained. In a way, the explanatory insight derives precisely from the realization that these few specific features and regularities are all you need to know, in order to be sure that phenomenon Y will occur; everything else is extraneous. Thus, the beauty of Newton's mechanics is that a few parameters and equational laws encapsulate everything that is relevant to the motions of a great many bodies. For example, the colors, textures, personalities, and so on of the planets can all safely be ignored in predicting and understanding their positions as a function of time.

In a systematic explanation, a comparable encapsulation is achieved in the specification of a few determinate modes of interaction among a few distinct components with particular specified abilities. Indeed, finding interfaces among portions of an object, such that this kind of encapsulation is possible, is the fundamental principle of individuation of functional components—

and hence a *sine qua non* of systematic explanation. For example, dividing the interior of a radio (or engine) into adjacent one-millimeter cubes would not be a decomposition into functional components; and the reason is exactly that the resulting "interfaces" would not yield any dividend of encapsulating what's relevant into a few highly specific interactions and abilities. By contrast, a resistor can be a functional component, because (almost) nothing about it matters except the way it resists the flow of electricity from one of its leads to the other. (Compare Simon, 1969, on "partial decomposability"; and Marr, 1977b, on "type 1" versus "type 2" theories.)

So if neurons are to be functional components in a system, some specific few of their countless physical, chemical, and biological interactions must encapsulate all that is relevant to understanding whatever ability of that system is being explained. This is not at all guaranteed by the fact that cell membranes provide an anatomically conspicuous gerrymandering of the brain. More important, however, even if neurons were components in some system, that still would not guarantee the possibility of "building back up." Not every contiguous collection of components constitutes a single component in a higher-level system; consolidation into a single higher component requires a further encapsulation of what's relevant into a few specific abilities and interactions—usually different in kind from those of any of the smaller components. Thus the tuner, pre-amp, and power amp of a radio have very narrowly specified abilities and interactions, compared to those of some arbitrary connected collection of resistors, capacitors, and transistors. The bare existence of functionally organized neurons would not guarantee that such higher level consolidations were possible. Moerover, this failure of a guarantee would occur again and again at every level on every dimension. There is no way to know whether these explanatory consolidations from below are possible without already knowing whether the corresponding systematic explanations and reductions from above are possible—which is the original circularity.

The second argument I will refute starts from the top rather than the bottom and is directed primarily at the intentional interpretation cornerstone, with its associated idea of "working out the rationale." Formally this argument amounts to the challenge: What else could it be?—but it is much more persuasive than that brazen rendition suggests. If one disregarded the intentional interpretation of any sophisticated IBB, it would be quite incredible to suggest that there was some elegant relation between the particular set of influences from the environment that we call inputs, and the particular set of influences on the environment that we call outputs. The relevant actual pattern can hardly even be described except in some way that is tantamount to specifying the cogency conditions which the object in fact meets. But since what we observe is that the object consistently meets these otherwise quite peculiar conditions, and since the conditions themselves are typically made explicit by spelling out some rationale, what else could explain the observations than that the object works the rationale out? How else would it happen to come upon those particular outputs time after time?

To show that a "what else could it be?" argument is inconclusive, one need only come up with a conceivably viable alternative; one need not make a case that the alternative is in fact more probable, just that it's viable. I will try to construct such an alternative, drawing on recent neurophysiological speculations about holographic arrangements and processes (van Heerden, 1968; Pribram, 1971, 1974; Pribram, et al., 1974; Pollen and Taylor, 1974). Fairly detailed hypothetical models have been proposed for how holograms might be realized in neuronal structures (Kabrisky, 1966; Baron, 1970; Cavanagh, 1972); and there is some empirical evidence that some neurons behave in ways that would fit the models (Campbell, 1974; Pollen and Taylor, 1974; and compare Erickson, 1974).

Optical holograms are photographs of interference patterns, which look kind of like the surface of a pond that has just had a lot of pebbles thrown in it. But they have some interesting properties (Leith and Upatnieks, 1965; Herriott, 1968; Cathey, 1974). First, they are prepared from the light bouncing off an ordinary object, and can subsequently be used to reconstruct a full three-dimensional image of that object. Second, the whole image can be reconstructed from any large enough portion of the hologram. (That is, there's no saying which portion of the hologram "encodes" which portion of the image). Third, a number of objects can be separately recorded on the same hologram, and there's no saying which portion records which object. Fourth, if a hologram of an arbitrary scene is suitably illuminated with the light from a reference object, bright spots will appear indicating (virtually instantaneously) the presence and location of any occurrences of the reference object in the scene (and dimmer spots indicate "similar" objects). So some neurophysiological holographic encoding might account for a number of perplexing features of visual recall and recognition, including their speed, some of their invariances, and the fact that they are only slightly impaired by large lesions in relevant areas of the brain.

What matters to us is that a pattern-recognizer based on these principles would not (or need not) be an IPS. There are no distinct functional components whose relevant interactions are confined to intentionally interpreted articulated typologies. That is, there is nothing going on which can be regarded as "working out a rationale" with quasilinguistic representations. By contrast a typical computer-based pattern-recognizer is an IPS. Thus, searching for discontinuities in luminance gradients, proposing that they are edges, checking for connexity among proposed edges, hypothesizing invisible edges so as to complete coherent objects, and so on are all rational procedures relative to the "problem" of identifying objects (see, e.g., Minsky and Papert, 1972; Waltz, 1972).

The neurophysiologists cited have rightly confined their speculations to recognition and recall processes, because there one at least has shreds of evidence to work with. (But see Yevick, 1975, for a mathematician's tentative proposal of a holographically based "logic.") We, however, who are answering a "what else could it be?" argument needn't be so circumspect.

Another interesting property of optical holograms is that if a hologram of two objects is illuminated with the light from one of them, an image of the other (absent) object appears (Gabor, 1969; Firth, 1972). Thus such a hologram can be regarded as a kind of "associator" of (not ideas, but) visual patterns. So imagine a set of such associated patterns, in which the first member of each is a common important substructure in chess positions, and the other is one or two moves which are generally powerful or dangerous around such structures. It seems to me that a set-up like that could be a nearly instantaneous "plausible move generator" for chess positions in general. In fact, it would mesh nicely with some of what is known about how human chess players perceive the board and their options (de Groot, 1965; Hearst, 1967; Frey and Adesman, 1976). Implementation of such a device by optical means might well be impossible; but it is worth pointing out how much more general the neural medium (potentially) is. In the first place, transforms other than the Fourier transform could be implemented just as easily—including, perhaps, "custom" transforms for particular problems. Second, n-dimensional transforms are easily possible. Third, since neurons are connected "point-to-point," even the analog of an ordinary hologram wouldn't have to be arrayed as a surface—physically, the "dots" could be distributed *ad libitum*, making possible all kinds of mingling and interaction among distinct "images." I have no clear idea what difference any of this would make; but it seems likely that the differences could be substantial. And, after all, the capabilities of regular holograms would have been difficult to visualize not so long ago.

Again, the point is that no "plausible-move generator" based on principles anything like this speculation would be an IPS. Nothing in it would "reason through" the move and counter-move alternatives that rationalize any move it proposed. Yet a chess player is a paradigm of what the "what-else-could-it-be" argument should apply to. (It's no accident that chess players are the most common IPS example.) I therefore take that argument to be refuted. I am not envisioning, of course, that humans (chess players included) engage in no cognitive "reasoning a problem through"; introspection, for all its ills, is enough to scotch that. But cognitive psychology is exciting and important for the unobvious thesis that cognitive information processing can explain much more than deliberate cogitation and reasoning; and for that larger thesis, the argument considered is inconclusive.

This last observation should put the whole present section in perspective. All I claim is that a few commonplace assumptions will not suffice to demonstrate that Cognitivism is the right approach to psychology. That should offend no one, since it only means that the position is not trivial and obvious—as clearly it isn't.

7. Potentially Serious Hurdles

In this section, I want to mention three issues which it seems to me may be serious hurdles for Cognitivism—serious in the sense of being equally hard to duck or get over. They are: moods, skills, and understanding. I cannot prove that Cognitivist accounts of these phenomena are impossible. My aim is rather to show that such accounts are going to be required if Cognitivism is to succeed, and that it's dubious whether they will be possible.

I will try to illustrate the nature of the difficulty with moods by contrasting it with another, which is superficially similar but more plausibly duckable. There is a long and tortured tradition in philosophy for distinguishing two kinds of mental phenomena: roughly, cognitive or intellectual states vs. felt qualities or the purely sensuous given (see Sellars, 1963, chap. 5, for a discussion of this distinction in the context of a different issue). Paradigm "felt qualities" would be pains or mere awarenesses of present red (not categorized or conceptualized as such). Several recent articles have argued that such states have some kind of determinate immediate character which is independent of any interpretation and/or any role in a systematic organization (Shoemaker, 1975; Block and Fodor, 1972; but see Dennett, 1978a). It would follow that they do not accord with the Cognitivist notion of a mental state or process.

But without even taking sides on the particular issue, I think we can see that it doesn't matter much to Cognitivism—which is, after all, only a theory of cognitive states and processes. In other words, if felt qualities are fundamentally different, so be it; explaining them is somebody else's business. This amounts to a kind of "segregation" of psychological phenomena, along roughly traditional lines. Such segregation can be legitimate (not a fudge) given one important assumption: Segregated noncognitive states can be effective in determining intelligent behavior only insofar as they somehow generate quasilinguistic representations ("red there now," "left foot hurts") which can be accepted as *inputs* by the cognitive IPS. This assumption is plausible enough for felt qualities, and perhaps for some other states as well. I have in mind the much disputed "mental images" (Shepard and Metzler, 1971; Pylyshyn, 1973, 1978a; Paivio, 1975; Kosslyn and Pomerantz,

1977; Dennett, 1978c). Since any Cognitivist theory must include some mechanism for getting from retinal images to cognitive descriptions of what is seen, I don't see why that same mechanism couldn't also take inputs from some precognitive visual "tape recorder" (perhaps one with "adjustments" for orientation, size, and location). Then playbacks from the recorder would have whatever nondiscursive, "image-y" quality perception has, and Cognitivism would be unruffled. Finally, it may even be that some emotions (e.g., gratitude and regret) can be accommodated with a standard elaboration of this same segregation strategy: roughly, by treating them as compound states, with a cognitive (representational, propositional) component, and a separate non-cognitive (qualitative, feeling) component.

But I am much less sanguine about a similar segregation for moods. The difference is that moods are pervasive and all-encompassing in a way that felt qualities and images are not. The change from being cheerful to being melancholy is much more thorough and far-reaching than that from having a painless foot to having a foot that hurts. Not only does your foot seem different, but everything you encounter seems different. The whole world and everything in it, past, present, and future, becomes greyer, duller, less livable. Minor irritations and failings are more conspicuous and less remediable; ordinary things are no longer fun, lovely, or pleasing. If melancholy were an input representation ("melancholy here now") it would have to accompany and infect every other input, and transform the meanings of them all. But moods not only affect how things look, they affect how one thinks. What seems reasonable when you're cheerful seems foolish when you're melancholy, and *vice versa*. Likelihoods and improbabilities invert, as do what seems relevant to an issue and what seems beside the point.

Moods come upon us, but they are neither direct observations nor inferences. Many things affect our moods, but our moods also affect how things affect us; and in neither case is it quasilinguistic or rational. We do not state or believe our moods, or justify them on the basis of evidence or goals; they are just the way things are. In sum: Moods permeate and affect all kinds of cognitive states and processes, and yet, on the face of it, they don't seem at all cognitive themselves. That suggests, at least until someone shows otherwise, that moods can neither be segregated from the explanation of cognition, nor incorporated in a Cognitivist explanation.

The second hurdle I want to mention concerns skills. I see three *prima facie* (not conclusive) reasons for doubting that the etiology of skillful behavior is cognitive. First, with rare exceptions, articulateness about a skill, no matter how detailed nor in what specialized quasilinguistic notation, is neither necessary nor sufficient for having it; it always takes practice, and often expert examples and talent ($\neq$ intelligence). Even a Rhodes scholar could not learn to play good ping-pong just from listening to thousands of detailed lectures about it; and even a Rhodes scholar ping-pong champion might be hard pressed to give a single detailed lecture on the subject. Second, a person who is acquiring or upgrading a skill may deliberately and thoughtfully try to execute certain maneuvers, but the thought and deliberation cease at just about the time the maneuvers become skillful and "natural"; the expert doesn't have to think about it. Third, skillful activity is faster than thought. Not only do skilled typists and pianists not have to think about what they're doing with their fingers; they can't. If they turn their attention to their fingers, as a novice must, their performance slows down and becomes clumsy, rather like a novice's.

A Cognitivist can explain these phenomena away by postulating some "unconscious" information processing which is somehow more efficient than, and immiscible with, that conscious thinking which is archetypically cognitive. But Dreyfus asks an interesting pointed question about this ploy, in the special case of chess skills (Dreyfus, 1979, p. 106). It is known that intermediate, advanced, and great chess players are alike in consciously considering on the order of a hundred plays in thinking out a move; they differ in their "skill in problem conception" (de Groot, 1965)—i.e., in preselecting which moves to think about. Now the rationales for these good preselections would be enormously long if they were spelled out (many thousands of plays). It's possible that players have some marvelously efficient unconscious information processor which works through these rationales; but if so, then why would anyone with such a splendid unconscious ever bother to deliberate consciously and tediously over a hundred plays? The implication is that the skillful preselection and the tedious cogitation differ not just in efficiency and consciousness, but in kind, and that neither could adequately substitute for the other. I think it would take powerful arguments (or prejudices) to outweigh this natural construal of the evidence—and only slightly less so in the case of skills in general.

But so what? If skillful behavior has to be explained in some non-Cognitivist way—call it "X" (maybe something to do with holograms)—then why not employ the segregation strategy introduced above for felt qualities and images? I think the danger here is not that the segregation strategy wouldn't work, but that it might work too well. "Skill" is such a broad and versatile notion that all kinds of things might fall under it. For example, the ability to act appropriately and adroitly in various social situations is a sort of skill, as is the art of conversation, and even everyday pattern recognition; moreover, these are like our earlier examples in that, to whatever degree one has mastered the skill, one needn't think about it to exercise it. But if very many such things turned out to be explainable in way X, rather than as the abilities of an IPS, then cognitive psychology would narrow dramatically in scope and interest. In the worst case, little would remain to call "cognitive" except conscious deliberation and reasoning—and that's hardly news.

The third hurdle I want to raise for Cognitivism is understanding; but this needs immediate qualification. In one sense, IPSs undoubtedly can understand, because computers programmed to be IPSs can do it. We could build a chess player, for example, that "understands" entered moves in any of three notations. What that means is that it responds appropriately (sensibly) to inputs in any of those forms. This is the same sense in which existing programs "understand" selected English sentences about colored blocks (see e.g., Winograd, 1972; and compare Greeno, 1977), airline reservations, and what not. Such usage is perfectly legitimate, but it's not all there is to understanding.

There is another notion of understanding, which, for convenience, I will call "insight" into why certain responses make sense, or are reasonable. As any teacher of arithmetic or logic knows, many students can learn the routines for getting the right answers, without the slightest insight into what's going on. And when original scientists struggle to find new and better theories, they grope for new "insights" into the phenomena, or new accounts which "make sense." Whether or not a new account, perhaps expressed in an unprecedented formulation, makes sense or is intelligible, is something which great scientists (and then their colleagues) can "just tell." Of course, whether an account is scientifically acceptable also depends on how well it accords with observations; but that does not determine whether it makes sense in the first place—both are necessary in science. The ability to tell when a whole account, a whole way of putting things, makes sense, is what I mean by insight.

The intelligibility of the whole account (or way of talking) then determines which particular utterances make sense, and what sense they make. Thus it is only because quantum mechanics is an intelligible theory that one can make sense of talking about the wavelength of a particular electron (but not about the rest mass of a photon). And this brings us back to the conditions on interpreting something as an IBB. The testable requirement is that individual outputs make sense in the context of prior inputs and other outputs. But what determines which outputs would and would not make sense in which contexts? That is, what determines which overall patterns render their constituents intelligible under an interpretation, or which input/output constraints count as cogency conditions? I have said that in appropriate circumstances, people can "just tell"; they can come to understand insightfully.

This is not to say that insight is itself some "transcendental" or impenetrable mystery, which we are forever barred from explaining. But once we appreciate that it is a genuine problem we can ask whether an IPS explanation could account for it. Now, we can understand how an IPS comes up with the reasonable outputs that it does, because we know how it works; in particular, we know that it works through a rationale for each output, and we know that it makes sense to say this of it because each of its interacting component IBBs consistently accords with certain cogency conditions. If we did not have that kind of a story to tell, then we would have no IPS explanation of the overall IBB's abilities.

So if an IPS explanation is to account for an object's having insight, then there must be a rationale for the insightful outputs. More specifically, if the insight is that certain new constraints constitute a kind of cogency, then there must be a rationale, according to the kind of cogency that the object and its components already exhibit, for why the new conditions count as cogency conditions. It seems to me that there could be such a rationale only if the new conditions were equivalent to, or a special case of, the established ones. For example, there could be no rationale according to chess player cogency conditions for why adding machine outputs make sense, or *vice versa*. If this is right, then an IPS with general insight into what makes sense would itself have to operate according to some cogency conditions that are ultimately general (so that the others which it recognizes could be given rationales as special cases).

There are two reasons to doubt that human insight can be explained that way. First, there is a sense in which it would preclude any radically new ways of understanding things; all new developments would have to be specializations of the antecedent general conditions. But I think the invention, say, of derivational-nomological explanation (around the time of Galileo) did comprise a "radical" advance in *ways* of understanding, in just the sense that the cogency of the new accounts could not be defended with a rationale which was cogent by prior standards. Medieval Aristotelians had explained (and understood) the motions of various kinds of bodies in terms of their efforts to get where they belonged, and their thwarting of each others' efforts. Galileo, Kepler, Newton, et al., didn't simply add to or modify those views. They invented a totally new way of talking about what happens, and a new way of rendering it intelligible; mathematical relationships and operations defined on universal measurable parameters became the illuminating considerations, rather than the goals and strivings of earth, air, fire, and water. I don't think a medieval IPS could have come to understand the new theory unless it had had it latently "built-in" all along. The same would be true of every IPS child who comes eventually to understand science, the arts, politics, and so on.

The second doubt has to do with this latent building-in—essentially, the ultimate general cogency conditions. We really have no reason to believe that there is any final characterization of what it is to make sense, except that it would facilitate a tidy account of intelligence. Barrels of philosophical ink have been spilt in the search for it, but so far without success. People who regularly make convergent decisions about the reasonableness of theories and interpretations don't explicitly work through rationales for their judgments. So we're back to postulating some mysterious and magnificent unconscious IPS. But once we admit that the phenomenon of insight is simply mysterious and unexplainable at present, then all we have to go on are the *prima facie* indications that IPS explanation is inadequate to the task.

It seems to me, however, that there is yet a deeper side to this: understanding pertains not primarily to symbols or rules for manipulating them, but the world and to living in it. Linguistic articulation can be a vehicle for such understanding; and perhaps articulateness is prerequisite to any elaborate understanding. But cases where facility with the symbols is plausibly sufficient—like well-defined games, mathematics, and AI "micro-worlds"—are very peculiar, and (I think) parasitic. Paradigms of understanding are rather our everyday insights into friends and loved ones, our sensitive appreciation of stories and dramas, our intelligent handling of paraphernalia and commerce. It is far from clear that these are governed by fully explicable rules at all. Our talk of them is sensible because we know what we are talking about, and not just because the talk itself exhibits some formal regularities (though that too is doubtless essential).

When the rationalists took cognition as the essence of being human (*res cogitans*), they meant especially theoretical cognition, as in mathematics and mathematical physics. The understanding manifested in arts and crafts was not, in their view, a different phenomenon, but just imperfect theory, sullied by obscurity and confusion. Cognitivism is heir to this tradition: to be intelligent is to be able to manipulate (according to rational rules) "clear and distinct" quasi-linguistic representations—but now they're sullied by omissions, probabilities, and heuristics. Deported from the immortal soul, however, they forfeit their original epistemic anchorage in the honesty of God and the natural light of Reason. So, bereft of credentials from above, the distinction of certain procedures as "reasonable" floats adrift, unless it can otherwise be explained. Evolution comes vaguely to mind, but much more needs to be said. My own hunch is that the intelligibility of rational "theorizing" is a derivative special case of an antecedent, atheoretical, intelligent practice—a prior "grasp" of how to get along in a multifarious existence. If articulate theory is one developed derivative, there can be others: the appreciation of fine art, a subtle sense of personality, the "mastery of metaphor" (Aristotle), even creativity and wisdom. We will understand understanding when we understand its many forms, primordial and refined. In the commerce of understanding, words are only money.

In this section I have raised three issues which it seems to me Cognitivists must face, and which it is not yet clear they can handle. It is of course possible that successful treatments will eventually be found. On the other hand, if the approach is doomed to failure, I suspect that these are tips of some of the icebergs on which it will founder.

8. The State of the Art

Needless to say, the eventual fate of cognitive psychology will be settled empirically—not by armchair philosophizing. But the way in which experimental results bear on scientific theories, let alone whole approaches to the form that such theories should take, is seldom straightforward. In this concluding section, I will venture a few general points about Cognitivism and its relation to empirical observations.

It is illustrative to begin with cognitive simulation, a subdiscipline where cognitive psychology overlaps with artifical intelligence. A generation ago, the prospect of building intelligent computers inspired a lot of enthusiasm and brilliant work; but everyone must agree that results to date fall well short of early expectations. General problem solving programs have long since hit a plateau. Mechanical language translation has proven so elusive and frustrating that even military funding has dwindled. Advances in pattern recognition are painfully small, and mainly confined to contrived special "universes." Even game playing, a relative bright spot, is a disappointment against once confident hopes and predictions. About the only thing which exceeds original forecasts is the amount of computing power which has become available—and yet isn't enough. Does all this constitute an empirical refutation of the possibility of artificial intelligence? Not at all.

Perhaps the lesson is just that the problem was initially underestimated; soberer judges are now gratified by smaller steps in a longer trek, and disillusioned pessimists may still be exposed as carpenters who blamed their tools. On the other hand, if there were indeed something fundamentally misguided about the whole project, then recurrent bottlenecks and modest sparse successes are just what you would expect. The empirical record is simply ambiguous, and the real problem is to wrest from it whatever moral it does hold, as clearly and as helpfully as possible.

Cognitive simulation is not merely an incidental offshoot of cognitive psychology. It is a powerful and important research tool, because it provides a new and unprecedented empirical testing ground. Any IPS, or at least any one which is reducible to some level or dimension on which component input/output functions are expressible mathematically, can in principle be simulated on a computer. That means that simulations can function as concrete checks on whether particular proposed IPSs in fact have the abilities which they are supposed to explain. This is valuable when the proposed explanations are so complex that it is otherwise practically impossible to determine whether the things would actually work as claimed. In effect, the computer makes it feasible for Cognitivist theories to be more intricate and complicated than their predecessors could be in the past, and still remain under detailed empirical control.

By the same token, however, computer simulation serves as the front line where fundamental difficulties not resolvable by further complication would first show themselves. This is not to say that psychological experiments, and programmatic theories formulated with their guidance, are beside the point; quite the contrary, they form an essential high-level ingredient in the whole endeavor. But if one were genuinely to entertain the hypothesis that Cognitivism is misconceived, then the stumbling blocks empirically discovered by cognitive simulationists would be the first place to look for clues as to what went wrong. How else than by struggling to build chess players could we have found out so definitively that the skill of deciding which moves to consider is not a simple matter of a few readily ascertained heuristics? What laboratory experiment could have shown more clearly than the mechanical translation effort that the hardest thing to account for in linguistic performance is understanding what the discourse is all about?

If Cognitivism proves to be the wrong approach after all (that's still a big "if," of course), then the genius who makes the next basic breakthrough in psychology will probably take his or her cue from difficulties like these. Empirical indications of what cannot be done often pave the way for major scientific progress; think of efforts to weigh phlogiston, to build a perpetual motion machine, or to measure the speed of the Earth through the luminiferous aether.

A sense of history can give us perspective in another way. Until the rise of Cognitivism, Behaviorism reigned almost unchallenged in American psychology departments. It could boast established experimental methods, mountains of well-confirmed and universally accepted results, speciality journals carrying detailed technical reports, texts and curricula for teaching people to read and write those reports, and a coherent "philosophy" within which it all fit together and seemed inevitably right. In short, it had all the institutional earmarks of an advanced and thriving science. In retrospect, however, Behaviorism seems to have made little positive contribution to our understanding of the human psyche, and to be hopelessly inadequate to the task.

Kuhn's notion of a scientific paradigm can be extended in a way that sheds light on a situation like this (Kuhn, 1970). A *paradigm* is a major scientific triumph, so impressive in breaking new ground, and yet so pregnant with unfulfilled possibilities, that a technical research tradition coalesces around it as a model. Thus the achievements of Thorndike and Pavlov inspired a vigorous and sophisticated investigation of the conditioning of birds, dogs, and rats—and also of people, to the extent that they are similar. But most of the interesting and important aspects of intelligent behavior, exhibited especially by humans, turn out to involve processes qualitatively different from those discovered by Thorndike, Pavlov, and their followers. So when Behaviorism was taken as an approach to psychology in general, its paradigm became a kind of impostor; experiments, concepts, and methods which were genuinely illuminating in a limited domain posed as the model for illumination in a quite different domain, where they had virtually no demonstrated credentials, and really didn't belong.

Cognitivism is a natural development from Behaviorism. It retains the same commitment to publicly ch   ~~ ble and verifiable data, the same rejection of posits and postulates that cannot be treated experimentally, and the same ideal of psychology as a natural science. Its advantage is having shown, via the systematicity and intentional interpretation "cornerstones," how to make good empirical sense of meaningful or rational internal processes—which gives it a much richer and more powerful explanatory framework. And not surprisingly, it has now acquired the institutional earmarks of an advanced and thriving science. But cognitive psychology too can be accused of having an impostor paradigm. The concrete achievements which inspire the notion of IPS explanation, and prove it to have application in the real world, come originally and almost entirely from the fields of computer science and automatic data processing. The few cases in which people explicitly and deliberately work through a rationale do suggest an analogy; but so did the cases in which people responded to conditioning.

Like their predecessors, Cognitivists have made undeniably important and lasting discoveries. But also as before, these discoveries are conspicuously narrow, even small, compared to the depth and scope of psychology's pretheoretic purview. The brilliance of what has been done can blind us to the darkness that surrounds it, and it is worth recalling how many shadows Cognitivism has not (yet) illuminated. How is it, for example, that we recognize familiar faces, let alone the lives reflected in them, or the greatness of Rembrandt's portrayals? How do we understand conversational English, let alone metaphors, jokes, Aristotle, or Albee? What is common sense, let alone creativity, wit, or good taste? What happens when we fall asleep, let alone fall under a spell, fall apart, or fall in love? What are personality and character, let alone identity crises, schizophrenia, the experience of enlightenment, or moral integrity? We turn to psychology if we think these questions have scientific answers; and if we shouldn't, why shouldn't we? Cognitivists are as vague and impressionistic on such issues as psychological theorists have always been. Of course, they too can buy time with the old refrain: "be patient, we're only just beginning (though so-and-so's preliminary results are already encouraging)." Promissory notes are legitimate currency in vigorous sciences, but too much deficit spending only fuels inflation.

The human spirit is its own greatest mystery. Perhaps the idea of an information processing system is at last the key to unlocking it; or perhaps the programmable computer is as shallow an analogy as the trainable pigeon—the conditional branch as sterile as the conditioned reflex. There is no way to tell yet, but we should be as ready to follow up on partial failures as we are on partial successes. The clues could be anywhere.

Acknowledgments: In preparing this paper I have incurred more of a debt than I can properly express to the inspiration and constant guiding criticism of H. L. Dreyfus. I am also thankful to several students and colleagues for directing my attention to weaknesses in earlier drafts (some of which, no doubt, remain)—especially Bob Brandom, Dan Dennett, Jay Garfield, Allan Gibbard, Bill House, and Zenon Pylyshyn. Finally, I am grateful to the University of Pittsburgh Faculty Grants Committee for research support during the summer of 1975.

10

Minds, Brains, and Programs

JOHN R. SEARLE

Abstract: I distinguish between strong and weak AI. According to strong AI, appropriately programmed computers literally have cognitive states, and therefore the programs are psychological theories. I argue that strong AI must be false, since a human agent could instantiate the program and still not have the appropriate mental states. I examine some arguments against this claim, and I explore some consequences of the fact that human and animal brains are the causal bases of existing mental phenomena.

WHAT PSYCHOLOGICAL and philosophical significance should we attach to recent efforts at computer simulations of human cognitive capacities? In answering this question I find it useful to distinguish what I will call "strong" AI from "weak" or "cautious" AI. According to weak AI, the principal value of the computer in the study of the mind is that it gives us a very powerful tool. For example, it enables us to formulate and test hypotheses in a more rigorous and precise fashion than before. But according to strong AI the computer is not merely a tool in the study of the mind; rather the appropriately programmed computer really is a mind in the sense that computers given the right programs can be literally said to *understand* and have other cognitive states. And, according to strong AI, because the programmed computer has cognitive states, the programs are not mere tools that enable us to test psychological explanations; rather, the programs are themselves the explanations. I have no objection to the claims to weak AI, at least as far as this article is concerned. My discussion here will be directed to the claims I have defined as strong AI, specifically the claim that the appropriately programmed computer literally has cognitive states and that the programs thereby explain human cognition. When I refer to AI, it is the strong version as expressed by these two claims which I have in mind.

I will consider the work of Roger Schank and his colleagues at Yale (cf. Schank and Abelson, 1977), because I am more familiar with it than I am with any similar claims, and because it provides a clear example of the sort of work I wish to examine. But nothing that follows depends upon the details of Schank's programs. The same arguments would apply to Winograd's (1972) SHRDLU, Weizenbaum's (1965) ELIZA, and, indeed, any Turing machine simulation of human mental phenomena.

Briefly and leaving out the various details, one can describe Schank's program as follows: the aim of the program is to simulate the human ability to understand stories. It is characteristic of the abilities of human beings to understand stories that they can answer questions about the story even though the information they give was not explicitly stated in the story. Thus, for example, suppose you are given the following story: "A man went into a restaurant and ordered a hamburger. When the hamburger arrived, it was burned to a crisp, and the man stormed out of the restaurant angrily without paying for the hamburger or leaving a tip." Now, if you are given the question "Did the man eat the hamburger?", you will presumably answer, "No, he did not." Similarly if you are given the following story: "A man went into a restaurant, and ordered a hamburger; when the hamburger came, he was very pleased with it; and as he left the restaurant he gave the waitress a large tip before paying his bill," and you are asked the question "Did the man eat the hamburger?", you will presumably answer, "Yes, he ate the hamburger." Now Schank's machines can similarly answer questions about restaurants in this fashion. In order to do so, they have a "representation" of the sort of information that human beings have about restaurants which enables them to answer such questions as those above, given these sorts of stories. When the machine is given the story and then asked the question, the machine will print out answers of the sort that we would expect human beings to give if told similar stories. Partisans of strong AI claim that in this question-and-answer sequence, not only is the machine simulating a human ability but also:

(a) the machine can literally be said to *understand* the story and provide answers to questions; and

(b) what the machine and its program do *explains* the human ability to understand the story and answer questions about it.

Claims (a) and (b) seem to me totally unsupported by Schank's work, as I will attempt to show in what follows.[1]

A way to test any theory of the mind is to ask oneself what it would be like if one's own mind actually worked on the principles that the theory says all minds work on. Let us apply this test to the Schank program with the following *Gedankenexperiment*. Suppose that I'm locked in a room and suppose that I'm given a large batch of Chinese writing. Suppose furthermore, as is indeed the case, that I know no Chinese either written or spoken, and that I'm not even confident that I could recognize Chinese writing as Chinese writing distinct from, say, Japanese writing or meaningless squiggles. Now suppose further that after this first batch of Chinese writing, I am given a second batch of Chinese script together with a set of rules for correlating the second batch with the first batch. The rules are in English and I understand these rules as well as any other native speaker of English. They enable me to correlate one set of formal symbols with another set of formal symbols, and all that "formal" means here is that I can identify the symbols entirely by their shapes. Now suppose also that I am given a third batch of Chinese symbols together with some instructions, again in English, that enable me to correlate elements of this third batch with the first two batches, and these rules instruct me how I am to give back certain Chinese symbols with certain sorts of shapes in response to certain sorts of shapes given me in the third batch. Unknown to me, the people who are giving me all of these symbols call the first batch 'a script,' they call the second batch a 'story,' and they call the third batch 'questions.'

---

1. I am not saying, of course, that Schank himself is committed to these claims.

Furthermore, they call the symbols I give them back in response to the third batch 'answers to the questions,' and the set of rules in English that they gave me they call 'the program.' To complicate the story a little bit, imagine that these people also give me stories in English which I understand, and they then ask me questions in English about these stories, and I give them back answers in English. Suppose also that after a while I get so good at following the instructions for manipulating the Chinese symbols and the programmers get so good at writing the programs that from the external point of view—that is, from the point of view of somebody outside the room in which I am locked—my answers to the questions are indistinguishable from those of native Chinese speakers. Nobody looking at my answers can tell that I don't speak a word of Chinese. Let us also suppose that my answers to the English questions are, as they no doubt would be, indistinguishable from those of other native English speakers, for the simple reason that I am a native speaker of English. From the external point of view, from the point of view of someone reading my 'answers,' the answers to the Chinese questions and the English questions are equally good. But in the Chinese case, unlike the English case, I produce the answers by manipulating uninterpreted formal symbols. As far as the Chinese is concerned, I simply behave like a computer; I perform computational operations on formally specified elements. For the purposes of the Chinese, I am simply an instantiation of the computer program.

Now the claims made by strong AI are that the programmed computer understands the stories and that the program in some sense explains human understanding. But we are now in a position to examine these claims in light of our thought experiment.

(a) As regards the first claim it seems to me obvious in the example that I do not understand a word of the Chinese stories. I have inputs and outputs that are indistinguishable from those of the native Chinese speaker, and I can have any formal program you like, but I still understand nothing. Schank's computer for the same reasons understands nothing of any stories whether in Chinese, English, or whatever, since in the Chinese case the computer is me; and in cases where the computer is not me, the computer has nothing more than I have in the case where I understand nothing.

(b) As regards the second claim—that the program explains human understanding—we can see that the computer and its program do not provide sufficient conditions of understanding, since the computer and the program are functioning and there is no understanding. But does it even provide a necessary condition or a significant contribution to understanding? One of the claims made by the supporters of strong AI is this: when I understand a story in English, what I am doing is exactly the same—or perhaps more of the same—as what I was doing in the case of manipulating the Chinese symbols. It is simply more formal symbol manipulation which distinguishes the case in English, where I do understand, from the case in Chinese, where I don't. I have not demonstrated that this claim is false, but it would certainly appear an incredible claim in the example. Such plausibility as the claim has derives from the supposition that we can construct a program that will have the same inputs and outputs as native speakers, and in addition we assume that speakers have some level of description where they are also instantiations of a program. On the basis of these two assumptions, we assume that even if Schank's program isn't the whole story about understanding, maybe it is part of the story. That is, I suppose, an empirical possibility, but not the slightest reason has so far been given to suppose it is true, since what is suggested—though certainly not demonstrated—by the example is that the computer program is irrelevant to my understanding of the story. In the Chinese case I have everything that artificial intelligence can put into me by way of a program, and I understand nothing; in the English case I understand everything, and there is so far no reason at all to suppose that my understanding has anything to do with computer programs—i.e., with computational operations on purely formally specified elements. As long as the program is defined in terms of computational operations on purely formally defined elements, what the example suggests is that these by themselves have no interesting connection with understanding. They are certainly not sufficient conditions, and not the slightest reason has been given to suppose that they are necessary conditions or even that they make a significant contribution to understanding. Notice that the force of the argument is not simply that different machines can have the same input and output while operating on different formal principles—that is not the point at all—but rather that whatever purely formal principles you put into the computer will not be sufficient for understanding, since a human will be able to follow the formal principles without understanding anything, and no reason has been offered to suppose they are necessary or even contributory, since no reason has been given to suppose that when I understand English, I am operating with any formal program at all.

What is it, then, that I have in the case of the English sentences which I do not have in the case of the Chinese sentences? The obvious answer is that I know what the former mean but haven't the faintest idea what the latter mean. In what does this consist, and why couldn't we give it to a machine, whatever it is? Why couldn't the machine be given whatever it is about me that makes it the case that I know what English sentences mean? I will return to these questions after developing my example a little more.

I have had occasions to present this example to several workers in artificial intelligence and, interestingly, they do not seem to agree on what the proper reply to it is. I get a surprising variety of replies, and in what follows I will consider the most common of these (specified along with their geographical origins). First I want to block out some common misunderstandings about "understanding." In many of these discussions one finds fancy footwork about the word "understanding." My critics point out that there are different degrees of understanding, that "understanding" is not a simple two-place predicate, that there are even different kinds and levels of understanding, and often the law of the excluded middle doesn't even apply in a straightforward way to statements of the form 'x understands y,' that in many cases it is a matter for decision and not a simple matter of fact whether x understands y. And so on. To all these points I want to say of course, of course; but they have nothing to do with the points at issue. There are clear cases where "understanding" applies and clear cases where it does not apply; and such cases are all I need for this argument.[2] I understand stories in English; to a lesser

2. Also, "understanding" implies both the possession of mental (intentional) states and the truth (validity, success) of these states. For the purposes of this discussion, we are concerned only with the possession of the states.

degree I can understand stories in French; to a still lesser degree, stories in German; and in Chinese, not at all. My car and my adding machine, on the other hand, understand nothing; they are not in that line of business. We often attribute "understanding" and other cognitive predicates by metaphor and analogy to cars, adding machines, and other artifacts, but nothing is proved by such attributions. We say, "The door *knows* when to open because of its photoelectric cell," "the adding machine *knows how (understands how, is able)* to do addition and subtraction but not division," and "the thermostat *perceives* changes in the temperature." The reason we make these attributions is interesting and has to do with the fact that in artifacts we extend our own intentionality;[3] our tools are extensions of our purposes, and so we find it natural to make metaphorical attributions of intentionality to them; but I take it no philosophical ice is cut by such examples. The sense in which an automatic door "understands instructions" from its photoelectric cell is not at all the sense in which I understand English. If the sense in which Schank's programmed computers understand stories is supposed to be the metaphorical sense in which the door understands, and not the sense in which I understand English, the issue would not be worth discussing. Newell and Simon write that the sense of "understanding" they claim for computers is exactly the same as for human beings. I like the straightforwardness of this claim, and it is the sort of claim I will be considering. I will argue that in the literal sense the programmed computer understands what the car and the adding machine understand, viz. exactly nothing. The computer understanding is not just (like my understanding of German) partial or incomplete; it is zero.

Now to the replies:

I. *The Systems Reply* (Berkeley): "While it is true that the individual person who is locked in the room does not understand the story, the fact is that he is merely part of a whole system

3. Intentionality is by definition that feature of certain mental states by which they are directed at or about objects and states of affairs in the world. Thus beliefs, desires, and intentions are intentional states; undirected forms of anxiety and depression are not. For further discussion, see Searle (1979).

and the system does understand the story. The person has a large ledger in front of him in which are written the rules, he has a lot of scratch paper and pencils for doing calculations, he has "data banks" of sets of Chinese symbols. Now, understanding is not being ascribed to the mere individual, rather it is being ascribed to this whole system of which he is a part."

My response to the systems theory is simple: Let the individual internalize all of these elements of the system. He memorizes the rules in the ledger and the data banks of Chinese symbols, and he does all the calculations in his head.The individual then incorporates the entire system. There isn't anything at all to the system which he does not encompass. We can even get rid of the room and suppose he works outdoors. All the same, he understands nothing of the Chinese, and *a fortiori* neither does the system, because there isn't anything in the system which isn't in him. If he doesn't understand, then there is no way the system could understand because the system is just a part of him.

Actually I feel somewhat embarrassed even to give this answer to the systems theory because the theory seems to me so implausible to start with. The idea is that while a person doesn't understand Chinese, somehow the *conjunction* of that person and bits of paper might understand Chinese. It is not easy for me to imagine how someone who was not in the grip of an ideology would find the idea at all plausible. Still, I think many people who are committed to the ideology of strong AI will in the end be inclined to say something very much like this; so let us pursue it a bit further. According to one version of this view, while the man in the internalized systems example doesn't understand Chinese in the sense that a native Chinese speaker does (because, for example, he doesn't know that the story refers to restaurants and hamburgers, etc.), still "the man as formal symbol manipulation system" *really does understand Chinese.* The subsystem of the man which is the formal symbol manipulation system for Chinese should not be confused with the subsystem for English.

So there are really two subsystems in the man; one understands English, the other Chinese, and "it's just that the two systems have little to do with each other." But, I want to reply, not only do they have little to do with each other, they are not even remotely alike. The subsystem that understands English (assuming we allow ourselves to talk in this jargon of "subsystems" for a moment) knows that the stories are about restaurants and eating hamburgers, etc.; he knows that he is being asked questions about restaurants and that he is answering questions as best as he can by making various inferences from the content of the story, and so on. But the Chinese system knows none of this; whereas the English subsystem knows that "hamburgers" refers to hamburgers, the Chinese subsystem knows only that "squiggle-squiggle" is followed by "squoggle-squoggle." All he knows is that various formal symbols are being introduced at one end and are manipulated according to rules written in English, and that other symbols are going out at the other end. The whole point of the original example was to argue that such symbol manipulation by itself couldn't be sufficient for understanding Chinese in any literal sense because the man could write "squoggle-squoggle" after "squiggle-squiggle" without understanding anything in Chinese. And it doesn't meet that argument to postulate subsystems within the man, because the subsystems are no better off than the man was in the first place; they still don't have anything even remotely like what the English-speaking man (or subsystem) has. Indeed, in the case as described, the Chinese subsystem is simply a part of the English subsystem, a part that engages in meaningless symbol manipulation according to rules in English.

Let us ask ourselves what is supposed to motivate the systems reply in the first place—that is, what *independent* grounds are there supposed to be for saying that the agent must have a subsystem within him which literally understands stories in Chinese? As far as I can tell, the only grounds are that in the example I have the same input and output as native Chinese speakers, and a program that goes from one to the other. But the point of the example has been to show that that couldn't be sufficient for understanding, in the sense in which I understand stories in English, because a person, hence the set of systems that go to make up a person, could have the right combination of input, output, and program and still not understand anything in the relevant literal sense in which I understand English. The only motivation for saying there *must* be a subsystem in me which understands Chinese is that I have a program and I can pass the Turing test;

I can fool native Chinese speakers (cf. Turing, 1950). But precisely one of the points at issue is the adequacy of the Turing test. The example shows that there could be two "systems" both of which pass the Turing test but only one of which understands; and it is no argument against this point to say that since they both pass the Turing test, they must both understand, since this claim fails to meet the argument that the system in me which understands English has a great deal more than the system which merely processes Chinese. In short the systems reply simply begs the question by insisting without argument that the system must understand Chinese.

Furthermore, the systems reply would appear to lead to consequences that are independently absurd. If we are to conclude that there must be cognition in me on the grounds that I have a certain sort of input and output and a program in between, then it looks as though all sorts of noncognitive subsystems are going to turn out to be cognitive. For example, my stomach has a level of description where it does information processing, and it instantiates any number of computer programs, but I take it we do not want to say that it has any understanding. Yet if we accept the systems reply, it is hard to see how we avoid saying that stomach, heart, liver, etc. are all understanding subsystems, since there is no principled way to distinguish the motivation for saying the Chinese subsystem understands from saying that the stomach understands. (It is, by the way, not an answer to this point to say that the Chinese system has information as input and output and the stomach has food and food products as input and output, since from the point of view of the agent, from my point of view, there is no information in either the food or the Chinese; the Chinese is just so many meaningless squiggles. The information in the Chinese case is solely in the eyes of the programmers and the interpreters, and there is nothing to prevent them from treating the input and output of my digestive organs as information if they so desire.)

This last point bears on some independent problems in strong AI, and it is worth digressing for a moment to explain it. If strong AI is to be a branch of psychology, it must be able to distinguish systems which are genuinely mental from those which are not. It must be able to distinguish the principles on which the mind works from those on which nonmental systems work; otherwise it will offer us no explanations of what is specifically mental about the mental. And the mental-nonmental distinction cannot be just in the eye of the beholder—it must be intrinsic to the systems, for otherwise it would be up to any beholder to treat people as nonmental and, e.g., hurricanes as mental, if he likes. But quite often in the AI literature the distinction is blurred in ways which would in the long run prove disastrous to the claim that AI is a cognitive inquiry. McCarthy, for example, writes: "Machines as simple as thermostats can be said to have beliefs, and having beliefs seems to be a characteristic of most machines capable of problem solving performance" (McCarthy, 1979). Anyone who thinks strong AI has a chance as a theory of the mind ought to ponder the implications of that remark. We are asked to accept it as a discovery of strong AI that the hunk of metal on the wall which we use to regulate the temperature has beliefs in exactly the same sense that we, our spouses, and our children have beliefs, and furthermore that "most" of the other machines in the room—telephone, tape recorder, adding machine, electric light switch, etc.—also have beliefs in this literal sense. It is not the aim of this article to argue against McCarthy's point, so I will simply assert the following without argument. The study of the mind starts with such facts as that humans have beliefs and thermostats, telephones, and adding machines don't. If you get a theory that denies this point, you have produced a counter-example to the theory, and the theory is false. One gets the impression that people in AI who write this sort of thing think they can get away with it because they don't really take it seriously and they don't think anyone else will either. I propose, for a moment at least, to take it seriously. Think hard for one minute about what would be necessary to establish that that hunk of metal on the wall over there has real beliefs, beliefs with direction of fit, propositional content, and conditions of satisfaction; beliefs that have the possibility of being strong beliefs or weak beliefs; nervous, anxious or secure beliefs; dogmatic, rational, or superstitious beliefs; blind faiths or hesitant cogitations; any kind of beliefs. The thermostat is not a candidate. Neither are stomach, liver, adding machine, or telephone. However, since we are taking the idea seriously, notice that its truth would be fatal to the claim of strong AI to be a science of the mind, for now the mind is everywhere. What we wanted to know is what distinguishes the mind from thermostats, livers, etc. And if McCarthy were right, strong AI hasn't a hope of telling us that.

II. *The Robot Reply* (Yale): "Suppose we wrote a different kind of program from Schank's program. Suppose we put a computer inside a robot, and this computer would not just take in formal symbols as input and give out formal symbols as output, but rather it would actually operate the robot in such a way that the robot does something very much like perceiving, walking, moving about, hammering nails, eating, drinking—anything you like. The robot would, for example, have a television camera attached to it that enabled it to see, it would have arms and legs that enabled it to act, and all of this would be controlled by its computer brain. Such a robot would, unlike Schank's computer, have genuine understanding and other mental states."

The first thing to notice about the robot reply is that it tacitly concedes that cognition is not solely a matter of formal symbol manipulation, since this reply adds a set of causal relations with the outside world. But the answer to the robot reply is that the addition of such "perceptual" and "motor" capacities adds nothing by way of understanding, in particular, or intentionality, in general, to Schank's original program; and to see this, notice that the same thought experiment applies to the robot case. Suppose that instead of the computer inside the robot, you put me inside the room and you give me again, as in the original Chinese case, more Chinese symbols with more instructions in English for matching Chinese symbols to Chinese symbols and feeding back Chinese symbols to the outside. Suppose unknown to me, some of the Chinese symbols that come to me come from a television camera attached to the robot, and other Chinese symbols that I am giving out serve to make the motors inside the robot move the robot's legs or arms. It is important to emphasize that all I am doing is manipulating formal symbols: I know none of these other facts. I am receiving "information" from the robot's "perceptual" apparatus, and I am giving out "instructions" to its motor apparatus without knowing either of these facts. I am the robot's homunculus, but unlike the traditional homunculus, I don't know what's going on. I don't understand anything except the rules for symbol manipulation. Now in this case I want to say that the robot has no intentional states at all; it is simply moving about as a result of its electrical wiring and its program. And furthermore, by instantiating the program, I have no intentional states of the relevant type. All I do is follow formal instructions about manipulating formal symbols.

III. *The Brain Simulator Reply* (Berkeley and M.I.T.): "Suppose we design a program that doesn't represent information that we have about the world, such as the information in Schank's scripts, but simulates the actual sequence of neuron firings at the synapses of the brain of a native Chinese speaker when he understands stories in Chinese and gives answers to them. The machine takes in Chinese stories and questions about them as input, it simulates the formal structure of actual Chinese brains in processing these stories, and it gives out Chinese answers as outputs. We can even imagine that the machine operates not with a single serial program but with a whole set of programs operating in parallel, in the manner that actual human brains presumably operate when they process natural language. Now surely in such a case we would have to say that the machine understood the stories; and if we refuse to say that, wouldn't we also have to deny that native Chinese speakers understood the stories? At the level of the synapses what would or could be different about the program of the computer and the program of the Chinese brain?"

Before addressing this reply, I want to digress to note that it is an odd reply for any partisan of artificial intelligence (functionalism, etc.) to make. I thought the whole idea of strong artificial intelligence is that we don't need to know how the brain works to know how the mind works. The basic hypothesis, or so I had supposed, was that there is a level of mental operations that consists in computational processes over formal elements which constitute the essence of the mental and can be realized in all sorts of different brain processes in the same way that any computer program can be realized in different computer hardwares: on the assumptions of strong AI, the mind is to the brain as the program is to the hardware, and thus we can understand the mind without doing neurophysiology. If we had to know how the brain worked in order to do AI, we wouldn't bother with AI. However, even getting this close to the operation of the brain is still not sufficient to produce understanding. To see that this is so, imagine that instead of a monolingual man in a room shuffling symbols we have the man operate an elaborate set of water pipes with valves connecting them. When the man receives the Chinese symbols he looks up in the program, written in English, which valves he has to turn on and off. Each water connection corresponds to a synapse in the Chinese brain, and the whole system is rigged up so that after doing all the right firings—that is, after turning on all the right faucets—the Chinese answers pop out at the output end of the series of pipes.

Now where is the understanding in this system? It takes Chinese as input, it simulates the formal structure of the synapses of the Chinese brain, and it gives Chinese as output. But the man certainly doesn't understand Chinese, and neither do the water pipes, and if we are tempted to adopt what I think is the absurd view that somehow the *conjunction* of man *and* water pipes understands, remember that in principle the man can internalize the formal structure of the water pipes and do all the "neuron firings" in his imagination. The problem with the brain simulator is that it is simulating the wrong things about the brain. As long as it simulates only the formal structure of the sequence of neuron firings at the synapses, it won't have simulated what matters about the brain, namely its causal properties, its ability to produce intentional states. And that the formal properties are not sufficient for the causal properties is shown by the water pipe example: we can have all the formal properties carved off from the relevant neurobiological causal properties.

IV. *The Combination Reply* (Berkeley and Stanford): "While each of the previous three replies might not be completely convincing by itself as a refutation of the Chinese room counter-example, if you take all three together they are collectively much more convincing and even decisive. Imagine a robot with a brain-shaped computer lodged in its cranial cavity; imagine the computer programmed with all the synapses of a human brain;

imagine that the whole behavior of the robot is indistinguishable from human behavior; and now think of the whole thing as a unified system and not just as a computer with inputs and outputs. Surely in such a case we would have to ascribe intentionality to the system."

I entirely agree that in such a case we would find it rational and indeed irresistible to accept the hypothesis that the robot had intentionality, as long as we knew nothing more about it. Indeed, besides appearance and behavior the other elements of the combination are really irrelevant. If we could build a robot whose behavior was indistinguishable over a large range from human behavior, we would attribute intentionality to it, pending some reason not to. We wouldn't need to know in advance that its computer brain was a formal analogue of the human brain.

But I really don't see that this is any help to the claims of strong AI, and here is why: According to strong AI, instantiating a formal program with the right input and output is a sufficient condition of, indeed is constitutive of, intentionality. As Newell (1980) puts it, the essence of the mental is the operation of a physical symbol system. But the attributions of intentionality that we make to the robot in this example have nothing to do with formal programs. They are simply based on the assumption that if the robot looks and behaves sufficiently like us, we would suppose until proven otherwise that it must have mental states like ours which cause and are expressed by its behavior, and it must have an inner mechanism capable of producing such mental states. If we knew independently how to account for its behavior without such assumptions, we would not attribute intentionality to it, especially if we knew it had a formal program. And this is the point of my earlier reply to objection II.

Suppose we knew that the robot's behavior was entirely accounted for by the fact that a man inside it was receiving uninterpreted formal symbols from the robot's sensory receptors and sending out uninterpreted formal symbols to its motor mechanisms, and the man was doing this symbol manipulation in accordance with a bunch of rules. Furthermore, suppose the man knows none of these facts about the robot; all he knows is which operations to perform on which meaningless symbols. In such a case we would regard the robot as an ingenious mechanical dummy. The hypothesis that the dummy has a mind would now be unwarranted and unnecessary, for there is now no longer any reason to ascribe intentionality to the robot or to the system of which it is a part (except of course for the man's intentionality in manipulating the symbols). The formal symbol manipulations go on, the input and output are correctly matched, but the only real locus of intentionality is the man, and he doesn't know any of the relevant intentional states; he doesn't, for example, *see* what comes into the robot's eyes, he doesn't *intend* to move the robot's arm, and he doesn't *understand* any of the remarks made to or by the robot. Nor, for the reasons stated earlier, does the system of which man and robot are a part.

To see the point contrast this case with cases where we find it completely natural to ascirbe intentionality to members of certain other primate species, such as apes and monkeys, and to domestic animals, such as dogs. The reasons we find it natural are, roughly, two: we can't make sense of the animal's behavior without the ascription of intentionality, and we can see that the beasts are made of stuff similar to our own—an eye, a nose, its skin, etc. Given the coherence of the animal's behavior and the assumption of the same causal stuff underlying it, we assume both that the animal must have mental states underlying its behavior, and the mental states must be produced by mechanisms made out of the stuff that is like our stuff. We would certainly make similar assumptions about the robot unless we had some reason not to, but as soon as we knew that the behavior was the result of a formal program, and that the actual causal properties of the physical substance were irrelevant, we would abandon the assumption of intentionality.

There are two other responses to my example which come up frequently (and so are worth discussing) but really miss the point.

V. *The Other Minds Reply* (Yale): "How do you know that other people understand Chinese or anything else? Only by their behavior. Now the computer can pass the behavioral tests as well as they can (in principle), so if you are going to attribute cognition to other people, you must in principle also attribute it to computers."

The objection is worth only a short reply. The problem in this discussion is not about how I know that other people have cognitive states, but rather what it is that I am attributing to them when I attribute cognitive states to them. The thrust of the argument is that it couldn't be just computational processes and their output because there can be computational processes and their output without the cognitive state. It is no answer to this argument to feign anesthesia. In "cognitive sciences" one presupposes the reality and knowability of the mental in the same way that in physical sciences one has to presuppose the reality and knowability of physical objects.

VI. *The Many Mansions Reply* (Berkeley): "Your whole argument presupposes that AI is only about analogue and digital computers. But that just happens to be the present state of technology. Whatever these causal processes are that you say are essential for intentionality (assuming you are right), eventually we will be able to build devices that have these causal processes and that will be artificial intelligence. So your arguments are in no way directed at the ability of artificial intelligence to produce and explain cognition."

I have no objection to this reply except to say that it in effect trivializes the project of strong artificial intelligence by redefining it as whatever artificially produces and explains cognition. The interest of the original claims made on behalf of artificial intelligence is that it was a precise, well defined thesis: mental processes are computational processes over formally defined elements. I have been concerned to challenge that thesis. If the claim is redefined so that it is no longer that thesis, my objections no longer apply, because there is no longer a testable hypothesis for them to apply to.

Let us now return to the questions I promised I would try to answer: Granted that in my original example I understand the English and I do not understand the Chinese, and granted therefore that the machine doesn't understand either English or Chinese; still there must be something about me that makes it the case that I understand English and a corresponding something lacking in me which makes it the case that I fail to understand Chinese. Now why couldn't we give those somethings, whatever they are, to a machine?

I see no reason in principle why we couldn't give a machine the capacity to understand English or Chinese, since in an important sense our bodies with our brains are precisely such machines. But I do see very strong arguments for saying that we could not give such a thing to a machine where the operation of the machine is defined solely in terms of computational processes over formally defined elements; that is, where the operation of the machine is defined as an instantiation of a computer program. It is not because I am the instantiation of a computer program that I am able to understand English and have other forms of intentionality (I am, I suppose, the instantiation of any number of computer programs), but as far as we know it is because I am a certain sort of organism with a certain biological (i.e., chemical and physical) structure, and this structure under certain conditions is causally capable of producing perception, action, understanding, learning, and other intentional phenomena. And part of the point of the present argument is that only something that had those causal powers could have that intentionality. Perhaps other physical and chemical processes could produce exactly these effects; perhaps, for example, Martians also have intentionality, but their brains are made of different stuff. That is an empirical question, rather like the question whether photosynthesis can be done by something with a chemistry different from that of chlorophyl.

But the main point of the present argument is that no purely formal model will ever be by itself sufficient for intentionality, because the formal properties are not by themselves constitutive of intentionality, and they have by themselves no causal powers except the power, when instantiated, to produce the next stage of the formalism when the machine is running. And any other causal properties which particular realizations of the formal model have are irrelevant to the formal model because we can always put the same formal model in a different realization where those causal properties are obviously absent. Even if by some miracle Chinese speakers exactly realize Schank's program, we can put the same program in English speakers, water pipes, or computers, none of which understand Chinese, the program notwithstanding.

What matters about brain operation is not the formal shadow cast by the sequence of synapses but rather the actual properties of the sequences. All the arguments for the strong version of artificial intelligence that I have seen insist on drawing an outline around the shadows cast by cognition and then claiming that the shadows are the real thing.

By way of concluding I want to state some of the general philosophical points implicit in the argument. For clarity I will try to do it in a question-and-answer fashion, and I begin with that old chestnut:

"Could a machine think?"

The answer is, obviously, yes. We are precisely such machines.

"Yes, but could an artifact, a man-made machine, think?"

Assuming it is possible to produce artificially a machine with a nervous system, neurons with axons and dendrites, and all the rest of it, sufficiently like ours, again the answer to the question seems to be obviously 'yes'. If you can exactly duplicate the causes, you could duplicate the effects. And indeed it might be possible to produce consciousness, intentionality and all the rest of it using chemical principles different from those human beings use. It is, as I said, an empirical question.

"OK, but could a digital computer think?"

If by "digital computer" we mean anything at all which has a level of description where it can correctly be described as the instantiation of a computer program, then again the answer is, of course, yes, since we are the instantiations of any number of computer programs and we can think.

"But could something think, understand, etc. *solely* by virtue of being a computer with the right sort of program? Could instantiating a program, the right program of course, by itself be a sufficient condition of understanding?"

This I think is the right question to ask, though it is usually confused with one or more of the earlier questions, and the answer to it is "no."

"Why not?"

Because the formal symbol manipulations by themselves don't have any intentionality; they are meaningless; they aren't even *symbol* manipulations, since the symbols don't symbolize anything. In the linguistic jargon they have only a syntax but no semantics. Such intentionality as computers appear to have is solely in the minds of those who program them and those who use them, those who send in the input and who interpret the output.

The aim of the Chinese room example was to try to show this by showing that as soon as we put something into the system which really does have intentionality, a man, and we program the man with the formal program, you can see that the formal program carries no additional intentionality. It adds nothing, for example, to a man's ability to understand Chinese.

Precisely that feature of AI which seemed so appealing—the distinction between the program and the realization—proves fatal to the claim that simulation could be duplication. The distinction between the program and its realization in the hardware seems to be parallel to the distinction between the level of mental operations and the level of brain operations. And if we could describe the level of mental operations as a formal program, it seems we could describe what was essential about the mind without doing either introspective psychology or neurophysiology of the brain. But the equation "Mind is to brain as program is to hardware" breaks down at several points, among them the following three:

First, the distinction between program and realization has the consequence that the same program could have all sorts of crazy realizations which had no form of intentionality. Weizenbaum (1976), for example, shows in detail how to construct a computer using a roll of toilet paper and a pile of small stones. Similarly, the Chinese story-understanding program can be programmed into a sequence of water pipes, a set of wind machines, or a monolingual English speaker, none of which thereby acquires an understanding of Chinese. Stones, toilet paper, wind, and water pipes are the wrong kind of stuff to have intentionality in the first place (only something that has the same causal powers as brains can have intentionality), and though the English speaker has the right kind of stuff for intentionality, you can easily see that he doesn't get any extra intentionality by memorizing the program, since memorizing it won't teach him Chinese.

Second, the program is purely formal, but the intentional states are not in that way formal. They are defined in terms of their content, not their form. The belief that it is raining, for example, if defined not as a certain formal shape, but as a certain mental content, with conditions of satisfaction, a direction of fit (cf. Searle, 1979), etc. Indeed, the belief as such hasn't even got a formal shape in this syntactical sense, since one and the same belief can be given an indefinite number of different syntactical expressions in different linguistic systems.

Third, as I mentioned before, mental states and events are a product of the operation of the brain, but the program is not in that way a product of the computer.

"Well if programs are in no way constitutive of mental processes, then why have so many people believed the converse? That at least needs some explanation."

I don't know the answer to that. The idea that computer simulations could be the real thing ought to have seemed suspicious in the first place because the computer isn't confined to simulating mental operations, by any means. No one supposes that computer simulations of a five-alarm fire will burn the neighborhood down or that a computer simulation of a rainstorm will leave us all drenched. Why on earth would anyone suppose that a computer simulation of understanding actually understood anything? It is sometimes said that it would be frightfully hard to get computers to feel pain or fall in love, but love and pain are neither harder nor easier than cognition or anything else. For simulation, all you need is the right input and output and a program in the middle that transforms the former into the latter. That is all the computer has for anything it does. To confuse simulation with duplication is the same mistake, whether it is pain, love, cognition, fires, or rainstorms.

Still, there are several reasons why AI must have seemed and to many people perhaps still does seem in some way to reproduce and thereby explain mental phenomena, and I believe we will not succeed in removing these illusions until we have fully exposed the reasons that give rise to them.

First, and perhaps most important, is a confusion about the notion of "information processing." Many people in cognitive science believe that the human brain with its mind does something called "information processing," and analogously the computer with its program does information processing, but fires and rainstorms on the other hand don't do information processing at all. Thus though the computer can simulate the formal features of any process whatever, it stands in a special relation to the mind and brain because when the computer is properly programmed, ideally with the same program as the brain, the information processing is identical in the two cases, and this information processing is really the essence of the mental. But the trouble with this argument is that it rests on an ambiguity in the notion of "information." In the sense in which people "process information" when they reflect, say, on problems in arithmetic or when they read and answer questions about stories, the programmed computer does not do "information processing." Rather, what it does is manipulate formal symbols. The fact that the programmer and the interpreter of the computer output use the symbols to stand for objects in the world is totally beyond the scope of the computer. The computer, to repeat, has a syntax but no semantics. Thus if you type into the computer "2 plus 2 equals?" it will type out "4." But it has no idea that "4" means 4 or that it means anything at all. And the point is not that it lacks some second-order information about the interpretation of its first-order symbols, but rather that its first-order symbols don't have any interpretations as far as the computer is concerned. All the computer has is more symbols. The introduction of the notion of "information processing" therefore produces a dilemma: Either we construe the notion of "information processing" in such a way that it implies intentionality as part of the process or we don't. If the former, then the programmed computer does not do information processing, it only manipulates formal symbols. If the latter, then although the computer does information processing, it is only in the sense in which adding machines, typewriters, stomachs, thermostats, rainstorms, and hurricanes do information processing—namely, they have a level of description where we can describe them as taking information in at one end, transforming it, and producing information as output. But in this case it is up to outside observers to interpret the input and output as information in the ordinary sense. And no similarity is established between the computer and the brain in terms of any similarity of information processing in the two cases.

Secondly, in much of AI there is a residual behaviorism or operationalism. Since appropriately programmed computers can have input/output patterns similar to human beings, we are tempted to postulate mental states in the computer similar to human mental states. But once we see that it is both conceptually and empirically possible for a system to have human capacities in some realm without having any intentionality at all, we should be able to overcome this impulse. My desk adding machine has calculating capacities but no intentionality, and in this paper I have tried to show that a system could have input and output capabilities which duplicated those of a native Chinese speaker and still not understand Chinese, regardless of how it was programmed. The Turing test is typical of the tradition in being unashamedly behavioristic and operationalistic, and I believe that if AI workers totally repudiated behaviorism and operationalism, much of the confusion between simulation and duplication would be eliminated.

Third, this residual operationalism is joined to a residual form of dualism; indeed, strong AI only makes sense given the dualistic assumption that where the mind is concerned the brain doesn't matter. In strong AI (and in functionalism, as well) what matters are programs, and programs are independent of their realization in machines; indeed, as far as AI is concerned, the same program could be realized by an electronic machine, a Cartesian mental substance, or a Hegelian world spirit. The single most surprising discovery that I have made in discussing these issues is that many AI workers are shocked by my idea that actual human mental phenomena might be dependent on actual physical-chemical properties of actual human brains. But I should not have been surprised; for unless you accept some form of dualism, the strong AI project hasn't got a chance. The project is to reproduce and explain the mental by designing programs; but unless the mind is not only conceptually but empirically independent of the brain, you cannot carry out the project, for the program is completely independent of any realization. Unless you believe that the mind is separable from the brain both conceptually and empirically—dualism in a strong form—you cannot hope to reproduce the mental by writing and running programs since programs must be independent of brains or any other particular forms of instantiation. If mental operations consist of computational operations on formal symbols, it follows that they have no interesting connection with the brain, and the only connection would be that the brain just happens to be one of the indefinitely many types of machines capable of instantiating the program. This form of dualism is not the traditional Cartesian variety that claims there are two sorts of *substances,* but it is Cartesian in the sense that it insists that what is specifically mental about the mind has no intrinsic connection with the actual properties of the brain. This underlying dualism is masked from us by the fact that AI literature contains frequent fulminations against "dualism"; what the authors seem to be unaware of is that their position presupposes a strong version of dualism.

"Could a machine think?" My own view is that *only* a machine could think, and indeed only very special kinds of machines, namely brains and machines that had the *same causal powers* as brains. And that is the main reason why strong AI has had little to tell us about thinking: it has nothing to tell us about machines. By its own definition it is about programs, and programs are not machines. Whatever else intentionality is, it is a biological phenomenon and it is as likely to be as causally dependent on the specific biochemistry of its origins as lactation, photosynthesis, or any other biological phenomena. No one would suppose that we could produce milk and sugar by running a computer simulation of the formal sequences in lactation and photosynthesis; but where the mind is concerned, many people are willing to believe in such a miracle, because of a deep and abiding dualism: the mind they suppose is a matter of formal processes and is independent of specific material causes in the way that milk and sugar are not.

In defense of this dualism, the hope is often expressed that the brain is a digital computer (early computers, by the way, were often called "electronic brains"). But that is no help. Of course the brain is a digital computer. Since everything is a digital computer, brains are too. The point is that the brain's causal capacity to produce intentionality cannot consist in its instantiating a computer program, since for any program you like it is possible for something to instantiate that program and still not have any mental states. Whatever it is that the brain does to produce intentionality, it cannot consist of instantiating a program, since no program by itself is sufficient for intentionality.

Acknowledgments: I am indebted to a rather large number of people for discussion of these matters and for their patient attempts to overcome my ignorance of artificial intelligence. I would especially like to thank Ned Block, Hubert Dreyfus, John Haugeland, Roger Schank, Robert Wilensky, and Terry Winograd.

11

Methodological Solipsism Considered as a Research Strategy in Cognitive Psychology

JERRY A. FODOR

> . . . to form the idea of an object and to form an idea simply is the same thing; the reference of the idea to an object being an extraneous denomination, of which in itself it bears no mark or character.
>
> —Hume (1888), p. 20

THE PAPER distinguishes two doctrines, both of which inform theory construction in much of modern cognitive psychology: the representational theory of mind (according to which propositional attitudes are relations that organisms bear to mental representations) and the computational theory of mind (according to which mental processes have access only to formal (nonsemantic) properties of the mental representations over which they are defined.

It is argued that the acceptance of some such formality condition is warranted, at least for that part of psychology which concerns itself with the mental causation of behavior. The paper closes with a discussion of the prospects for a "naturalistic" psychology: one which defines its generalizations over relations between mental representations and their environmental causes. Two related arguments are proposed, both leading to the conclusion that no such research strategy is likely to prove fruitful.

Your standard contemporary cognitive psychologist—your thoroughly modern mentalist—is disposed to reason as follows. To think (e.g.,) that Marvin is melancholy is to represent Marvin in a certain way; viz. as being melancholy (and not, for example, as being maudlin, morose, moody, or merely moping and dyspeptic). But surely we cannot represent Marvin as being melancholy except as we are in some or other relation to a representation of Marvin; and not just to *any* representation of Marvin, but, in particular, to a representation the content of which is *that* Marvin is melancholy; a representation which, as it were, expresses the propoposition that Marvin is melancholy. So, a fortiori, at least some mental states/processes are or involve at least some relations to at least some representations. Perhaps, then, this is the *typical* feature of such mental states/processes as cognitive psychology studies; perhaps all such states can be viewed as relations to representations and all such processes as operations defined on representations.

This is, prima facie, an appealing proposal, since it gives the psychologist two degrees of freedom to play with and they seem, intuitively, to be the right two. On the one hand, mental states are distinguished by the *content* of the associated representations, and we therefore can allow for the difference between thinking that Marvin is melancholy and thinking that Sam is (or that Albert isn't, or that it sometimes snows in Cincinnati); and, on the other hand, mental states are distinguished by the *relation* that the subject bears to the associated representation (so we can allow for the difference between thinking, hoping, supposing, doubting and pretending that Marvin is melancholy). It's hard to believe that a serious psychology could make do with fewer (or less refined) distinctions than these, and it's hard to believe that a psychology that makes these distinctions could avoid taking the notion of mental representation seriously. Moreover, the burden of argument is clearly upon anyone who claims that we need *more* degrees of freedom than just these two: the least hypothesis that is remotely plausible is that a mental state is (type) individuated by specifying a relation and a representation such that the subject bears the one to the other.[1]

---

1. I shall speak of 'type identity' (distinctness) of mental states to pick out the sense of 'same mental state' in which, for example, John and Mary are in the same mental state if both believe that water flows. Correspondingly, I shall use the notion of 'token identity' (distinctness) of mental state to pick out the sense of 'same mental state' in which it's necessary that if x and y are in the same mental state, then x = y.

I'll say that any psychology that takes this line is a version of the REPRESENTATIONAL THEORY OF THE MIND. I think that it's reasonable to adopt some such theory as a sort of working hypothesis, if only because there aren't any alternatives which seem to be even *remotely* plausible and because empirical research carried out within this framework has, thus far, proved interesting and fruitful.[2] However, my present concern is neither to attack nor to defend this view, but rather to distinguish it from something other—and stronger—that modern cognitive psychologists *also* hold. I shall put this stronger doctrine as the view that mental states and processes are COMPUTATIONAL. Much of what is characteristic of cognitive psychology is a consequence of adherence to this stronger view. What I want to do in this paper is to say something about what this stronger view is, something about why I think it's plausible, and, most of all, something about the ways in which it shapes the cognitive psychology we have.

I take it that computational processes are both *symbolic* and *formal*. They are symbolic because they are defined over representations, and they are formal because they apply to representations in virtue of (roughly) the *syntax* of the representations. It's the second of these conditions that makes the claim that mental processes are computational stronger than the representational theory of the mind. Most of this paper will be a meditation upon the consequences of assuming that mental processes are formal processes.

I'd better cash the parenthetical 'roughly'. To say that an operation is formal isn't the same as saying that it is syntactic since we could have formal processes defined over representations which don't, in any obvious sense *have* a syntax. Rotating an image would be a timely example. What makes syntactic operations a species of formal operations is that being syntactic is a way of *not* being semantic. Formal operations are the ones that are specified without reference to such semantic properties of representations as, for example, truth, reference and meaning. Since we don't know how to complete this list (since, that is, we don't know what semantic properties there are), I see no responsible way of saying what, in general, formality amounts

2. For extensive discussion, see Fodor (1975, 1978b).

to. The notion of formality will thus have to remain intuitive and metaphoric, at least for present purposes: formal operations apply in terms of the, as it were, shapes of the objects in their domains.[3]

To require that mental processes be computational (viz. formal-syntactic) is thus to require something not very clear. Still, the requirement has some clear consequences, and they are striking and tendentious. Consider that we started by assuming that the *content* of representations is a (type) individuating feature of mental states. So far as the *representational* theory of the mind is concerned, it's possibly the *only* thing that distinguishes Peter's thought that Sam is silly from his thought that Sally is depressed. But, now, if the *computational* theory of the mind is true (and if, as we may assume, content is a semantic notion par excellence) it follows that content alone cannot distinguish thoughts. More exactly, the computational theory of the mind requires that two thoughts can be distinct in content only if they can be identified with relations to formally distinct representations. More generally: fix the subject and the relation, and then mental states can be (type) distinct only if the representations which constitute their objects are formally distinct.

Again, consider that accepting a formality condition upon mental states implies a drastic narrowing of the ordinary ontology of the mental; all sorts of states which look, prima facie, to be mental in good standing are going to turn out to be none of the psychologist's business if the formality condition is endorsed. This point is one that philosophers have made in a number of contexts, and usually in a deprecating tone of voice. Take, for example, knowing that such-and-such, and assume that you can't know what's not the case. Since, on that assumption, knowledge is involved with truth, and since truth is a semantic notion, it's going to follow that there can't be a psychology of *knowledge* (even if it is consonant with the formality condition to hope for a psychology of *belief*). Similarly, it's a way of making a point

---

3. This is *not*, notice, the same as saying 'formal operations are the ones that apply mechanically'; in this latter sense, *formality* means something like *explicitness*. There's no particular reason for using 'formal' to mean both 'syntactic' and 'explicit', though the ambiguity abounds in the literature.

of Ryle's to say that, strictly speaking, there can't be a psychology of perception if the formality condition is to be complied with. Seeing is an achievement; you can't see what's not there. From the point of view of the representational theory of the mind, this means that seeing involves relations between mental representations *and their referents;* hence, semantic relations within the meaning of the act.

I hope that such examples suggest (what, in fact, I think is true) that even if the formality condition isn't very clear, it is quite certainly very strong. In fact, I think it's not all *that* anachronistic to see it as the central issue which divides the two main traditions in the history of psychology: 'Rational psychology' on the one hand, and 'Naturalism' on the other. Since this is a mildly eccentric way of cutting the pie, I'm going to permit myself a semihistorical excursus before returning to the main business of the paper.

Descartes argued that there is an important sense in which how the world is makes no difference to one's mental states. Here is a well known passage from the first *Meditation:*

> At this moment it does indeed seem to me that it is with eyes awake that I am looking at this paper; that this head which I move is not asleep, that it is deliberately and of set purpose that I extend my hand and perceive it . . . But in thinking over this I remind myself that on many occasions I have been deceived by similar illusions, and in dwelling on this reflection I see so manifestly that there are no certain indications by which we may clearly distinguish wakefulness from sleep that I am lost in astonishment. And my astonishment is such that it is almost capable of persuading me that I now dream.   (1967; p. 146)

At least three sorts of reactions to this kind of argument are distinguishable in the philosophical literature. First, there's a long tradition, including both Rationalists and Empiricists, which takes it as axiomatic that one's experiences (and, a fortiori, one's beliefs) might have been just as they are even if the world had been quite different from the way that it is. See, for example, the passage from Hume which serves as an epigraph to this paper. Second, there's a vaguely Wittgensteinian mood in which one argues that it's just *false* that one's mental states might have been what they are had the world been relevantly different. For example, if there had been a dagger there, Macbeth would have been *seeing*, not just hallucinating. And what could be more different than that? If the Cartesian feels that this reply misses the point, he is at least under an obligation to say precisely which point it misses; in precisely *which* respects the way the world is is irrelevant to the character of one's beliefs, experiences, etc. Finally there's a tradition which argues that—epistemology to one side—it is at best a strategic mistake to attempt to develop a psychology which individuates mental states without reference to their environmental causes and effects (e.g., which counts the state that Macbeth *was* in as type-identical to the state he would have been in had the dagger been supplied.) I have in mind the tradition which includes the American Naturalists (notably Pierce and Dewey), all the learning theorists, and such contemporary representatives as Quine in philosophy and Gibson in psychology. The recurrent theme here is that psychology is a branch of biology, hence that one must view the organism as embedded in a physical environment. The psychologist's job is to trace those organism/environment interactions which constitute its behavior. A passage from William James (1890) will serve to give the feel of the thing:

> On the whole, few recent formulas have done more service of a rough sort in psychology than the Spencerian one that the essence of mental life and of bodily life are one, namely, 'the adjustment of inner to outer relations.' Such a formula is vagueness incarnate; but because it takes into account the fact that minds inhabit environments which act on them and on which they in turn react; because, in short, it takes mind in the midst of all its concrete relations, it is immensely more fertile than the old-fashioned 'rational psychology' which treated the soul as a detached existent, sufficient unto itself, and assumed to consider only its nature and its properties.   (p. 6)

A number of adventitious intrusions have served to muddy the issues in this long-standing dispute. On the one hand, it may well be that Descartes was relying on a specifically introspectionist construal of the claim that the individuation of mental states is independent of their environmental causes. That is, Descartes' point may have been that (a) mental states are (type) identical if and only if they are introspectively indistinguishable, and (b) introspection cannot distinguish (e.g.,) perception from hallucination, or knowledge from belief. On the other hand, the naturalist, in point of historical fact, is often a behaviorist as well. He wants to argue not only that mental states are individuated by reference to organism/environment relations, but also that such relations constitute the mental. In the context of the present discussion, he is arguing for the abandonment not just of the formality condition, but of the notion of mental representation as well.

If, however, we take the computational theory of the mind as what's central to the issue, we can reconstruct the debate between rational psychologists and naturalists in a way that does justice to both their points; in particular, in a way which frees the discussion from involvement with introspectionism on the one side and behaviorism on the other.

Insofar as we think of mental processes as computational (hence as formal operations defined on representations) it will be natural to take the mind to be, *inter alia,* a kind of computer. That is, we will think of the mind as carrying out whatever symbol manipulations are constitutive of the hypothesized computational processes. To a first approximation, we may thus construe mental operations as pretty directly analogous to those of a Turing machine. There is, for example, a working memory (corresponding to a tape) and there are capacities for scanning and altering the contents of the memory (corresponding to the operations of reading and writing on the tape). If we want to extend the computational metaphor by providing access to information about the environment, we can think of the computer as having access to "oracles" which serve, on occasion, to enter information in the memory. On the intended interpretation of this model, these oracles are analogs to the senses. In particular, they are assumed to be transducers, in that what they write on the tape is determined solely by the ambient environmental energies that impinge upon them. (For elaboration of this sort of account, see Putnam, 1960; it is, of course, widely familiar from discussions in artificial intelligence.)

I'm not endorsing this model, but simply presenting it as a natural extension of the computational picture of the mind. Its present interest is that we can use it to see how the formality condition connects with the Cartesian claim that the character of mental processes is somehow independent of their environmental causes and effects. The point is that, so long as we are thinking of mental processes as purely computational, the bearing of environmental information upon such processes is exhausted by the formal character of whatever the oracles write on the tape. In particular, it doesn't matter to such processes whether what the oracles write is *true;* whether, for example, they really are transducers faithfully mirroring the state of the environment, or merely the output end of a typewriter manipulated by a Cartesian demon bent on deceiving the machine. I'm saying, in effect, that the formality condition, viewed in this context, is tantamount to a sort of methodological solipsism. If mental processes are formal, they have access only to the formal properties of such representations of the environment as the senses provide. Hence, they have no access to the *semantic* properties of such representations, including the property of being true, of having referents, or, indeed, the property of being representations *of the environment.*

That some such methodological solipsism really is implicated in much current psychological practice is best seen by examining what researchers actually do. Consider, for example, the well-known work of Professor Terry Winograd. Winograd was primarily interested in the computer simulation of certain processes involved in the handling of verbal information; asking and answering questions, drawing inferences, following instructions and the like.The form of his theory was a program for a computer which 'lives in' and operates upon a simple world of block-like geometric objects. (Cf. Winograd, 1971) Many of the capacities that the device exercises vis-à-vis its environment seem impressively intelligent. It can arrange the blocks to order, it can issue 'perceptual' reports of the present state of its environment and 'memory' reports of its past states, it can devise simple plans for achieving desired environment configurations, and it can discuss its undertakings (more or less in English) with whoever is running the program.

The interesting point for our purposes, however, is that the machine environment which is the nominal object of these actions and conversations actually isn't there. What actually happens is that the programmer so arranges the memory states of the machine that the available data are whatever they would be *if* there were objects for the machine to perceive and manipulanda for it to operate upon. In effect, the machine lives in an entirely notional world; all its beliefs are false. Of course, it doesn't matter to the machine that its beliefs are false since falsity is a semantic property and, qua computer, the device satisfies the formality condition; viz. it has access only to formal (non-semantic) properties of the representations that it manipulates. In effect, the device is in precisely the situation that Descartes dreads; it's a mere computer which dreams that it's a robot.

I hope that this discussion suggests how acceptance of the computational theory of the mind leads to a sort of methodological solipsism as a part of the research strategy of contemporary cognitive psychology. In particular, I hope it's clear how you get that consequence from the formality condition alone, without so much as raising the introspection issue. I stress this point because it seems to me that there has been considerable confusion about it among the psychologists themselves. People who do machine simulation, in particular, very often advertise themselves as working on the question how thought (or language) is related to the world. My present point is that, whatever else they're doing, they certainly aren't doing *that.* The very assumption that defines their field—viz. that they study mental processes *qua* formal operations on symbols—guarantees that their studies won't answer the question how the symbols so manipulated are semantically interpreted. You can, for example, build a machine that answers baseball questions in the sense that (e.g.) if you type in "Who had the most wins by a National League pitcher since Dizzy Dean?" it will type out "Robin Roberts, who won 28." But you delude yourself if you think that a machine which in this sense answers baseball questions is thereby answering questions *about* baseball (or that the machine has somehow referred to Robin Roberts). If the *programmer* chooses to interpret the machine inscription "Robin Roberts won 28" as a statement about Robin Roberts (e.g., as the statement that he won 28), that's all well and good, but it's no business of the machine's. The machine has no access to that interpretation, and its computations are in no way affected by it. The machine doesn't know what it's talking about, and it doesn't care; *about* is a semantic relation.[4]

4. Some fairly deep methodological issues in AI are involved here. See Fodor (1978a), where this surface is lightly scratched.

This brings us to a point where, having done some sort of justice to the Cartesian's insight, we can also do some sort of justice to the naturalist's. For, after all, mental processes are supposed to be operations on representations, and it is in the nature of representations to represent. We have seen that a psychology which embraces the formality condition is thereby debarred from raising questions about the semantic properties of mental representations; yet surely such questions ought *somewhere* to be raised. The computer which prints out 'RR won 28" is not thereby referring to RR. But, surely, when I think *RR won 28,* I *am* thinking about RR, and if not in virtue of having performed some formal operations on some representations, then presumably in virtue of something else. It's perhaps borrowing the least tendentious fragment of causal theories of reference to assume that what fixes the interpretation of my mental representations of RR is something about the way that he and I are embedded in the world; perhaps not a causal chain stretching between us, but anyhow *some* facts about how he and I are causally situated; *Dasein,* as you might say. Only a *naturalistic* psychology will do to specify these facts, because here we are explicitly in the realm of organism/environment transactions.

We are on the verge of a bland and ecumenical conclusion: that there is room both for a computational psychology—viewed as a theory of formal processes defined over mental representations—*and* a naturalistic psychology, viewed as a theory of the (presumably causal) relations between representations and the world which fix their semantic interpretations of the former. I think that, in principle, this is the right way to look at things. In practice, however, I think that it's misleading. So far as I can see, it's overwhelmingly likely that computational psychology is the only one that we are going to get. I want to argue for this conclusion in two steps. First, I'll argue for what I've till now only assumed: that we must *at least* have a psychology which accepts the formality condition. Then I'll argue that there's good reason to suppose that that's the most that we can have; that a naturalistic psychology isn't a practical possibility and isn't likely to become one.

The first move, then, is to give reasons for believing that at least *some* part of psychology should honor the formality condition. Here too the argument proceeds in two steps. I'll argue first that it is typically under an *opaque* construal that attributions of propositional attitudes to organisms enter into explanations of their behavior; and second that the formality condition is intimately involved with the explanation of propositional attitudes so construed: roughly, that it's reasonable to believe that we can get such explanations only within computational theories. *Caveat emptor:* the arguments under review are, in large part, nondemonstrative. In particular, they will assume the perfectibility in principle of the kinds of psychological theories now being developed, and it is entirely possible that this is an assumption contrary to fact.

Thesis: when we articulate the generalizations in virtue of which behavior is contingent upon mental states, it is typically an opaque construal of the mental state attributions that does the work; for example, it's a construal under which believing that *a is F* is logically independent from believing that *b is F,* even in the case where a = b. It will be convenient to speak not only of opaque construals of propositional attitude ascriptions, but also of *opaque taxonomies* of mental state types; e.g. of taxonomies which, *inter alia,* count the belief that the Morning Star rises in the East as type distinct from the belief that the Evening Star does. (Correspondingly, *transparent* taxonomies are such as, *inter alia,* would count these beliefs as type identical.) So, the claim is that mental states are typically opaquely taxonomized for purposes of psychological theory.[5]

The point doesn't depend upon the examples, so I'll stick to the most informal sorts of cases. Suppose I know that John wants to meet the girl who lives next door; and suppose I know that this is true when 'wants to' is construed opaquely. Then, given even

5. I'm told by some of my friends that this paragraph could be read as suggesting that there are *two kinds* of beliefs: opaque ones and transparent ones. That is not, of course, the way that it is intended to be read. The idea is rather that there are two kinds of conditions that we can place on determinations that a pair of belief tokens count as tokens of the same belief type. According to one set of conditions (corresponding to transparent taxonomy), a belief that the Morning Star is such and such counts as the same belief as a belief that the Evening Star is such and such; whereas, according to the other set of conditions (corresponding to opaque taxonomy), it does not.

rough-and-ready generalizations about how people's behaviors are contingent upon their utilities, I can make some reasonable predictions (/guesses) about what John is likely to do: he's likely to say (viz. utter), "I want to meet the girl who lives next door". He's likely to call upon his neighbor. He's likely (at a minimum, and all things being equal) to exhibit next-door-directed behavior. None of this is frightfully exciting, but it's all I need for present purposes, and what more would you expect from folk psychology?

On the other hand, suppose that all I know is that John wants to meet the girl next door where 'wants to' is construed transparently. I.e., all I know is that it's true of the girl next door that John wants to meet her. Then there is little or nothing that I can predict about how John is likely to proceed. And this is *not* just because rough and ready psychological generalizations want *ceteris paribus* clauses to fill them in; it's also for the deeper reason that I can't infer from what I know about John to any relevant description of the mental causes of his behavior. For example, I have no reason to predict that John will say such things as "I want to meet the girl who lives next door" since, let John be as cooperative and as truthful as you like, and let him be utterly a native speaker, still, he *may believe* that the girl he wants to meet languishes in Latvia. In which case, "I want to meet the girl who lives next door" is the last thing it will occur to him to say. (The contestant wants to say 'suspender', for 'suspender' is the magic word. Consider what we can predict about his probable verbal behavior if we take this (a) opaquely and (b) transparently. And, of course, the same sorts of points apply, *mutatis mutandis*, to the prediction of *non*verbal behavior).

Ontologically, transparent readings are stronger than opaque ones; for example, the former license existential inferences which the latter do not. But psychologically, opaque readings are stronger than transparent ones; they tell us more about the character of the mental causes of behavior. The representational theory of mind offers an explanation of this anomaly. Opaque ascriptions are true in virtue of the way that the agent represents the objects of his wants (intentions, beliefs, etc.) *to himself*. And, by assumption, such representations function in the causation of the behaviors that the agent produces. So, for example, to say that it's true *opaquely* that Oedipus did such-and-such because he wanted to marry Jocasta, is to say something like (though not, perhaps, *very* like; see Fodor, 1978b): "Oedipus said to himself, 'I want to marry Jocasta', and his so saying was among the causes of his behavior". Whereas to say (only) that it's true transparently that O. wanted to marry J. is to say no more than that among the causes of his behavior was O's saying to himself 'I want to marry . . .' where the blank was filled by *some* expression that denotes J.[6] But now, what O. *does,* how he in the proprietary sense behaves, will depend on which description he (literally) had in mind.[7] If it's 'Jocasta', courtship behavior follows *ceteris paribus.* Whereas, if it's 'my Mum', we have the situation towards the end of the play and Oedipus at Colonus eventually ensues.

I dearly wish that I could leave this topic here, because it would be very convenient to be able to say, without qualification, what I strongly implied above: the opaque readings of propositional attitude ascriptions tell us how people represent the objects of

6. I'm leaving it open that it may be to say still less than this (e.g., because of problems about reference under false descriptions). For purposes of the present discussion, I don't need to run a line on the truth conditions for transparent propositional attitude ascriptions. Thank Heaven, since I do not have one.

7. It's worth emphasizing that the sense of 'behavior' *is* proprietary, and that that's pretty much what you would expect. Not every true description of an act can be such that a theory of the mental causation of behavior will explain the act under that description. (In being rude to Darcy, Elizabeth is insulting the man whom she will eventually marry. A theory of the mental causation of her behavior might have access to the former description, but not, surely, to the latter.)

Many philosophers—especially since Wittgenstein—have emphasized the ways in which the description of behavior may depend upon its context, and it is a frequent charge against modern versions of Rational psychology that they typically ignore such characterizations. So they do, but so what? You can't have explanations of everything under every description, and it's a question for empirical determination which descriptions of behavior reveal its systematicity vis-à-vis its causes. The Rational psychologist is prepared to bet that—to put it *very* approximately—behavior will prove to be systematic under some of the descriptions under which it is intentional.

At a minimum, the present claim goes like this: there is a way of taxonomizing behaviors and a way of taxonomizing mental states such that, given these taxonomies, theories of the mental causation of behavior will be forthcoming. And that way of taxonomizing mental states construes them nontransparently.

their propositional attitudes. What one would like to say, in particular, is that if two people are identically related to formally identical mental representations, then they are in opaquely type identical mental states. This would be convenient because it yields a succinct and gratifying characterization of what a computational cognitive psychology is about: such a psychology studies propositional attitudes opaquely taxonomized.

I think, in fact, that this is *roughly* the right thing to say, since what I think is *exactly* right is that the construal of propositional attitudes which such a psychology renders is nontransparent. (It's nontransparency that's crucial in all the examples we have been considering). The trouble is that nontransparency isn't quite the same notion as opacity, as we shall now see.

The question before us is: 'What are the relations between the pretheoretic notion of type identity of mental states opaquely construed and the notion of type identity of mental states that you get from a theory which strictly honors the formality condition?' And the answer is: complicated. For one thing, it's not clear that we have *a* pretheoretic notion of the opaque reading of a propositional attitude ascription: I doubt that the two standard tests for opacity (failure of existential generalization and failure of substitutivity of identicals) so much as pick out the same class of cases. But what's more important are the following considerations. While it's notorious that extensionally identical thoughts may be opaquely type distinct (e.g. thoughts about the Morning Star and thoughts about the Evening star) there are nevertheless some semantic conditions on opaque type identification. In particular:

(a) there are some cases of formally distinct but coextensive token thoughts which count as tokens of the same (opaque) type (and hence as identical in content at least on one way of individuating contents); and

(b) *non*-coextensive thoughts are *ipso facto* type distinct (and differ in content at least on one way of individuating contents.)

Cases of type (a): (1) I think I'm sick and you think I'm sick. What's running through my head is 'I'm sick'; what's running through your head is 'he's sick'. But we are both having thoughts of the same (opaque) type (and hence of the same content.)

(2) You think: 'that one looks edible'; I think: 'this one looks edible.' Our thought are opaquely type identical if we are thinking about the same one.

It connects with the existence of such cases that pronouns and demonstratives are typically (perhaps invariably) construed as referring, even when they occur in what are otherwise opaque constructions. So, for example, it seems to me that I can't report Macbeth's hallucination by saying: "Macbeth thinks that's a dagger' if Macbeth is staring at nothing at all. Which is to say that "that's a dagger" doesn't report Macbeth's mental state even though "that's a dagger may be precisely what is running through Macbeth's head (precisely the representation his relation to which is constitutive of his belief).

Cases of type (b): (1) Suppose that Sam feels faint and Misha knows he does. Then what's running through Misha's head may be 'he feels faint.' Suppose too that Misha feels faint and Alfred knows he does. Then what's running through Alfred's head, too, may be 'he feels faint.' I have no, or rather no univocal, inclination to say, in this case, that Alfred and Misha are having type identical thoughts even though the principle of type individuation is, by assumption opaque and even though Alfred and Misha have the same things running through their heads. But if this is right, then formal identity of mental representations cannot be sufficient for type identity of opaquely taxonomized mental states.[8] (There is an interesting discussion of this sort of case in Geach

---

8. One might try saying: what counts for opaque type individuation is what's *in* your head, not just what's running through it. So, for example, though Alfred and Misha are both thinking, 'he feels faint,' nevertheless different counterfactuals are true of them: Misha would cash his pronoun as: 'he, Sam', whereas Alfred would cash *his* pronoun as: 'he, Misha.' The problem would then be to decide *which* such counterfactuals are relevant, since, if we count all of them, it's going to turn out that there are few, if any, cases of distinct organisms having type identical thoughts.

I won't, in any event, pursue this proposal, since it seems clear that it won't, in principle, cope with all the relevant cases. Two people would be having different thoughts when each is thinking, 'I'm ill' even if *everything* in their heads were the same.

(1957). Geach says that Aquinas says that there is no 'intelligible difference' between Alfred's thought and Misha's. I don't know whether this means that they are having the same thought or that they aren't.)

(2) Suppose that there are two Lake Eries (two bodies of water so-called). Consider two tokens of the thought 'Lake Erie is wet,' one of which is, intuitively speaking, about the Lake Erie in North America and one of which is about the other one. Here again, I'm inclined to say that the aboriginal, uncorrupted, pretheoretical notion of type-wise same thought wants these to be tokens of *different* thoughts and takes these thoughts to differ in content. In this case, though, as in the others, I think there's also a countervailing inclination to say that they count as type identical—and as identical in content—for some relevant purposes and in some relevant respects. How like aboriginal, uncorrupted, pretheoretical intuition!

I think, in short, that the intuitive opaque taxonomy is actually what you might call 'semi-transparent'. On the one hand, certain conditions on coreference are in force (Misha's belief that he's ill is type distinct from Sam's belief that *he's* ill, and my thought *this is edible* may be type identical to your thought *that is edible*. On the other hand, you don't get free substitution of coreferring expressions (beliefs about the Morning Star are type distinct from beliefs about the Evening Star) and existential generalization doesn't go through for beliefs about Santa Claus.

Apparently, then, the notion of same mental state that we get from a theory which honors the formality condition is related to, but not identical to, the notion of same mental state that unreconstructed intuition provides for opaque construals. And it would certainly be reasonable to ask whether we actually need both. I think the answer is probably: yes, if we want to capture *all* the intuitions. For, if we restrict ourselves to either one of the taxonomies we get consequences that we don't like. On the one hand, if we taxonomize *purely* formally, we get identity of belief compatible with difference of truth value. (Misha's belief that he's ill will be type identical to Sam's belief that *he's* ill, but one may be true while the other is false.) On the other hand, if we taxonomize solely according to the pretheoretic criteria, we get trouble with the idea that people act out of their beliefs and desires. We need, in particular, some taxonomy according to which Sam and Misha have the *same* belief in order to explain why it is that they exhibit the same behaviors. It is, after all, *part* of the pretheoretic notion of belief that difference in belief ought *ceteris paribus* to show up in behavior *somewhere* ('*ceteris paribus*' here means 'given relevant identities among other mental states'), whereas, it's possible to construct cases where differences like the one between Misha's belief and Sam's can't show up in behavior even in principle (see note 8, above). What we have, in short, is a tension between a partially semantic taxonomy and an entirely functional one, and the recommended solution is to use both.

Having said all this, I now propose largely to ignore it and use the term 'opaque taxonomy' for principles of type individuation according to which Misha and Sam are in the same mental state when each believes himself to be ill. When I need to distinguish this sense of opaque taxonomy from the pretheoretic one, I'll talk about *full* opacity and fully opaque type identification.

My claim has been that, in doing our psychology, we want to attribute mental states fully opaquely because it's the fully opaque reading which tells us what the agent has in mind, and it's what the agent has in mind that causes his behavior. I now need to say something about how, precisely, all this is supposed to constitute an argument for the formality condition.

Point one: it's just as well that it's the fully opaque construal of mental states that we need since, patently, that's the only one that the formality condition permits us. This is because the formality condition prohibits taxonomizing psychological states by reference to the semantic properties of mental representations and, at bottom, transparency is a semantic (viz. nonformal; viz. nonsyntactic) notion. The point is sufficiently obvious: if we count the belief that the Evening Star is F as (type) identical to the belief that the Morning Star is F, that must be because of the coreference of such expressions as 'The Morning Star' and 'The Evening Star'. But coreference is a semantic property, and not one which could conceivably have a formal Doppelgänger; it's inconceivable, in particular, that there should be a system of mental representations such that, in the general case, coreferring expressions are formally identical in that system. (This might be true for God's mind, but not, surely, for anybody else's (and

not for God's either unless he is an Extensionalist; which I doubt.))
So, if we want transparent taxonomies of mental states, we will
have to give up the formality condition. So it's a good thing for
the computational theory of the mind that it's not transparent
taxonomies that we want.

What's harder to argue for (but might, nevertheless, be true) is
point two: that the formality condition *can* be honored by a theory which taxonomizes mental states according to their content.
For, barring caveats previously reviewed, it may be that mental
states are distinct in content only if they are relations to formally
distinct mental representations; in effect, that aspects of content
can be reconstructed as aspects of form, at least insofar as appeals
to content figure in accounts of the mental causation of behavior.
The main thing to be said in favor of this speculation is that it
allows us to explain, within the context of the representational
theory of mind, how beliefs of different content *can* have different behavioral effects, even when the beliefs are transparently type
identical. The form of explanation goes: it's because different content implies formally distinct internal representations (via the
formality condition) and formally distinct internal representations
can be functionally different—can differ in their causal role.
Whereas, to put it mildly, it's hard to see how internal representations could differ in causal role *unless* they differed in form.

To summarize: transparent taxonomy is patently incompatible
with the formality condition; whereas taxonomy in respect of
content *may* be compatible with the formality condition, plus
or minus a bit. That taxonomy in respect of content *is* compatible
with the formality condition, plus or minus a bit, is perhaps *the*
basic idea of modern cognitive theory. The representational theory
of mind and the computational theory of mind merge here for, on
the one hand, it's claimed that psychological states differ in content only if they are relations to type-distinct mental representations; and, on the other, it's claimed that only formal properties
of mental representations contribute to their type individuation
for the purposes of theories of mind/body interaction. Or, to put
it the other way 'round, it's allowed that mental representations
affect behavior in virtue of their content, but it's maintained that
mental representations are distinct in content only if they are also
distinct in form. The first clause is required to make it plausible

that mental states are relations to mental representations and the second is required to make it plausible that mental processes are computations. (Computations just *are* processes in which representations have their causal consequences in virtue of their form.) By thus exploiting the notions of content and computation *together*, a cognitive theory seeks to connect the *intensional* properties of mental states with their *causal* properties vis-à-vis behavior. Which is, of course, exactly what a theory of the mind ought to do.

As must be evident from the preceding, I'm partial to programmatic arguments: ones which seek to infer the probity of a conceptual apparatus from the fact that it plays a role in some prima facie plausible research enterprise. So, in particular, I've argued that a taxonomy of mental states which honors the formality condition seems to be required by theories of the mental causation of behavior, and that that's a reason for taking such taxonomies very seriously.

But there lurks, within the general tradition of representational theories of mind, a deeper intuition: that it is not only *advisable* but actually *mandatory* to assume that mental processes have access only to formal (non-semantic) properties of mental representations; that the contrary view is not only empirically fruitless but also conceptually unsound. I find myself in sympathy with this intuition, though I'm uncertain precisely how the arguments ought to go. What follows is just a sketch.

I'll begin with a version that I *don't* like; an epistemological version.

Look, it makes no *sense* to suppose that mental operations could apply to mental representations in virtue of (e.g.) the truth or falsity of the latter. For, consider: truth value is a matter of correspondence to the way the world is. To determine the truth value of a belief would therefore involve what I'll call 'directly comparing' the belief with the world; i.e., comparing it with the way the world *is,* not just with the way the world is represented as being. And the representational theory of mind says that we have access to the world only *via* the ways in which we represent it. There is, as it were, nothing that corresponds to looking around (behind? through? what's the right metaphor?) one's beliefs to catch a glimpse of the things they represent.

Mental processes can, in short, compare representations, but they can't compare representations with what they're representations of. Hence mental processes can't have access to the truth value of representations or, *mutatis mutandis,* to whether they denote. Hence the formality condition.

This line of argument could certainly be made a good deal more precise. It has been in, for example, some of the recent work of Nelson Goodman (see especially Goodman, 1978). For present purposes, however, I'm content to leave it *im*precise so long as it sounds familiar. For, I suspect that all versions of the argument suffer from a common deficiency: they assume that you can't run a *correspondence* theory of truth together with a *coherence* theory of evidence. Whereas, I see nothing compelling in the inference from 'truth is a matter of the correspondence of a belief with the way the world is' to '*ascertaining* truth is a matter of "directly comparing" a belief with the way the world is.' Perhaps we ascertain the truth of our beliefs by comparing them with one another, appealing to inference to the best explanation whenever we need to do so.

Anyhow, it would be nice to have a *non*-epistemological defence of the formality condition; one which saves the intuition that there's something conceptually wrong with its denial but doesn't acquire the skeptical/relativistic commitments with which the traditional epistemic versions of the argument have been encumbered. Here goes:

Suppose, just for convenience, that mental processes are algorithms. So, we have rules for the transformation of mental representations, and we have the mental representations which constitute their ranges and domains. Think of the rules as being like hypothetical imperatives; they have antecedents which specify conditions on mental representation, and they have consequents which specify what is to happen if the antecedents are satisfied. And now consider rules *a* and *b*.

(a) If it's the case that P, do such and such.

(b) If you believe it's the case that P, do such and such.

Notice, to begin with, that the compliance conditions on these injunctions are quite different. In particular, in the case where P is *false but believed true,* compliance with *b* consists in doing such and such, whereas compliance with *a* consists in *not* doing it. But despite this difference in compliance conditions, there's something *very* peculiar (perhaps *pragmatically* peculiar, whatever precisely that may mean) about supposing that an organism might have different ways of going about attempting to comply with *a* and *b*. The peculiarity is patent in *c:*

> (c) Do such and such if it's the case that P, *whether or not* you believe that it's the case that P.[9]

To borrow a joke from Professor Robert Jagger, *c* is a little like the advice: 'buy low, sell high.' One knows just what it would be *like* to comply with either, but somehow knowing that doesn't help much.

The idea is this: when one has done what one can to establish that the belief that P is warranted, one has done what one can to establish that the antecedent of *a* is satisfied. And, conversely, when one has done what one can do to establish that the antecedent of *a* is satisfied, one has done what one can to establish the warrant of the belief that P. Now, I suppose that the following is at least *close* to being true: to have the belief that P is to have the belief that the belief that P is warranted; and conversely, to have the belief that the belief that P is warranted is to have the belief that P. And the upshot of *this* is just the formality condition all over again. Given that mental operations have access to the fact that P is believed (and hence that the belief that P is believed to be warranted, and hence that the belief that the belief that P is warranted is believed to be warranted, . . . etc.) there's nothing further left to do; there is nothing that corresponds to the notion of a mental operation which one undertakes to perform just in case one's belief that P is *true.*

This isn't, by the way, any form of skepticism, as can be seen from the following: there's nothing wrong with Jones having one mental operation which he undertakes to perform if it's the case that P and another *quite different* mental operation which he undertakes to perform if Smith (≠ Jones) believes that it's the case that P. (Cf. 'I promise . . . though I don't intend to . . .' vs.

---

9. I'm assuming, for convenience, that all the Ps are such that either they or their denials are believed. This saves having to relativize to time (e.g. having *b* and *c* read '. . . you believe or come to believe . . .').

'I promise . . . though Smith doesn't intend to . . .'). There's a first person/third person asymmetry here, but it doesn't impugn the semantic distinction between 'P is true' and 'P is believed true.' The suggestion is that it's the tacit recognition of this pragmatic asymmetry that accounts for the traditional hunch that you can't both identify mental operations with transformations on mental representations and at the same time flout the formality condition; that the representational theory of mind and the computational theory of mind are somehow conjoint options.

So much, then, for the formality condition and the psychological tradition which accepts it. What about Naturalism? The first point is that none of the arguments *for* a rational psychology is, in and of itself, an argument *against* a Naturalistic psychology. As I remarked above, to deny that mental operations have access to the semantic properties of mental representations is *not* to deny that mental representations *have* semantic properties. On the contrary, beliefs are *just* the kinds of things which exhibit truth and denotation, and the Naturalist proposes to make science out of the organism/environment relations which (presumably) fix these properties. Why, indeed, should he not?

This all *seems* very reasonable. Nevertheless, I now wish to argue that a computational psychology is the only one that we are likely to get; that qua research strategy, the attempt to construct a *naturalistic* psychology is very likely to prove fruitless. I think that the basis for such an argument is already to be found in the literature, where it takes the form of a (possibly inadvertent) reductio ad absurdum of the contrary view.

Consider, to begin with, a distinction that Professor Hilary Putnam introduces in "The Meaning of 'Meaning' " (1975a) between what he calls "psychological states in the wide sense" and "psychological states in the narrow sense". A psychological state in the *narrow* sense is one the ascription of which does not "[presuppose] the existence of any individual other than the subject to whom that state is ascribed" (p. 136). All others are psychological states in the wide sense. So, for example, *x's jealousy of y* is a schema for expressions that denote psychological states in the wide sense, since such expressions presuppose the existence not only of the *x*s who are in the states, but also of the *y*s who are its objects. Putnam remarks that methodological solipsism (the phrase, by the way, is his) can be viewed as the requirement that only psychological states in the narrow sense are allowed as constructs in psychological theories.

But it is perhaps Putnam's main point that there are at least *some* scientific purposes (e.g. semantics and accounts of intertheoretical reference) which demand the wide construal. Here, rephrased slightly, is the sort of example that Putnam finds persuasive.

There is a planet (call it 'Yon') where things are very much as they are here. In particular, by a cosmic accident, some of the people on Yon speak a dialect indistinguishable from English and live in an urban conglomerate indistinguishable from the Greater Boston Area. Still more, for every one of our Greater Bostonians, there is a Doppelgänger on Yon who has precisely the same neurological structure down to and including microparticles. We can assume that so long as we're construing 'psychological state' narrowly, this latter condition guarantees type identity of our psychological states with theirs.

However, Putnam argues, it doesn't guarantee that there is a corresponding identity of psychological states, hither and Yon, if we construe 'psychological state' *widely.* Suppose that there is this difference between Yon and Earth; whereas, over here, the stuff we call 'water' has the atomic structure H_2O, it turns out that the stuff that they call 'water' over there has the atomic structure XYZ ($\neq H_2O$). And now, consider the mental state *thinking about water.* The idea is that, so long as we construe that state widely, it's one that we, but not our Doppelgängers, can reasonably aspire to. For, construed widely, one is thinking about water only if it is water that one is thinking about. But it's water that one's thinking about only if it is H_2O that one's thinking about; water *is* H_2O. But since, by assumption, they never think about H_2O over Yon, if follows that there's at least one wide psychological state that we're often in and they never are, however neurophysiologically like us they are, and however much our narrow psychological states converge with theirs.

Moreover, if we try to say what they speak about, refer to, mention, etc.—if, in short, we try to supply a semantics for their dialect—we will have to mention XYZ, not H_2O. Hence it would be wrong, at least on Putnam's intuitions, to say that they have a word for water. A fortiori, the chemists who work in what they call 'M.I.T.' don't have theories about *water,* even though what runs through their head when they talk about XYZ may be identical to what runs through our heads when we talk about H_2O. The situation is analogous to the one which arises for demonstratives and token reflexives, as Putnam insightfully points out.

Well, what are we to make of this? Is it an argument against methodological solipsism? And, if so, is it a *good* argument against methodological solipsism?

To begin with, Putnam's distinction between psychological states in the narrow and wide sense looks to be very intimately related to the traditional distinction between psychological state ascriptions opaquely and transparently construed. I'm a bit wary about this, since what Putnam *says* about wide ascriptions is only that they "presuppose the existence" of objects other than the ascribee; and, of course *a believes Fb and b exists* does not entail *b is such that a believes F of him,* or even $\exists x$ *(a believes Fx)*. Moreover, the failure of such entailments is notoriously important in discussions of quantifying in. For all that, however, I don't *think* that it's Putnam's intention to exploit the difference between the existential generalization test for transparency and the presupposition of existence test for wideness. On the contrary, the burden of Putnam's argument seems to be precisely that 'John believes (widely) that water is F' is true only if water (viz. H_2O) is such that John believes it's F. It's thus unclear to me why Putnam gives the weaker condition on wideness when it appears to be the stronger one that does the work.[10]

But whatever the case may be with the wide sense of belief, it's pretty clear that the narrow sense must be (what I've been calling) fully opaque. This is because it is only full opacity which allows type identity of beliefs that have different truth conditions (Sam's belief that he's ill with Misha's belief that *he* is; Yon beliefs about XYZ with hither beliefs about H_2O). I want to emphasize this correspondence between narrowness and full opacity, and not just in aid of terminological parsimony. Putnam sometimes writes as though he takes the methodological commitment

10. I blush to admit that I had missed some of these complexities until Sylvain Bromberger kindly rubbed my nose in them.

to a psychology of narrow mental states to be a sort of vulgar prejudice: "Making this assumption is, of course, adopting a *restrictive program*—a program which deliberately limits the scope and nature of psychology to fit certain mentalistic preconceptions or, in some cases, to fit an idealistic reconstruction of knowledge and the world" (p. 137). But in light of what we've said so far, it should be clear that this is a methodology with malice aforethought. Narrow psychological states are those individuated in light of the formality condition; viz. without reference to such semantic properties as truth and reference. And honoring the formality condition is part and parcel of the attempt to provide a theory which explains (a) how the belief that the Morning Star is F could be different from the belief that the Evening Star is F despite the well-known astronomical facts; and (b) how the behavioral effects of believing that the Morning Star is F could be different from those of believing that the Evening Star is F, astronomy once again apparently to the contrary notwithstanding. Putnam is, of course, dubious about this whole project: "The three centuries of failure of mentalistic psychology is tremendous evidence against this procedure, in my opinion" (p. 137). I suppose this is intended to include everybody from Locke and Kant to Freud and Chomsky. I should have such failures.

So much for background. I now need an argument to show that a naturalistic psychology (a psychology of mental states transparently individuated; hence, presumably, a psychology of mental states in the wide sense) is, for practical purposes, out of the question. So far as I can see, however, Putnam has given that argument. For, consider: a naturalistic psychology is a theory of organism/environment transactions. So, to stick to Putnam's example, a naturalistic psychology would have to find some stuff S and some relation R, such that one's narrow thought that water is wet is a thought about S in virtue of the fact that one bears R to S. Well, *which* stuff? The natural thing to say would be: 'Water, of course.' Notice, however, that if Putnam is right, it may not even be *true* that the narrow thought that water is wet is a thought about water; it *won't* be true of tokens of that thought which occur on Yon. Whether the narrow thought that water is wet is about water depends on whether it's about H_2O; and whether it's about H_2O depends on 'how science turns out'—viz. on what *chemistry* is true. (Similarly, mutatis mutandis, *'water' refers to water* is *not*, on this view, a truth of any branch of linguistics; it's *chemists* who tell us what it is that 'water' refers to.) Surely, however, characterizing the objects of thought is methodologically prior to characterizing the causal chains that link thoughts to their objects. But the theory which characterizes the objects of thought is the theory of *everything*; it's all of science. Hence, the methodological moral of Putnam's analysis seems to be: the naturalistic psychologists will inherit the Earth, but only after everybody else is finished with it. No doubt it's alright to have a research strategy that says 'wait awhile'. But who wants to wait *forever*?

This sort of argument isn't novel. Indeed, it was anticipated by Bloomfield (1933). Bloomfield argues that, for all practical purposes, you can't do semantics. The reason you can't is that to do semantics you have to be able to say, for example, what 'salt' refers to. But what 'salt' refers to is NaCl, and that's a bit of chemistry, not linguistics:

> The situations which prompt people to utter speech include every object and happening in their universe. In order to give a scientifically accurate definition of meaning for every form of a language, we would have to have a scientifically accurate knowledge of everything in the speaker's world. The actual extent of human knowledge is very small compared to this. We can define the meaning of a speech-form accurately when this meaning has to do with some matter of which we possess scientific knowledge. We can define the names of minerals, as when we say that the ordinary meaning of the English word *salt* is 'sodium chloride (NaCl),' and we can define the names of plants or animals by means of the technical terms of botany or zoology, but we have no precise way of defining words like *love* or *hate,* which concern situations that have not been accurately classified . . . The statement of meanings is therefore the weak point in language-study, and will remain so until knowledge advances very far beyond its present state.
>
> (pp. 139–140)

It seems to me as though Putnam ought to endorse all of this *including the moral:* the distinction between wanting a naturalistic semantics (psychology) and not wanting any is real but academic.[11]

The argument just given depends, however, on accepting Putnam's analysis of his example. But suppose that one's intuitions run the other way. Then one is at liberty to argue like this:

1. They do too have water over Yon; all Putnam's example shows is that there could be two kinds of water, our kind (=H_2O) and their kind (=XYZ).
2. Hence, Yon tokens of the thought that water is wet are thoughts about water after all;
3. Hence, the way chemistry turns out is irrelevant to whether thoughts about water are about water.
4. Hence, the naturalistic psychology of thought need not wait upon the sciences of the objects of thought;
5. Hence, a naturalistic psychology may be in the cards after all.

Since the premises of this sort of reply may be tempting (since, indeed, they may be *true*) it's worth presenting a version of the argument which doesn't depend on intuitions about what XYZ is.

A naturalistic psychology would specify the relations that hold between an organism and an object in its environment when the one is thinking about the other. Now, think how such a theory would have to go. Since it would have to define its generalizations over mental states on the one hand and environmental entities on the other, it will need, in particular, some canonical way of referring to the latter. Well, *which* way? If one assumes that what makes my thought about Robin Roberts a thought *about Robin Roberts* is some causal connection between the two of us, then

11. It may be that Putnam *does* accept this moral. For example, the upshot of the discussion circa p. 153 of his article appears to be that a Greek semanticist prior to Archimedes *could* not (in practice) have given a correct account of what (the Greek equivalent of) 'gold' means—because the theory needed to specify the extension of the term was simply not available. Presumably *we* are in that situation vis-à-vis the objects of many of *our* thoughts and the meanings of many of our terms; and, presumably, we will continue to be so into the indefinite future. But then, what's the point of so defining psychology (semantics) that there can't be any?

we'll need a description of RR such that the causal connection obtains in virtue of his satisfying that description. And *that* means, presumably, that we'll need a description under which the relation between him and me instantiates a law.

Generally, then, a naturalistic psychology would attempt to specify environmental objects in a vocabulary such that environment/organism relations are law-instantiating when so described. But here's the depressing consequence again: we have no access to such a vocabulary prior to the elaboration (completion?) of the nonpsychological sciences. 'What Granny likes with her herring' isn't, for example, a description under which salt is law-instantiating; nor, presumably, is 'salt'. What we need is something like 'NaCl', and descriptions like 'NaCl' are available only *after* we've done our chemistry. What this comes down to is that, at a minimum, '*x*'s being F causally explains . . .' can be true only when 'F' expresses nomologically necessary properties of the *x*s. Heaven knows it's hard to say what *that* means, but it presumably rules out both 'Salt's being what Granny likes with herring . . .' and 'Salt's being salt . . . ;' the former for want of being necessary, and the latter for want of being nomological. I take it, moreover, that Bloomfield is right when he says (a) that we don't know relevant nomologically necessary properties of most of the things we can refer to (think about) and (b) that it isn't the linguist's (psychologist's) job to find them out.

Here's still another way to put this sort of argument. The way Bloomfield states his case invites the question: "Why *should* a semanticist want a definition of 'salt' that is "scientifically accurate" in your sense? Why wouldn't a 'nominal' definition do?' There is, I think, some point to such a query. For example, as Hartry Field has pointed out (1972), it wouldn't make much difference to the way that truth-conditional semantics goes if we were to say only " 'salt' refers to whatever it refers to". All we need for this sort of semantics is some way or other of referring to the extension of 'salt'; we don't, in particular, need a "scientifically accurate" way. It's therefore pertinent to do what Bloomfield notably does not: distinguish between the goals of *semantics* and those of a naturalistic psychology of language. The latter, by assumption, purports to explicate the organism/environment transactions in virtue of which relations like reference hold. It therefore requires, at a minimum, lawlike generalizations of the (approximate) form: *X's utterance of 'salt' refers to salt if X bears relation R to* Δ. Since this whole thing *is* supposed to be lawlike, what goes in for 'Δ' must be a projectible characterization of the extension of 'salt'. But in general we discover which descriptions are projectible only a posteriori, in light of how the sciences (including the nonpsychological sciences) turn out. We are back where we started. Looked at this way, the moral is that we can do (certain kinds of) semantics if we have a way of referring to the extension of 'salt'. But we can't do the naturalistic psychology of reference unless we have some way of saying what salt *is;* which of its properties determine its causal relations.

It's important to emphasize that these sorts of arguments do *not* apply against the research program embodied in 'Rational psychology'—viz. to the program that envisions a psychology that honors the formality condition. The problem we've been facing is: under what description does the object of thought enter into scientific generalizations about the relations between thoughts and their objects? It looks as though the naturalist is going to have to say: under a description that is law instantiating—e.g. under physical description. But the rational psychologist has a quite different answer. What *he* wants is *whatever description the organism has in mind* when it thinks about the object of thought, construing 'thinks about' fully opaquely. So for a theory of psychological states narrowly construed, we want such descriptions of Venus as, e.g., 'The Morning Star', 'The Evening Star', 'Venus', etc., for it is these sorts of descriptions which we presumably entertain when we think that the Morning Star is *F*. In particular, it is our relation to these sorts of descriptions which determine what psychological state type we're in insofar as the goal in taxonomizing psychological states is explaining how they affect behavior.

Final point under the general head: the hopelessness of naturalistic psychology. Practicing naturalistic psychologists have been at least dimly aware all along of the sort of bind that they're in. So, for example, the 'physical specification of the stimulus' is just about invariably announced as a requirement upon adequate formulations of S-R generalizations. We can now see why. Suppose, wildly contrary to fact, that there exists a human population (e.g. English speakers) in which pencils are, in the technical sense of the notion, discriminative stimuli controlling the verbal response 'pencil'. The point is that even if some such generalization were true, it wouldn't be among those enunciated by a naturalistic psychology; the generalizations of naturalistic psychology are presumably supposed to be nomological, and there aren't any *laws* about pencils *qua* pencils. That is, expressions like 'pencil' presumably occur in no true, lawlike sentences. Of course, there presumably is *some* description in virtue of which pencils fall under the organism/environment laws of a naturalistic psychology, and everybody (except, possibly, Gibson) has always assumed that those descriptions are, approximately, physical descriptions. Hence, the naturalist's demand, perfectly warranted by his lights, that the stimulus should be physically specified.

But though their theory has been consistent, their practice has uniformly not. In practice, and barring the elaborately circumscribed cases that psychophysics studies, the requirement that the stimulus be physically specified has been ignored by just about *all* practitioners. And, indeed, they were well advised to ignore it; how else could they get on with their job? If they really had to wait for the physicists to determine the descriptions(s) under which pencils are law-instantiators, how would the psychology of pencils get off the ground?

So far as I can see, there are really only two ways out of this dilemma:

1. We can fudge, the way that learning theorists usually do. That is, we can 'read' the description of the stimulus from the character of the organism's response. In point of historical fact, this has led to a kind of naturalistic psychology which is merely a solemn paraphrase of what everybody's grandmother knows: e.g. to saying 'pencils are discriminative stimuli for the utterance of "pencil"' where Granny would have said 'pencil' refers to pencils. I take it that Chomsky's review of *Verbal Behavior* demonstrated, once and for all, the fatuity of this course. What *would* be interesting—what would have surprised Grandmother—is a generalization of the form Δ *is the discriminative stimulus for utterances of* 'pencil' where Δ is a description that picks out pencils in some projectable vocabulary (e.g. in the vocabulary of physics). Does anybody suppose that such descriptions are

likely to be forthcoming in, say, the *next* three hundred years?

2. The other choice is to try for a computational psychology—
which is, of course, the burden of my plaint. On this view, what
we can reasonably hope for is a theory of mental states fully
opaquely type individuated. We can try to say what the mental
representation is, and what the relation to a mental representation
is, such that one believes that the Morning Star is F in virtue of
bearing the latter to the former. And we can try to say how that
representation, or that relation, or both, differ from the representation and the relation constitutive of believing that the Evening Star is F. A naturalistic psychology, by contrast, remains a sort
of ideal of pure reason; there must *be* such a psychology, since,
presumably, we do sometimes think of Venus and, presumably, we
do so in virtue of a causal relation between it and us. But there's
no practical hope of making science out of this relation. And, of
course, for methodology, practical hope is *everything.*

One final point, and then I'm through. Methodological solipsism isn't, of course, solipsism *tout court.* It's not part of the
enterprise to assert, or even suggest, that you and I are actually
in the situation of Winograd's computer. Heaven only knows what
relation between me and Robin Roberts makes it possible for me
to think of him (refer to him, etc.), and I've been doubting the
practical possibility of a science whose generalizations that relation instantiates. But I *don't* doubt that there *is* such a relation or
that I do sometimes think of him. Still more, I have reasons not
to doubt it; precisely the sorts of reasons I'd supply if I were asked
to justify my knowledge claims about his pitching record. In
short: it's true that Roberts won 28 and it's true that I know that
he did, and nothing in the preceding tends to impugn these truths.
(Or, contrariwise, if he didn't and I'm mistaken, then the reasons
for my mistake are philosophically boring; they're biographical,
not epistemological or ontological.) My point, then, is *of course*
not that solipsism is true; it's just that truth, reference, and
the rest of the semantic notions aren't psychological categories.
What they are is: they're modes of *Dasein.* I don't know what
Dasein is, but I'm sure that there's lots of it around, and I'm
sure that you and I and Cincinnati have all got it. What more
do you want?

Acknowledgments: I've had a lot of help with this one. I'm particularly indebted to Professors Ned Block, Sylvain Bromberger, Janet Dean Fodor, Keith Gundersen, Robert Richardson, and Judith Thomson; and to Mr. Israel Krakowski.

12

The Material Mind

DONALD DAVIDSON

I WISH TO DISCUSS some general methodological questions about the nature of psychology as a science by assuming we know very much more than we do about the brain and the nervous system of man. Suppose that we understand what goes on in the brain perfectly, in the sense that we can describe each detail in purely physical terms—that even the electrical and chemical processes, and certainly the neurological ones, have been reduced to physics. And suppose, further, that we see that because of the way the system is constructed, the indeterminacies of quantum physics are irrelevant to our ability to predict and explain the events that are connected with input from sensation or output in the form of motion of the body.

While we are dreaming, let us also dream that the brain, and associated nervous system, have come to be understood as operating much like a computer. We actually come to appreciate what goes on so well that we can build a machine that, when exposed to the lights and sounds of the world, mimics the motions of a man. None of this is absurd, however unlikely or discredited by empirical discoveries it may be.

Finally, partly for fun and partly to stave off questions not germane to the theme, let us imagine that *l'homme machine* has actually been built, in the shape of a man and out of the very stuff of a man, all synthesized from a few dollars' worth of water and other easily obtainable materials. Our evidence that we have built him right is twofold. First, everything we can learn about the physical structure and workings of actual human brains and bodies has been replicated. Second, Art (as I shall call him or it) has acted in all observable ways like a man: Art has had or seems to have had, appropriate expressions on his or its face, has answered questions (as it seems), and has initiated motions of a human sort when exposed to environmental change. Every correlation that has been discovered between what we know of mental processes, so far as this knowledge is reflected in physically describable ways, and what goes on in the human nervous system, every such correlation is faithfully preserved in Art. No one who did not know that Art was artificial would have discovered it by watching or listening, by prodding or talking. True, his makers could tell the observer exactly what was going on inside Art in terms of physics, and could explain in physical terms why Art moved as he did when subjected to various stimuli. But this should not put the observer on to the fact that Art came from the mad scientist's laboratory, since a similar explanation is possible in theory for men produced by more old-fashioned methods.

(The assumption that biology and neurophysiology are reducible to physics is not essential to the argument, and is probably false. Nor does anything really depend on the assumption that indeterminacy is irrelevant. Both assumptions could be eliminated, but at the expense of complicating the argument.)

And now the question is, what would all this knowledge of physics (and a fortiori of neurophysiology) tell us about psychology? Much less than might be expected, I shall argue, at least as long as we maintain a certain view of the subject matter of psychology.

For the scope of this paper, I shall treat psychology as a subject that deals with phenomena described by concepts that involve intention, belief, and conative attitudes like desire. I would include among these concepts action, decision, memory, perception, learning, wanting, attending, noticing, and many others. Attempts have been made, of course, to show that psychology can do without some or all of these concepts, for example by trying to define concepts like belief or desire in terms of concepts more behavioral, or otherwise more like the concepts used in the physical sciences. Direct elimination through definition of psychological terms no longer seems very plausible, and indeed if the line of argument I shall give is correct, definitional reduction is impossible. But of course other forms of reduction are imaginable. This fact marks a limit of the discussion: to the extent that psychology does not make essential use of the concepts I have described, the considerations that follow do not apply to it.

In any case, it would be foolish to maintain that the existence of Art would make no difference to psychology. It or he would show, for example, that determinism (to the extent that physics is deterministic) was compatible with every appearance of intentional action: aside from the matter of provenance, we would have as much reason to consider Art a voluntary agent as anyone else. Art would be as free as any of us, at least as far as could be told. And Art would prove that however different they may be, there is no conflict between the modes of explanation of physical science and of psychology.

Beyond these very general methodological questions, the existence of Art would no doubt have an influence on the direction and focus of research in the social sciences, on the design of experiments, and on the hypotheses considered worth testing. I take for granted that detailed knowledge of the neurophysiology of the brain will make a difference—in the long run, an enormous difference—to the study of such subjects as perception, memory, dreaming and perhaps of inference. But it is one thing for developments in one field to effect changes in a related field, and another thing for knowledge gained in one area to constitute knowledge of another. In a broad sense of relevance, I do not, of course, doubt the relevance of biology and the neurosciences to psychology. What interests me is that there seem to be limits to what can be directly learned from the other sciences (or from Art, as I am supposing) about psychology, and it is these limits I wish to explore.

It is time to be a little clearer about what did and what did not go into the manufacture of Art. Art is physically indistinguishable inside and out from a man, and he has reacted to changes in his environment by moving in ways indistinguishable from human behavior. Identifiable parts of the interior of Art are physically connected with his movements, in accord with everything known about the construction of the brain and the nervous system. All this falls short, however, of assuming that we have succeeded in identifying such things as beliefs, desires, intentions, hopes, inferences, or decisions with particular states of the brain or mechisms in it. Of course, there may be reason to connect *parts* of the brain with various cognitive processes; but parts are not mechanisms. And nothing in our description of Art requires that we be able to identify specific physical mechanisms with particular cognitive states and events. Since such states and events as thinking, believing, perceiving, and intending are conceptually central to all the psychological concepts (as I have arbitrarily designated them), we so far seem justified in saying that Art may not, directly at least, teach us much about psychology.

But how can this be? On a particular occasion, a pin penetrates the skin or surface of Art; he jumps away, wears the expression of pain and surprise, makes sounds like "Ouch!" Or so we are tempted to describe matters. I assume we can describe the penetration of the skin and all of Art's motions in purely physical terms—terms that can be incorporated into physical laws. Knowing the relevant structure of Art, we know *exactly* how the penetration of the skin caused the reaction (physically described). We also can describe cause and effect in more mundane ways—I just have. Now consider one pair of descriptions: the official physical description of the cause (or stimulus) and the psychological description of the effect (bodily movement, exclamation, facial expressions or surprise and pain). These are, we have agreed, descriptions of cause and effect and as such the events must fall under laws. If something like this holds for all psychological events—and we have been assuming nothing less—then are we not committed to the view that all psychological events are strictly predictable, and even that, for Art, we know how to predict them? Further, since we know both the physical and the psychological descriptions of the same events, why can we not correlate physical with psychological descriptions systematically? How then can we deny that in building Art we have reduced psychology to physics, and hence solved all the problems specific to psychology?

I would agree that we are committed to one important philosophical and, indeed, metaphysical thesis. If psychological events cause and are caused by physical events (and surely this is the case) and if causal relations between events entail the existence of laws connecting those events, and these laws are, as we have supposed in designing Art, physical, then it must follow that psychological events simply *are* (in the sense of *are identical with*) physical events. If this is materialism, we are committed to it in assuming the existence of Art.

Our commitments are less than might seem, however, for if I am right, we are not committed to the view that psychological events are predictable in the way physical events are; nor that psychological events can be reduced to physical events; nor that we have, in building Art, shown that we can explain psychological events as we can physical events. For I have not assumed, nor does anything I have assumed entail, that we can effectively correlate important open classes of events described in physical terms with classes of events described in psychological terms.

What I have supposed is that for any particular, dated psychological event we can give a description in purely physical terms; and so for any *given, finite* class of events, we can set up a correlation between psychological and physical descriptions. But although this can be done, it does not follow that such psychological predicates as 'x desires his neighbor's wife', or 'x wants a kaffee mit schlag', or 'x believes that Beethoven died in Vienna' or 'x signed a check for \$20' which determine, if not infinite classes, at least potentially infinite ones—it does not imply that such predicates have any nomologically corresponding physical predicates. Of course, if a certain class of psychological events is finite, and each psychological event has, as we are assuming, a physical description, then it follows trivially that there is a physical predicate that determines the same class as each psychological predicate. But this fact is in itself of no interest to science. Science is interested in nomological connections, connections that are supported by instances, whether or not the instances happen to exhaust the cases.

It should be easy to appreciate the fact that although every psychological event and state has a physical description, this gives us no reason to hope that any physical predicate, no matter how complex, has the same extension as a given psychological predicate—much less that there is a physical predicate related in a lawlike way to the given psychological predicate. To take an example from a different field than I have used before: consider some fairly rich language L that has the resources for describing any sentence of L. Assume in particular that L can pick out with a unique description each of the true sentences of L. But L cannot contain a predicate, no matter how complex, that applies to the true and only the true sentences of L—at least not if it is consistent. This fact would surprise someone who did not know about the semantic paradoxes. "Surely", he would say, "since I can pick out each true sentence I can specify the class". And he starts going through the true sentences, noticing what properties they have in common that none of the false sentences have. But he would be wrong; we know in advance that he cannot succeed. I think this is roughly the situation with psychological predicates in relation to physical: we know in advance that all the resources of physics will not suffice to pick out important (open or infinite) classes of events which are defined by psychological predicates.

We see, then, that complete knowledge of the physics of man, even if this covers, under its mode of description, all that happens, does not necessarily yield knowledge of psychology (a point made long ago by Plato's Socrates). Still, why should it not happen that there are inductively established correlations between physical and psychological events? Indeed, do we not already know that there are? We do, if by laws we mean *statistical generalizations.* The burned child avoids the flame (and psychology may contain more sophisticated examples). But these generalizations, unlike those of physics, cannot be sharpened without limit, cannot be turned into the strict laws of a science closed within its area of application. In giving my reasons for this conclusion, let me turn back again for a moment to the question what makes us think Art has been properly constructed from a psychological point of view. I think the answer has to be, Art gives every appearance of thinking, acting, feeling like a man. And not just the superficial appearances. If you cut him he bleeds, if you shine lights in his eyes, he blinks, and if you dissect his eyes, you discover rods and cones. It is important, in deciding that he has psychological traits, that he is made like a man. If we found a radio receiver inside, and learned that another person was sending out signals to make Art move, we would no longer be tempted to assign psychological characteristics to him. Any important difference under the skin might make us hesitate. Nevertheless, our detailed understanding of the physical workings cannot, in itself, force us to conclude that Art is angry, or that he believes Beethoven died in Vienna. In order to decide this, we would have first to observe Art's macroscopic movements, and decide how to interpret them, in just the way we decide for humans.

It would be easy to go wrong in our thinking here, partly because I have assumed we deliberately *built* Art to do what he does. And probably in building Art, we used circuits of the sort we would use if we wanted to build a machine that could process information, and so forth. But of course we must not jump to the conclusion that when those circuits go into play, then Art is processing information. It is very much part of what is at stake whether what would be information for us if Art were merely an extension of our own faculties (as a computer is) is information for him. To assume this point is to suppose Art sees things as we do, and means by the sounds he makes what we should mean. But this we can decide only be seeing how such assumptions fit into the total picture of Art's behavior. The point is a simple one. If we want to decide whether Art has psychological properties, we must stop thinking of him as a machine we have built and start judging him as we would a man. Only in this way can we study the question of possible correlations between physical and psychological properties.

It will be best to admit at this point that the fact that Art is artificial plays no essential part in the argument. The reason is that I have not supposed that he was built on the basis of knowledge of *laws* correlating psychological and physical phenomena: all that was known was the physical correlate of each *particular* movement or act. It is true that we can predict Art's physical movements. But if we want to know whether a particular one of these will be interpretable as an action or response, we can tell only by considering all the physical aspects in detail (including of course what the environment will be like) and then judging the case as we would a human movement. We have no clear reason to say that Art will continue to seem human. So Art proves no point that cannot be made as well by supposing we have the same sort of comprehensive knowledge of the physics of a man as we have pretended we have of Art. Art served the heuristic purpose of removing any mysterious unknown properties. But in fact all we removed was unknown *physical* properties, and we can suppose these removed from a man as easily as from Art. The supposition no more settles the question whether man has a soul (i.e., irreducible psychological properties) than it settles the question whether we *gave* Art a soul.

I return again to the question why we should not expect to discover sharp lawlike correlations (or causal laws) connecting psychological and physical events and states—why, in other words, complete understanding of the workings of body and brain would not constitute knowledge of thought and action. Before I give what I think is the correct reason, let me briefly mention some bad reasons that have commonly been offered. (I am embarrassed by the fact that here I accept a conclusion for which philosophers have generally given very bad, even downright shabby, arguments. I want to disassociate myself from them.)

It is very often said, especially in recent philosophical literature, that there cannot be a physical predicate with the extension of a verb of action (for example) because there are so many different ways in which an action may be performed. Thus a man may greet a woman by bowing, by saying any of a number of things, by winking, by whistling; and each of these things may in turn be done in endless ways. The point is fatuous. The particulars that fall under a predicate always differ in endless ways, as long as there are at least two particulars. If the argument were a good one, we could show that acquiring a positive charge is not a physical event, since there are endless ways in which this may happen.

There is a symmetrical argument that is equally common and equally bad: it is said that the same physical event may count as quite different actions. So, for example, exactly the same motion and sound emanating from an agent may on one occasion constitute a greeting and on another occasion constitute an insult. But of course if the occasions differ, the events must differ in some physical characteristics. The difference may lie within the agent. There may, for example, be a difference in intention: this difference, we assume, has its physical aspect, since it is reflected in the propensities to motion of the agent. Given a complete description of the brain, we must expect this difference to correspond to some difference in physiology—ultimately in physics, as we have been seeing it.

We can imagine cases, however, where even the intention is the same, and the beliefs and desires, and so, let us pretend, everything physical, too, in the agent; and yet different actions are performed. Thus a man might intend to keep a promise by going to the opera. Yet on one occasion his going to the opera with this intention might constitute the keeping of a promise, and on another occasion not (he might have forgotten the day). But again the physical situation is not identical in all physical respects. We simply must define the physical event or situation more broadly—just as keeping a promise depends on certain prior events having taken place, so the occurrence of a physical event of a certain sort may depend on a broad physical setting in which it takes place. If we pleased, we could define a supereclipse of the moon to be an eclipse that was preceded, within a week, by an eclipse of the sun. A supereclipse may not be of much interest to science, but it is surely a respectable physical concept.

Again, it is said that cultural relativism affects the classification of actions, but not of physical events. So the same gesture may indicate assent in Austria and dissent in Greece. Here we need only increase the frame of physical reference to find a relevant difference: Austria is physically distinct from Greece, and so any event in Austria is physically distinct from any event in Greece. Perhaps it will be suggested that the same *particular* gesture of a man may be judged to be an act of assent by an Austrian and an act of dissent by a displaced Greek. In this case, however, the two descriptions cannot contradict one another. Just as an object may accelerate relative to one frame of reference and not relative to another, so a gesture may count as assent *to an Austrian* and as dissent *to a Greek*. Only if we accept an unduly restricted view of the predicates that can be formed using physical concepts are we apt to be attracted by any of these arguments.

In these considerations, two important themes emerge. One is the necessity for distinguishing individual, dated, events from sorts of events. We may without error say that 'the same gesture' has one meaning in Austria and another in Greece: what we have in mind, of course, are gestures of *some relevant same sort*. The other theme concerns the relations between psychological descriptions and characterizations of events, and physical (or biological or physiological) descriptions. Although, as I am urging, psychological characteristics cannot be reduced to the others, nevertheless they may be (and I think are) strongly dependent on them. Indeed, there is a sense in which the physical characteristics of an event (or object or state) *determine* the psychological characteristics; in G.E. Moore's word, psychological concepts are *supervenient* on physical concepts. Moore's way of explaining this relation (which he maintained held between evaluative and descriptive characteristics) is this: it is impossible for two events (objects, states) to agree in all their physical characteristics (or in Moore's case, their descriptive characteristics) and to differ in their psychological characteristics (evaluative).

The two themes, of the distinction between individual events and sorts, and the supervenience of the psychological on the physical, are related. For what needs to be stressed is that it is the descriptions of individual psychological events, not sorts of events, that are supervenient on physical descriptions. If a certain psychological concept applies to one event and not to another, there must be a difference describable in physical terms. But it does not follow that there is a single physically describable difference that distinguishes any two events that differ in a given psychological respect. (Consider the example from semantics.)

There is another class of argument that I cannot deal with in any detail: these are arguments based on the claim that psychological concepts are essentially *evaluative,* while physical concepts are not. If this means that when we call an event an action, we are not, or not merely, describing, it, but are also judging it as good or bad, blameworthy or reasonable, then I think this is wrong. Whenever we say anything, we may be expressing a value of some sort; but this does not mean that what we say may not also be true or false. In any case, to make sense of the question why there are no strict laws connecting physical and psychological phenomena, we must assume that judgments concerning these phenomena are true or false in the same way.

In a quite different sense, evaluative considerations may be thought to enter our judgments about the actions people perform. It may be claimed that there are certain *regulative* or *constitutive* elements in the application of pyschological concepts. This is certainly right; but the same can be said for the application of physical concepts. Nevertheless, here we are much closer to the truth.

Let us consider a particular historical event, say David Hume's admitting in an appendix to his *Treatise* that he cannot see how to reconcile two of his theses. Making an admission is necessarily an intentional act, and it entails that what is admitted is the case—in our example, Hume's admission entails that he cannot see how to reconcile the two theses. Since making the admission was intentional, we also know that Hume must have *believed* that he did not see how to reconcile the two theses, and he must have *wanted* (probably for some further reason) to reveal this fact. Not only did Hume have this desire and this belief, but they were somehow efficacious in his making the admission—he made the admission *because* he had the desire and the belief. If we interpret this 'because' as implying (among other things) a causal relation—and I believe we must—then in describing an action as performed with a certain intention, we have described it as an action with a certain causal history. So in identifying the action with a physical event, we must at the same time be sure that the causal history of the physical event includes events or states identical with the desires and cognitive states that yield a psychological explanation of the action.

This is only the beginning of the complications, however, for most emotional states, wants, perceivings, and so on have causal connections with further psychological states and events or, at least, require that these other states exist. Therefore, in saying that an agent performed a single intentional action, we attribute a *very* complex system of states and events to him, and all this must be captured in giving the corresponding physical states and events. I am not arguing, of course, that there is not a corresponding physical description—I am sure there is. I am not even arguing that we could not produce the corresponding description in particular cases. I am only trying to show why we cannot establish general, precise, and lawlike correlations between physical and psychological descriptions. The complexity of psychological attributions does not in itself prove the point; but it will turn out that the quality of this complexity is germane.

Here it will help to turn to a psychological phenomenon one step more abstract—the ability to speak and understand language. We cannot hope in any case to cope with the full range and subtlety of psychological traits without taking account of language, for the finer distinctions among desires and beliefs, thoughts and fears, intentions and inferences depend on the assumption of a cognitive structure as complex as that of language and not to be understood apart from it.

In the end, we want to be able to explain speech acts that are intentional and have the characteristics of other actions recently touched on. Part of explaining such acts is interpreting them, in the sense of being able to say what the speaker's words expressed on an occasion of use—expressed in *his* language, of course. We have a full grasp of what a man said when he uttered certain sounds only if we know his language—that is, are prepared to interpret a large number of things he might say. For we do not understand a particular sentence uttered by a man unless we know the role the words in it play in other sentences he might utter. To interpret a single speech act, therefore, we must have a grasp of the speaker's unrealized dispositions to perform other speech acts. Indeed, we may think of having, or knowing, a language as a single, highly structured, and very complex disposition of the speaker. We describe the disposition by specifying what the speaker would mean by uttering any of a large number of sentences under specified conditions.

Described psychologically, a speaker's language ability is a complex disposition. Described physically, it is not a disposition, but an actual state, a mechanism. So here, if anywhere, it would seem that detailed knowledge of the physical mechanism should be a help to psychology. No doubt in each man there is some physical state, largely centered in the brain, that constitutes his language ability. But how can we identify this state? (I do not mean merely *locate* it, but describe in detail the relevant mechanism?) How do we know that a certain physical state of the brain, a certain mechanism, *is* the mechanism that accounts for the speaker's speech behavior, his saying and meaning what he does when he speaks? I assume, as before, that if the agent speaks, we can on each occasion identify the particular physical event that corresponds. Thus there is no problem about testing the claim that a particular physical mechanism (for example Art) is a language-speaking mechanism: we can test it just as we test a man for language ability, by noticing how it behaves in various circumstances. This will not, however, give us what we want: a lawlike

correlation between workings of the mechanism and speech behavior. We want to know what the physical property of the machine, of any machine, is—the property that would make it speak
like a man.

Why can we not simply say: the physical property is just the
one that produces the observed results? This is inadequate, because the required results outrun the observed ones: we want the
physical property that *would* produce linguistic behavior. Here we
do have *one* description of the physical property, but it is a description that uses psychological concepts. It is like saying man is
a language-speaking machine. True; but what does the word
'machine' tell us?

We interpret a single speech act against the background of a
theory of the speaker's language. Such a theory tells us (at least)
the truth conditions of each of an infinite number of sentences
the man might utter, these conditions being relative to the time
and circumstances of utterance.

In building up such a theory, whether consciously, like an an-
thropologist or linguist, or unwittingly like a child learning its
first language, we are never in a position directly to learn the
meanings of words one by one, and then independently to learn
rules for assembling them into meaningful wholes. We start rather
with the wholes, and infer (or contrive) an underlying structure.
Meaning is the operative aspect of this structure. Since the structure is inferred, from the point of view anyway of what is needed
and known for communication, we must view meaning itself as a
theoretical construction. Like any construct, it is arbitrary except
for the formal and empirical constraints we impose on it. In the
case of meaning, the constraints cannot uniquely fix the theory of
interpretation. The reason, as Quine has convincingly argued, is
that the sentences a speaker holds to be true are determined, in
ways we can only partly disentangle, by what the speaker means
by his words and what he believes about the world. A better way
to put this would be to say: belief and meaning cannot be uniquely reconstructed from speech behavior. The remaining indeterminacy should not be judged as a failure of interpretation, but rather
as a logical consequence of the nature of theories of meaning (just
as it is not a sign of some failure in our ability to measure temperature that the choice of an origin and a unit is arbitrary).

Underlying the indeterminacy of interpretation is a common-place fact about interpretation. Suppose someone says, "That's a shooting star". Should I take him to *mean* it really is a star, but that he *believes* some stars are very small and cold; or should I think he *means* it is not a star but a meteorite, and *believes* stars are always very large and hot? Additional evidence may resolve this case, but there will always be cases where all possible evidence leaves open a choice between attributing to a speaker a standard meaning and an idiosyncratic pattern of belief, or a deviant meaning and a sober opinion. If a speaker utters the words, "There's a whale", how do I know what he means? Suppose there is an object that looks like a whale in the offing, but I know it is not a mammal? There seems to be no absolutely definite set of criteria that determine that something is a whale. Fortunately for the possibility of communication, there is no need to force a decision. Having a language and knowing a good deal about the world are only partially separable attainments, but interpretation can proceed because we can accept any of a number of theories of what a man means, provided we make compensating adjustments in the beliefs we attribute to him. What is clear, however, is that such theory construction must be *holistic:* we cannot decide how to interpret a speaker's "There's a whale" independently of how we interpret his "There's a mammal", and words connected with these, without end. We must interpret the whole pattern.

At this point we might hope that knowledge of the physical correlate of the speech mechanism would be a help. After all, words are used as they are because of the way this mechanism works. Can we not locate *the physical correlates of meaning?* Can we not discover unambiguously on the physical level what we must merely infer, or treat as a construct, as long as we stick to observation of speech behavior?

Well, how might it work? We might find out exactly what patterns of sights and sounds and smells, described now in terms of physical inputs, suffice to dispose our artful machine to utter, "That's a whale", when asked, "What is that?" (And so on for endless further cases.) Would we then know what Art means? I think the answer is, we would know no more and no less about meaning than we do about human speakers now. For what would Art say if he 'learned' that an object with a cetaceous appearance was not a mammal? How can we decide without knowing what he means by 'mammal'? Suppose the whale were to appear very small, or upside down, but that Art 'believes' he is looking through the wrong end of a telescope, or inverting glasses? A few questions like this should make us realize that we cannot simply associate some fixed part of Art's brain, or aspect of it, with the criteria for the application of a word. It is the total pattern that must be interpreted.

Might we not identify the meaning of a sentence with the *intention* with which it is spoken, and hunt for the physical correlate of the intention, thus avoiding the problem of endless ramifications that seems to plague theories of meaning or interpretation? The difficulty is that specific intentions are just as hard to interpret as utterances. Indeed, our best route to the detailed identification of intentions and beliefs is by way of a theory of language behavior. It makes no sense to suppose we can *first* intuit all of a person's intentions and beliefs and *then* get at what he means by what he says. Rather we refine our theory of each in the light of the other.

If I am right, then, detailed knowledge of the physics or physiology of the brain, indeed of the whole of man, would not provide a shortcut to the kind of interpretation required for the application of sophisticated psychological concepts. It would be no easier to interpret what *l'homme machine* means by what it 'says' than to interpret the words of a man, nor would the problem be essentially different. (There would be one unimportant shortcut: where with a man we must gather our evidence by creating experimental situations, we could disassemble the machine. But after disassembly, we could only say, in psychological terms, what it would do under completely specified circumstances; no general laws about its behavior would be forthcoming.) With the machine, then, as with the man, we would have to interpret the total pattern of its observed (or predicted) behavior. Our standards for accepting a system of interpretation would also have to be the same: we would have to make allowance for intelligible error; we would have to impute a large degree of consistency, on pain of not making sense of what was said or done; we would have to assume a pattern of beliefs and motives which agreed with our own sufficiently to build a base for understanding and interpreting disagreements. These conditions, which include criteria of consistency and rationality, can no doubt be sharpened and made more objective. But I see no reason to think that they can be stated in a purely physical vocabulary.

Past discoveries about the nature of the brain and, even more, the discoveries we can expect from workers in this field throw a flood of light on human perception, learning, and behavior. But with respect to the higher cognitive functions, the illumination must, if I am right, be indirect. There is no important sense in which psychology can be reduced to the physical sciences.

Acknowledgments: I benefited from sage advice from David Lewis, Allison Ryan, Nancy Wiggins and Kathleen Wilkes.

References

The numbers in square brackets following each entry indicate the chapters in which the references are cited.

[1]	Newell and Simon	[7]	Putnam
[2]	Pylyshyn	[8]	Dennett
[3]	Minsky	[9]	Haugeland
[4]	Marr	[10]	Searle
[5]	McDermott	[11]	Fodor
[6]	Dreyfus	[12]	Davidson

Abelson, R. P. (1973). "The Structure of Belief Systems." In Schank and Colby, 1973. [3]

Anderson, Alan Ross, ed. (1964). *Minds and Machines,* Englewood Cliffs, N.J.: Prentice Hall. [7] [9]

Austin, John L. (1970). *How to Do Things with Words,* New York: Oxford University Press. [Intr.]

Banerji, R., and Mesarovic, M. D., eds. (1970). *Theoretical Approaches to Non-numerical Problem Solving,* New York: Springer-Verlag. [2]

Baron, Robert J. (1970). "A Model for Cortical Memory," *Journal of Mathematical Psychology,* 7 (1970), 37–59. [9]

Bartlett, F. C. (1932). *Remembering: A Study in Experimental and Social Psychology,* Cambridge, England: The University Press (revised 1961). [3]

Berliner, Hans (1975). Chess as Problem Solving: The Development of a Tactics Analyzer. Unpublished Ph.D. thesis, Carnegie-Mellon University. [1]

Binford, T. O. (1971). Visual Perception by Computer. Paper delivered at the IEEE Conference on Systems and Control, Miami, Florida, December 1971. [4]

Black, Max, ed. (1965). *Philosophy in America,* Ithaca: Cornell University Press. [9]

Block, Ned, and Fodor, Jerry (1972). "What Psychological States Are Not," *Philosophical Review,* 81 (1972), 159–181. [9]

Bloomfield, L. (1933). *Language,* London: George Allen and Unwin. [11]

Bobrow, Daniel G., and Collins, A. M., eds. (1975). *Representation and Understanding,* New York: Academic Press. [5]

Bobrow, Daniel G., and Raphael, Bertram (1974). "New Programming Languages for Artificial Intelligence Research," *Computing Surveys,* 6 (1974), 153–174. [2]

Bobrow, Daniel G., and Winograd, Terry (1977). "An Overview of KRL, a Knowledge Representation Language," *Cognitive Science,* 1 (1977), 3–46. [2] [6]

Bransford, J. D., and Johnson, M. K. (1973). "Considerations of Some Problems of Comprehension." In Chase, 1973. [2]

Campbell, F. S. (1974). "The Transmission of Spatial Information through the Visual System." In Schmitt and Worden, 1974. [9]

Capitan, W. H., and Merrill, D. D., eds. (1965). *Art, Mind, and Religion,* Pittsburgh: University of Pittsburgh Press. [7]

Care, N. S. and Landesman, C. (1968). *Readings in the Theory of Action,* Bloomington, Ind.: University of Indiana Press. [8]

Carroll, Lewis (1895). "What the Tortoise Said to Achilles," *Mind,* new series, 4 (1895), 278–280 (reprinted in Copi and Gould, 1964). [8]

Castañeda, Hector Neri, ed. (1967). *Intentionality, Minds and Perception,* Detroit: Wayne State University Press. [7]

Castellan, N. John; Pisoni, David B.; and Potts, George R., eds. (1977). *Cognitive Theory II,* Hillsdale, N.J.: Lawrence Erlbaum Associates. [9]

Cathey, W. T. (1974). *Optical Information Processing and Holography,* New York: John Wiley and Sons. [9]

Cavanaugh, J. P. (1972). Holographic Processes Realizable in the Neural Realm. Unpublished Ph.D. thesis, Carnegie-Mellon University. [9]

Charniak, E. (1974). Toward a Model of Children's Story Comprehension. Unpublished Ph.D. thesis, MIT, and AI Lab Tech Report 266. [3] [5]

Chase, W., ed. (1973). *Visual Information Processing,* New York: Academic Press. [2]

Chisholm, Roderick (1967). "Intentionality." In Edwards, 1967. [8]

Chomsky, Noam (1957). *Syntactic Structures,* The Hague: Mouton. [3]

―― (1964). *Current Issues in Linguistic Theory,* The Hague: Mouton. [2]

―― (1965). *Aspects of the Theory of Syntax,* Cambridge, Mass.: MIT Press. [4]

Cohen, L. Jonathan (1950–51). "Teleological Explanation," *Proceedings of the Aristotelian Society,* 51 (1950–51), 255–292. [8]

—— (1955–56). "Can There Be Artificial Minds?" *Analysis,* 16 (1955–56), 36–41. [8]

Collins, A. W. (1969). "Unconscious Belief," *Journal of Philosophy,* 66 (1969), 667–680. [8]

Cooley, J. M. and Tukey, J. W. (1965). "An Algorithm for the Machine Computation of Complex Fourier Series," *Mathematics of Computation,* 19 (1965), 297–301. [4]

Copi, I. M. and Gould, J. A. (1964). *Readings on Logic,* New York: MacMillan. [8]

Cummins, Robert (1975). "Functional Analysis," *Journal of Philosophy,* 72 (1975), 741–765. [9]

Davidson, Donald (1970). "Mental Events." In Foster and Swanson, 1970. [9]

—— (1973a). "The Material Mind." In Suppes, et al., 1973; reprinted in this volume as Chapter 12. [9]

—— (1973b). "Radical Interpretation," *Dialectica,* 27 (1973), 313–328. [Intr.] [9]

Davies, D. J. M., and Isard, S. D. (1972). "Utterances as Programs." In Meltzer and Michie, 1972. [2]

Davis, Martin (1958). *Computability and Unsolvability,* New York: McGraw Hill. [7]

de Groot, A. (1965). *Thought and Choice in Chess,* The Hague: Mouton. [9]

Dennett, Daniel (1969). *Content and Consciousness,* London: Routledge and Kegan Paul. [8]

—— (1971). "Intentional Systems," *Journal of Philosophy,* 68 (1971), 87–106; reprinted in Dennett, 1978b, and in this volume as Chapter 8. [9]

—— (1973). "Mechanism and Responsibility." In Honderich, 1973; reprinted in Dennett, 1978b. [8]

—— (1975). "Why the Law of Effect Will Not Go Away," *Journal for the Theory of Social Behavior,* 5 (1975), 169–187; reprinted in Dennett, 1978b. [9]

—— (1976). "Conditions of Personhood." In Rorty, 1976; reprinted in Dennett, 1978b. [8]

—— (1978a). "Why You Can't Make a Computer that Feels Pain," *Synthese,* 38 (1978), 415–456; reprinted in Dennett, 1978b. [9]

—— (1978b). *Brainstorms,* Montgomery, Vt.: Bradford Books. [Intr.] [8] [9]

—— (1978c). "Two Approaches to Mental Images." In Dennett, 1978b. [9]

—— (1978d). "Toward a Cognitive Theory of Consciousness." In Savage, 1978; reprinted in Dennett, 1978b. [Intr.]

—— (1981). "Three Kinds of Intentional Psychology." In Healey, 1981. [Intr.]

Descartes, Rene (1967). *The Philosophical Works of Descartes,* Vol. 1, trans.

Elizabeth S. Haldane and G. R. T. Ross, Cambridge, England: Cambridge University Press, 1st ed., 1911. [11]

Dreyfus, Hubert L. (1972; 2nd ed., 1979). *What Computers Can't Do*, New York: Harper and Row. Excerpts from the introduction to the 2nd ed. are included in this volume as Chapter 6. [5] [6] [9]

Edwards, Paul, ed. (1967). *The Encyclopedia of Philosophy*, New York: MacMillan. [8]

Elcock, E. W.; McGregor, J. J.; and Murray, A. M. (1972). "Data Directed Control and Operating Systems," *Computer Journal*, 15 (1972), 125–129. [2]

Erickson, R. P. (1974). "Parallel 'Population' Neural Coding in Feature Extraction." In Schmitt and Worden, 1974. [9]

Ernst, G. W. and Newell, Allen (1969). *GPS: A Case Study in Generality and Problem Solving*, New York: Academic Press. [5]

Evans, T. (1968). "A Program for the Solution of Geometric-Analogy Intelligence Test Questions." In Minsky, 1968. [4]

Fahlman, Scott (1975). Thesis Progress Report: A System for Representing and Using Real-World Knowledge. Cambridge, Mass.: MIT AI Lab Memo 331. [5]

Feigenbaum, Edward A. (1977). "The Art of Artificial Intelligence: Themes and Case Studies of Knowledge Engineering." In *IJCAI-77*, 1014–1029. [6]

Feigenbaum, E. A., and Feldman, J., eds. (1963). *Computers and Thought*. New York: McGraw-Hill. [4]

Field, Hartry (1972). "Tarski's Theory of Truth," *Journal of Philosophy*, 69 (1972), 347–375. [11]

Firth, I. M. (1972). *Holography and Computer Generated Holograms*, London: Mills and Boon. [9]

Fodor, Jerry A. (1965). "Explanation in Psychology." In Black, 1965. [9]

—— (1974). "Special Sciences (or: The Disunity of Science as a Working Hypothesis)," *Synthese*, 28 (1974), 97–115. [9]

—— (1975). *The Language of Thought*, New York: Thomas Y. Crowell. [11]

—— (1978a). "Tom Swift and his Procedural Grandmother," *Cognition*, 6 (1978), 229–247. [11]

—— (1978b). "Propositional Attitudes," *Monist*, 61 (1978), 501–521. [11]

Fodor, Jerry, and Pylyshyn, Zenon. How Direct Is Visual Perception? Some Reflections on Gibson's "Ecological Approach." In preparation. [2]

Foster, Lawrence, and Swanson, J. W., eds. (1970). *Experience and Theory*, Amherst: University of Massachusetts Press. [9]

Frey, P., and Adesman, P. (1976). "Recall Memory for Visually Presented Chess Positions," *Memory and Cognition*, 4 (1976), 541–547. [9]

Gabor, D. (1969). "Associative Holographic Memories," *IBM Journal of Research and Development*, 13 (1969), 156–159. [9]

Geach, Peter (1957). *Mental Acts*, London: Routledge and Kegan Paul. [11]

Gibson, J. J. (1979). *An Ecological Approach to Visual Perception*, Boston: Houghton Mifflin. [2]

Gödel, Kurt (1931). "Über formal unentscheidbare Sätze der Principia Mathematica und verwandter Systeme I," *Monatshefte für Mathematik und Physik*, 38 (1931), 173–198. [Intr.]

Goldmeier, Erich (1972). *Similarity in Visually Perceived Forms*, New York: International Universities Press. [6]

Goldstein, Ira (1974). Understanding Simple Picture Programs. Unpublished Ph.D. thesis, MIT, and AI Lab Tech Report 294. [3] [5]

Goldstein, Ira, and Papert, Seymour (July 1975; revised March 1976). Artificial Intelligence, Language and the Study of Knowledge. Cambridge, Mass.: MIT AI Lab Memo 237. [6]

Goodman, Nelson (1968). *Languages of Art*, Indianapolis: Bobbs-Merrill. [9]

—— (1978). *Ways of World Making*, Indianapolis: Hackett. [11]

Grandy, Richard (1973). "Reference, Meaning and Belief," *Journal of Philosophy*, 70 (1973), 439–452. [9]

Greeno, James (1977). "Process of Understanding in Problem Solving." In Castellan, Pisoni, and Potts, 1977. [9]

Gregg, L., ed. (1974). *Knowledge and Cognition*, Potomac, Md.: Lawrence Erlbaum Associates. [2] [5]

Gregory, R. L. (1966). *Eye and Brain*, London: World University Library. [8]

Grice, H. Paul (1975). "Logic and Conversation." In Harmon and Davidson, 1975. [Intr.]

Griffiths, A. Phillips (1962–63). "On Belief," *Proceedings of the Aristotelian Society*, 63 (1962–63), 167–186; reprinted in Griffiths, 1967. [8]

—— ed. (1967). *Knowledge and Belief*, New York: Oxford. [8]

Groen, G. J. and Parkman, J. M. (1972). "A Chronometric Analysis of Simple Addition," *Psychological Review*, 79 (1972), 329–343. [2]

Gunderson, Keith, ed. (1975). *Language, Mind and Knowledge*, Minnesota Studies in the Philosophy of Science, 7, Minneapolis: University of Minnesota Press. [11]

Guzman, Adolfo (1968). Computer Recognition of Three-Dimensional Objects in a Visual Scene. Unpublished Ph.D. thesis, MIT, and Project MAC Tech Report 59. [6]

Hampshire, Stuart (1966). *Philosophy of Mind*, New York: Harper and Row. [8]

Harman, Gilbert (1973). *Thought*, Princeton: Princeton University Press. [9]

Harman, Gilbert, and Davidson, Donald, eds. (1975). *The Logic of Grammar,* Encino, Cal.: Dickenson. [**Intr.**]

Haugeland, John (1979). "Understanding Natural Language," *Journal of Philosophy,* 76 (1979), 619–632. [**Intr.**]

Hawkinson, L. (1975). The Representation of Concepts in OWL. Cambridge, Mass.: Project MAC Automatic Programming Group Memo 17. [5]

Healey, R. A. (1981). *Reduction, Time and Reality: Studies in the Philosophy of the Natural Sciences,* Cambridge, England: Cambridge University Press. [**Intr.**]

Hearst, E. (1967). "Psychology across the Chessboard," *Psychology Today,* June 1967. [9]

Heidegger, Martin (1962). *Being and Time,* New York: Harper and Row. [6]

Hempel, Carl (1962). "Rational Action," *Proceedings and Addresses of the American Philosophical Association,* 35 (1962), 5–23; reprinted in Care and Landesman, 1968. [8]

Hempel, Carl, and Oppenheim, Paul (1948). "Studies in the Logic of Explanation," *Philosophy of Science,* 15 (1948), 135–175. [9]

Herriot, D. R. (1968). "Applications of Laser Light," *Scientific American,* 218 (September 1968), 140–156. [9]

Hewitt, C. E. (1972). Description and Theoretical Analysis (Using Schemata) in PLANNER: A Language for Proving Theorems and Manipulating Models in a Robot. Cambridge, Mass.: MIT AI Lab Tech Report 258. [5]

—— (1977). "Viewing Control Structures as Patterns of Passing Messages," *Artificial Intelligence,* 8 (1977), 323–364. [2]

Hintikka, Jaakko (1962). *Knowledge and Belief,* Ithaca: Cornell University Press. [8]

Hobbes, Thomas (1651). *The Leviathan.* [**Intr.**]

Honderich, Ted, ed. (1973). *Essays on Freedom of Action,* London: Routledge and Kegan Paul. [8]

Hook, Sydney, ed. (1960). *Dimensions of Mind: A Symposium,* New York: New York University Press. [7]

Horn, B. K. P. (1975). "Obtaining Shape from Shading Information." In Winston, 1975. [4]

Hudson, Liam (1972). *The Cult of the Fact,* London: Cape. [9]

Hume, David (1888). *A Treatise of Human Nature,* ed. L. A. Selby-Bigge, Oxford: Oxford University Press. [11]

Husserl, Edmund (1960). *Cartesian Meditations,* The Hague: Martinus Nijhoff. [6]

IJCAI-73 (1973). Third International Joint Conference on Artificial Intelligence, *Proceedings,* Menlo Park, Cal.: SRI International, Publications Department, 333 Ravenswood Avenue, Menlo Park, Cal. 94025. [2]

IJCAI-77 (1977). Fifth International Joint Conference on Artificial

Intelligence, *Proceedings*, Available through Department of Computer Science, Carnegie-Mellon University, Pittsburgh, Penn. 15213. [6]

James, William (1890). *Principles of Psychology*, Vol. 1, New York: Dover Publications. [11]

Jardine, N., and Sibson, R. (1971). *Mathematical Taxonomy*, New York: Wiley. [4]

Johnson, N. F. (1972). "Organization and the Concept of a Memory Code." In Melton and Martin, 1972. [2]

Julesz, B. (1975). "Experiments in the Visual Perception of Texture," *Scientific American*, 232 (April 1975), 34–43. [4]

Kabrisky, M. (1966). *A Proposed Model for Visual Information Processing in the Human Brain*, Urbana: University of Illinois Press. [9]

Kenny, K. (1963). *Trixie Belden and the Mystery of the Blinking Eye*, Racine, Wis.: Western Publishing Company. [5]

Kiefer, H. E. and Munitz, M. K., eds. (1970). *Language, Belief, and Metaphysics*, Albany, N.Y.: SUNY Press. [8]

Kosslyn, Steven, and Pomerantz, J. R. (1977). "Imagery, Propositions and the Form of Internal Representations," *Cognitive Psychology*, 9 (1977), 52–76. [9]

Krantz, D. H., et al., eds. (1974). *Contemporary Developments in Mathematical Psychology*, Vol. 2, San Francisco: W. H. Freeman. [9]

Kuhn, Thomas (1970). *The Structure of Scientific Revolutions*, 2nd ed., Chicago: University of Chicago Press. [Intr.] [3] [6] [9]

Lambert, K. (1969). *The Logical Way of Doing Things*, New Haven, Conn.: Yale University Press. [8]

Langer, S. (1962). *Philosophical Sketches*, Baltimore: The Johns Hopkins Press. [2]

Lavoisier, A. (1949). *Elements of Chemistry*, Chicago: Regnery. [3]

Leith, E. N., and Upatnieks, J. (1965). "Photography by Laser," *Scientific American*, 212 (June 1965), 24–35. [9]

Levin, M. I.; McCarthy, J.; Abrahams, P. W.; Edwards, D. J.; and Hart, T. P. (1965). *LISP 1.5 Programmer's Manual*, 2nd ed., Cambridge, Mass.: The MIT Press. [5]

Levitt, M., and Warshel, A. (1975). "A Computer Simulation of Protein Folding," *Nature*, 253 (1975), 694–698. [4]

Lewis, David (1974). "Radical Interpretation," *Synthese*, 27 (1974), 331–344. [8] [9]

Lighthill, J. (1973). "Artificial Intelligence: A General Survey." In *Artificial Intelligence: A Paper Symposium*, London: Great Britain–Science Research Council. [5]

Lucas, J. R. (1961). "Minds, Machines and Gödel," *Philosophy*, 36 (1961), 120–124; reprinted in Anderson, 1964. [Intr.]

Marr, David (1974). A Note on the Computation of Binocular Disparity in a Symbolic, Low-level Visual Processor. Cambridge, Mass.: MIT AI Lab Memo 327. [4]

—— (1976). "Early Processing of Visual Information," *Philosophical Transactions of the Royal Society,* 275 (1976), 483–524. [4]

—— (1977a). "Analysis of Occluding Contour," *Proceedings of the Royal Society of London,* Series B, 197 (1977), 441–475. [4]

—— (1977b). "Artificial Intelligence—A Personal View," *Artificial Intelligence,* 9 (1977), 37–48; also published as MIT AI Memo 355, and included in this volume as Chapter 4. [9]

Marr, David, and Nishihara, H. K. (1977). "Representation and Recognition of Spatial Organization of Three Dimensional Shapes," *Proceedings of the Royal Society of London,* Series B, 200 (1978), 269–294. [4]

Marr, David, and Poggio, T. (1976). "Cooperative Computation of Stereo Disparity," *Science,* 194 (1976), 283–287. [4]

Martin, W. (1974). Memos on the OWL System. Cambridge, Mass.: Project MAC, MIT. [3]

Mayo, Bernard (1964). "Belief and Constraint," *Proceedings of the Aristotelian Society,* 64 (1964), 139–156; reprinted in Griffiths, 1967. [8]

McCarthy, John (1960). "Recursive Functions of Symbolic Expressions and Their Computation by Machine," *Communications of the Association for Computing Machinery,* 3 (April 1960), 184–195. [1]

—— (1979). Ascribing Mental Qualities to Machines. Stanford, Cal.: Stanford AI Lab Memo 326; reprinted in Ringle, 1979. [9] [10]

McCulloch, W. S. (1961). "What Is a Number, That a Man May Know it, and a Man, That He May Know a Number?" *General Semantics Bulletin,* Nos 26 and 27 (1961), 7–18. [1]

McDermott, Drew (1974a). Assimilation of New Information by a Natural Language-Understanding System. Cambridge, Mass.: MIT AI Lab Tech Report 291. [5]

—— (1974b). Advice on the Fast-Paced World of Electronics. Cambridge, Mass.: MIT AI Lab Working Paper 71. [5]

—— (1976). "Artificial Intelligence Meets Natural Stupidity," *SIGART Newsletter,* No. 57 (April 1976), 4–9; reprinted in this volume as Chapter 5. [6]

Melton, A. W., and Martin, E., eds. (1972). *Coding Processes in Human Memory,* New York: Winston. [2]

Meltzer, B., and Michie, D., eds. (1970). *Machine Intelligence,* Vol. 5, Edinburgh: Edinburgh University Press. [2] [3]

—— (1972). *Machine Intelligence,* Vol. 7, Edinburgh: Edinburgh University Press. [2]

Melville, Herman (1952). *Moby Dick,* New York: Modern Library College Editions. [6]

Michie, D. (1971). *On Not Seeing Things,* School of Artificial Intelligence, University of Edinburgh, EPR-22. [2]

Miller, G. A., Galanter, E., and Pribram, K. H. (1960). *Plans and the Structure of Behavior,* New York: Holt, Rinehart and Winston. [2]

Minsky, Marvin, ed. (1968). *Semantic Information Processing,* Cambridge, Mass.: MIT Press [4] [5] [6]

—— (1970). "Form and Content in Computer Science," *Journal of the Association for Computing Machinery,* 17 (January 1970), 197–215. [3]

—— (1974). A Framework for Representing Knowledge. Cambridge, Mass.: MIT AI Lab Memo 306; excerpts reprinted in Winston, 1975; other excerpts reprinted in: *TINLAP-75;* and still others included as Chapter 3 of this volume. [4] [6]

Minsky, Marvin, and Papert, Seymour (1970). Draft of a proposal to ARPA for research on artificial intelligence at MIT, 1970–71. [6]

—— (1972). Progress Report on Artificial Intelligence. Cambridge, Mass.: MIT AI Lab Memo 252. [3] [9]

—— (1973). *Artificial Intelligence,* Condon Lectures, Oregon State System of Higher Education, Eugene, Oregon. [6]

Moore, J., and Newell, Allen (1974). "How Can Merlin Understand?" In Gregg, 1974. [2] [5]

Moses, J. (1974). "MACSYMA—The Fifth Year," *SIGSAM Bulletin,* 8 (1974), 105–110. [4]

Nevins, A. (1974). A Relaxation Approach to Splitting in an Automatic Theorem Prover. Cambridge Mass.: MIT AI Lab Memo 302. [5]

Newell, Allen (1962). "Some Problems of Basic Organization in Problem-Solving Programs." In Yovitts, Jacobi, and Goldstein, 1962. [2] [5]

—— (1970). "Remarks on the Relationship between Artificial Intelligence and Cognitive Psychology." In Banerji and Mesarovic, 1970. [2]

—— (1972). "A Theoretical Exploration of Mechanisms for Coding the Stimulus." In Melton and Martin, 1972 [2]

—— (1973a). "Artificial Intelligence and the Concept of Mind." In Schank and Colby, 1973. [3]

—— (1973b). "You Can't Play 20 Questions with Nature and Win." In Chase, 1973. [2]

—— (1973c). "Production Systems. Models of Control Structures." In Chase, 1973. [2]

—— (1980). Physical Symbol Systems. *Cognitive Science,* (1980), 135–183. [10]

Newell, Allen, and Simon, Herbert (1972). *Human Problem Solving,* Englewood Cliffs, N.J.: Prentice-Hall. [2] [3]

Nilsson, Nils J. (1971). *Problem Solving Methods in Artificial Intelligence,* New York: McGraw Hill. [1]

Norman, Donald (1973). "Memory, Knowledge and the Answering of Questions." In Solso, 1973. [3]

Norman, D. A., and Rumelhart, D. E. (1974). *Explorations in Cognition,* San Francisco: W. H. Freeman. [4]

Papert, Seymour (1972). "Teaching Children to be Mathematicians vs. Teaching about Mathematics," *International Journal of Mathematical Education for Science and Technology,* 3 (1972), 249–262. [3]

Papert, Seymour, and Minsky, Marvin (1973). Proposal to ARPA for Research on Intelligent Automata and Micro-Automation. Cambridge, Mass.: MIT AI Lab Memo 299. [6]

Pavio, Allen (1975). "Imagery and Synchronic Thinking," *Canadian Psychological Review,* 16 (1975), 147–163. [9]

Poggio, T., and Reichardt, W. (1976). "Visual Control of the Orientation Behavior of the Fly: Towards the Underlying Neural Interactions," *Quarterly Reviews of Biophysics,* 9 (1976), 377–438. [4]

Pollen, D. A., and Taylor, J. H. (1974). "The Striate Cortex and the Spatial Analysis of Visual Space." In Schmitt and Worden, 1974. [9]

Pribram, Karl H. (1971). *Languages of the Brain,* Englewood Cliffs, N.J.: Prentice-Hall. [9]

—— (1974). "How Is It That Sensing So Much We Can Do So Little?" In Schmitt and Worden, 1974. [9]

Pribram, Karl H.; Nuwer, M.; and Baron, Robert J. (1974). "The Holographic Hypothesis of Memory Structure in Brain Function and Perception." In Krantz, et al., 1974. [9]

Price, H. H. (1954). "Belief and Will," *Proceedings of the Aristotelian Society,* Supplementary Vol. 28 (1954), 1–26; reprinted in Hampshire, 1966. [8]

Putnam, Hilary (1960). "Minds and Machines." In Hook, 1960; reprinted in Anderson, 1964, and in Putnam, 1975b. [7] [9] [11]

—— (1965). "Psychological Predicates." In Capitan and Merrill, 1965. [7]

—— (1967). "The Mental Life of Some Machines." In Castañeda, 1967; reprinted in Putnam, 1975b. [7]

—— (1973). "Reductionism and the Nature of Psychology," *Cognition,* 2 (1973), 131–146; abridged version included in this volume as Chapter 7. [9]

—— (1975a). "The Meaning of 'Meaning.'" In Gunderson, 1975; reprinted in Putnam, 1975b. [11]

—— (1975b). *Mind, Language and Reality—Philosophical Papers,* Vol. 2, Cambridge, England: Cambridge University Press. [7] [9] [11]

Pylyshyn, Zenon (1973). "What the Mind's Eye Tells the Mind's Brain: A Critique of Mental Imagery," *Psychological Bulletin,* 80 (1973), 1–24. [9]

—— (1978a). "Imagery and Artificial Intelligence." In Savage, 1978. [9]

—— (1978b). "Computational Models and Empirical Constraints," *Behavioral and Brain Sciences,* 1 (1978), 93–99. [2]

—— (1980). "Computation and Cognition: Issues in the Foundations of Cognitive Science," *Behavioral and Brain Sciences*, 3 (1980), 111–132. [2]

Quillian, M. R. (1968). "Semantic Memory." In Minsky, 1968. [4] [5]

—— (1969). "The Teachable Language Comprehender," *Communications of the Association for Computing Machinery*, 12 (1969), 459–476. [5]

Quine, W. V. O. (1960). *Word and Object*, Cambridge, Mass.: MIT Press. [Intr.] [8] [9]

Raphael, B. (1968). "SIR: Semantic Information Retrieval." In Minsky, 1968. [4]

Ringle, Martin, ed. (1979). *Philosophical Perspectives in Artificial Intelligence*, Atlantic Highlands, N.J.: Humanities Press. [2] [9] [10]

Robinson, J. A. (1965). "A Machine-Oriented Logic Based on the Resolution Principle," *Journal of the Association for Computing Machinery*, 12 (1965), 23–41. [5]

Rorty, Amelie O., ed. (1976). *The Identities of Persons*, Berkeley: University of California Press. [8]

Rosch, Eleanor (1976). "Classifications d'objets du monde réel: origines et représentations dans la cognition," *Bulletin de Psychologie* (1976), 242–250. [4]

—— (1977). "Human Categorization." In Warren, 1977. [4] [6]

Sacerdoti, E. D. (1973). "Planning in a Hierarchy of Abstraction Spaces." In *IJCAI-73*, 412–422; also published in *Artificial Intelligence*, 5 (1974), [2]

Sandewall, E. (1970). "Representing Natural Language Information in Predicate Calculus." In Meltzer and Michie, 1970. [3]

Savage, C. Wade, ed. (1978). *Perception and Cognition: Issues in the Foundations of Psychology*, Minnesota Studies in the Philosophy of Science, Vol. 9, Minneapolis: University of Minnesota Press. [Intr.] [9]

Schank, Roger C. (1972). "Conceptual Dependency: A Theory of Natural Language Understanding," *Cognitive Psychology*, 3 (1972), 552–631. [6]

—— (1973a). The Fourteen Primitive Actions and Their Inferences. Stanford, Cal.: Stanford AI Lab Memo 183. [3]

—— (1973b). "Identification of Conceptualizations Underlying Natural Language." In Schank and Colby, 1973. [4]

—— (1975a). "The Primitive Acts of Conceptual Dependency." In *TINLAP-75*. [6]

—— (1975b). "Using Knowledge to Understand." In *TINLAP-75*. [6]

—— (1975c). *Conceptual Information Processing*, Amsterdam: North-Holland. [4]

—— (1979). "Natural Language, Philosophy and Artificial Intelligence." In Ringle, 1979. [2]

Schank, Roger C., et al. (1977). "Panel on Natural Language Processing." In *IJCAI-77*, pp1007–1013. [6]

Schank, Roger C., and Ableson, Robert P. (1977). *Scripts, Plans, Goals and Understanding,* Hillsdale, N.J.: Laurence Erlbaum Associates. [6] [10]

Schank, Roger C., and Colby, Kenneth, eds. (1973). *Computer Models of Thought and Language,* San Francisco: W. H. Freeman. [3] [4] [6]

Schmitt, F. O., and Worden, F. G., eds. (1974). *The Neurosciences: Third Study Program,* Cambridge, Mass.: MIT Press. [9]

Searle, John R. (1969). *Speech Acts: An Essay in the Philosophy of Language,* Cambridge, England: Cambridge University Press. [Intr.]

—— (1979). "What Is an Intentional State?" *Mind,* 88 (1979), 72–94. [10]

Sellars, Wilfrid (1963). *Science, Perception and Reality,* London: Routledge and Kegan Paul. [2] [9]

Shepard, Roger (1975). "Form, Formation, and Transformation of Internal Representations." In Solso, 1975. [4]

Shepard, Roger, and Metzler, J. (1971). "Mental Rotation of Three-Dimensional Objects," *Science,* 171 (1971), 701–703. [9]

Shoemaker, Sydney (1975). "Functionalism and Qualia," *Philosophical Studies,* 27 (1975), 291–315. [9]

Simmons, R. F. (1973). "Semantic Networks: Their Computation and Use for Understanding English Sentences." In Schank and Colby, 1973. [3]

Simon, Herbert A. (1969). *The Sciences of the Artificial,* Compton Lectures, Cambridge, Mass.: MIT Press. [2] [9]

—— (1977). "Artificial Intelligence Systems That Understand." In *IJCAI-77,* 1059–1073. [6]

Slagle, J. R. (1963). "A Heuristic Program That Solves Symbolic Integration Problems in Freshman Calculus." In Feigenbaum and Feldman, 1963. [4]

Solso, R. L., ed. (1973). *Contemporary Issues in Cognitive Psychology: The Loyola Symposium,* Washington, D.C.: V. H. Winston and Sons. [3]

—— , ed. (1975). *Information Processing and Cognition: The Loyola Symposium,* Hillsdale, N.J.: Lawrence Erlbaum Associates. [4]

Stansfield, J. L. (1975). Programming a Dialogue Teaching Situation. Unpublished Ph.D. thesis, University of Edinburgh. [5]

Sternberg, S. (1967). "Two Operations in Character Recognition," *Perception and Psychophysics,* 2 (1967), 43–53. [2]

Sunguroff, A. (1975). Unpublished paper on the OWL system. [5]

Suppes, Pat, et al., eds. (1973). *Logic, Methodology and Philosophy of Science IV,* Amsterdam: North-Holland. [9]

Sussman, Gerald J. (1973). *A Computational Model of Skill Acquisition.* MIT Ph.D. thesis and AI Lab Tech Report 297; published by American Elsevier, New York, 1975. [3] [5]

Sussman, Gerald J., and McDermott, Drew V. (1972). "From PLANNER to CONNIVER—A Genetic Approach (Or: Why Conniving Is Better Than Planning)," *AFIPS Conference Proceedings,* 41 (1972), 1171–1180. [5]

Sussman, G. J., and Stallman, R. M. (1975). "Heuristic Techniques in Computer-Aided Circuit Analysis," *IEEE Transactions on Circuits and Systems, CAS-22* (1975), 857–865. [4]

Taylor, Charles (1964). *The Explanation of Behavior*, London: Routledge and Kegan Paul. [8]

TINLAP-75 (1975). *Theoretical Issues in Natural Language Processing*, Cambridge, Mass.: June 10–13, 1975. [6]

Turing, A. M. (1937). "On Computable Numbers, with an Application to the *Entscheidungsproblem*," *Proceedings of the London Mathematical Society*, 42 (1937), 230–265. [Intr.] [2]

—— (1950). "Computing Machinery and Intelligence," *Mind*, 59 (October 1950), 433–460; reprinted in Anderson, 1964. [1] [10]

Ullman, S. (1976). "On Visual Detection of Light Sources," *Biological Cybernetics*, 21 (1976), 205–212. [4]

van Heerden, P. J. (1963). "A New Method of Storing and Retrieving Information," *Applied Optics*, 2 (1963), 387–392. [9]

Vickers, John (1969). "Judgement and Belief." In Lambert, 1969. [8]

Waltz, David (1972). *Generating Semantic Descriptions from Drawings of Scenes with Shadows*. MIT Ph.D. thesis; published in Winston, 1975. [4] [6] [9]

Warren, N., ed. (1977). *Advances in Cross-Cultural Psychology*, Vol. 1, London: Academic Press. [6]

Warrington, E. K. (1975). "The Selective Impairment of Semantic Memory," *Quarterly Journal of Experimental Psychology*, 27 (1975), 635–657. [4]

Weizenbaum, Joseph (1965). "ELIZA—A Computer Program for the Study of Natural Language Communication between Man and Machine," *Communications of the Association for Computing Machinery*, 9 (1965), 36–45. [4] [10]

—— (1976). *Computer Power and Human Reason*, San Francisco: W. H. Freeman. [4] [5] [10]

Wertheimer, M. (1959). *Productive Thinking*, New York: Harper and Row. [3]

Williams, B. A. O. (1970). "Deciding to Believe." In Kiefer and Munitz, 1970. [8]

Wilson, N. L. (1959). "Substances without Substrata," *Review of Metaphysics*, 12 (1959), 521–539. [9]

Winograd, S. (1976). "Computing the Discrete Fourier Transform," *Proceedings of the National Academy of Science*, 73 (1976), 1005–1006. [4]

Winograd, Terry (1971). Procedures as a Representation for Data in a Computer Program for Understanding Natural Language. Cambridge, Mass.: MIT AI Lab Tech Report 84. [5] [11]

—— (1972). "Understanding Natural Language," *Cognitive Psychology*, 1

(1972), 1–191; also published by Academic Press, New York, 1972. [2] [6] [9] [10]

—— (1973). "A Procedural Model of Language Understanding." In Schank and Colby, 1973. [6]

—— (1974). Five Lectures on Artificial Intelligence. Stanford, Cal.: Stanford AI Lab Memo 246. [3] [6]

—— (1975). "Frame Representations and the Declarative/Procedural Controversy." In Bobrow and Collins, 1975. [5]

—— (1976a). "Artificial Intelligence and Language Comprehension." In *Artificial Intelligence and Language Comprehension*, Washington, D.C.: National Institute of Education. [6]

—— (1976b). "Towards a Procedural Understanding of Semantics," *Revue Internationale de Philosophie*, Nos. 117–118 (1976), 260–303, Foundation Universitaire de Belgique. [6]

Winston, Patrick H., ed. (1975). *The Psychology of Computer Vision*, New York: McGraw Hill. [4] [6]

Winston, Patrick H., and the staff of the MIT AI Laboratory (May, 1976). Proposal to ARPA, Cambridge, Mass.: MIT AI Lab Memo 366. [6]

Wittgenstein, Ludwig (1953). *Philosophical Investigations*, Oxford: Basil Blackwell. [6]

Woods, William A. (1975). "What's in a Link: Foundations for Semantic Networks." In Bobrow and Collins, 1975. [5]

Yevick, Miriam L. (1975). "Holographic or Fourier Logic," *Pattern Recognition*, 7 (1975), 197–213. [9]

Yovitts, M.; Jacobi, G. T.; and Goldstein, G. D. (1962). *Self-Organizing Systems*, New York: Spartan. [2] [5]

Zucker, S. W. (1976). Relaxation Labeling and the Reduction of Local Ambiguities. College Park, Md.: University of Maryland Computer Science Tech Report 451. [4]